There was no stronger advocate than Malcolm Fraser during the Cold War years for the rewards of Australia's alliance with the US. But in this fascinating book, he makes a passionate case that, in today's very different world, the risks of Australia's strategic dependence on Washington now far exceed any returns. His core argument—that the only aggression for which we are likely to need American defence will be that prompted by the alliance itself—will startle many readers, and enrage many more, but it certainly compels attention. Some of Fraser's judgments are, I think, unarguable: that unthinking reflex commitment to America's perceived interests is never likely to be reciprocated with reflex commitment to our own, and that Australia could and should have been a much more independent and less subservient alliance partner in recent years. Others—in particular, his conclusion that we should now go it completely alone—are much more problematic. But on any view, Malcolm Fraser has made in this book a major contribution to a debate that Australia has to have.

Gareth Evans, Australian Foreign Minister 1988–96,
President of the International Crisis Group 2000–09

DANGEROUS
ALLIES
MALCOLM
FRASER

WITH CAIN ROBERTS

MELBOURNE
UNIVERSITY
PRESS

MELBOURNE UNIVERSITY PRESS
An imprint of Melbourne University Publishing Limited
11–15 Argyle Place South, Carlton, Victoria 3053, Australia
mup-info@unimelb.edu.au
www.mup.com.au

First published 2014
Reprinted 2014 (three times)
Text © Malcolm Fraser, 2014
Design and typography © Melbourne University Publishing Limited, 2014

Edited by Cathryn Game
Cover design by Design by Committee
Typeset in Bembo 12/15pt by Cannon Typesetting
Printed in Australia by McPherson's Printing Group

National Library of Australia Cataloguing-in-Publication entry

Fraser, Malcolm, 1930– author.
Dangerous allies/Malcolm Fraser with Cain Roberts.

9780522862652 (hardback)
9780522862669 (ebook)

Includes bibliographical references and index.

International relations.
National security—Australia.
Dependency.
Australia—Foreign relations.

Roberts, Cain, author.

327.0994

Contents

Acknowledgements

A book of this kind cannot be written without a great deal of research and without resources. Melbourne University Publishing had wanted me to write the book. I am grateful for its support and encouragement and for the resources they made available.

Cain Roberts applied for and was chosen principally to do the basic research that would be required. He has, in fact, been much more than a researcher. His capacity to sort out facts and details is great. He has assisted in drafting. He has advised on the strength of an argument and where a paragraph might need modification. His point of view was always worth considering. I was fortunate that he has a basic interest in foreign policy and in the way in which foreign policy decisions are made. He understands the arguments, and at all times seemed interested in what the book was trying to say. His advice, his counsel and his research has done a great deal to help bring the book to completion. Thank you, Cain.

A number of people have assisted with certain aspects of the book. There are one or two who do not want to be named, but whose advice I value greatly. They will know who they are. The Parliamentary Library has also been very helpful in chasing sources and clarifications. The bibliography is testimony to the depth of research that has been undertaken.

Petro Georgiou and Denis White, two long-time friends and former staff members, read some early chapters, and their comments and criticisms were all thoughtful and helpful and very much to the point.

Richard Tanter, a professor in the School of Social and Political Sciences at the University of Melbourne, is a specialist in advanced techniques of modern warfare and strategic planning. The sections relating to naval capability, to missile technology, to the role of bases in Australia, have been checked for technical accuracy. His knowledge lends authority to those sections of the book. Tim McCormack, Professor of Law at the Melbourne Law School and the Special Adviser on International Humanitarian Law to the prosecutor of the International Criminal Court in The Hague, on anything with legal implications, has helped me on a number of occasions. He did a great deal of work in drafting the Statutes of the International Criminal Court. His advice has been wise and helpful, and again has assisted in maintaining accuracy in important parts of the book. I would like to thank both of them for their help.

Sally Heath, Executive Publisher at Melbourne University Publishing, gave advice on the structure and shape of the book, as the chapters unfolded. I would also like to thank Cathryn Game, copy-editor, for working assiduously and drawing attention to some important matters of detail that needed clarification.

I would especially like to thank Louise Adler, CEO of Melbourne University Publishing, who was instrumental in persuading me to write the book in the first place.

Julie Gleeson, who runs my office and has been with me for very nearly a quarter of a century, was absolutely central to the production of the book. I could not have done it without her assistance and her willing acceptance of an enormously increased workload. Julie is a first-class Executive Assistant. Through the course of writing this book she has shown a capacity for accurate research, which was helpful and, in some cases critical, in enabling the book to progress. I thank Julie very much indeed for all the help that she has given. Christine Walker has also been a willing and constructive help.

As always, Tamie has helped in innumerable ways and made it easier to bring the book to a conclusion. Thank you, Tamie.

Introduction

Australia has always been a dependent nation. We were a child of the British Empire and were brought up to believe that the Empire would protect us, should we ever need it. This was the beginning of a policy of strategic dependence, a policy that made sense from Australia's colonial beginnings until the end of the Cold War. For the entirety of our history, Australia has been reliant on 'great and powerful friends' for our sense of national security and for direction on our foreign policy priorities. I call this strategic dependence.

In the early days, Australia did not seek an independent voice. We argued for greater authority within the councils of the British Empire, to make sure that the Empire took note of Australia's needs. Our success was somewhat limited. Even so, from the birth of the colonies, through Federation and both world wars, we recognised Britain as the final determinant of our foreign and security policy. It was indeed a grand bargain. Australia accepted that Britain would be the final determinant of Empire policy, which would give Britain the power to take Australia to war resulting in the most terrible casualties. In return, the Empire had an obligation to defend Australia, should we ever need help. We were strategically dependent.

As it happened, when we did need help during World War II, Britain had its back to the wall in Europe. Britain could not fulfil its part of the bargain. The Empire was unable to support Australia. The policy of strategic dependence had failed. It failed in what was the darkest hour, both for Britain and for Australia.

Australia then appealed to the United States for support. Our sense of strategic dependence, our need for protection by a great power, was then fulfilled by America. In the mind of many Australians, the United States became our protector through the instrument of ANZUS and through the long years of the Cold War, until the break-up of the Soviet Union in 1991.

After the end of the Cold War, Australia had a real opportunity to enact an independent foreign policy, a foreign policy that reflected the change in the global strategic context, which would cast away the country's history of strategic dependence on great and powerful friends. Not only has the post-Cold War era provided an opportunity for an independent foreign policy but also it has provided an imperative for one—changes across the globe, within America, within our region and within Australia, make continuing our strategic dependence on the United States increasingly difficult and questionable.

Strategic dependence was once necessary. The first part of this book will show that as a young, small, newly federated country, with few resources and reliance on Britain, adherence to the rules of the Empire made sense. This was understood by Australia's leaders of that era. The policy of strategic dependence was right for the strategic context of those times. As with other nations, Australia did not realise the extent to which Britain's power had been weakened by World War I and so, between the wars, that sense of strategic dependence continued. Australians still felt that we were part of the British Empire. We refused to apply the provisions of the Statute of Westminster,[1] which was passed by Britain in 1931, because we believed it would dilute Britain's obligation to defend us should we ever need it. We also argued that Britain should not give guarantees to Eastern European states and become embroiled in the affairs of Eastern Europe because to do so would reduce Britain's capacity to act in other parts of the world—notably our own.

As World War II dawned, Australian leaders slowly began to recognise that Britain no longer had the power to guarantee our security. Nevertheless, the policy of strategic dependence on Britain remained. It was not until Curtin made his historic appeal to the United States in 1942, about three weeks after Japan attacked Pearl Harbor, that Australia's sense of strategic dependence shifted.

In the late 1930s, Robert Menzies, when he became Prime Minister, decided that Australia should establish its own missions and be advised by our own people. Yet it was Dr Herbert Vere Evatt, however, who had been Justice of the High Court of Australia for ten years until September 1940, and was Minister for External Affairs from October 1941 to December 1949, who really established a separate foreign policy for Australia. Missions were established in many countries, and Australia slowly began to play an active role in world politics for the first time. Evatt's role in the formation of the United Nations was substantial. Although established at Federation, the Department of External Affairs was finally given a policy-making and information-gathering mandate and was expanded and equipped to provide Australia with proper representation in countries important to us. Australian representation, for Australians. Nobody any longer thought of operating through Britain.

Yet the strategic context Australia faced was no less threatening than in the past. The growing tensions of the Cold War, insurgencies in many parts of the world, the Soviet Union's brutal suppression of nationalism in different countries in Eastern Europe, and communist insurrections in countries of East and South-East Asia, all weighed heavily on the strategic thinking of Australian leaders. Australia almost desperately wanted to be able to rely on a major power for strategic defence—the United States, replacing the United Kingdom, became that major power. Our policy of strategic dependence transitioned to a new protector, but continued in much the same fashion as it had before World War II. Australia's strategic dependence on the United States will form the focus of the second part of the book.

The policy of strategic dependence continued to make sense during the years of the Cold War. It was a realistic and pragmatic policy, a policy that suited the strategic context and international situation of the time. It was by no means a perfect policy, and it was a policy for which Australia paid a high price, but it was a required policy. We had little other choice.

With the break-up of the Soviet Union, however, the world started to change substantially. There was no other nation or group of nations that might take the Soviet Union's place as a major threat to our security or, indeed, to world peace from the point of view of the West. The opportunity for a more independent Australian policy became a reality, a possibility, even a necessity, that we should have seized avidly. A more independent standing in strategic affairs would have allowed Australia to participate more fully in the affairs of our own region and to establish better relations as an independent and productive partner with East and South-East Asia. It would have allowed the region to listen to a uniquely Australian view on important issues, not an Australian view circumscribed by obligations to great and powerful friends.

We did not take that course; we did not fashion a new role for ourselves in the region and on the broader world stage. Australia, much as our earlier history suggested we would, remained with the status quo and chose to continue to follow the United States. This would lead Australia into wars of no strategic consequence for our nation, in an effort simply to be closer to and court the favour of the United States. Following the United States into Iraq particularly, as one of three nations to contribute ground troops to the invasion force, was a major error not only because the justifications for that war were based on falsehoods but also because the result is, and was always going to be, disastrous. The argument that invading Iraq was a necessary action in the fight against terrorism is untrue— Saddam Hussein's Iraq had no significant links with Al Qaeda.[2]

It is against this backdrop that the final part of this book is set. The post-Cold War era provided Australia with a change in strategic context that should have facilitated abandonment of our strategic dependence. I examine four interrelated themes that provide Australia not only with an opportunity to move to a more independent foreign policy—an opportunity we have thus far failed to grasp—but also reasons why we must. First, I will discuss the changes in the broader global context since the fall of the Berlin Wall. These changes include the expansion of NATO, the War on Terror and the new global role of the United States, all three of which make strategic dependence less desirable.

Second, I will examine how, in a world where American power is no longer balanced by any other superpower, notions of manifest destiny and exceptionalism have become key features of American foreign policy. Although these concepts have been present since the earliest days of the republic, America's unchecked power and the rise of neo-conservatives have brought these notions to the fore. Domestic politics within America have changed, and Australia needs to consider whether the values of our two nations continue to align and whether the changed American polity is conducive to our ongoing security and foreign policy needs.

Third, I will look at how the Asia–Pacific region has matured and developed in the two decades since the end of the Cold War. The achievements of both the nations and institutions of the region have occurred largely without the assistance of the West—ASEAN, the East Asia Forum and the dynamism of regional economies are all underpinning stability in the region. Yet the strategic pivot by the United States and the West's response to the rise of China could potentially undo much of this work. Tensions between nations over specks of rock in the South and East China seas and the Korean peninsula continue to be potential flashpoints requiring management. Will Australia carve a unique role for itself in this changed region we call home, or will our priorities be predicated on the wishes of policy-makers in Washington?

Finally, I will discuss Australia's missed opportunities to build on the efforts of the 1980s and early 1990s, in building a place for ourselves in Asia; how our continued strategic dependence on America led us to make policy choices that ostracised us from the region, cast us as a deputy sheriff to Washington and a willing participant in US strategic aims, both in the region and around the world.

Our integration with US defensive systems and over-enthusiastic bipartisan support for ANZUS—above and beyond what ANZUS actually should entail—further emphasise our estrangement from the region in which we live. Have we come to a point whereby our strategic dependence on the United States is a paradox? We need the United States for defence, but we only need defence because of the United States. It is a consideration of great importance.

These three themes and Australia's failure to make the most of its post–Cold War opportunities all go towards the need to reassess our policy of strategic dependence not only because the time is right, but also because we must.

Part I

Loyal to the Crown, dependent on Empire

'… there is no pretence of claiming the power of peace or war, or exercising power outside our territories.'

ALFRED DEAKIN

1

Colonial foundations of strategic dependence

Australia's history of strategic dependence pre-dates the creation of the Commonwealth of Australia, taking root in the early years of the individual colonies. The one thing that stands out in reading our colonial history is the limitation on the aspirations of our legislators for independence over foreign and defence policy. The connection of the colonies to Great Britain and the British Empire was through the Colonial Office, an institution that colonial leaders felt did not always have their best interests at heart.

The colonies wanted to be able to do what they thought was best within their own boundaries but, with rare exceptions, colonists and colonial politicians had no ambition for separate action in relation to foreign affairs or defence. They did, however, wish to strengthen their position within the Empire to make their voice stronger than it might otherwise have been. Although the Colonial Office was the key link to imperial affairs, it was also an impediment to a stronger voice for the colonies.

The notions of what it meant to be a colonist were very different from the way Australians feel about themselves today. Colonists regarded themselves as British, and this overriding sentiment of imperial allegiance remained for many years after Federation.[1] Many referred to Britain as home despite the fact that they might not have been born there and might never have visited the United Kingdom. The sense of being British was overwhelming, and led directly to obligations to Britain to help fight Britain's wars and to dependence on Britain for our own defence. Ties to Britain through race, through economic dependence, through genuine affection for and belief in the Empire would all have made any push for full independence quite impossible. There was a sense of 'pride of race' or 'British race patriotism'. The colonies strongly felt they were part of the best in the world.[2]

The issues that arose in those earlier years, however, led colonists to believe that they would be better off in one federation. The development of the self-governing colonies, the influence of foreign policy and defence on the attitudes of the colonists and the moves to Federation itself, all influence each other. The themes move in and out of the story reinforcing and leading inevitably to Federation. There was no one reason for Federation.

Yet one thing that stands out clearly throughout the history of the self-governing colonies to their unification in 1901 is that the argument for a fully strategically independent nation, standing free and in its own right, was never part of the story. Although the colonists wanted greater influence and greater authority over their futures, they wanted influence within the Empire, in the belief that dependence upon a great power offered them the best chance of a stable and secure future. That desire for protection, that fear of standing alone, were never openly expressed, but they were very much part of the Australian story. They remain so to this day.

By the end of the 1850s, all Australian colonies, with the exception of Western Australia, had been granted self-government yet, until Federation, the United Kingdom maintained legal and constitutional control of foreign affairs and defence.[3] The powers defined, for example in the constitutions of New South Wales and Victoria in 1855, were broad and vague in the extreme; in New South Wales's case, 'to make laws for the peace, welfare and good government of the said colony'.[4] There were limitations on the powers of the self-governing colonies because certain payments needed to be paid to the United Kingdom for services and for administration. Such matters could not be altered without the approval of the Imperial Parliament. It says much about the attitude of the time that there was no mention in these constitutions of the self-governing colonies of Aboriginals—a sentiment that has yet to be remedied in the Australian Constitution.

Despite being self-governing, the power of the colonies was in many ways strictly limited, particularly when it came to foreign and defence policies. The powers to declare war, negotiate treaties or exchange diplomats with other states were not afforded to the colonies.[5] Their only 'legitimate point of contact' with the international system was via agents general appointed to London to facilitate business such as immigration and loan funds, which had to be raised in the United Kingdom.[6] Even these officers had limited, if any, direct communication with key institutions of the British Government, let alone the British Prime Minister, as colonial matters were strictly managed through the Colonial Office. Direct communication with other states would have been unthinkable. Although the colonial governments might have felt at times restricted by the Colonial Office, they valued the ties to the Mother Country, and the Colonial Office was their conduit to imperial policy.

The separate colonies therefore had no aspirations beyond the domestic provisions enshrined in their individual constitutions— the notion of greater autonomy, let alone strategic independence, was non-existent. The unstated bargain was that the government of the United Kingdom would protect the self-governing colonies and the colonies would themselves fulfil their duty to respond to the call of the Empire.[7] Foreign affairs and defence matters were regarded as the exclusive province of the Imperial Parliament.

This might seem a naive position for colonial governments to have taken, yet the colonies were very conscious of the worldwide dominance of the Royal Navy. Colonial leaders believed that it was 'the solid basis on which the defence policy of Australia may safely rest'.[8] This was particularly so because none of the colonies had the industrial capacity nor the population to support significant military forces of their own. Colonial governments took great comfort in the security provided by such a powerful protector, believing that the British Government had a responsibility to protect them and that, in reward, London could regard the colonies of the South Pacific as a British preserve.[9] This colonial sense of strategic dependence would act as a tie to the Mother Country for decades to come. Yet during this period communication was obviously slow and understanding often imperfect and, as these self-governing colonies matured, they came to resent what they regarded as the heavy hand of the Colonial Office. Despite having achieved self-governing status, which for some colonies occurred not long after their settlement, it was not long before leading colonial politicians started to look to the future.

The colonies slowly understood that they needed greater influence with imperial policy-making structures if they were to preserve and enhance their own identity and avoid dangers for the future. This was true even in the area of external affairs and defence, with reluctant colonial governments voicing concerns over actions of European powers in Australia's vicinity throughout the 1800s. The colonies' concern with foreign affairs seemed very much restricted to the actual or possible ownership of territories close to Australia by potentially hostile powers. This included the French, the Germans and later the Japanese. Papua New Guinea, the New Hebrides and Fiji were mentioned on a number of occasions.[10] It was the view of all the colonies that British control of these territories was the best guarantee to avoid a potentially hostile neighbour.

Of particular strategic importance to the colonies was the status of New Guinea, specifically the eastern regions that were not under Dutch control. In 1874 Henry Parkes, Premier of New South Wales, wrote a sharply worded memo to the British Government drawing attention to the possible colonisation of New Guinea by a foreign power. He argued that such an event would be 'an embarrassment' and emphasised that Australians would approve colonisation of the territory by Britain. In 1875 the Parliament of Queensland, the colony most concerned about the future status of New Guinea, passed a resolution urging all parts of the island not under Dutch authority to be annexed by the British.[11] New Guinea was the largest island close to Australia and was both productive and fertile. It was important for it to be in friendly hands to preserve freedom of the seas surrounding it, which were increasingly important to Australian trade. For this territory to be in the hands of a foreign power would have been intolerable for political, trade and cultural reasons. Parkes' approach and the Queensland resolution were both rejected by the British Government.

In 1882 a number of colonies expressed concern regarding French activities in the New Hebrides. The British did no more than inform the French that annexation would 'give offence to Australia'.[12] It did, however, lead to a declaration by both Great Britain and France that the New Hebrides would be neutral territory and to the establishment of a joint naval commission in 1887 to protect the rights of their respective citizens.[13] This would ultimately lead to the Anglo-French Condominium, which was agreed to in 1906 and was negotiated without reference to the new Federation.[14] It was designed to limit the rights of both powers and to limit competition between them.

More broadly, the self-governing colonies, especially New South Wales, Queensland and Victoria, showed special concern at the activities of other European powers in the Pacific. For example, New South Wales appealed to Britain to annex the Fijian Islands.[15] Lord Kimberley, Secretary of State for the Colonies, replied in 1871 that New South Wales could act on its own account if it wished to take responsibility for so doing.[16] New South Wales took no action, and Britain finally annexed Fiji in 1874.[17]

The concern of the colonies over the fate of the Pacific Islands had intensified as the British had withdrawn their military regiments from all colonies by 1870. The colonial governments raised small forces of volunteers 'supplemented gradually by small bodies of permanent colonial soldiers for safeguarding fixed defences'.[18]

Any proposed annexation in the Pacific was not for the purpose of colonisation but was rather related to the protection of Britain's colonies in Australia. While annexation of New Guinea was raised by the colonies in 1874, Australia was unwilling to cover the costs of such an undertaking, and the British desire for expansion seemed to have waned.[19] However, when German newspapers indicated that there was real German interest in New Guinea, Queensland took full possession of southern New Guinea in 1883.[20] This action was beyond Queensland's powers and was rejected by Britain as 'altogether indefinite and unfounded'.[21] Victoria then pushed for annexation of all Pacific Islands between New Guinea and Fiji. Britain in part agreed and declared a protectorate over the south coast of New Guinea on 6 November 1883.

The colonies certainly had pressed harder to persuade Britain to act more effectively in relation to the territories or islands close to Australia, which, if not held by Britain, could be held by a hostile power. The colonies realised that they had to do something on their own account and therefore Queensland, New South Wales and Victoria guaranteed the cost of administration of the protectorate.[22]

What is important here is that the colonies, even when given specific permission to implement foreign policy as New South Wales had been regarding New Guinea, would not take action on their own account. They needed and desired a British imprimatur to act. They expected Britain to act and provide the kind of shelter that British ownership of the islands close to Australia was intended to provide. Yet British policy in the Pacific was shifting, with London having no desire for further colonisation, having already established an extensive empire and viewing the commercial opportunities for further colonies as insignificant—'it was an age of retrenchment and colonies cost money'.[23]

This situation was exacerbated at the end of 1884 when Bismarck, Chancellor of Germany, informed Britain that the German flag had been raised over northern New Guinea. This took the British Government by surprise as the Foreign Office had not anticipated a vigorous German colonial policy. The unsurprised Australian colonial governments were 'aspirated beyond measure and not slow in expressing their feelings'. Many colonial leaders had felt that London's lack of foreign policy foresight and poor negotiations with Germany had sacrificed colonial interests.[24]

This action by Germany highlighted the vulnerability of the colonies. They were totally dependent upon Britain for defence and for foreign policy decision-making. The colonies would have no capacity to withstand an attack by a major power on their own account.[25]

In addition, more colonial leaders were beginning to believe that they needed greater weight and greater influence in imperial affairs in order to best serve their interests. They did not want to be independent of the British Empire, but rather wanted to create a more robust mechanism for engaging with the various policy-making arms of the Imperial Government in London. They wanted a larger voice in foreign and defence policy-making, a way to ensure that voice would be heard by Whitehall. Although not the only influence, such sentiments were certainly part of the motivation for Federation. This was underlined in 1885 by General Henry MacIver, who argued that the islands of the Pacific were 'geographically the birthright of Australasia' and that encroachment on any island, including New Guinea, by other European powers must be resisted. MacIver declared that 'Australasia must awake to her responsibilities of self-defence' and that the British Empire had an obligation to protect Australia and its interests, particularly if imperial blundering was to drag the colonies into a war with unfriendly neighbours through no act of their own.[26]

The confluence of these events and similar issues in other colonies in the British Empire led to a Colonial Conference in 1887 in London coinciding with Queen Victoria's jubilee. Edward Stanhope, Secretary of State for the Colonies, described it as the 'first attempt to bring all parts of Her Majesty's Empire into joint deliberation' with defence and commerce being the first-order issues.[27] The conference was also in part a concession to consult with the colonies in an effort to ward off any sentiments towards independence.

One attendee was Alfred Deakin, who was representing the Colony of Victoria when he put forward what was regarded as an impassioned plea for Britain to take greater account of colonial wishes. Deakin wanted a system whereby colonial policy would be considered imperial policy.[28] He spoke of the frustration the colonies felt with the Colonial Office and the seemingly impenetrable wall it put around the central British institutions of government—such as the Foreign Office and the Cabinet—that could assist the colonies in achieving their aspirations. Deakin expressed that what was good for the colonies was ultimately good for the British Empire and that, should the colonies suffer, it would be to the detriment of imperial ambition. He did not want to be independent of Empire, but rather have the role played by the colonies appreciated in London and rewarded by adequate consultation and consideration. The colonial policies of Great Britain as compared to France and Germany were also raised by Deakin, who lamented 'the disdain and indifference' bestowed upon them by the Colonial Office.[29] It was a remarkable display by a colonial politician.

Yet Deakin's speech was not entirely popular with the British elite. It was deemed too outspoken for the time, particularly for a politician and colonial from a far-flung colony.[30] Many delegates thought it was inappropriate, and British Prime Minister Salisbury was apparently not amused.[31] It was, however, the voice of the colonies speaking out strongly, not for independence but for greater authority within the imperial system.

Along with territorial concerns in the Pacific and constant fears about colonial defence, two significant conflicts embroiled the colonies before Federation. The first was the Boer War in South Africa in 1899, the second the Boxer Rebellion in China in 1900. The colonies, both government and citizens, seemed proud to become involved in both conflicts. There was an outpouring of loyalty to Great Britain: 'demonstrations of patriotic fervour, volunteers marched through the Australian city streets to the tunes of "Rule Britannia" and "Soldiers of the Queen"'.[32] It was again a sign of how strong was the sense of being British within the colonies.[33]

The Boer War was regarded as an opportunity by many Australians to show loyalty to the Mother Country in difficult times. It was also hoped that support would enhance Australia's prestige.[34] There was a hope that such a display would give the colony some influence in imperial affairs by proving an able and loyal contributor to imperial ambitions.

Deakin wrote in the *Morning Post*: 'The Mother Country stood alone. In an instant the cry was "Australia for the Empire".'[35] For the first time there was a significant interest in military affairs. Australia's colonial forces acquitted themselves with distinction in this war, with ingenuity and great courage.

The execution of Lieutenant Harry 'Breaker' Morant by Lord Kitchener in 1902 caused a great deal of resentment, and the colonies passed resolutions noting that in future the Australian military would be responsible for disciplinary actions involving Australian forces.[36] This showed a healthy concern to protect people who were shortly to become Australian citizens once the act of Federation had been consummated.

Despite the fact that Australia offered to send troops to South Africa, Joseph Chamberlain, Secretary of State for the Colonies, was not particularly enthusiastic. He thought war was a serious business and that untrained men from the colonies would not be much help. He did not want too many; he thought they would have to be looked after.[37]

Britain showed a significantly changed attitude when the Boxer Rebellion occurred in 1900, with the initial request to the Australian colonies coming from Joseph Chamberlain.[38] He asked for naval forces as shallow-draft vessels were required to navigate Chinese rivers. This followed views expressed by a former Governor of Victoria who had said that, in his view, the colonies would 'readily cooperate with the Imperial authorities in the Chinese war'.[39]

Australia's willingness to contribute to these wars, as in later wars, was in part fuelled by a desire to gain greater influence in the Empire and to create obligations from the Empire as a whole to Australia for Australian defence.

The issue of defence was omnipresent during the colonial years. In 1889 Major General Bevan Edwards provided Parkes and other colonial premiers with recommendations for continental defence. Edwards' report suggested that the colonies were indefensible as separate entities but that, as one nation, with one army and a unified command and structure, we would have a much greater chance of providing an adequate defence. His report was accepted by Parkes, although others described it as alarmist.[40] As Major General Bevan Edwards stated,

> If the Australian colonies had to rely at any time solely on their own resources, they would offer such a rich and tempting prize that they would certainly be called upon to fight for their independence, and isolated as Australia would be—without a proper supply of arms and ammunition, with forces which cannot at present be considered efficient in comparison with any moderately trained army, and without any cohesion or power of combination for mutual defence among the different colonies—its position would be one of great danger. Looking to the state of affairs in Europe, and so the fact that it is the unforeseen which happens in war, the defence forces should at once be placed on a proper footing; but this is, however, quite impossible without a federation of the forces of the different colonies.[41]

Edwards' report obviously motivated a number of premiers and particularly Parkes. It called for unified services and for central-ised control of those services, so there would be one cohesive and powerful fighting force. For such a proposal to work, a centralised body representing all six colonies would need to be established and operate effectively, allowing all colonial governments to participate in decision-making.

There was already a central body called the Federal Council, but it was appointed, it had no authority, no executive powers and no resources, and it certainly could not provide the centralised control of the defence force that Edwards had so strongly recommended.[42] Indeed it did not even include all of the colonies as members, with both New South Wales and South Australia being absent for most of the council's existence. The Federal Council was not a suitable body for Edwards' proposal.

The inadequacies of the Federal Council, together with the need to have some sort of centralised body, caused Parkes and other colonial statesmen to consider whether the time had now arisen for the creation of an Australian government. In his famous Tenterfield address in 1889, Parkes asked 'whether the time had not now arisen for the creation on this Australian continent of an Australian Government'.[43] He drew parallels to the American experience, arguing that what was achieved by blood and conflict in the United States could be achieved through peaceful means in Australia. Parkes also raised the issue of collective defence, highlighting the benefits of a federated force in ensuring the security and integrity of all the colonies.

By 1891 Parkes' ambition seemed to have expanded into the area of foreign affairs. He proclaimed that a federal government would 'undertake on behalf of Australia the intercourse with other parts of the world'.[44] Imagining a federation of colonies free to execute power and influence in its own interests on the international stage was ambitious and far more than any individual colony could ever hope to achieve in its own right.

Yet this ambition was, of course, not achieved. Although the Parkes idea of a federal government would be realised, Britain would remain master of foreign policy and of defence. Even after Federation Australia's communications with the rest of the world would still be through London and coordinated by the Colonial Office.

Although colonial leaders bickered about the best way to form a centralised coordinating body for the continent, many colonists continued to be concerned at the activities of other European powers around Papua New Guinea and the New Hebrides.[45] Later there was concern for trade and communication routes as the Russian Navy appeared off South Africa.[46] Issues of security and the strong desire to maintain British dominance of both the waters and the territories close to Australia gave a new impetus to moves for Federation in addition to aspirations being espoused by colonial leaders such as Parkes. The main purpose was always to seek a stronger voice within imperial circles and to put the self-governing colonies in the position to contribute even more to the strength of the British Empire—there was never any widespread desire to move outside imperial circles. So Parkes' fleeting mention of a wider authority over external policy in his 1891 speech was put aside and did not become a major part of the Federation story. Indeed, the ambitions expressed in those words were not really achieved until after World War II.

So the march towards Federation had begun. In 1891 a convention was held in Sydney prompted by Parkes' Tenterfield speech. A constitution, drafted largely by Sir Samuel Griffith, laid out four federal principles. It is notable that the external affairs power was not included. The four principles were:

- 'That the powers of the several colonies should remain intact, except for such surrenders as were necessary to the power of the national Government.'
- 'That trade and intercourse between the colonies by land and sea, should be absolutely free.'
- 'That the power to impose customs duties should be exclusively federal, subject to such disposal of the customs revenue as should be agreed upon.'
- 'That the naval and military defence of Australia be under federal control.'[47]

In 1897 Sir Edmund Barton made an important speech in which he sought to take the issue of Federation further, but he was cautious and his aspirations for the new Federation were strictly limited. He recognised quite clearly that foreign policy would be the prerogative of the Imperial Government and that the duty of a federated Australia would be to help implement that policy. He pushed for the exclusion of treating-making powers, arguing that although certain trade arrangements could be made by the proposed Commonwealth, such powers concerning foreign affairs should remain the prerogative of the Crown.[48] Barton had probably recognised that, if Australia had wished to exercise powers over foreign affairs and defence, there would have been major problems with the United Kingdom. It would have been a sticking point that Britain would not have approved.

In the next year, 1898, Deakin launched a campaign for Federation in Victoria and suggested that an Australian identity and a sense of belonging to an empire were principal objectives. It was also a rallying call to Victorian voters to vote yes for Federation. He suggested that the Empire was under siege and that a federal Australia would gain greater benefit and be able to do more to support that Empire. He spoke of unity and liberalism, enlightenment and opportunity, and raised the spectre of foreign foes. Only through unity would Australia outface the future, and it was a future that Deakin believed the Australian people should be free to create and control.[49] Yet it was a future that firmly involved Australia being a loyal member of the British Empire and not a strategically independent nation in its own right.

In the period leading to Federation another dominant theme along with security seemed to be that of an Australian identity—in particular a more effective and a more powerful identity as part of and within the British Empire. There was never any suggestion that Federation should carry with it any weakening of imperial ties. Indeed, from the outset it was understood, not only by Britain but also by such strong advocates of Federation as Deakin and Barton, that in matters of foreign affairs and defence a new Australia would defer to the United Kingdom. Australia's duty was to carry out the foreign policy determined by Britain itself.[50]

When the Constitution was finally agreed to, there was a provision that gave the new Australia control over external affairs, but it was unclear what that meant, what authority it involved. There was never a suggestion that it involved the making of a foreign policy that would be Australian rather than British. It was interpreted that the external affairs power gave Australia a capacity to play its part in supporting the foreign policy of Britain and international treaties made by Britain.

Along with security and identity, other reasons for Federation were problems with trade, customs and taxation. One of the most important matters to be agreed was that trade between the states would be absolutely free. There was no mention of what today would be called human rights. The basis of the Constitution was the division of power between the new Commonwealth of Australia and the states themselves. It was a bargain between the governing classes, a bargain that had to be approved by the British Government.

In some respects the proposed Constitution was far in advance of its time, and it is worth examining the desire for Australians to show independence of mind in terms of the nation they wanted—irrespective of the strategic dependence desired on the international stage. For example, one very important provision in the Constitution is Section 116, which, unlike in Britain, insists that the Commonwealth is to have no established church. The Commonwealth was denied the power that would have established any religion, which would have related to religious observance or which would have prohibited the free exercise of any religion. No religious test was to be allowed as a qualification for any office of public trust under the Commonwealth. Compared to the British experience, this was liberal and far-sighted. Although Australia had no desire to be independent in the international sense, it certainly exhibited independent thought when developing many domestic policies.

In earlier drafts of the Constitution, colonial leaders wanted legal appeals to the Privy Council to end, insisting that the High Court of Australia be the final arbiter of Australian law. Yet, at the insistence of the British Government, appeal to the Privy Council was included in the final text.[51] However, in a concession to the colonies, appeal to the Privy Council on constitutional matters could not occur unless the Australian High Court gave its own prior consent.[52] On constitutional matters the main determinant of the Constitution would be the Australian court.[53] It is interesting that the British were most concerned to maintain full appeals to the Privy Council for corporate and commercial matters. It was much later that the Commonwealth Parliament first limited appeals to the Privy Council quite substantially by the *Privy Council (Limitation of Appeals) Act 1968* and the *Privy Council (Appeals from the High Court) Act 1975*. These two Acts virtually ended appeals from the High Court.[54] Appeals from state Supreme Courts were not ended until 1986—eight decades for complete legal independence from the Crown.

In many ways, the Australian Constitution was unlike any modern constitution, because it had no overt protection of the rights of individuals within it. It was indeed a division of power between the new Commonwealth and the states of the Federation, a division of power sanctioned by the British Parliament. It was nevertheless in a number of respects an enlightened document. It was certainly more liberal than the constitutions of the respective colonies that pre-dated it, and in many ways the attitudes of the document's authors were well in advance of public opinion in Britain or, for that matter, the United States. Indeed, Deakin would claim that the Constitution accepted by the colonies and sent to the British Parliament for approval was more liberal than the Constitution of any of the colonies it was replacing.[55]

Although foreign affairs and defence represented a significant part of the motivation for Federation, they were certainly not the only factors. The prevailing view, very strongly held at the time, was that if the self-governing colonies at Federation could do more to strengthen the Empire and to achieve a greater voice within that Empire, then they would make themselves much more secure than if they were on their own, in charge of their own affairs. The fact that the new Constitution left foreign affairs and defence in British hands did not therefore minimise the importance of these issues in the minds of the colonists. Yet it does go towards establishing that the notion of strategic dependence has been present since our colonial days and was certainly a part of shaping Federation.

Australian citizens on Federation were proud of having achieved what they regarded as independence by peaceful means, and they considered themselves as members of the British Empire, which they wanted to strengthen. Alfred Deakin, who was staunchly national-istic, wrote in his anonymous London column in 1901 that Britain had 'nowhere among his dominions a more loyal people than those in the Southern Seas'.[56] Our early leaders did not know the impact that such strategic dependence on Britain was soon to have, nor of the long-lasting policy implications such dependence would have on generations of Australian leaders and policy-makers to come.

The major elements that bound the newly federated Australia to Britain was one of race, the need for a sense of security and a desire to have a more powerful voice in imperial circles. It is doubtful that the desire for a more powerful voice ever materialised. In many ways the new Federation, while combining the voices of the states, had no more influence than those states had as individual colonies.

There was also a mark of pride that we had achieved Federation by negotiation, whereas the United States had had to fight for its separation from Britain. The marked difference between the two, however, was that the United States achieved true independence and true sovereignty whereas our sovereignty was heavily circumscribed. And it established a dichotomy within the Australian polity as there was an absolute determination that the United Kingdom should not interfere in the internal management of Australia, but for a considerable period the new Federation was content to allow Britain to conduct foreign and defence policy on behalf of Australia. The arguments for Federation had not been arguments for independence and freedom as a fully sovereign or strategically independent state. They had been arguments to establish a more powerful entity that would have greater influence in the imperial voice.

So, the newly federated Australia controlled its domestic concerns but abdicated responsibility for foreign affairs, as well as the majority of defence, to the British Empire. The roots of strategic dependence had been planted. Yet it was probably the right decision for the time—given our isolation, our small population and our lack of industrial capacity, what choice did Australian leaders have? This policy, however, would not be without its faults and would not be without its costs. Indeed, there is one final prescient remark that has a resonance to this very day, one that should be recorded, and it also leads us on to the next chapter. Victorian parliamentarian H.B. Higgins declared at the time of Federation: 'The people will be wanting to know whether we in these colonies are to be expected to volunteer each time to contribute valuable lives and money in aid of wars which may not interest us directly.'[57]

2

Strategic dependence consolidated

Australia emerged from its colonial era wanting to build a nation that was very different from Great Britain. For the time, it had progressive ideals but still wanted the comfort of protection by the world's dominant imperial power. We were a new nation, but we were not an independent nation and had no real passion to be one. Britain still had command of our present and of our future, and Australia's early leaders took comfort in the protection this provided.

This chapter examines how the young Australia attempted to reconcile what it wanted to achieve domestically while attempting to carve a role for itself at the imperial table; aiming to ensure that British foreign policy took note of Australia's needs and wants. It was a period in which Australia would still not push for an independent foreign and defence policy but rather consolidate the notion of strategic dependence. Australia would pay greatly for this consolidation, with the Great War costing so many thousands of Australian lives less than twenty years after the creation of our nation.

Yet the policy of dependence remained the best option in the context of a newly formed nation, geographically isolated and industrially under-developed. Within this policy, Australia's early leaders, particularly Alfred Deakin and Billy Hughes, manoeuvered for a greater say in imperial policy-making, for a greater outcome for Australia within the imperial structure. Their efforts were usually met with disdain from the Colonial Office. It was a price we had to pay for our strategic dependence. Although Australian leaders never envisaged any foreign or defence policy resembling independence, the latitude afforded to Australia by Britain in those early years to influence imperial efforts in areas of concern to Australia was strictly limited.

During the initial years post-Federation, the Commonwealth was significantly concerned with building a new and different society. Class structures of Britain were to have no part in Australia. The architects of Federation wanted Australia to be different. The federated nation would respect its British heritage, but develop a more egalitarian society devoid of entrenched privilege. Alfred Deakin himself would emphasise this desire by always refusing any imperial honour. It would be differentiated from the American experience by its peaceful union and its continual commitment to the British Empire. It was to be a nation of both Australians and imperial citizens. Although the policy of strategic dependence meant Australia had little say over the defence and foreign policy of the Empire, it did provide the security to pursue its domestic agenda relatively unhindered.

One of the early priorities was an attempt to establish a sense of social justice within Australia, of a kind that had never existed in Britain and which would set an example to the world. Deakin, supported by others, was one of the chief protagonists of this approach. For example, the *Franchise Act 1902*, although it was not contained in the Constitution, was passed early in the life of the new Parliament by the new Federation. Its purpose was to give adult suffrage to women.

The Act did two things, one good and one bad. It gave adult suffrage to women on the same basis as applied to men. There were no property restrictions, the same age limit applied to both and its passing by the Parliament put Australia nearly two decades ahead of Britain. Indeed, it was not until 1918 that British women received a limited right to vote, but it was heavily circumscribed, women had to be older than thirty, as opposed to twenty-one for men, and they either had to be married or to have owned property. In the United States women did not gain the right to vote until 1919. Australia, at least in the English-speaking world, was a world leader.

Yet the Franchise Act was also bad for Indigenous Australians. Male Aboriginal people and Torres Strait Islanders had had a right to vote in all states with the exception of Queensland and Western Australia. In South Australia, where women had won the right to vote before Federation, Indigenous women also had suffrage. Neither of these rights was propagated throughout Indigenous communities and they were little known and little understood, and therefore very few Aboriginal people or Torres Strait Islanders actually voted.[1] The introduction of the Franchise Act abolished those rights for all Indigenous Australians.[2] Section 41 of the Constitution should have protected the right of all Indigenous Australians to vote after Federation,[3] yet there was very little debate concerning the constitutional validity of the Franchise Act at the time. Such disregard was consistent with the new Federation's determination to establish the White Australia Policy.

The strength of feeling of the time, at least among some Australians, towards both the White Australia policy and removing the Indigenous vote, is exhibited in a quote by Senator Alexander Matheson from Western Australia: 'Surely it is absolutely repugnant to the greater number of the people of the Commonwealth that an aboriginal man, or aboriginal lubra or gin—a horrible, degraded, dirty creature—should have the same rights, simply by virtue of being 21 years of age, that we have, after some debate today, decided to give to our wives and daughters.' Senator De Largie from Western Australia also said that 'it would be as sensible to give votes to the lunatics in an asylum as to the aboriginals'.[4] Clearly feelings ran very strongly on the question of Aboriginals fulfilling their natural right as citizens, which they were denied for well over half a century.

In addition to the racial limitation the Franchise Act facilitated on voting rights, the new Parliament legislated for the White Australia

Policy, further enshrining in legislation the racial prejudices of the time. Sadly, we see remnants of that policy in the refugee debates that take place at the present time.

There was also legislation designed to have a lasting positive social influence. One of the most important acts in this regard was to establish the Court of Conciliation and Arbitration.[5] The purpose of the court was to settle conflicts between employees and employers and to determine just reward for labour. Perhaps the most famous judgment of all time from that commission was the Harvester judgment in 1907.[6] It determined the just wage, which was seven shillings a day in 1907, based on the lowest realistic wage that could reasonably sustain a husband, a wife and two children.

Such a determination was wider in its scope and more all-encompassing than equivalent determinations in other countries. Britain enacted a similar policy only in 1909, and the United States did not introduce national statutory minimum wages until 1938.[7] Canada had established a fair wages policy in 1900, but its coverage was extraordinarily limited.[8] So, by the standard of the time, the new Commonwealth performed well in this area. Furthermore, an age and invalid pension was established under new legislation in 1908.[9]

The Constitution and the attitudes of our first parliamentarians had a significant influence on the way Australians would lead their lives. The social attitudes and underpinning social philosophy of Australians were from the beginning—and remain to this day—quite different from those of the United Kingdom and the United States.

Yet the attempts to differentiate Australian society and policy from Great Britain did not extend to all areas of Commonwealth Government activity. The early post-Federation politicians had not wanted to establish a separate foreign or defence policy, despite the fact that defence was an element in persuading the colonies that they should federate. It was argued in those days that Federation would give Australia a stronger voice within the Imperial Council, that Federation would enable us to influence imperial policy, or at least influence it to a greater extent than an individual colony might hope to. At the first Colonial Conference Australia attended as a federated nation in 1902, our leaders were still content to allow matters of foreign and defence policy to be decided by Britain.[10] The new Federation, as the individual colonies had before it, wanted to support the aims of Empire and believed that these aims would provide the best protection for Australia. This was not done reluctantly but with enthusiasm and a belief in Empire coupled with a naive faith in the wisdom and righteousness of the United Kingdom.

Accordingly, defence and foreign policy did not receive much attention from the new Australia.[11] Australia felt no real sense of urgency to craft an independent defence and foreign policy position. Its reliance on the United Kingdom and on the imperial power was substantial. Its ability to influence matters of foreign policy was virtually non-existent. The Commonwealth Government did not possess a genuinely independent capacity to execute external affairs as London controlled foreign representations, major trade negotiations, defence issues and matters of high policy with foreign nations.[12] Although the Department of External Affairs was one of the first Commonwealth departments created, it did not function in a manner consistent with the modern department we have today. External affairs during the first decades of Federation meant 'a miscellany of "overseas" functions such as immigration, off-shore fisheries, exploration of Papua New Guinea and Antarctica, and Commonwealth Government publicity'.[13]

Even the extraordinarily limited rights over foreign policy-making afforded to Australia—such as limited representation over matters of trade—were exercised only sparingly and usually through the Department of Trade,[14] again highlighting the Commonwealth's reluctance to act independently over external affairs. Our window to the world was through London and, although an officer was appointed in 1906,[15] a High Commissioner was not appointed until 1910 when Sir George Reid of New South Wales became Australia's first High Commissioner to Great Britain. It would take close to half a century after Federation before Australia built a substantial department of external affairs and set about establishing significant overseas representation.

The Colonial Conferences held in the later stages of the nineteenth century were to continue during the early decades of the twentieth. At these conferences Dominion leaders slowly, gradually and hesitatingly sought to exercise some influence over imperial foreign and defence policy. On the face of it the conferences were held to allow them a voice. Another interpretation of why these conferences were held, and one which I prefer, was to try to maintain British dominance of foreign and defence policy.

Coinciding with the coronation of Edward VII in 1902, the first Colonial Conference of the twentieth century was again held in London. It was also the first time that the newly federated Australia joined Canada as a Dominion of the British Empire. Despite the growing stature of the two Dominions and the other self-governing colonies within the Empire, continual reference to 'Colonial' in the name of the conference emphasised that Britain did not really regard the status of Australia as having changed, merely that the colonies now had one united voice. The Colonial Conference was symbolic of Britain's mindset, of its attitude to the colonies, of its belief that self-government did not really alter their status in the wider world. The British would have believed that the Dominions had no greater power and no greater authority than that which had been accorded the self-governing colonies before Federation. This is a position that nations dependent upon another for defence and foreign policy should come to expect. Why should we expect a great power to treat a dependent nation, even if an ally, as an equal?

When he was opening the conference, Chamberlain as Secretary of State of the Colonies quite bluntly told the Dominion prime ministers that Britain could not bear the whole burden of defence indefinitely and that the position of the Dominions 'was inconsistent with their dignity as nations'.[16] Chamberlain did not seem to notice the contradiction in his own statement. Chamberlain seemingly wanted to shift some of the cost of defence onto the colonies, but not provide any mechanism for the colonies to have a greater say in policy priorities. How is this any more dignified? There was an assumption by the British, which was probably correct, that the colonies were still content to allow Britain, on behalf of the Empire, to manage foreign policy. Cost-sharing made sense for London if Whitehall was to provide the bulk of the imperial defences, yet it should have been predicated on giving the colonies a greater say in how the resources were to be spent.

The Colonial Conference of 1907 was the last under that name, with New Zealand joining Australia and Canada as a Dominion. The conferences had so far achieved little, and the 1907 conference in particular emphasised very clearly the limitation of the power of the new Australian Government. One of the main objectives of Australia at the 1907 conference had been to achieve greater influence on imperial policy and decision-making.[17] Australian leaders accepted that although Britain might have the ultimate say in determining policy for the Empire, there was scope for more Dominion input into that policy.

As such, the Australian delegates advanced the concept of the British and Dominion prime ministers forming an Imperial Council to integrate foreign policy and foreign policy decision-making.[18] The United Kingdom, of course, did not take kindly to this idea. The relatively minor changes achieved by the Dominions did not go far enough for Deakin, who subsequently warned that 'if some way could not be found to admit the dominions to imperial decision-making, Australia would be obliged to go it alone in foreign policy'.[19] Deakin did not wish for a completely independent Australian stance, but rather a greater role in shaping a shared imperial approach to international events. Deakin's words were prophetic; it was the force of circumstances at the end of World War II that forced Australia to reconsider its policy of strategic dependence on Britain. It resulted in a decision to maintain the policy of strategic dependence but to transfer it to the United States.

In 1911 the first Imperial Conference was held. The Australian Prime Minister Andrew Fisher took a very quiet line over foreign policy. He asked for greater Dominion say in policy issues affecting Australia but qualified this request by saying 'we do not desire in any way to restrict the final arbitrary powers of the Mother Country'.

Again, Fisher expressed a desire for more influence within, rather than independence from, the British Empire. This was the standard line for leaders of the era. Nonetheless, such an attitude was most unlikely to have any influence on the United Kingdom or to advance Australia's influence in the international policy of the Empire. As far as Britain was concerned the Empire rested on 'the local autonomy of its white members and the prestige and strength of the metropolitan power'.[20] It was at this conference that it was agreed that Dominion warships would be placed under British control in the event of war.[21]

Despite varying attempts by Australian leaders to carve out a greater role for Australia in imperial affairs through the conferences, the general malaise towards defence and foreign policy was still very evident on the domestic front. Bickering over the potential for an Australian naval force is one such example. Australia's Prime Minister Barton did not want to establish an Australian naval force, although others in his government would have wished to do so. Instead, he recommended paying a larger sum—around £200,000— to the British to enable provision of a less out-of-date squadron in Australian waters.[22]

There was still a fervent belief that one imperial navy would best serve the interests of all parts of the Empire. As West Australian Premier John Forrest put it, 'If the British nation is at war, so are we; if it gains victories or suffers disasters, so do we … There is only one sea to be supreme over, and we want one fleet to be mistress over that sea … Our aim and object should be to make the Royal Navy the Empire's Navy, supported by the whole of the self-governing portions of the Empire …'[23]

Australia did not like and did not really want the cost of defence. Although the government was content to be dependent on the Royal Navy, they wanted some say in how a continental defence policy might be implemented. By 1902 they had become quite unimpressed with the efficiency of the War Office. They were disenchanted with Britain because the Admiralty kept only old, obsolete war ships on the Australian station in return for the annual fee paid by Australia.[24] Deakin would push for the building of Australian ships of war, building on public disquiet over defence after a series of Japanese naval victories.[25]

Deakin's efforts were not entirely unsuccessful. In 1909 Prime Minister Fisher said that Australia intended to obtain a flotilla of twenty-three naval destroyers, which would allow the Commonwealth Government to 'take over the responsibility of coastal defence, and ... relieve the Admiralty of the cost of the present squadron ... thus making Australia a great self-defended naval base for the Empire and the Pacific'.[26] Deakin's actions were a sign of some independent thought, but even this nationalistic Prime Minister saw Australia's squadron as forming part of imperial forces for imperial defence. It was an example of some independent thinking within a policy of dependence.

It was not just naval concerns that early governments had to contend with as some held the broader view that Australia was in a more difficult position than other Dominions in attempting to establish effective armed forces. Australian forces had never participated in a major war, as had other Dominions.[27] New Zealand had had major wars against the Maoris. South Africa had done so both against the Boers and against indigenous nations. Canada had participated in multiple military campaigns across North America in efforts to subject the local Indian population. Australia's subjection of Aboriginal people was quieter and more dispersed. It in fact involved that part of the population which moved inland, but there was no major military campaign. As was clearly shown by Chamberlain's reaction to the offer to colonial troops to fight in the Boer War, the United Kingdom regarded Australians as not versed in military matters, with no adequate training or experience.

Against this backdrop, a number of foreign policy issues were emerging with implications for defence policy of concern to the Commonwealth Government. Australian leaders began to be significantly frustrated, not so much by their lack of diplomatic independence—they did not seek independent representation outside London—but rather by their incapacity to influence imperial policy with an Australian point of view. A greater voice within the

Empire had been one of the drivers of Federation. It was disappointing to find that Britain regarded the newly federated nation as having no more say in imperial foreign policy and defence than the self-governing colonies had had.

Despite the frustrations, Britain's positions on these matters were accepted by the Australian political leadership of the times. Yet it made the process of raising foreign policy issues overly complicated. For example, during the 1907 Colonial Conference Australia had raised with London concerns about French activities in the New Hebrides, and particularly about France sending convicts to New Caledonia, yet the government had no mechanism to raise them directly with Paris. Instead, Deakin had to contact the Colonial Office, who then referred his request to the Foreign Office, who then had the issue investigated by the British ambassador in Paris, who then reported back to the Foreign Office, who relayed the information to the Colonial Office, who provided it to the Governor General in Melbourne, who then finally passed it on to Deakin.[28] No leader of a truly independent nation would suffer such a process. Indeed it took so long that by the time the Colonial Office was in a position to report back on French activities in the New Hebrides, Deakin had returned to Melbourne.

Although operating within a policy of dependence and the processes established by the Colonial Office, Australia did on occasion act directly, often receiving rebuke from London as a result. For example, Deakin asked the United States, which was sending the Great White Fleet on a world tour, to call on Australian ports. Deakin made direct representations to American officials in both London and Melbourne, inviting the fleet to visit Australian ports not only as a demonstration of American naval power in the Pacific but also to indicate to the United Kingdom its growing concern about imperial naval policy in the region—particularly given the growing strength of Japanese military power. Deakin ultimately asked London to issue a formal invitation, but the visit was a *fait accompli*, with Washington having responded favourably to Australian overtures. Both Whitehall and the Foreign Office were appalled, with the

British Foreign Secretary, Sir Edward Grey, sternly reminding Deakin that 'invitations to foreign governments should not be given except through us'.[29]

This exchange emphasised that, although Australia was federated as one nation, in the British mind we were still a colony. While we could do largely whatever we wanted within our own boundaries, if we wanted to be in the Empire, we were bound by British rules, by British decisions and by British control. This is far short of nationhood, and such a perception by the great power of the smaller ally is symbolic of the relationship inherent in a policy of strategic dependence.

During this time other events started to cause concern among Australians. In 1904–05 the Russo-Japanese War took place, and resulted in an easy victory for Japan. This led to a reluctant Commonwealth legislating for its own navy.[30]

In subtle ways the Russo-Japanese War had most unfortunate consequences. Japan had all along wanted to be regarded as a Western nation, accepted into the halls of the West on equal terms. Japan was a sophisticated nation with a well-ordered and, for the time, well-governed society. Japan thought it necessary to demonstrate military power to gain acceptance by the West, but when Japan exhibited military strength, they found that it caused greater concern and even fear. The Japanese victory did not advance its relationships with the West and certainly caused Australia to be concerned.

These events led Deakin to undertake a concerted campaign to stimulate public defiance of Admiralty opposition to a local navy and prepared the ground for Australia's first ships of war.[31] Again, Deakin showed a willingness to act for Australian interests within the context of broader imperial defence policy.

Despite growing concerns about Japanese influence and increasing power, Japan was on the side of the Allies during World War I as Tokyo was aligned to Britain. Britain had signed the first Anglo-Japanese Alliance in London at the end of January 1902. The Alliance was renewed and expanded in scope in 1905 and in 1911. An alliance between Britain and Japan had been discussed for a number of years.

Britain was in better standing with Japan than France, Germany or Russia, which intervened against the Japanese occupation on the Liaodong Peninsula.

Britain was also helpful in assisting Japan in its drive to modernise its industry. Japan had been cooperative in helping to put down the Boxer Rebellion. This probably had less to do with relationships between Britain or the other powers than it did with Japan's own perception of itself and of its relations with China. It would have been in Japan's interests to keep China weak. Therefore support of Britain and other Western powers during the Boxer Rebellion is more a function of its policy towards China than it was a desire to be friendly to Britain.

The deepening of the relationship between Britain and Japan happened without significant discussions with the Dominions, especially with Canada or Australia, two Dominions in the Pacific and both fearful of Japanese expansion, immigration and militarisation.[32] Nonetheless, after long-drawn-out discussions, London and Tokyo came to an agreement and the alliance was signed, but Japan's interests and dominance over Korea was excluded from any British obligation.[33] In 1905 the Treaty was amended, again without discussions with the Dominions. The reservations in relation to Korea were removed, and Japan acknowledged British interests in India, thereby expanding the obligations of both parties.[34] Korea at this time was under Japanese control.

As one might expect, the United States and China were both at various stages very strongly opposed to the Anglo-Japanese Alliance, but the fact that it existed kept France out of the Russo-Japanese War in 1904–05.[35] This was because the terms of the Anglo-Japanese Alliance meant that any involvement in the war by France would probably mean going to war also with Britain. The Anglo-Japanese Alliance would have been highly significant in persuading Japan to enter World War I on the side of Britain and its allies.

All of this was high policy, policy that Britain reserved entirely for itself. As a great power one could not have expected anything else. London probably would have believed that the Dominions did not have the diplomatic experience or skills to contribute anything to discussions concerning it, but also might well have believed that Australia in particular, and perhaps Canada, would have different interests and might provide an impediment to the UK–Japanese treaty.[36] The Anglo-Japanese Alliance was on the British agenda before Federation.[37] However, with the 1902 and later Colonial and Dominion conferences, it was never a substantive matter for discussion. The idea of the Dominions contributing to Empire policy was no more than an idea.

In 1914, when war broke out in Europe, Britain's declaration of war encompassed the Empire and all its constituent parts—Australia included. In the environment of the time, it would have been unthinkable for the Australian Government to make a separate declaration of war. In the British view, we had no capacity to do so, since Britain made decisions relating to foreign policy and defence for and on behalf of the Empire. Our policy of dependence meant we were also at war. The policy would exact a severe and bloody toll on Australia.

Instead of announcing a declaration like a sovereign nation, in August 1914 the Australian Governor General, Sir Ronald Munro Ferguson, sent the Secretary of State for the Colonies a message indicating that Australia stood ready: 'In the event of war Common-wealth of Australia prepared to place vessels of the Australian Navy under control of British Admiralty when desired. Further prepared to despatch expeditionary force 20,000 men of any suggested com-position to any destination desired by Home Government. Force to be at complete disposal Home Government. Cost of despatch and maintenance would be borne by this Government. Australian press notified accordingly.'[38]

At this time, the total Australian army strength was a little more than 45,000 men, but the expeditionary force promised to Britain would have to be volunteers alone because the Defence Act did not permit compulsory service beyond Australian shores.[39] Volunteers would be required to fulfil Australia's promise to Great Britain. This also was an issue that not only resonated during the two plebiscites concerning conscription during World War I but also had repercussions during World War II, especially on relationships between Australia and the United States.

The Australian Government did insist on one thing. During the Boer War small numbers of Australians had been dispersed through the British forces, reflecting Chamberlain's view that they would be totally untrained, not of much use and would have to be looked after. Australia insisted that the force, to be called the Australian Imperial Force, would have a commander responsible to the Australian Government and that it would be a national force that would be fighting as a national unit and not to be dispersed through other elements of British forces.[40]

Australia's first major involvement in the war related to Gallipoli. The Launceston *Daily Telegraph* reported in 1915: 'The manner in which our Australian military members of the British family have borne the first severe test proves conclusively that the sons of the Empire … are of the same mettle as the founders and builders of our race.'[41] At the time, Australia's attitude to Gallipoli might have in part been influenced because we had not fought for independence and we had not been involved in major wars on our own account, as had other Dominions.

This lack of military experience had some resonance when we participated in the Gallipoli campaign and in our own memories of that campaign, as perhaps the major 'bloodying' of Australia as a nation. There are still those who say that a nation does not find its full identity until it has indeed been blooded in war. It is an old view and one that I do not accept, especially so as we were involved in the Gallipoli campaign as a result of British decisions, as a result of British planning, a plan that involved inadequate forces and incompetent command. Many also had serious doubts about the underlying strategy of the Gallipoli campaign. In accord with the practice of the times we made no contribution to the strategy, to the tactics, to the execution of a campaign that cost 8709 Australian lives.[42]

Gallipoli should not be remembered as something that contributed to the founding of Australia as a nation because, from the Australian point of view, the whole operation was subject to British decision and control. Gallipoli should be remembered for the courage of the Australian soldiers, for the mateship they showed, for their ingenuity, for their skill, for their endurance and for their extraordinary bravery as soldiers. A nation needs more than these characteristics to be called a nation. The earlier achievements of Australia in seeking to establish a new and egalitarian society offer, in many ways, a better basis for describing the nature of Australian society.

It is also again worth recording an attitude expressed for a second time by Victorian federal parliamentarian H.B. Higgins, who would later become a High Court Justice, in an early parliamentary debate in the Federal Parliament on foreign policy: 'Are we ... to adopt the principle that we should actively side with Great Britain, no matter what is done? ... commit Australia to the principle that she must aid the Imperial Government in all wars ... although she has no voice in the negotiations which precede the war, and is not to be consulted in regard to its expedience or necessity.'[43] It is clear that Higgins' words accurately depicted the reality. If one had been able to say to Higgins that his fears would be relevant well into the twenty-first century with every prospect of that lack of independence continuing, he would have been appalled at that, and at the lack of strength of Australian leaders.

Whatever great qualities Australian soldiers exhibited at Gallipoli, that campaign did not represent Australia's coming of age. Coming of age also involves independence of mind, of spirit, of decision-making in foreign affairs and defence, attributes we were denied.

As the war progressed, other issues emerged. Prime Minister Billy Hughes became greatly concerned at the possibility of Japan being given control of islands formerly occupied by Germany in any peace settlement. Japan would have expected some benefits, some reward for having supported the Allies during the war, but, as it all ended, Japan found itself subjected to very considerable hostility, particularly from Australia.

The British Government wanted to ask Japan for naval assistance in the Mediterranean theatre and gave this pursuit priority over

Australian concerns regarding Japanese territorial expansion. The British thought the Australian position against friendship with Japan, especially the rights of Japanese individuals to enter Australia as a part of any new arrangement, as somewhat of a double standard. London told the Australian Government they could hardly say to the Japanese that Britain valued their contribution to winning this war but we will not grant you concessions in China or most favoured nation treatment as recompense for your participation.[44] Japan could hardly be expected to take Britain's protestations of friendship seriously.

Hughes was absolutely adamant about not allowing Japanese to enter Australia. He told the British Foreign Secretary, Sir Edward Grey, that 'Australia would fight to the last ditch rather than allow Japanese to enter Australia'.[45] In terms of territorial acquisition, Hughes was slightly less vociferous, arguing that Australia was willing to consider the Equator as a line of demarcation, with the Australian Government controlling the islands to the south. London was eventually successful in getting Tokyo to agree to the British Empire's right over German territories south of the Equator after the war, with Great Britain duly acknowledging Japan's claims over the territories to the north and in Shantung.[46] The Japanese further agreed to send naval forces to assist the British effort in the Mediterranean and South Atlantic.

The casualty rate on the Western Front was horrific. In order to meet Australia's commitments, five thousand volunteers were needed each month to keep pace with casualties.[47] At times Australian divisions were not fully manned because volunteerism was not providing sufficient troops. Hughes came to believe that conscription was needed if our commitment to Britain to maintain five fully equipped divisions on the Western Front was to be kept. Indirectly, this question was to lead to great sectarian bitterness, even hatred, throughout Australia between Catholics and Protestants. It was a bitterness that did not start to die until significantly after World War II.

A young Catholic bishop had arrived from Ireland shortly before the war, Daniel Mannix. He was reported as having said that, although he was not against the German war and wanted to see a just peace, he was against conscription because it would make an unequal commitment on Australia's part even more unequal.[48] He based those comments on the extent of Australian casualties, which provided full justification for his comments.

The first plebiscite that would have enabled conscription to go ahead failed. The British Government then asked Australia to provide a 6th Division, which would require seven thousand replacements a month.[49] Hence there was a second plebiscite. Although Mannix, at the request of the Catholic hierarchy, had not said very much during the first plebiscite, because of Hughes' attack he decided to ignore the injunction of the Catholic hierarchy. During this second plebiscite he spoke strongly against conscription. However, it should be remembered that he was never against the war as such. Prime Minister Hughes claimed that Mannix 'preached sedition in season and out of season' and that 'behind Dr Mannix are arrayed the Independent Workers of the World and the reckless extremists responsible for the recent strike, the pacifists and the pro-Germans'.[50] Such attacks on Mannix caused deep bitterness within Australia's Catholic community. The consequences represent a clear lesson to politicians who play politics with race and religion. Such actions can create serious divisions that will take decades to overcome. As a result of such actions by Hughes, a sectarian divide was created in Australia between Catholic and Protestant that did not start to disappear until the late 1950s.

By 1917 the idea of consultation between different parts of the Empire was gathering greater traction. Britain established the Imperial War Cabinet and the Imperial War Conference, which would include all Dominion prime ministers.[51] Although William Morris Hughes was in today's terms an outrageous, religious and racist bigot, he made his presence felt and argued passionately for interests that he believed were important for Australia. Yet he was still very much an Empire man and wanted Australia's voice to be effective within the Empire. The policy of dependence on Britain continued under Hughes. There is no doubt that he influenced the outcome of the peace settlements and, perhaps almost single-handedly,

41

prevented the racial non-discrimination clause being introduced in the preamble to the League of Nations. These are not necessarily achievements to be proud of. Yet his efforts to speak for Australia gained much support in Australia and should have served as a clear warning to Britain that its dominance and control of foreign affairs and defence would not long endure.

It is hard to generalise about the attitudes of any particular Dominion, but the extent of Australian casualties, which were extraordinarily high, coupled with the bitterness and hatreds aroused during the conscription debates, caused many people to question the price that Australia was paying for devotion to Empire. Some were beginning to question the good sense of Australia automatically following Britain to war.[52]

Despite the questioning of imperial wisdom, most of Hughes' Cabinet colleagues were stalwart Empire men, and many still argued that strong imperial cohesion added to the strength of them all. Participation in Britain's wars was the key to maintaining this cohesion. Yet Hughes throughout was unpredictable and tended to go his own way and rarely consulted his colleagues.[53] This trait was to become very evident at the conclusion of the war when Hughes led Australia's delegation to the Paris Peace Conference.

As the end of the war drew near and an Allied victory became likely, thoughts turned to how the post-conflict international landscape might look. If Australia was to have any say in the new global order, its voice needed to be heard both within and outside the imperial family. Hughes was determined not only to make Australia's position on a number of key issues known, and the best place to do this was in Europe, but also to push Australia's position through the structures of Empire.[54] Hughes knew that, to make Australia's view known, he had to do so as a member of the British Empire. If Britain would not accept an independent Australian position on the post-war order, the other powers, particularly America, certainly would not.

In 1918 he left for London via the United States, where he met President Woodrow Wilson. Hughes was concerned to impress upon the President the importance of extracting reparations from Germany and the importance of detaching Germany from Papua New Guinea or from any islands in the Pacific. He emphasised the necessity of such territories belonging only to the British Empire and friendly powers. In these discussions Wilson was apparently non-committal, but he also would have understood that Hughes had another agenda, namely to limit Japanese influence throughout the Pacific.[55] Wilson would have been well aware of Hughes' general attitude to Japan and had to balance that with American aspirations on policy throughout the Pacific, which would involve views not necessarily held by Australia. This applied in particular to Australian attitudes to Japan but also to the United Kingdom.

At this time, Hughes, in advance of other Australians, became convinced that we should have our own embassy in the United States. He spoke of the British ignorance of Australia's importance, and he spoke disparagingly of the senior British officials in New York, particularly the Consul General.[56]

Hughes and Joseph Cook, as Minister for the Navy, attended the Imperial War Conference and the Imperial War Cabinet and remained in London until the armistice was signed. That meant Hughes was absent from Australia for well over a year. At the Imperial War Conference and the Imperial War Cabinet he argued strongly for a united Empire policy and for maximum reparations to be made by Germany. He argued that all German colonies should be detached from Berlin's control. Hughes persuaded British Prime Minister Lloyd George to make him chairman of the Imperial Reparations Committee. Its purpose was to decide how much Germany should pay to members of the Empire, and Hughes was adamant that the Germans would incur a heavy financial penalty for their actions.

Hughes pushed an Australian position within the Imperial War Conference and wanted the ability to voice his concerns at the forthcoming peace conference on behalf of an Australian representation. Yet his own Cabinet had cabled him advice that 'claim for representation of Dominions as Dominions, either at Versailles or Peace Conference, is not reasonable and cannot be supported by Cabinet'.[57] It is strange that an Australian Cabinet, even at that time, and after the horrific casualties suffered during the war, was prepared quietly to argue that it was not reasonable for the Dominions to be directly represented at the Peace Conference and that such an idea should not be supported. On this issue Hughes was a maverick, in contrast to his staunchly imperial Cabinet. If Hughes was attempting to exert an independent Australian standpoint, bucking against automatic acquiescence to London's demands, his Cabinet was certainly opposed, being cautious of upsetting standard practice. The only justification for such an argument would be that separate representation as Dominions would in fact weaken the Empire and thus weaken their own ultimate position.

Hughes as chairman of the Imperial Reparations Committee, as well as Prime Minister of Australia and part of the British delegation, argued strongly against Wilson's Fourteen Points, particularly against calls for no annexations, reparations and indemnities, for the so-called freedom of the seas (I suppose unless it diminished the range of British sea power) and for a utopian League of Nations, which would outlaw war. Hughes told British audiences that they should not listen 'to the babble of talk from visionaries and doctrinaires'.[58] There is no doubt that Hughes' influence as chairman of the Imperial Reparations Committee contributed to one of the most vindictive and later damaging aspects of a peace treaty with Germany. The weight of reparations was beyond reason and opened the door to the most extreme views within Germany itself. Yet, by and large, the post-war order was decided by nations other than Australia, despite Hughes' efforts. Australia was still seen as a part of the British Empire, with Britain its rightful representative.[59] Strategic dependence and recognition as a nation with its own views and agendas do not often come hand in hand.

Lloyd George, against Hughes' wishes, had been given permission by the British Cabinet to present Wilson's Fourteen Points as the basis for the Armistice with exception to freedom of the seas and reparations. As his prime ministerial predecessors before him had done (and many more after him would do), Hughes complained to the British that the Dominions had not been properly consulted.[60]

He had concerns on many areas of imperial foreign policy, including the state of former German Pacific islands and terms at the forthcoming Paris Peace Conference, and generally disliked the proposed League of Nations.[61] Hughes' concerns about the consequences at the end of the war were increased by activities of the Japanese, who claimed islands north of the Equator, formerly in German possession. This caused Hughes again to press Australia's strategic concerns on Lloyd George.[62]

The Japanese had prepared a preamble to the League of Nations arguing for racial non-discrimination.[63] Hughes opposed it.[64] The Japanese produced a second draft trying to overcome the difficulties. The second draft contains these words: 'The equality of nations being a basic principle of the League of Nations, the High Contracting Parties agree that concerning the treatment and rights to be accorded to aliens in their territories, they will not discriminate, either in law or in fact, against any person or persons on account of his or her race or nationality.' Today these words would be regarded as unexceptional. It is probable that, if left to themselves, Woodrow Wilson would have accepted this preamble, although he had been warned especially by west coast Democrats in the United States that, on issues of race, the President would have to tread carefully if he wanted to be re-elected.[65]

Yet the Japanese proposal would ultimately be undermined by the Dominions, especially by Australia and Prime Minister Hughes.[66] It seemed that Britain did not want a major argument with the Dominions on these issues and really left the running of policy on such matters to the Dominions, which meant to Hughes.[67] A number of members of the Peace Conference tried to organise a meeting to reach compromise words in relation to the Japanese preamble. When approached about this, Hughes said that he would not attend because they did not understand. It was not the words that were at fault but the very idea of racial equality that was so repugnant and offensive.[68]

A number of other people made it plain that they did not think too highly of William Morris Hughes. Wilson called him a 'pestiferous varmint'.[69] Hughes said he had been called a lot worse and did not care what the President called him. The Australian Labor Party had called him a 'rat', which was totally predictable, and expelled him from its ranks, about which he recalled years later: 'I did not leave the Labor party. The party left me.'[70] Lord Robert Cecil described him as 'that shrimp'. President Clemenceau of France referred to him as a 'cannibal'; maybe that was just Gallic humour.[71]

Hughes' relationship with President Wilson was not at all friendly, largely because of their differences concerning the ex-German territories. There was never a chance that Hughes and Wilson could get on together. Hughes was the ultimate pragmatic; he defined his particular interest or interpreted what he thought were Australian interests in narrow and harshly practical terms. Wilson was in many ways a dreamer, remote from the harsh realities of that world; he was too far ahead of his time. He dreamed of a world without war, the peace being held by the League of Nations. Many years after the destruction of the League of Nations, despite the development of the United Nations we still do not know whether Wilson's high aspirations will ever be fulfilled. While discussing whether German territories should be placed under the control of the League of Nations, 'Wilson asked whether the Australasians insisted on presenting an ultimatum to "the whole civilised world".'

Hughes impudently replied, 'That's about the size of it, President Wilson.'[72]

There was no love lost between the Australian Prime Minister and the American President—imagine if such an exchange were to occur today. Such independence displayed by Hughes was more down to his personality than a concerted effort by the Australian Government to exert a more independent position. His conflicts with his own Cabinet point to this.

Nonetheless, it is clear, perhaps largely from Hughes' own character, that, revolving around the Peace Treaty in Versailles, differences were beginning to emerge between Australia and imperial policy. Hughes clearly saw that, at times, Australian interests would be separate from Britain's. For example, he wanted an Australian ambassador in the United States to push Australian interests. Hughes knew that the British Ambassador would always push London's interests first and foremost, and this would be problematic for occasions when these interests did not completely align with Australia's. Nothing was done about that, however. His colleagues in Australia would not have supported him, taking such a step in defiance of British desires. His attitude to reparations and to former German colonies related not only to the terrible price Australia had had to pay for its participation in the war but also to what he perceived to be necessary for Australia's security. On this last point, his attitude to Japan not being part of the white races became very apparent.

Australia punched above its weight during the Peace Conference but not to the advantage of Australia and not due to a broadly supported desire for Australia to enact an independent stance on key issues. Rather, Hughes' reputation was awkward, rough and unwilling to compromise, unwilling to listen to others' views. The volume of our position on key issues rather than content of our solutions resulted in our views being heard to an extent greater than could otherwise have been expected. On matters of race, one can only say that Hughes was a hard-line racist who did much damage. There were many at the conference who would have believed that his views reflected the racism—and indeed the bigotry—of Australians.[73] Then, as now, it was an unfortunate representation.

Although in these conferences Hughes had started to articulate strong views, especially about reparations and race, it was always in the context of influencing imperial policy and thus the conduct of Britain itself. He might have spoken out of turn from time to time and he might not have always liked it, but Hughes knew that Australia's view on issues could only be put through Britain. Unlike Deakin, who, many years before, mentioned the prospect of developing our own foreign policy and defence, such thoughts seemed to be inimical to Hughes. Despite his difference of opinion, he was very much an Empire man and wanted the protection of Empire for Australia.

The first twenty years of Australia post-Federation saw much of our policy-making and political energy focused on domestic reform.

With a few notable exceptions, the White Australia Policy and disenfranchisement of Indigenous Australians being two poignant examples, the drive for reform was focused on making Australian society fairer and more egalitarian than Britain. Australia did not want class divisions to be re-established in Australia, and worked positively to prevent it. Yet, on matters of defence, Australia relied on Britain and did not want to commit substantial resources.

Although such leaders as Deakin and Hughes would push for a greater role for Australia in imperial decision-making, they never dreamed of a truly independent Australian foreign policy. They manoeuvred within the policy of strategic dependence, never seeking to overthrow it. Strategic dependence was an ensconced part of Australia's polity, unquestionable and with no real alternative available. The ravages of World War I should have made Australia realise that the perceived comfort that this policy brought could exact a cruel and severe toll. Yet it did not. In the decades following the Great War, Australia continued in much the same fashion as it had—loyal to Britain and to the Crown.

3

Hanging on too long

Our early political leaders were only being realistic when they accepted that Britain would be the ultimate determinant of foreign policy for Britain, for Australia, for the Empire. They might have hoped for some influence over issues directly affecting Australia, but they were fully aware that the final decision would not be theirs to make.

They accepted that their influence would be minimal. It was, in a sense, a grand bargain. Britain had the capacity to make foreign policy for the Empire as a whole and, in return, the colonies, and later the Dominions, expected protection should they ever need it. The price of this bargain was of course to supply support, to find men and money when Britain needed assistance in its wars. It was in anticipation of this bargain that Australian forces were offered to support Britain in the Boer War and were supplied in support of Britain and other powers in relation to the Boxer Rebellion. When one looks at the Australia of those days, with its small population and lack of industrial resources, the grand bargain suited Australia well. Strategic dependence was in many ways a necessary evil.

This chapter will look at how Australia's policy of strategic dependence continued through the 1920s and 1930s. At a time when other Dominions were ready to move towards greater autonomy, Australia would not follow. Australia's commitment to Empire blinded it as to how damaged Britain was as result of World War I and how ineffective London would be in protecting its own direct interests, let alone those of the entire Empire, should war break out again. As the world hurtled towards conflict in the mid-1930s, Australia still counted on Britain for defence and foreign policy.

At the various Colonial Conferences and at the first Imperial Conference held in 1911, the Federation leaders were pressing for a true Empire policy and for procedures that would enable the Dominions, as they had become, to make an adequate contribution to and influence the development of that policy. This was a trend that would continue at Imperial Conferences during the 1920s and 1930s.

Yet it was an ideal never achieved. Empire policy was, and would remain, British policy. Great powers do what they perceive to be in their own interests. They might consult others, but they will not act contrary to their perception of their own interests because others seek to persuade them to a different course.

The development of foreign and defence policy was nearly always on the agenda at Colonial, and later Imperial, Conferences, but little was achieved in those early years. Lack of consultation on matters affecting the Dominions was commonplace. In communications with the Dominions and with Australia, Britain gave the impression that it would consult, that the views of the Colonies or Dominions were important, but ultimately they were never given much weight. There was no formal structure that gave the Dominions access to the real policy-making arena in the United Kingdom, such as the Foreign Office or the Cabinet.

As a result of inadequate consultation processes and a genuine lack of desire to involve the Dominions, there are many examples of Britain not taking much notice of Empire views, not only in the relationship between Britain and Australia but also in British relations with South Africa, Canada and the Irish Free State after the 1922 Settlement.[1] The development of the Anglo-Japanese Alliance is a good example of the deficiencies present in imperial foreign policy-making. Another is the decision by Britain to engage in the North Russian Intervention.

In the final months of World War I in 1918, through to the end of 1919, Britain and other powers intervened in Russia after the October Revolution. The Russian Provisional Government, led by Alexander Kerensky, a Democrat, pledged to continue fighting imperial Germany on the Eastern Front. The United States began providing economic and technical support to the Russian Provisional Government. The Russian offensive was crushed by Germany. Lenin came to power in October 1917 and established a communist government, and five months later what became the Soviet Union made a separate peace with Germany through the Treaty of Brest-Litovsk.

The British in particular were concerned that this would lead to a reinforcement of German forces on the Western Front, and therefore they planned to invade Russia through the north, Murmansk and Archangel, and take control of a significant cache of supplies and secure two ice-free northern ports.[2] The British in the end relied upon the Americans as their own forces were fully committed.

The British were initially not concerned with the Boshevik forces. They believed that the Bolsheviks were weak and would be overcome.[3] They were focused on the Germans. When it became apparent that Germany desired to establish a submarine base at Murmansk, British Foreign Secretary Balfour appealed to the Americans, and President Wilson acquiesced, dispatching several thousand troops to northern Russia. The force was considerable; however, it was far too small to achieve its major objective, the defeat of the Bolshevik Revolution.[4]

Hughes was firmly against the intervention and believed that only external aggression by the Bolsheviks should concern Great Britain, arguing in the Imperial War Cabinet of 23 December 1918 that the Allies should leave Russia and its people to decide what government it wanted for itself.[5] Hughes did not want Australian soldiers sent elsewhere following the defeat of the Germans—he felt they had done enough. He was joined by Canada's Prime Minister Borden in believing that the Bolsheviks had firmer support within Russia than their opposing forces. The Dominion prime ministers had made their position clear—'they were not interested in providing forces for quixotic imperial adventures in north Russia'.[6]

The venture was doomed to failure, and it was one more major strategic blunder by Sir Winston Churchill. Indeed, when Allied losses to the Red Army started to mount and the Americans and French decided to withdraw their forces, Churchill was put in charge of the British withdrawal. He took liberties with the authority he had been given over the withdrawal and pushed through the British Cabinet a plan for a relief force to extricate forces hemmed down by the Russian winter.[7]

The campaign was ultimately futile as any attempt to change the course of events in the Russian Civil War would require forces substantially greater than the Allied governments, including Britain, were willing to commit.

This was not the only military intervention in which Britain, and Churchill in particular, sought to involve the Empire, virtually without any consultation. The 'Chanak Crisis' provides a better example of the way in which the British refused to improve imperial consultation and of the way in which a client state can potentially become involved in a disastrous operation. The Chanak Crisis arose in the latter part of 1922 and had the potential to throw the Empire into another costly war so soon after the Armistice.

The remnants of the Ottoman Empire had been disposed of in the Treaty of Sèvres. Turkey remained quite powerful and was thoroughly dissatisfied with the dispositions made under this treaty. Turkey had been dealt with very harshly. Allied forces had occupied Constantinople and Greek forces controlled most of European Turkey and Ionia.[8]

The Chanak Crisis began when Mustafa Kemal Ataturk, rejecting the Treaty of Sèvres, destroyed the Greek forces in Izmir, a key battle in what was becoming an increasingly bloody campaign. He was determined to establish more acceptable boundaries for modern Turkey. Turkish forces had made considerable advances against the Greeks and were marching on Constantinople in the neutral zone, established by the Allies under the Treaty of Sèvres.[9] The British Cabinet decided to maintain its position in guarding the Dardanelles.

A message was sent by Prime Minister Lloyd George to Prime Minister Hughes requiring Australia's support.[10] The request was sent to the media before the Dominion prime ministers, with Hughes hearing about the British cable from news reports before he actually received it.[11] Lloyd George evoked the sacrifice made by ANZAC forces in defending the freedom of the Dardanelles and that, should the Empire fail, he reminded Australian leaders that thousands of war graves would 'fall into the ruthless hands of the Kemalists'.[12] Although this message was sent by Lloyd George, it is believed to have been penned by Churchill himself. The message was clearly less than tactful, reminiscent of Churchill's previous involvement in the Gallipoli campaign.

Similar requests were put to other Dominions. Canada was to insist that its Parliament would decide on any involvement of its forces. It is almost certain that Canada would have denied the use of its forces. South Africa played for time, and only New Zealand immediately responded positively. Hughes' response was reported to have been restrained, and there appears to have been no 'official' agreement to provide assistance.[13]

Perhaps for the first time Australia, under Hughes, had refused to respond to an important cable from London. Hughes believed that the communication between London and the Dominions was much less than ideal. Publicly, Hughes said that Australia would join necessary action.[14] Privately, he sent a message to Lloyd George, making it clear that Australia was not prepared to support such a dangerous course with no clear objective or end point, or without access to strategic information.[15] Hughes was clearly dissatisfied, once again, with a lack of British consultation.

Both Churchill himself and Lloyd George responded to Hughes' comments and denied that there had been poor consultation. Hughes was attacked by the Opposition in Parliament. Hughes was thoroughly dissatisfied with the rationale presented by the Colonial Office. He cabled London directly insisting that information come straight from the Prime Minister or the Foreign Office. Churchill, then Secretary of State for the Colonies, rejected that proposal. Australia would have to abide by the processes Britain, and Britain alone, determined appropriate for consultation.

This whole issue was thoroughly unpopular in Britain and played a significant part in Lloyd George's political downfall shortly there-after. The incident emphasises in the clearest possible terms that the presumed strategic interests of Britain were not always identical to those of Australia. Although no action was taken for many years, it was the strongest sign the young Dominion had yet received that Australia needed its own well-resourced and appropriately man-dated foreign affairs department, its own ability to gather diplomatic information, the capacity to develop its own foreign policy. Australia needed to be cut free from automatically following British decisions. Hughes put it this way:

> If the Empire is only another name for Britain, and the Dominions are to be told that things are done after they have been done, that Britain had decided upon war, and asking whether they wish to be associated with her and stand by her side, when in fact they have no other alternative, then … it is perfectly clear that all talk about the Dominions having a real share in deciding foreign and Imperial policy is empty air …
>
> The position in which the action of the British Government placed the Dominions was not only embarrassing but deeply humiliating. That they should again be brought to the very brink of war without even knowing the long train of events which led to the crisis held them up to the ridicule of a world almost deafened by their loud declarations that they were nations equal in status and authority to Great Britain. In the face of what had happened, their claim to be regarded as nations appeared only the pretentious vapourings of adolescence.[16]

That comment seems to suggest that Hughes still believed Britain had the power or the capacity to require a Dominion such as Australia to go to war. If that view had been put to the test over an incident such as Chanak, I suspect that very major opposition would have occurred in Australia.

The threat ultimately passed, and new terms were made between the Empire and the Turks, with British and French troops ultimately withdrawing following the ratification of the Treaty of Lausanne in 1923. Yet it signified that the agreements on consultation between Britain and the Dominions established at the 1921 Imperial Conference had failed their first test—the 'British government had publicly assumed dominion support without dominion concurrence'.[17] This was not soon forgotten in Australia, with officials long being annoyed by Britain's request for Australia to go to war without any form of consultation as to the virtues of such war.

Alongside these international incidents, the development of the Empire continued, with the first post-war Imperial Conference being held in 1921. Their purpose again was to decide a unified international policy for the Empire. The extension of the Anglo-Japanese Alliance was a major item on the agenda. Perhaps for the first time in these Imperial Conferences, major differences arose. The Canadian Prime Minister, Arthur Meighan, was firmly opposed to a continuation of the Anglo-Japanese Alliance in its current form.[18] He was concerned that a conflict could develop between Japan and the United States and was determined that the Empire should avoid being caught in a war between the two nations as a result of the Alliance. Indeed, the United States had been critical of the Alliance, as it meant Britain encouraged Japan's expansion in the Far East and also preserved the United Kingdom's trade and financial interests, especially in China.[19]

At the beginning of the conference all other members, including Australia, had supported the immediate renewal of the Anglo-Japanese Alliance but, as discussions continued, more and more problems were seen with that course of action. Australia would have liked the Alliance to continue while it sought to build up naval resources of its own. Hughes believed that the Alliance was indispensable to the security of Australia as it gave Great Britain a means to restrict an ambitious ally. Yet Hughes also knew that the Alliance was anathema to the United States and that support from Washington would be necessary should the Japanese become belligerent. Hughes' strategy was to advocate for the renewal of the Alliance, but in a form acceptable to Britain, America and Japan.[20] From outside the Imperial Conference, the US view had been made very clear. The United States had obviously influenced Canada significantly. America feared that the treaty would lead to a Japanese-dominated market in the Pacific and close China off from American trade. The issue became too difficult, and the Imperial Conference decided to shelve the Alliance, which was put aside in favour of courting America's favour. A decision regarding the Alliance would eventually be made in the signing of the Four-Power Treaty at the Washington Conference.[21]

The negotiations over the Anglo–Japanese Treaty made it perfectly plain that the Dominions were all anxious to curry favour with America. They were not prepared to take any steps of which America would disapprove. This was a precursor to future international conferences where the United States would clearly have great influence as an emerging and growing power. Although there was disagreement between the various members of the Empire, the result of the conference was that there was broad consensus over the need to include the United States in any future treaty arrangement. Yet symbolically, 'British policy was shaped by the opinions of all rather than just one of the dominions'.[22] Perhaps for the first time, London was forced to seriously consider the demands of Ottawa and Melbourne in a foreign policy decision.

These events also had consequences for the 1921 Washington Naval Conference, which was designed to limit an arms race for control of the seas. The Washington Naval Conference, so far as Australia was concerned, was attended by the four powers but more were added: Italy, Belgium, the Netherlands, Portugal and China, as all had interests in the Pacific Ocean and East Asia. Soviet Russia was not invited. The Dominions, Canada and Australia, were not asked to attend the Washington Conference in their own right but were able to participate as part of the British delegation.[23] The United States still tended to look upon the British Empire as one entity; another consequence of being strategically dependent.

The Washington Conference had a number of objectives. The United States wished to prevent a new arms race and thus limit the development of the navies, especially of Japan and Britain, and of the United States itself. The conference was also designed to eliminate Anglo-American tension, which had arisen as a result of the Anglo-Japanese Alliance. The United States was not part of that Alliance nor involved in it, and it believed it could prove an impediment to its own wider ambitions. It might have been the first example of the United States opposing international arrangements that it had not framed and of which it was not a part. It played into the dissolution of the Anglo-Japanese Alliance as discussed at the 1921 Imperial Conference.

The Washington Conference had minimal influence on the arms race that occurred in those years and on competition for power and influence in the wider world. It was clearly an attempt to establish American superiority in the Pacific, to maintain British superiority in the Atlantic and to keep the Japanese Navy significantly short of the power of either Britain or the United States.

At this time, Australia did not have a proper department to advise on foreign policy. It had no missions overseas apart from our window in London, and direct communication with other governments still occurred through the British Government. The Empire was still operating in a phase in which Britain believed it was master of Empire policy on major matters, believing that Britain had the power to take the Empire to war without separate decisions by the Dominions.

Discussions over the Anglo-Japanese Alliance, the result of the Washington Conference and the attempt to control the shifting balance of power were not conducive to long-term peace. Britain still believed it was a great pre-eminent imperial power, not diminished by World War I. London's understanding of shifting events throughout the Pacific was inadequate. Britain was no longer a great power in the Pacific. Yet, like Britain, Australia failed to appreciate this, instead persisting with the policy of strategic dependence when it should have begun questioning whether London could realistically provide security for Australia.

In 1923 another Imperial Conference was held which decided that the negotiation, signature and ratification of treaties affecting only part of the Empire would depend on the individual government concerned and that no obligation would be imposed on any other part of the Empire.[24] The discussion had a greater emphasis given the Chanak Crisis, which showed that the agreements reached at the Imperial Conference in 1921 concerning consultation between Britain and the Dominions were worthless.

The conference sought to place an obligation on each government to consider whether a treaty being considered could potentially affect other members of the Empire. As R. G. Casey put it, 'the right of Commonwealth members to pursue their separate policies was tempered by their duty to harmonise those separate policies by consultation with each other'.[25] The conference again called 'on the need for renewed defence efforts and common principles on which it should be organised'.[26] Prime Minister Bruce said, in 1923, 'if Australia is to be part of the Empire, and responsible for some share in its defence, Australia must have every reasonable opportunity to criticise and to help in formulating the foreign policy of the Empire as a whole'.[27] The Dominions were still expected to act with a policy of strategic dependence within the Empire, even if they were to be given a larger say in decision-making.

Yet only a year after this conference, Britain took another action with implications for the Empire without any consultation whatsoever: full diplomatic recognition of the Soviet Union. Indeed, the head of the British Foreign Office, Sir Eyre Crowe, would describe the need to consult the Dominions as 'a disease of the mind', with Prime Minister Ramsay MacDonald reportedly agreeing with this comment.[28]

Significant and far-reaching changes were underway that led to the Balfour Declaration in 1926 and to the Statute of Westminster in 1931. Canada and South Africa both had strong domestic and geographical reasons to want a greater degree of independence and did not want to be bound by British policy or by decisions of the Westminster Parliament. The Irish Free State had also joined as a result of the 1922 Settlement. It too did not want to be too close to Britain and to be bound by its policies.[29] This meant that one foreign and defence policy for the Empire was beyond reach. Although Australia wanted a greater say in imperial policy, it fought against the trend to independence for many years.

Another Imperial Conference was held in 1926 to coincide with the meeting of the League of Nations in Geneva. Here Prime Minister Bruce was still pushing for a more consultative and co-operative set of institutions within the British Empire, as he had done three years earlier. He would also insist that, in wanting a cohesive and institutionalised Empire, Australia must not accept a lower status than other Dominions.[30] Australia still clung to the belief that its best protection and defence was in a united Empire in which Australia would participate in the making of policy. Australia did not and was not able to spell out how that would come about.

In the larger measure, Australia was fighting against an objective that Canada, South Africa and Ireland all wanted to achieve.[31] They wanted greater independence from Britain and, in the case of Ireland, complete independence—the capacity to make their own policies and not be bound by policies set by Britain. This is not to say that they would not be conscious of British policy, but they could ignore it if they wished.

The Balfour Declaration was contained in a report resulting from the 1926 Imperial Conference. Its central point was: 'The Dominions are autonomous communities within the British Empire, equal in status, in no way subordinate one to another in any aspect of their domestic or external affairs, although united by a common allegiance to the Crown and freely associated as the members of the British Commonwealth of Nations.'[32] It meant that for the first time, the Dominions were, on paper at least, equal to Britain. An Inter-Imperial Relations Committee chaired by Balfour had drawn up the document, expecting and achieving unanimous approval by the Dominions in November 1926.

It also had another significant recommendation: that the governors general, representatives of the monarch, who up to this time had acted for the Crown as head of state in each Dominion, would no longer automatically serve as the principal representative of the British Government. Thus Britain came to appoint high commissioners who were quite separate from the governors general. Their responsibilities were equivalent to those of ambassadors. The Dominions would appoint their own high commissioners to London.

The Balfour Declaration went on to say: 'Every self-governing member of the Empire is now master of its destiny. In fact if not always in form, it is subject to no compulsion whatever.'[33] This was not to say that each member was to be independent in all areas of policy. In many subtle ways, and some not so subtle, the Dominions would still be subject to considerable pressures from London from time to time over issues of foreign affairs and defence.[34] It also proclaimed that the Empire depended essentially on positive ideals; free institutions, free cooperation, peace, security and progress were among its objectives. It recognised that while each Dominion would remain the sole judge of the extent of any cooperation in any venture, it was also stated that 'no common cause would, in their opinion, be thereby imperilled'.[35]

Technically the Dominions were freed of British restraint, but history, custom, loyalty to Britain and a common association in the Empire, all placed significant restraints on that freedom, certainly so far as Australia was concerned. Australia was still content to be strategically dependent on Britain and follow London's lead on important international issues. Canada with its French population, South Africa with English and Boer, and the new Irish Free State felt much less restrained and less inclined to acquiesce blindly to London's whims.

The Balfour Declaration tried to define the nature of international conferences, when it would be appropriate for a Dominion to be represented and when not,[36] which was again an anachronism, a reversion to the past and inappropriate after the Declaration had been accepted. Any truly independent nation would have been free to attend conferences as it deemed necessary to its foreign policy needs.

The Dominions had repeatedly appeared before the League of Nations and would obviously continue to do so. Despite the fact that, as late as 1929, it was still argued that Australia's membership of the League of Nations depended upon the grace and favour of Britain.[37] A point, cherished by Australia in particular, recognised that in the conduct of foreign affairs generally, and of defence, the major responsibility continued to rest with the United Kingdom.

The Balfour Declaration, in reality, was by no means a statement of true equality. It was a significant step in that direction, but true independence as we understand it in today's world was still beyond reach. Australia was uneasy at the trend to greater independence, which was the substance of the Balfour Report, because Australia believed it would weaken the Empire's obligation to defend its constituent members.[38]

The next major step was the Statute of Westminster (1931), which stemmed from resolutions from the Imperial Conference of 1930. The statute gave legal effect to the substance of the Balfour Declaration and other decisions made at the Imperial Conferences that pointed to greater independence for the Dominions. The central point was to declare that the Parliament of the United Kingdom no longer had any legislative authority over any of the Dominions.[39] Before that the Dominions were still legally under British law, colonies of the United Kingdom. Canada, South Africa and the Irish Free State, as one would have expected with their respective domestic pressures, gave immediate effect to the Statute of Westminster. They did not need separate legislation or ratification. Australia, New Zealand and Newfoundland did need to ratify the statutes by legislation through their own parliaments.

Here Australia and New Zealand stood apart from other Dominions. John Latham, Attorney General and Minister for External Affairs under Prime Minister Joseph Lyons, opposed ratifying the statute. He thought it would weaken Britain's obligation to Australia, especially its obligation to defend Australia. He did not want the relationship between Britain and Australia codified in any way at all.[40]

Ratification of the Statute of Westminster in Australia did not occur until 1942. By that time it was plain for the world to see that our reliance on Britain for defence was false, misguided and deceptive. Indeed it had become dangerous. It was a Labor Government in Australia under John Curtin that passed the necessary legislation through Parliament. As doubts had been raised about the validity of Australia's war powers, the *Statute of Westminster Adoption Act 1942*, adopting the statute, was backdated to 3 September 1939, to coincide with the outbreak of World War II.

The Statute of Westminster Act put the Balfour Declaration into legislative form and was a consummation of a movement that really began slowly and hesitantly with the first Imperial Conference in 1911 but which was given some impetus in the immediate years after World War I. It was a movement that Australia was always reticent to embrace.

In the early 1930s, the level of staff dedicated to the Department of External Affairs and the relevant minister was minuscule.[41] Without separate representation in a number of countries overseas, it was impossible for Australia to develop a public service or a foreign office tuned to Australia's interests and concerns. Even if the Commonwealth had wanted to chart an independent path for Australian foreign policy, it would have been reliant on British information to do so.

In the early 1930s Australia was little interested in foreign affairs, but events were moving in unfortunate ways. As a result of the severity of the reparations placed on the defeated powers, the financial crash of 1929 and the ensuing depression, deflation and hardship raged throughout much of Europe. Germany was not spared this hardship; the resultant social and political struggles contributing to Hitler's rise to power.

Indeed, events in other nations of Europe indicated that the relative stability the continent had achieved post-Versailles was under strain. This in turn put pressure on the League of Nations to resolve increasing tensions and growing disputes. For example, Italy regarded itself as having a considerable interest in much of North Africa. Mussolini, the nation's dictatorial leader since 1922, set about establishing a greater colonial presence across North Africa, sparking the Abyssinian Crisis, which led to war and eventually to the creation of Italian East Africa.

The Italo-Ethiopian War, along with the Mukden incident in Manchuria[42] and inaction over the Spanish Civil War, are three major incidents that exposed the weakness of the League of Nations and its inability to influence the actions of a significant power.

Although the League included many European powers, America of course was not a member. President Wilson had been its principal advocate, yet his own Congress denied him and refused to ratify the League of Nations. The United States was out of the equation so far as policy in Europe and North Africa was concerned. Yet these years were not entirely isolationist for the United States. Washington wanted to cut itself off from what it regarded as old quarrels in Europe, although that did not diminish its desire for influence throughout the Western Pacific, especially in relation to the Philippines and China.

Although Australia was not part of European events, the weakness of the League of Nations made the Empire all the more important for Britain. From Federation through to World War II, Australia had believed in and had wanted to maintain the grand bargain between the United Kingdom and the Dominions.

After World War I, Britain had established what was called the Singapore Strategy. It was discussed in the 1923 Imperial Conference, with Bruce being unsure of how the strategy would work but accepting British assurances that it would.[43] Singapore was to be developed into a major naval base that would protect Empire interests in what was then called the Far East. As a consequence, much of Australia's defence plans depended on the Singapore Strategy.

Defence planners in those years believed that the only likelihood of a war would be with Japan and that such a war would have three phases. First, the Singapore garrison would be defended. Second, the fleet would make its way from home waters to the Pacific, then relieve or recapture Hong Kong if it were under threat and, third, blockade Japanese home islands to force the Japanese to come to acceptable terms.[44] They never believed that Singapore would be attacked from the land, that Japan would march down through the Malay Peninsula and that Singapore itself would fall almost without a fight. But before World War II began, even in 1937, some recognised that the Singapore Strategy was impractical and incapable of fulfilment.[45] Nonetheless, as a result of the Singapore Strategy Australia and New Zealand did not establish adequate defence forces on their own account.[46]

To be fully effective, the Singapore Strategy depended upon the British having a navy large enough to be split between home waters and the Pacific. Through the 1930s and leading to World War II, the British Navy never had that strength. It had never recovered from the ravages of World War I. Australian defence planners, by and large, had so much faith in our dependence on Britain that they failed to acknowledge the inadequacy of the Royal Navy.[47] As World War II unfolded, Britain was beleaguered and needed the fleet to fight for its own survival. The Singapore Strategy was in reality worthless. The planners had prepared for a time past, not for the future. In military planning, in strategic thinking, that happens all too often. As loyal members of the Empire, as a Dominion that was not prepared to ratify the 1931 Statute of Westminster, it is not surprising that Australia accepted the policy dictates stemming from Britain—yet we were going to pay a high price for our acceptance.

The last Imperial Conference before the war was held in 1937, and it was becoming increasingly understood that the Royal Navy was inadequate to deal with hostilities in home waters and in the Pacific, and that any requirements from the Far East would be secondary to needs closer to Britain.[48] Prime Minister Lyons raised the idea of a non-aggression pact in the Pacific.[49] It was ultimately endorsed by the conference, but Japan would certainly oppose it if it was a mechanism to maintain the status quo, and China would have been highly sceptical. The Americans took the view that there were enough pacts around. Russia supported the proposal, believing that collective security in the Pacific would play a significant—possibly a decisive—role in ensuring European peace. Russia foresaw Hitler's intentions, perhaps more clearly than some others.[50]

A non-aggression pact in the Pacific, which in reality was never accepted by Britain, was part of an Australian proposal designed to mollify the British Empire's two most dangerous potential enemies, Japan and Germany. The non-aggression pact in the Pacific might have been relatively uncontroversial, but the Lyons Government's proposal in relation to Europe was far ahead of anything that the British might have accepted. The Australian position argued that the primary danger to peace was the emergence of an axis between Fascist Italy and Nazi Germany, with the key question being how to stop that from happening. The Australian view of the time, pre-dating the Munich crisis, suggested that Britain should not oppose a union between Germany and Austria and that it should also acknowledge Germany's predominance in Eastern Europe. Casey himself proposed that the United Kingdom 'cease to offer any further opposition to the realisation of "Anschluss" provided always that Germany could attain this objective peacefully and without the shedding of blood'.[51]

Casey also wanted a public declaration from Britain that the British Empire had no interest in the affairs of central Europe, and he was critical of London for highlighting the defence obligations to small nations on the continent. He said the Australian Government opposed any British commitment to defend the status quo in Eastern and central Europe.[52] That, of course, would have required a dramatic reversal of British policy, one that Australia did not have the influence to force. Australia would push Britain on these issues because it still believed our security was pegged to British authority and to British naval power, and guaranteed by our allegiance to the Crown. Strategic dependence can be blinding and insidious, shielding leaders from hard decisions needed to ensure our safety and prosperity.

Prime Minister Lyons threw his weight behind these proposals, offering platitudes and calling for imperial unity and friendship with all. The plan never had any chance of getting off the ground, because it attacked two important planks of British European policy: an independent Austria, and an active interest in central European affairs. London's relationship with France and French treaty obligations to Eastern European nations also made such a plan quite impossible.

Although Australia maintained faith in the Empire, it also understood the vulnerability of the Empire in a fast-changing world. Bruce, as High Commissioner in London, tried to reopen discussions and arrangements in Europe that might avoid war.[53] He argued that Britain had failed to anticipate Germany's many breaches of the Versailles Treaty, which meant that London was merely reacting to events in Europe rather than seeking to shape them. He rehashed the proposals that would have given Hitler dominance over Austria, Czechoslovakia and Eastern Europe. It appeared that Chamberlain and other members of the British Cabinet had come to similar views.

By 1938 Eden, as British Foreign Secretary, had resigned from Chamberlain's government, and some efforts were made to seek an accommodation with Hitler. Chamberlain was still not prepared to go as far as the earlier proposals suggested by Lyons. When relationships with Czechoslovakia developed into a crisis, the Lyons Government declared that Sudetenland was not worth going to war over.[54] War over the Sudetenland Crisis was avoided only by the agreements Chamberlain made with Hitler at Munich.

Australia's role in all of this might well have been to try to avoid war in Europe so that Britain would still have some capacity to provide naval and other forces to the Far East. It was, however, far, far too late. The policy of interlocking alliances had existed for too long.

After the Munich Crisis, Menzies reiterated that he had always believed 'that the British Empire exercises its greatest influence in the world ... when it speaks with one concerted voice ... This involves prior consultation, enabling the Australian Government to say useful things at the right time to the Government of the United Kingdom ... In that sense, of course, we are bound to have a foreign policy.'[55] That was still placing Australia's future in the hands of another country. Bridge sums up the Australian appeasement positions nicely by stating that 'Bruce, Lyons, Casey, Pearce, Page and Menzies were revisionists over Versailles and saw no major difficulty with Germany taking back the Rhineland, annexing the Sudetenland, and conducting Anschluss with Austria'.[56] From today's perspective, we know that such a policy would not have led to peace, and would not have enhanced Britain's capacity to assist Australia once the Japanese war was begun. The power of the British Empire had declined too far.

Britain still probably believed in the power and authority of Empire, as it had been before, and up to, World War I. As it turned out, the pact between a great power and a smaller, lesser power can draw the great power into conflict with devastating consequences. Britain's relationship with Poland did just that in 1939 and, once again, the Empire was at war.

Menzies became Prime Minister in 1939, after the death of Prime Minister Lyons. In a speech at the time, Menzies said he had become convinced 'that in the Pacific Australia must regard herself as a principal providing herself with her own information and maintaining her own diplomatic contacts with foreign powers'. He still claimed that this must be done within the context of Empire. He also spoke in that speech of '[looking] forward to the day when we will have a concert of Pacific powers, pacific in both senses of the word'.[57] He was speaking specifically of the United States, China and Japan, but including the Netherlands, East Indies and other countries that fringe the Pacific.

This was not a move away from his position that the Empire is strongest when it speaks with one voice, but rather to make sure that, on issues of importance to Australia, information was gathered and verified by officials with no allegiance other than to Australia.[58] It was, if you like, a substantial criticism of Britain's understanding of policy issues in the Western Pacific. This attitude was confirmed in letters between Menzies and Bruce, as High Commissioner.[59]

After the Non-Aggression pact between Nazi Germany and the Soviet Union, Menzies reaffirmed the unity of Empire. The idea of Empire offering adequate protection for Australia was still strong despite the fact that it had, by that time, become outdated.

In September 1939, following the outbreak of war, Menzies made a statement: 'Fellow Australians, it is my melancholy duty to inform you officially, that in consequence of a persistence by Germany in her invasion of Poland, Great Britain has declared war upon her and that, as a result, Australia is also at war.'[60] He came in for some criticism because it appeared as though Australia had not made an independent decision.[61]

There was no doubt that Australia would have joined in the fight against Nazi Germany in support of Britain, in spite of the fact that Australia had not been consulted by Great Britain before its decision to guarantee Poland, and Australia was not party to that guarantee. This was just one more serious example of a lack of consultation between Britain and the Dominions on a matter that was to have far-reaching consequences.

Paul Hasluck explained the reasons in a more nuanced way. Hasluck argues that there were three reasons for Australia's acceptance of war.[62] There was little doubt that Menzies regarded it as a consequence of the constitutional position of Australia within the British Commonwealth. He could not have held that view if Australia had ratified the Statute of Westminster. Second, and with more veracity, Menzies believed that should Great Britain be defeated, the threat to Australia would be increased. Third, the government had a view about the need for a stable community of nations. In my mind there is no doubt that the Australian Cabinet itself should have considered the matter and made its decision and on announcement, Menzies should have announced the Australian reasons for joining the conflict.[63]

Australia was continuing to pay a high price for automatically following a major power. Australia's policy of strategic dependence was again about to incur a most costly and devastating toll. Whatever the constitutional developments, it is worth again recalling the words of H.B. Higgins at Federation. Higgins' view was mirrored by John Curtin, Leader of the Opposition, in a speech during the Abyssinia Crisis when he said, 'It is sheer folly ... for Australia to regard herself as a major element in the settlement of international antagonisms begotten of the racial prejudices and economic conflicts which still dominate European relationships. Our business is to keep Australia aloof from the wars of the world.'[64]

Australia's immediate declaration of support for Britain was in stark contrast to South Africa and Canada, where a declaration of war was made only after Parliament had fully discussed the issue.[65]

Churchill expressed impatience with Australia's war effort, and Casey was dispatched to London seeking assurances that should the Japanese become aggressive and enter the war, the British Navy would be sent to Singapore in accordance with past arrangements.[66] Britain and Churchill, as Prime Minister, gave Australia assurances that they very well knew they would be unlikely to keep. Australia nevertheless agreed to send three divisions to the Middle East, and one division was dispatched to Malaya, in the expectation that Britain would come to Australia's assistance if Japan were to enter the war.[67]

The communications between Australia and Britain were clearly unsatisfactory. Menzies cabled Casey: 'It is the general feeling of Cabinet that there has been ... a quite perceptible disposition to treat Australia as a colony [strong words for such a lover of the Empire] ... it is for the Government of Australia to determine whether and when Australian Forces shall go out of Australia.'[68]

The most persuasive argument with Menzies remained something he regarded as a self-evident truth: that Australia could remain 'independent' only by continued dependence on Britain and on the strength of the Empire. Menzies believed that our independence depended upon belonging to 'a family of nations, the central nation of which is still ... the most powerful and the most resolute country in the world'.[69] That, of course, was the great misunderstanding.

Menzies was referring to Britain as Britain had been before World War I. Powerful and relatively unrivalled before that war, and still a force in the interwar years, Britain would never regain the kind of power it wielded before the Great War. Menzies failed to appreciate this and, as a consequence of his belief in the Empire, failed to understand that no country can be secure unless it can rely primarily on its own efforts. Our overdependence on Britain, particularly in its weakened state, was soon to place Australia in great peril.

Menzies decided to travel to London.[70] I believe he did so because he wanted improved assurances from Britain concerning support for Australia. Bruce cabled Menzies warning of the treatment he would be likely to receive:

> [Churchill is] little influenced by other members of the War Cabinet who frankly are not prepared to stand up to him. My view is Prime Minister would endeavour treat you in much same way—most cordial welcome—utmost courtesy—invitation to attend meetings of War Cabinet and apparently every possibility of consultation. When however you tried to pin him down to definite discussions of fundamental questions of major war policy I am inclined to think you would find him discursive and elusive necessitating you either (a) taking a line that would mean a considerable show down between you or (b) leaving with a sense of frustration.[71]

Casey at this time also was made Australia's first Minister to the United States. Casey's appointment to Washington was timely because there were continual differences between British and American policy in relation to the Far East. Menzies, in communications with Bruce, High Commissioner in London, was much concerned with these issues. Menzies wrote on 22 February 1940, long before Pearl Harbor, of the fear in Australian minds of Japan entering the war against the Allies. He wrote:

> I would feel more satisfied about it if I really believed that the British Foreign Office had a practical and realistic view of the Far Eastern position. One's instinctive judgement is that the Japanese have a marked inferiority complex and that a real gesture of friendship with some real assistance in the settlement of the Chinese Question, accompanied by a proper recognition of Japanese trading ambitions, might very easily produce peace

in the Far East, particularly if Japan was, by that time, feeling the impact of Russian Bolshevism.[72]

Menzies was clearly in his own mind exploring other options to the policies that were in place. Japan had withdrawn from the League of Nations in 1933 because of the League's condemnation of Japan as a result of a military invasion of Manchuria. Japan's military activities throughout Asia were expanding, and in 1937 full-scale war broke out between Japan and China. Again, the League of Nations was impotent and unable to secure any resolution. The League's impotence, which was by then obvious to the entire world, concerned the Australian leadership.

One of the problems in managing the diplomacy of the Far East was the competing views of Britain and the United States. The United States had regarded the Anglo-Japanese Alliance as a device that would enable Japan and Britain to expand their markets throughout Asia, almost certainly at the expense of the United States. The United States was not prepared to allow that to happen. The Washington Conference broke that alliance and contributed very much to Japan's feelings that it would never really be accepted by the white races. In the early stages of the war, before Pearl Harbor, American policy was supporting China and opposing Japan. The United States had sanctions in place against Japan, designed to inhibit its war effort. Any attempt to end that conflict to accommodate Japan in any way would have been bitterly opposed by the United States.

On the way to London in 1941 Menzies visited Australian troops in Egypt. British General Wavell discussed the invasion of Greece using Australian forces, to which Menzies agreed without consulting his Cabinet or his Commander-in-Chief, General Blamey.[73] General Blamey, having a sceptical view of the consequences of British command, pushed for an independent commander of Australian troops.

In Australia, by August 1941, Menzies had been replaced and Fadden had become Prime Minister. Blamey had been pushing for the relief of our troops in Tobruk, and Churchill cabled Fadden:

'I think … that you will weigh very carefully the immense responsibility which you would assume before history by depriving Australians of the glory of holding Tobruk till victory was won, which otherwise by God's help will be theirs for ever.'[74]

This cable was typical of the kind of message that came from Churchill: judging everything against the grand design and intending to make it psychologically difficult to refuse his request. The Fadden Cabinet was not amused by Churchill's rhetoric and again asked for Australian troops in Tobruk to be relieved. Blamey pushed the issue with the British commander, General Auchinleck, pointing out that if French or Americans made the request they would not be refused. Auchinleck replied in the most offensive fashion possible: 'Oh, but it isn't.' Australia was still not regarded as independent and still not treated as independent by the government and authorities of Britain. Blamey had remembered all too well that in World War I, every success won by Australian troops was described in the British press as a success won by British troops.[75]

The policy of appeasement that had been supported by Australia had quite clearly failed. The British guarantee to Poland, as German troops marched, not only involved Britain but also led the Empire to war. Menzies never spoke about it publicly, but in private he believed that British diplomacy had failed seriously. For some years Britain had only reacted to Hitler and had not tried to shape events. France had done nothing to improve relations with Italy nor try to prevent the development of an alliance between Germany and Italy. Menzies also believed that Whitehall underestimated the problem that Japan posed for Australia saying 'frankly I have not been impressed with British diplomacy of late.'[76]

With the changing political scene in Australia, Fadden's government was short-lived, and John Curtin became Prime Minister on 3 October 1941. He faced some of the most difficult times in Australia's history, especially during the attacks on Darwin. He continued to deny Churchill's request that troops stay in Tobruk. There were three Australian divisions in the Middle East and another in Malaya; a large part of the navy was in the Mediterranean and around

12,000 airmen were overseas. As Leader of the Opposition he had been highly critical of the conduct of the war in the Middle East. He had been outspoken about Greece and Crete and the losses that both campaigns involved.[77] The rapidity with which the British changed their Commander-in-Chief in North Africa lends more than a little justification to Curtin's criticism.

On 7 December 1941 Pearl Harbor was attacked, and only two days later, British naval forces in the Pacific were crippled by the sinking of the *Prince of Wales* and the battle cruiser *Repulse*. Churchill later wrote, 'Over all this vast expanse of waters, Japan was supreme, and we everywhere were weak and naked.'[78] Japan had entered the war.

Before Churchill, Chamberlain had repeated the assurance that the fleet was large enough to be formidable in the Pacific should Japan enter the war. Casey had earlier secured assurances in 1939, and Menzies' own visit to Britain was to try to cement those assurances, to be more convinced that Britain would be able to fulfil her undertaking. A year before the sinking of the British capital ships, Churchill had cabled Menzies:

> ... should the Italian Fleet be knocked out as a factor, and Italy herself broken as a combatant, as she may be, we could send strong naval forces to Singapore without suffering any serious disadvantages. We must try to bear out Eastern anxieties patiently and doggedly until this result is achieved, it always being understood that if Australia is seriously threatened by invasion we should not hesitate to compromise or sacrifice the Mediterranean position for the sake of our kith and kin.[79]

The day after Pearl Harbor, Curtin broadcast to Australia that we were also at war with Japan. Curtin asked that a specific war council of allied nations be established in Washington, but the British refused. Churchill himself tried to prevent any direct discussions between Australia and the United States, and he made no secret in his memoirs that he feared America would concentrate its forces on the Pacific after it entered the war.[80]

On Christmas Day 1941, Hong Kong fell to the Japanese, and on the following day Curtin made his famous announcement appealing to the United States. He said, 'The Australian Government therefore regards the Pacific struggle as primarily one in which the United States and Australia must have the fullest say in the direction of the democracies' fight plan ... I make it quite clear that Australia looks to America, free of any pangs as to our traditional links or kinship with the United Kingdom.'[81] He said he was well aware of the dangers that Britain faced, but also made it clear that events in Australia were his primary concern. This is an important point in Australian history, as it is the point at which our policy of strategic dependence changed. Australia transferred its dependence to America with Curtin's speech. It was a necessary transferral. Australia faced its darkest days, with Japan seeming unstoppable in its advance through Asia. Australian leaders felt it necessary to continue its policy of strategic dependence, only this time it would no longer be with the British Empire, it would be with the United States of America. It was a decision made in the face of a real and major threat to Australia.

Churchill reacted very badly to Curtin's statement, saying that Britain should stand 'firm against this misbehaviour'. Churchill even went so far as to suggest that Curtin's statements released Britain from her obligation to defend Australia. Some of the reactions from Britain were complimentary.[82] The *Evening Standard* published an article sympathetic both to Australia's desire for a larger say in relation to strategic policy throughout the Pacific and to the gravity of the threats Australia faced.[83]

The first attack on Australian territory came when the RAAF base at Rabaul was bombed by the Japanese air force. On the same day a unified command for the South West Pacific was established under Wavell and Generalissimo Chiang Kai-Shek. These were British arrangements. Australia still had no say in plans that involved Australia. Curtin issued a statement in which he made it clear that the Australian Government considered its first duty was to Australia and that Australia should be fully consulted in plans that would affect Australia's destiny. He said: 'No single nation can afford to risk its future on the infallibility of one man, and no nation can afford to submerge its right of speaking for itself because of the assumed omniscience of another.'[84]

Churchill replied to a cable from Curtin asking for reinforcement of Malaya since much of it had already been overrun. In his cable Curtin implied criticism of the campaigns in Greece and Crete. Churchill replied, 'I do not accept any censure about Crete and Greece.'[85] Curtin had chosen the wrong way to argue with Churchill, who went on to recap the dedication of the British war effort, implying, albeit unstated, a stark contrast with Australian efforts and reminding Curtin: 'We have successfully disengaged Tobruk after the previous relief of all your men who gallantly held it for so long. I hope therefore that you be considerate in the judgement which you pass upon those to whom Australian lives and fortunes are so dear.'[86] Churchill had once more 'scratched the Tobruk scab'.[87]

By Sunday 15 February, Singapore had fallen. In Churchill's words, it was the 'worst disaster and largest capitulation in British history'.[88] If Churchill had listened more to other people and not been so sure of himself, that disaster might have been averted. Within the following week, Darwin itself was bombed.

It was against this background that Prime Minister Curtin engaged in a difficult and extensive exchange of cables with Churchill, who described the communication as 'daily cable battles'.[89] Curtin pushed Churchill for the 6th, 7th and 9th Divisions to return from North Africa to Australia. Churchill, as history has recorded, used every device and every lever to try to prevent that happening. One cannot entirely blame Churchill for his attitude. His primary task was the defence of Britain. He would sacrifice anything, everything, including Australia, if necessary, to prevent the defeat of Britain by Germany. As he saw it, he would have been doing his duty. But Curtin would have been failing in his duty if he had not pressed for the return of troops to Australia and if he had not in fact ordered that they return.

Churchill knew little of the Far East. The region was remote from his consciousness. Menzies was to write caustically in his memoirs:

'But of the Far East he knew nothing, and could not imagine it. Australia was a very distant country which produced some great fighting men and some black swans for the pond at Chartwell … I sometimes think that he regarded the Japanese attack in the South West Pacific as a rather tiresome intrusion, distracting attention from the great task of defeating Hitler.'[90]

By March, the Dutch East Indies had fallen and an Allied fleet had been lost in the Battle of the Java Sea. Churchill wrote later implying a significant criticism of Curtin and of Australia regarding our devotion to broader war efforts.[91] It is clear at that time from Churchill's writings that he believed the withdrawal of Australian divisions, for the protection of Australia, represented a betrayal of the Empire.

When Curtin ordered the 6th and 7th Divisions to return, Churchill used every device again to divert those divisions to Burma, to help secure the road to China and to India. At this time, Churchill said that Australia's greatest support must come from the United States.[92] He continued implying that if Curtin did not allow our troops to be diverted to Burma, it would affect American readiness to do anything to support Australia. Churchill persuaded Roosevelt also to weigh in and urge Curtin to allow the troops to land in Burma. The troops did not have the equipment or the weapons required to fight in Burma, and Curtin responded, despite objections from both Churchill and Roosevelt, that Australia had every right to require its troops to be returned to Australia to shore up its defences against the Japanese.[93]

Churchill had written that he could not contemplate that Curtin would deny his request and Roosevelt's, and Churchill ordered the ships to be diverted north to Rangoon. As one can imagine, Curtin was furious. He emphasised the speed of the Japanese advance and that Australia's defences were vanishing. Australia had a primary obligation to save Australia, not only for Australia but also as a base from which a counter-attack against Japan could be launched. He made it plain it was quite impossible to reverse the decision that he had made.[94] Churchill's request was in fact out of time because Burma was lost on 22 February 1942 and Australian forces could not have arrived before the end of the month.

While the ships were crossing the Indian Ocean, Curtin had a tense time. The ships were without escorts. They were vulnerable to Japanese attack, and the divisions could so easily have been lost. When Curtin first received news that the troops had arrived in safe harbour, it would have been an overwhelming relief from days of great stress and concern for him.

Curtin prevailed over Churchill in contrast to the New Zealand Prime Minister, Peter Fraser, who agreed to delay the return of the New Zealand division.

In March, General MacArthur and American forces arrived in Australia, and Curtin publicly recognised that, as Churchill had told the British Parliament, Britain could not carry the burden of the Pacific while engaging in a life-and-death struggle with Germany and Italy.[95] That certainly was true. These disputes between Churchill and Curtin did not represent a question of right or wrong. Churchill, it can be well argued, was correct in doing what he believed necessary for the defence of Britain, but Curtin was equally right in doing what he believed necessary for the defence of Australia. The days were long past when an independent Dominion could be expected to risk invasion to supply forces for the defence of Britain.

After the German war began, conflict with Japan became inevitable. Australia, Britain and the United States had done much to make Japan believe that it could not carve out a partnership with Western nations and that it would have to create its own zone of influence. Indeed, in 1940, Japan had instituted the Greater East Asia Co-Prosperity Sphere, with senior Japanese leaders guaranteeing 'Asia for the Asiatics' and to 'break the shackles of Western imperialist control'.[96] The 1940 declaration saw the sphere defined as China, Manchukuo, the Dutch East Indies and French Indo-China; by January 1942 it also included Malaya, Burma and the Philippines.

Japan had hoped for better terms with the West, yet such issues as hostility towards the racial equity clause in the preamble of the League of Nations, the destruction of the Anglo-Japanese Alliance and failure to recognise Japanese efforts in World War I, all reinforced the view of the Japanese leadership that their future was in Asia, and in Asia alone.

Japan had also become severely affronted in the mid-1920s when the United States virtually banned Japanese immigration, in a measure that I understand banned all immigration from Asia. The white races were seen as racist and exclusive. If there had been a broader view of the human race, an acceptance of non-discrimination and of equality between races, and if that had been clearly understood by Japan, would that have been enough to stop Japan entering the war on the side of Germany? It is a question we will never be able to answer. It is significant that one Japanese Prime Minister on his retirement, in unofficial discussions told me that he really thought Australia had changed and put aside the racism of earlier times. That Prime Minister is no longer with us, but no Japanese leader would make such a comment today.

The other great question to which we will never know the answer is what would the United States have done if Japan had not attacked Pearl Harbor. Would Washington have inevitably been drawn into the war, or would it have stood aside? America had already let Britain stand alone against Nazi Germany for the best part of two and a half years, knowing the policies that Germany was pursuing in Europe. As it was, after Pearl Harbor, the United States declared war on Japan, as was inevitable, but not on Germany. It was indeed Germany that declared war on the United States in support of Japan.

I have debated many times with Americans I trust and regard as friends the question of what would America have done without Pearl Harbor. Many have told me that without Pearl Harbor the United States might well have stayed out of the war.

With General MacArthur's arrival in Australia, planning began in earnest to push Japan back from the land and the islands it had taken in the Pacific. It was a bloody and difficult campaign, and its course has been well chronicled. The arguments that John Curtin had with the British Prime Minister demonstrated in the starkest terms that Australia needs leaders and governments that will stand for Australia's interests. It is only natural that the leader of any country will place that country ahead of all others. This is true for an ally, a neighbour or an important part of the Empire, as we were with Britain. We should not be surprised at any part of this. Nations, especially great and powerful nations, make decisions perceived to be in their own interest. If Australia's interest coincides with that of a great power, then we could expect support in the venture, but if it does not, we would be wrong to expect support and foolish to rely on it.

The reliance we had placed on the United Kingdom and the Empire, since Federation, whatever guarantees we had—and there were many—as events were to prove, carried no weight; they were indeed worthless, because larger events had intervened. The lesson to this stage in Australia's history is a simple one. When the difficulties are great and seem insurmountable, you must rely on yourself, your own efforts. That is the one sure thing on which you can base plans for the future.

The newly federated Australia pursued domestic policies that, with a few notable exceptions, were for the great benefit of Australian society. We wanted to be different. We wanted to stand apart from the nations of Europe. We did not want the social inequalities inherent in early twentieth-century European societies. Yet this desire to be different, to lead the world and stand apart, did not translate to the international policy level. Indeed, the first four decades of Australia's existence enshrined the policy of strategic dependence in our national psyche. Australia felt comfortable as a part of the British Empire and relied on our imperial membership for defence and foreign policy. Although it was a policy suitable to the context of the time, it was a policy that was too blindly followed. We did not question British intentions nearly as hard as we should have, and we too easily assumed that the strategic priorities of London aligned with our own.

Some leaders, Deakin and Hughes most notably, attempted to carve a more influential role for Australia within this dependence, but they both believed in the virtues of imperial membership. Any greater say that they were to push for was always firmly within the policy of dependence and imperial policy-making mechanisms. It was not until Curtin turned to America as the Japanese marched through Asia that Australia began to realise that its reliance on Britain had been misplaced.

Yet in the decades following the war, Australia did not base its future plans on self-reliance. Both international and domestic events would mean that, once again, Australia would place its security and interests in the hand of a great power; a great power that still influences our foreign policy decisions to this day. Although the nation might have cast away the remnants of imperial decision-making during World War II, the strategic calculations of America and its interests would soon become a persuasive influence on Australian leaders. A policy of strategic dependence would remain a dominant element of our foreign and defence policies.

Part II

All the way
with the USA

'I make it quite clear that Australia looks to America ...'
JOHN CURTIN

4

Securing post-war Australia

Because the American fleet had been put out of action by the Japanese attack on Pearl Harbor, it was some time before the American counter-offensive was able to begin. The first turning point came with the Battle of the Midway and, although not a decisive victory, it nevertheless halted the Japanese advance and helped to relieve pressure on Australian troops in New Guinea. The first land victory against the Japanese was achieved by Australian troops fighting at Milne Bay in 1942. The first major reinforcement of Australia as a base from which territories and islands conquered by the Japanese could be recaptured occurred in December 1942 when American troops first arrived.

There is no point in recounting here the long, difficult and bloody battles that took place across the Pacific—there are many thorough accounts of Australia's role in World War II.[1] Great heroism was shown by Australian troops and by Americans in some of the most difficult battles of the entire war against the Axis powers. The Pacific War ended when the United States dropped atomic weapons on Hiroshima and Nagasaki on 6 and 9 August 1945 respectively. That decision was not controversial in Australia at the time, with the entire nation being relieved that war was over. It has, of course, become controversial in the years since.

Understanding the circumstances that Australia faced in those early post-war years is important. It was a very different Australia— and a very different world—from that which exists today. We still regarded ourselves largely as a community made up of Anglo-Saxon and Celtic heritage. We were still a community in which the sectarian differences created hostility, even enmity, between Australians. These differences were all the greater because of the way in which Prime Minister Billy Hughes attacked Catholics and the Catholic Church during the conscription debates held during World War I. The White Australia Policy was still in effect, and the rights of Indigenous Australians were still restricted.

The post-war leaders in Australia understood that we had so nearly been invaded. They understood that with seven million people, Australia did not have the strength, the resources, the infrastructure and, more importantly, the men and women necessary to mount a credible defence effort by itself. On all sides there was a major commitment to increase Australia's population and to invest heavily in resources for the future. A larger Australia with a greater industrial capacity was seen as a way to strengthen our defences against future aggressors, as well as ensuring our economic prosperity. They also realised that, after so much suffering, the nation needed a strong statement that the future was bright and that the fighting and sacrifice necessitated by the war would not be in vain.

The Chifley Government commenced the post-war reconstruction effort designed to transform Australia from a war-time economy with the establishment of the Department of Post-War Reconstruction under the directorship of H.C. 'Nugget' Coombs. At the same time, Immigration Minister Arthur Calwell initiated a major migration scheme that worked in tandem with the government's nation-building policies.[2] Calwell had hoped that Australia's population would grow at a rate of two per cent per annum, with one per cent of this growth coming from immigration.[3] Growth at this rate would require some 70,000 arrivals per annum.[4]

To gain the support of the union movement, he expressed aspirations for the migration scheme that he really could not fulfil. He had wanted 90 per cent of immigrants to come from traditional sources; in other words, from the United Kingdom and Ireland.[5] With the number of displaced people in Europe, the beginning of the Cold War and Soviet domination over Eastern Europe, Calwell's desire for such a high proportion of British immigrants was never possible. The vast majority of immigrants came from Europe, although Britain remained the largest source of immigrants until 1953.

Australian political parties still adhered to the White Australia Policy. For both parties, adherence to the White Australia Policy was an article of faith. This included Calwell, who began the migration program, and Robert Menzies, leader of the Liberal Party and Opposition. The policy would continue once the Menzies Government took office, with Menzies exclaiming in 1950 that it was 'well justified as it is on the grounds of national homogeneity and economic standards'.[6] The White Australia Policy did not start to lose force until the end of that decade. I can remember conversations that I had with Harold Holt, as Minister for Immigration, in which he made the point very strongly that the White Australia Policy was doing us a good deal of damage throughout East and South-East Asia. The grossly discriminatory nature of that policy was often raised with him in South-East Asia. According to that conversation, he had had discussions in Cabinet trying to find some amelioration of the policy. Putting that divisive and inexcusable policy aside, Australians were determined to make new citizens feel at home.

The Department of Immigration had been established in 1945. Calwell established an immigration advisory council in 1947.[7] Many voluntary organisations were involved in facilitating contact between old and new Australians in all areas of life. The Good Neighbour Movement was established on a nationwide basis in 1950. New settlers' leagues had been established in the early 1920s for much the same purpose. There was a desire among Australians to see that new citizens could integrate, understand and be made to feel welcome in Australia. Church organisations, philanthropic bodies, commercial associations, trade unions, education and sporting bodies, almost the whole of Australian community life, became involved. It was a major contributor to the success of the migration program in those early years. A Citizenship Convention was held annually in Canberra. Again, the motivation behind all of these initiatives was to advance relationships and to encourage immigrants to take out Australian citizenship.

A significant part of the work of the Immigration Advisory Council was concerned with social integration of migrants into the Australian community. An Immigration Planning Council was first formed in 1949 to advise the minister on the relationship between migration and national development and to make sure that there was adequate accommodation and employment for immigrants. In 1962 the Commonwealth established an Immigration Publicity Council to make sure that all relevant information was made readily available.[8]

It is quite clear that the acceptance of new Australians by the Australian community did not just happen by chance. It did not just happen because the political parties did not play politics with race or religion. There was a community groundswell designed to make new Australians feel at home, to become part of the general community, to participate in public life and, above all, to be made to feel welcome.

The purpose of these bodies was to give non-political advice to government on the progress of a great planned movement of people, to help build Australia's strength, but also to assist the arriving immigrants. These bodies also came to be a major protector of the migration program. If it looked as though a movement was growing against migration, for whatever reason, they would often weigh into the debate in a non-political way. They played an important role in maintaining Australia's commitment to the migration program and in helping to avoid divisive debate. It was not always perfect, but the initiatives consecutive governments established to ease the transition of new immigrants into Australian society had a positive influence.

More important than that, however, was the commitment of the major political parties not to play politics with race or religion.

Without that commitment, it would have been extraordinarily difficult to sustain the program. That commitment endured until razor-wire detention centres were established in the late 1980s. Up to this point, Australia's post-war migration policies were a remarkable achievement, especially in a country where politics is often played roughly with no holds barred and where race politics has, unfortunately, been a part of our political history.

This is not to say that some aspects of the migration program did not come in for debate. There was a famous case concerning a Filipino, Sergeant Gamboa.[9] Sergeant Gamboa fought with the American forces and was in fact a naturalised American. He was demobilised in Australia and had married in Melbourne. Arthur Calwell, as Immigration Minister, decided he should be deported. There were vigorous debates as a consequence. During the debates, the Immigration Minister was highly criticised for not allowing Sergeant Gamboa and his wife to live as Australians. Menzies made a speech in which he, on the one hand, defended the White Australia Policy and, on the other, attacked Calwell for weakening an important principle through bad administration.[10]

Australian politicians also showed a great commitment to investing in the future of this country. The thinking was, and still should be, that we cannot use all our wealth for today; we must invest, build, expand, make it a better and stronger country for our children and for those to come after us. For example, the Snowy Mountains Hydro Electric Scheme, providing power to cities and water for Australian farms, was a major landmark development of historic proportions. The commitment to build Australia should be replicated in today's Australia. In addition, there were moves to establish greater social justice, greater equity in the life of the nation; a better life for Australians who had just sacrificed so much.[11] Much of this represented the positive side of developments in Australia in the early years after the war.

The story, however, is not all positive. There were deep divisions in Australian society that had to be overcome. Australian trade unions had caused great concern in the early stages of the war. Some unions were under communist control, such as the Federated Ironworkers

Association, while others, such as the Seamen's Union of Australia, had strong links to the Communist Party.[12] The Waterside Workers Federation was unwilling to load military supplies intended for our troops in North Africa because in their view it was an imperial capitalist war. That changed only after Hitler launched his offensive against the Soviet Union. It was the Labor Prime Minister, Curtin, who put troops on the wharfs to load the ships when the Waterside Workers Federation would not.

These activities sharpened the ideological divide within Australia. I have already mentioned the sectarianism that was rampant between Catholic and Protestants. There was also an ugly side to the divide between capitalism and labour. The Labor Party and the union movement would have feared that the conservative parties, as they were believed to be, and capitalists themselves, would seek to exploit labour and deny a fair wage. These discussions came in the wake of a war that had engulfed the nation for the best part of six years, which had followed by far the worst depression in Australia's history, with unemployment reaching unthinkable levels of 29 per cent in 1932.[13]

The union movement was far more powerful in those days than it has been in more recent times. It was led with great responsibility by President of the Australian Council of Trade Unions, Albert Monk. He knew that working with the government was vitally important. In those days in the early 1950s, about 50 per cent of the labour force was unionised. By the 1960s, during the period of the Menzies Government, that figure rose to about 60 per cent.[14] Today, the percentage of the workforce that is unionised has fallen to 18 per cent.[15] The union movement now has far less influence on Australian affairs than it has ever had.

There are many people who spent the 1930s walking Australia's roads looking for work, looking for a way to survive. This army of swagmen came to have a secret language. I knew one of the people who existed during the 1930s in this way. He told me that there were signs on the gates of farms and properties; signs that he would not tell me, even then, of a time that was long past. 'At this property you can get food, a bit of work chopping wood. You will be shown a swagman's hut down by the creek where you can stay for a night or two.' Other signs would be not so positive. 'A waste of time going on to this farm. Watch out. He will set the dogs on you.' This particular person joined the Second Australian Imperial Force during World War II—his first job in ten years—and served with the Australian forces in North Africa. Many of those who joined the army were in a similar position.

Everyone was concerned that the depression days should not return. After the sacrifices that had been made during World War II, the nation yearned for an economic opportunity and a prosperous future. When the migration program began there were 600,000 service men and women in uniform waiting to be demobilised.[16] That Calwell was able to persuade the movement to accept migration in the face of that challenge was all the more remarkable.

It was a time when many believed that socialism was inevitable and that the best that could be done was to slow down its approach. This was a common view among academics at Oxford during my time there (1949–52). Many of the economists really believed in socialism and that capitalism had had its day. There was an unfortunate by-product of that view. Many of the newly emerging countries of Africa were given extraordinarily bad economic advice by allegedly reputable economists from the United States and from the United Kingdom. African countries were later blamed for having made very bad decisions in terms of economic management. Many had merely followed the advice they had been given.

There were also many who believed that communism and socialism were remarkably similar. The difference really related to the means that the respective parties would use.[17] In too many countries the communist parties had shown that they were prepared to use any means, including revolution, to achieve their objective. On the other hand, socialists such as the Labor Party were firmly committed to democracy. Many believed that the end point would be similar.

The Australian Labor Party had in its platform an objective of nationalising 'the socialisation of industry, production, distribution and exchange'.[18] When in 1947 Prime Minister Chifley therefore decided to nationalise Australia's banking system, many people became extraordinarily concerned. This was regarded as a major step in advancing the socialist democrat dream. Many people became very frightened of the Labor Party. Those with savings in the banks thought the government was going to steal their savings for its own purposes. The *Banking Act 1947* was introduced with the express intention of taking over the banking activities of private banks by the Commonwealth Bank.[19] Australia's private banking system would be bought out by the Commonwealth Bank and owned by the Commonwealth Government. The bank nationalisation proposals put forward by Chifley made it very easy for people to believe that the Labor Party was absolutely serious in wanting to fulfil its platform and nationalise, not only the banks but also the means of production, distribution and exchange. Nationalisation of the banks would have been the single most serious and most important step in achieving that overall objective. The legislation was appealed in the High Court by the banks and certain state governments, with the court finding in favour of the plaintiffs in 1948.[20] Under the advice of Evatt, Chifley took the matter to the Privy Council, which would ultimately uphold the High Court's decision. Those on the right of politics had their worst fears confirmed by these actions of the Labor Party and of Prime Minister Chifley, in particular. The attempts to nationalise the banking system contributed greatly to Labor's fall in 1949.

In addition to these domestic policy issues that our post-war leaders had to contend with, there were many foreign policy concerns facing Australia. The post-war leadership wanted to secure Australia's economic and social prosperity with significant domestic reform. Yet this was all predicated on ensuring that the international environment was stable and that global trade recovered. In the early post-war years both political parties wanted a tough peace treaty with Japan, preferably one that would prevent Japan's rearmament. They also wanted the protection of a defence treaty with the United States. On both issues Australia demonstrated an independence of mind and determination in the execution of foreign policy, specifically tuned to Australia's interest and freed of the old links to the British Empire.

As the previous chapters of this book attest to, pushing this kind of independence over foreign policy was a new direction for Australian leaders. There were differences between Evatt and Menzies. Evatt believed in Australia as an independent nation acting entirely in our own interests. Menzies still tended to the view that we could exert the greatest influence when working through the Commonwealth and the Empire connection.

It is important to put Australia's views in the broader international context. Australia was concerned with the future of the Western Pacific. Australia also understood that it could not achieve its objectives acting alone, and initially thought that common action with other Commonwealth powers, particularly New Zealand and Britain, might help Australia achieve its objectives.[21] It was reminiscent of a bygone age, and British influence was minimal as events were to unfold. The United States was inflexible in pursuit of its own objectives and was prepared to make concessions on the periphery only so long as they did not interfere with major objectives of American policy.[22]

The first severe differences with the United States came quite early in the piece. As Japanese surrender approached, Evatt was determined for Australia to take its place at the ceremony where the surrender would be signed. Australia had sacrificed much in the fight against the Japanese, and Evatt would accept nothing less than equal representation at the ceremony. Yet the Americans proposed that Australia and other Dominions be attached to the British delegation. The tactic was designed to minimise Australia's influence. Evatt bluntly disagreed with that proposition, refusing to concede to American demands. There were even suggestions that if Australia did not have an appropriate place at the surrender ceremony, it would heavily influence Australia's attitude in relation to the Japanese Peace Treaty, which was still to be negotiated.[23] Australia's signature was going to be needed for that purpose, and that gave Australia some leverage.

Evatt, who at this stage in his career showed a remarkable understanding of Australia's interests, understood that, for those interests to be pursued adequately, Australia would have to show determination—even bluntness—to break through the monopoly of international decision-making, formerly held by Britain, but now held by the United States. Evatt recognised that British power in the Pacific had been grievously weakened, although London was determined to maintain its position in Hong Kong. Australia could no longer look to Britain. Yet it still yearned for security and surety provided by the protection of a great power. Therefore, Evatt developed a three-point plan to achieve what he saw as necessary to ensure Australia's security as well as involvement in the post-war settlement.[24] Evatt's first point was a security arrangement with the United States. He wanted it to be formalised, not merely relying on the word of a President that might mean nothing to a later President. Second, Evatt wanted Japan to be permanently disarmed. Third, Australia wanted a significant say in the post-war settlements and arrangements, especially in relation to Japan.

To the end of Evatt's Labor Government, these objectives were pressed firmly, vigorously, but without success. The British themselves showed little sympathy and the United States rebuffed Australia's efforts on all sides.[25] From their point of view, Australia was probably making a nuisance of itself, but it really showed how little regard a victorious America had for the concerns of a smaller country such as Australia. At this stage, America reigned supreme over the post-war world, with the Soviet Union having yet to detonate an atomic bomb.

In 1949 the government changed. Evatt was replaced by Percy Spender, who was an adept and probably more skilful negotiator.[26] While the new Menzies Government adopted a softer position in relation to the United States and moved closer to its views, the main lines of Australian policy did not change. Through Spender and Casey, the new government pursued much the same policy as that set out by Chifley and Evatt before them.[27]

Australia's main concern continued to be the fear of a militarily resurgent Japan.[28] General MacArthur described such fears as 'irrational'. Australia's view was quite different from that of the

United States.[29] Australia had been profoundly affected by the war. As a consequence of that, we not only had a determination to build and strengthen Australia by internal development but also sought to pursue policies that would create an international environment more conducive to Australia's safety and to peace in the Western Pacific. Australia knew these matters had to be made its own concern. Yet Australia also knew that our relationship with America was key to ensuring peace and security in our region. The days of reliance on the British Empire were well and truly in the past.

While it had suffered a humiliation at Pearl Harbor, the United States had never come close to invasion. The continental United States had never been bombed and had never feared invasion and occupation.

In Australia, that fear was very real. As a young child I can remember going into a room with adults discussing various matters. There would be a sudden silence. I had heard somebody say, 'Would it be safer in the country or safer in a large city where other people are around?'

I can remember asking, 'Safe from what?'

As was quite common in those days, it was believed that young children should be kept in a state of ignorance and that too much knowledge would be a bad thing. It was not until a good year later that I realised they were talking about the time in which they believed Australia would be occupied by the Japanese. So the fear was real and had bitten into the Australian psyche. Both Britain and America believed that our fears were grossly exaggerated. New Zealand gave us support.[30]

As the war drew to a close, there were discussions about a larger Pacific pact involving several powers, which would involve a NATO-type commitment to defend any power that was threatened or came under attack.[31] That argument was ultimately put aside because it was believed that many Pacific countries had unstable governments.[32] The United States at that time 'distrusted any proposal that might have led to further involvement on the Asian mainland or entanglement with declining European colonialism'.[33] It was the latter reason that weighed most heavily with the United States. Therefore a more limited treaty in our case involving Australia, New Zealand and the United States was pursued.

Australia was left with two of Evatt's three objectives: a continuing security arrangement with the United States and a peace treaty that would make sure Japan would not again be a threat to Australia's security.[34] Australia found it difficult to influence the post-war settlement outside its immediate area of concern. The dual objectives became harder and harder to achieve. America by this time was becoming obsessed by the Soviet Union, by the need to keep Japan out of the Soviet orbit and by the need to make Japan an ally in the broader international environment. Therefore, Washington was determined on a soft peace and determined not to prevent Japanese rearmament. Australia could not alter this resolve, so the one objective left to Australia was a continuing treaty with the United States.

After war broke out on the Korean Peninsula and after the communist victory in China, the Americans wished to conclude the peace treaty with Japan as a matter of urgency. Australia gained some greater weight in these negotiations because we supported the United Nations' decisions in relation to Korea and made a commitment to provide substantial ground forces.

The American idea of a soft peace with Japan, in the larger order of events, was probably correct. They wanted to make Japan an ally in the impending Cold War against the Soviet Union.[35] This attitude would also have been common in the United Kingdom. It was a view that Evatt, and the Labor Party in particular, would have rejected. The Menzies Government had a different emphasis. It tended to share America and Europe's concerns with communist aggression. In any case, on these matters, the United States was inflexible. Japan was to be allowed to rearm and, in the decades that followed, became a successful democracy and economic power.

Australia gave up its arguments against the rearmament of Japan only when the ANZUS pact itself was close to reality.[36] Even in those days, Australia trusted its war experience with Japan much more than Washington's grand designs.[37] The grand designs of great powers had cost Australian lives in the past, and our leaders were determined to avoid such sacrifices again.

The timing and circumstances of Australia's commitment to Korea was managed by Spender, as Foreign Minister. He persuaded acting Prime Minister Arthur Fadden to act and send troops to Korea. Menzies was absent, travelling from the United Kingdom. Spender was determined to make sure that the world knew that this was an Australian decision and not a decision consequent on British action.[38] Spender was in part motivated by his belief that the British were acting to frustrate the successful development of a treaty with the United States. The British were clearly arguing with John Foster Dulles, the American Secretary of the State, that an ANZUS treaty was unnecessary or undesirable. From the British perspective, they feared that such a treaty would weaken the Empire connection. From an Australian perspective, our participation in Korea would assist in assuring a defence treaty with Washington.

It was Spender who short-circuited the arguments by giving an ultimatum to the United States over the defence treaty, a courageous act for the young Australia.[39] He made it clear that we would not support a peace settlement with Japan without an adequate defence and security arrangement with the United States. Only after that did the Americans come to the table and realise that they would have to enter into an agreement with Australia. They were therefore most reluctant partners, and this became clear as the terms of ANZUS developed.[40] While at some point Spender had hoped for a NATO-type commitment, which is an absolute commitment to defend a member country under attack, the best that could be achieved was a commitment to consult, a commitment to inform the United Nations and a commitment to consider further action in accordance with each country's constitutional processes. That would potentially require a resolution through the US Congress before the ANZUS Treaty could result in military support for an Australia under attack.

While successive Australian governments have spoken of ANZUS as though it is a guarantee of American support, should we ever be in trouble, it is in fact nothing of the sort. It was Spender's ultimatum that resulted in ANZUS, limited as it is. It is also interesting to note that, were it not for Spender's determination, we might well not have even achieved that much. The Department of Foreign Affairs and Trade's historical assessment of the period highlights differences between Menzies and Spender, suggesting that Menzies was prepared to take the United States on trust; he would have settled for a Presidential Statement of support.[41] Spender, being more realistic, thought that such a commitment might well be temporary, a position that depended on the mood of the President of the day. In any case, it would lack any accompanying planning machinery that could lead to implementation of effective support should a crisis arise. Spender would never have acquiesced merely in a Presidential Statement.

There had been other differences between Menzies and Spender. Menzies was more concerned to make sure that Australia's relationship with the United Kingdom would not be damaged by new relationships with the United States. Spender was looking more to the future, Menzies looking, to some extent, to the past.

ANZUS was signed on 12 July 1951. The treaty mentioned a Council of Foreign Ministers, which would be charged with decisions concerning the implementation of ANZUS. That council has led to the planning arrangements that have been developed over the following years. The United States also made separate treaties with Japan and the Philippines, which were signed at roughly the same time.

Of the initial aims expressed by Evatt, Australia achieved only one, a permanent and formal treaty arrangement with the United States. It was, however, a much lesser arrangement than Evatt or Spender would have wanted. During its negotiation there were significant differences between Spender and Menzies, and I have no doubt that Menzies was delighted when he was able to persuade Spender to take on the post of Ambassador to the United States with Casey becoming Foreign Minister.

It was a time in which Australia pursued its own diplomacy based on Australia's perception of Australia's interests. It is not to our credit but, since that time, we have tended to slip little by little into a belief that ANZUS will protect us, no matter what. We once believed that the British Empire could protect us no matter what the danger. We learnt to our cost that that was seriously mistaken. It would be ironic if just as that reliance on Empire left us unprepared and vulnerable to invasion, reliance on ANZUS and the American connection, in changed and differing circumstances, were also to lead Australia into grave and serious danger.

For the time, which we need to remember is more than sixty years ago, the policy was right. The Cold War was a reality. The Soviet expansion was real, the future was unpredictable. I have no doubt that ANZUS would have been effective if Australia were attacked by a communist power, but if we were attacked by something else, or needed support for another reason, the result would be much more problematic and open to debate. Nonetheless, the signing of ANZUS completed the transferral of strategic dependence from Britain to America—a situation that persists to this day.

5

Dr H.V. Evatt

Although Australian initiatives on the domestic policy front and our relationship with America were all geared towards securing our future, Australia's post-war leaders also appreciated that Australia had to carve a role out for itself in the broader new world order that was forming from the ashes of the old. From the dying days of the League of Nations through to the foundation of the United Nations Organisation, Dr Herbert Vere Evatt was an internationalist who believed devoutly in an independent Australia. Evatt believed that only Australia was in the best position to argue for Australia's interests. Only Australia could make judgements solely motivated by the interests of this country. He had pushed for the ratification of the Statute of Westminster, even before the war. He had argued that 'close Imperial relations were not inconsistent with independence'.[1] Evatt achieved much as Minister for External Affairs and should be remembered for the kind of foreign policy Australia can achieve when we follow what is in our interests, based on our values and based on the needs of our region.[2]

When he became Minister for External Affairs, first of all under Curtin and later under Chifley, Evatt enjoyed almost exclusive control over foreign policy.[3] The department he inherited was minuscule and, although Menzies had recognised in his time the need for Australia to be advised by its own people, who had Australia's interests at heart, it was Evatt who was first in an emphatic way to give voice to that.

Evatt sought to project a more prominent Australian identity abroad, and sought Australian representation at key conferences so that Australia's concerns and opinions could be advanced.[4] As an Australian nationalist, he objected to the common practice at the end of the war when the great powers came together to reach their own agreement on how a post-war world should look, believing glibly that other countries would have to accept what they had determined.

Proposals for a new world organisation had been canvassed well before the end of the war. The proposal was drafted at Dumbarton Oaks, a historic estate in Washington DC, and later affirmed by agreement at Yalta between Churchill, Stalin and Roosevelt in February 1945. Evatt had been concerned about the great powers dominating the new organisation and, in particular, the voting formula for the Security Council, which assigned major powers a right of veto.[5]

Evatt was prominent at a Commonwealth meeting in London to discuss the proposals. He had three major concerns.[6] First, Evatt was worried about the powers given to the World Court and Security Council to settle disputes between nations. Second, and perhaps more pressingly, he was worried about the provisions that would enable the charter to be amended from time to time. The inability in later decades to achieve any substantial change in the organisation probably justifies Evatt's original objection. Finally, he was also opposed to the veto power and pressed the Commonwealth to ask for its removal at the San Francisco conference. At the very least, Evatt wanted an amendment which stated that a veto could only be used in an emergency—a provision that, if adopted, would have done much to improve the operation of the Security Council. Evatt also argued about the perception and impact of the veto power in dispute settlement, arguing that there 'is no reason why one great power should be able to veto an attempt to settle a dispute through negotiation and arbitration, particularly when that dispute might be in an area outside the power's sphere of influence'.[7] Such a power could mean that an agreement reached between two disputing nations that met the needs of both parties could fail to materialise if one of the veto powers did not concur with the agreement's terms or outcomes. It would make some negotiations untenable.

Evatt also suggested that if a majority of great powers believed that there should be enforcement action, it could be taken even if one power wielded its veto. Evatt also wanted a more flexible method for amending the charter, which can be amended only if the five veto powers agreed. It was clear that none of those five would agree to any amendment that would diminish its own special privileges. Evatt also argued that a periodic revision of the charter would be necessary so that the world organisation could keep pace with changing circumstances.[8] Evatt knew that the world was not static and that, if the United Nations was to have any chance of keeping up with changing global politics, it too needed to be able to change.

For example, the time of decolonisation was fast approaching. Many new nations were being created out of the old European colonial empires. These new nations would need to be accommodated into the new international organisation, and they would need to feel a part of it. They would need to feel that it belonged to them as much as the original fifty-one nations that brought it into being.

For Evatt, for Australia, the Dumbarton Oaks draft was a good starting point, but it was not without fault. In San Francisco, Evatt's efforts succeeded in having Australia placed on the powerful, fourteen-member Executive Committee. In a broadcast made on the eve of the San Francisco conference he argued: 'While security is the first task, it is not enough to plan for security alone; economic and social conditions are potent factors in international relations.'[9]

The great powers had not wanted to discuss the mingling of welfare and security, and Britain, in particular, was annoyed,[10] I suppose because Australia had stepped outside Empire policy. New Zealand supported this move. It was ironic that on this issue the British complained that we had not consulted them, yet for so much of our history it had been the other way around.

It is not surprising Evatt failed to achieve any modification of the veto. It was unfortunately the cement that brought the great powers into the organisation, great powers that probably foresaw the rivalry that was to develop. It is an issue that troubles the UN to this day. Yet Evatt was an Australian leader who, for the first time, stepped outside the policy of strategic dependence and pushed policies that were in Australia's interests irrespective of the consequences for what was left of the British Empire. It was a commendable attempt.

Evatt also managed to secure for Australia one of the first non-permanent seats on the Security Council and defeated a Russian demand to limit the scope of discussion on international issues.[11] He was extraordinarily busy in the formative stage of the United Nations. The *New York Times* said of Evatt: 'When Dr Evatt came here he was a virtually unknown second-string delegate, with the background of a professor and Labor politician. He leaves, recognised as the most brilliant and effective voice of the Small Powers, a leading statesman for the world's conscience, the man who was not afraid to force liberalisation of the League charter, and who had sense enough not to press his threat so far as to break up the conference.'[12]

When the Steering Committee passed a special resolution of thanks to Evatt, all delegates, including the Big Five, stood and applauded. He ultimately became the third President of the General Assembly. How many Australians know today that Herbert Vere Evatt, who in his later political career in Australia made some serious mistakes, had stood in such high regard in the international environment? The quality of his argument, on a number of issues, carried the day and won a respected place for Australia.

The United States had obviously shown significant leadership in the development of this organisation and in the development of the Universal Declaration of Human Rights, which was accepted in 1948. This was a remarkable about-turn from the days in which the US Congress turned its back on its then President Wilson and never participated in the League of Nations. If the United Nations was to be successful the major powers had to be involved, and the

United States was very heavily involved. This time the United States recognised the error of keeping out of the League of Nations.

Many good things happened at this time under US leadership. In addition to the founding of the United Nations and acceptance of the Universal Declaration of Human Rights in 1948, this period also saw the establishment of such global institutions as the International Monetary Fund and the World Bank, both of which pointed to an optimistic and shared desire for a more peaceful future.

But the great hopes that political leaders had as peace was declared, first in Europe and then in the Pacific, soon faded. The democratic nations of the world soon realised that they were facing a most determined and powerful opponent prepared for long-drawn-out and often bitter ideological struggle. It was a struggle that would not end until the fall of the Soviet Union in 1991.

Regardless, Evatt's record as Foreign Minister was a constructive one and one in which Australia should feel a sense of deep pride, that we had played an independent role constructively. It had been recognised by the international community as a role of substance that carried great merit. This is not the way Australians would remember Evatt. His important place in history was secured by his execution of foreign policy. He showed that Australia could be independent, bowing neither to Britain nor to America. It was an example that should be followed. Sadly, it has been an exception rather than the norm.

6

Strategic dependence through the Cold War prism

Despite the independence of mind shown by Dr Evatt over the United Nations and, indeed, the peace with Japan and the formulation of ANZUS, Australia found itself strategically dependent in the post-war era. The desire to transition from the British to the Americans as our great and powerful friend was in no small part due to the international political situation that eventuated in the post-war world. The Cold War was beginning, and Australia once again felt the need to be linked to a great power. Much like in our earlier years, the policy of strategic dependence that was continued through this era made sense—our leaders had very little choice. Yet, as it had with the British, the policy would have consequences and costs, and would embed the desire for strategic dependence firmly within the Australian psyche—a condition that exists to this day.

At the Potsdam and Yalta conferences, Stalin and Roosevelt, who was suffering from great ill-health at the time, virtually sidelined Churchill. As a result, Roosevelt conceded to Stalin's domination and communisation of Eastern Europe.[1] Instead of being governed as one entity, Berlin was governed under four zones that became an East and a West, a very sharp and dangerous divide. It did not take long for the Cold War to be cemented in place. Not surprisingly, Stalin made an attempt to strangle Berlin to have it all embraced as part of the Soviet Empire in East Germany. When he established a ground blockade of Berlin, the Allies, including the Royal Australian Air Force, did what the Soviet leader thought was impossible: they kept Berlin supplied by air.

A body that later became CARE International, of which Australia was very much a part, under contract to the United States, flew thousands upon thousands of food parcels into Berlin to help keep Berliners alive. I am told they actually carried more food into Berlin than any other single organisation. Some years after I left Parliament, I was asked if I would help establish a CARE organisation in Australia. On the basis of the organisation's record, I was very happy to do so. CARE Australia has become one of Australia's most significant overseas aid and development organisations. Forty years after the Berlin airlift, CARE International had its major annual meeting in Berlin, and I was present as vice-president of CARE International and chairman of CARE Australia. I then met people who claimed they had been kept alive by the CARE food packages. All in all, the Berlin airlift was the largest single airlift in history. Beginning on 24 June 1948, the blockade would last almost a year before the Soviets realised their blocking of supply was useless, with the Allies transporting more supplies in by air than had previously arrived by land. It ended on 12 May 1949.

The Soviet Union's takeover of Eastern Europe was not entirely peaceful, and a number of countries suffered greatly when opposing the will of the Kremlin. Czechoslovakia, in particular, showed great courage in opposing the Soviet Union. The 1948 *coup d'état* had seen the Soviet-backed Communist Party of Czechoslovakia overthrow the last remaining democracy in Eastern Europe. By 1968, economic downturn and the process of de-Stalinisation had started political machinations within the Czech Communist Party. The Prague Spring uprising was brought about when reformist Alexander Dubcek introduced reforms aimed at providing Czech citizens with more rights in such areas as freedom of speech and a more open press.[2] The Soviet response was swift, with Warsaw Pact troops and tanks overrunning the country within a day and NATO largely turning a blind eye to the events.

There was also an uprising in Hungary in 1956, which was in part caused by Radio Free Europe. The radio broadcasts carried propaganda across Europe, including exhortations to rise and oppose communism. The broadcasts implied that if there was sufficient strength to rebel against communist rule, then those brave freedom fighters would get help from the West. Indeed the London *Observer* reported the radio broadcast as saying: 'If the Soviet troops really attack Hungary, if our expectations should hold true and Hungarians hold out for three or four days, then the pressure upon the government of the United States to send military help to the Freedom Fighters will become irresistible!'[3]

Radio Free Europe encouraged many to believe that help would be forthcoming when it most certainly would not. There was a full policy review of the influence of that American-backed program on the events at the end of 1956. Radio Free Europe had been accused of promoting the revolution by virtually promising American aid. There was an internal investigation, which included a report by Radio Free Europe political adviser William Griffith, into the Voice for Free Hungary programming during the Hungarian uprising. The report shows that 'RFE broadcast in several cases had implied that foreign aid would be forthcoming if the Hungarians succeeded in establishing a "central military command"'. The broadcasts also appealed to the Hungarians to 'continue to fight vigorously'.[4] Radio Free Europe, according to this American review, gave tactical advice to the rebels.

It was clear that many in Hungary were justified in believing that American support would be forthcoming, that they would get significant help and would be freed from communist rule. That was never going to happen. In the conditions of the times, American intervention would have meant a major war against the Soviet Union.

Both inside Europe and more broadly across the globe, the nuclear stand-off between the United States and the Soviet Union established an uneasy balance, which became known as Mutually Assured Destruction; clearly, a consequence that neither side wanted. The existence of the Soviet Union meant that the United States was not the sole superpower and hence could not dictate terms to the world as it has since the break-up of the Soviet Union. The international system had become bipolar, with many nations falling under the sphere of influence of either one of the two superpowers. Australia was no exception.

The Soviet Union's technological advances had a clear message for the United States. Although Moscow's initial development of nuclear weapons had trailed America's program, it quickly caught up, detonating a hydrogen bomb within a year of the United States and making rapid progress in intercontinental ballistic missile technology. It also demonstrated an edge in space technology, launching the first artificial satellite into space, Sputnik 1, as well as the first man in space, Yuri Gagarin. The Soviet Union's space program through the 1950s was probably ahead of America's. In such a world, the United States could exercise great influence, but there would have to be an accommodation with the Soviet Union if war was to be avoided. The two powers balanced each other.

As George F. Kennan reported in his 'Long Telegram' from Moscow to the Secretary of State in February 1946, 'In summary, we have here a political force committed fanatically to the belief that with US there can be no permanent *modus vivendi*, that it is desirable and necessary that the internal harmony of our society be disrupted, our traditional way of life be destroyed, the international authority of our state be broken, if Soviet power is to be secure.'[5] In plain language, the Soviets did not accept America's right to exist as a democracy.

If today's attitudes had then prevailed, America would have said, well, we are not going to talk with you about anything until you change your attitude and recognise that we exist and will continue to do so. Yet despite those inflammatory and unrealistic remarks expressed in Kennan's telegram, American presidents sat down and talked with Soviet leaders about ways and means of limiting the arms race, mechanisms to avoid nuclear war and how to make the world a little safer. That attitude, exhibited by many American presidents during the Cold War and, in fairness, in some of their Soviet counterparts, was an attitude that should be applied and replicated in today's world. Unfortunately it is not.

These were also uneasy times in the Pacific. While the great decolonisation processes went ahead rapidly in Africa, the colonies of both the Dutch and the French in South-East Asia that had been conquered by the Japanese found themselves in a more complicated situation. Although the international community had been lukewarm in providing authority for both colonial powers to retake their colonies, there were divergent opinions on how to best manage the transition from Japanese-occupied territories to new nation states.

For example, Evatt, as Foreign Minister, had wanted to maintain good relations with Holland and the Netherlands East Indies but, at the same time, clearly showed sympathy for the nationalist cause in Indonesia.[6] Australia's position was quite different from that of the British, who fully supported Dutch sovereignty over the archipelago. The decision of London to support Amsterdam's claim created some difficulty for British commanders stationed in Indonesia after the Japanese surrender.[7] Australia's standing in Indonesia was quite high as a consequence.

During the San Francisco Conference in 1945, Evatt had pointed to the need to foster the goodwill of people throughout South-East Asia. He underlined the fact that, for three years, these people had been under Japanese military dictatorship. They had, of course, been under colonial rule for many years before. In that speech he showed sympathy for the nationalist cause.[8]

In August 1945 Sukarno became the first President and Mohammad Hatta became the first Vice-President when they declared the independent Republic of Indonesia. The Dutch were weakened with minimal military forces and showed good sense in not fighting against the declaration by Sukarno and Hatta. Australia's policy was in part ambivalent, wanting to preserve a good relationship with the Dutch East Indies, although it was soon to disappear, but wanting at the same time to give moral support to the emerging Indonesia. Menzies, in Opposition, opposed Evatt's unwillingness to blindly follow British foreign policy, which, of course, supported continued Dutch ownership of the Netherlands East Indies.[9] Menzies' judgement on the issue was severely at fault.

In these matters, although Evatt did not embrace the future wholeheartedly, he at least showed some sympathy for an emerging and changing world. Evatt recognised that colonial emancipation throughout Asia was proceeding at a pace that was inevitable and could not be reversed and that, as European powers withdrew, Australia should enter councils of the new Asia. He urged Australians to regard Asian nationalism 'realistically and with understanding'.[10] Conversely, Menzies' remarks in the Parliament made it plain that he wished to re-establish the old order. He claimed that Australia had seriously offended the Dutch and that Evatt's policies were dominated by communist-led wharf labourers.[11] It was not his proudest hour. He misjudged the direction in which the world was heading.

Other parts of East and South-East Asia were in turmoil. In Indo-China armed resistance began against the French in late 1946. The resistance was initially regarded as nationalistic, until the leaders declared themselves to be communist and purged anti-communist elements from the Vietminh army. The French military were unexpectedly defeated in a major battle at Dien Bien Phu in 1954. I will discuss the issues arising from this situation in a later chapter.

In addition, there was also a communist insurgency in Malaya, which extended from 1948 to 1960 and delayed independence for about ten years.[12] From the point of view of the United Kingdom—and indeed of Australia—it suited the politics of the time to depict what was happening in Malaysia as a communist insurgency. It fitted into the paradigm of the West versus global communism. There is no doubt that communists were heavily involved and that communist parties gave very considerable support to the insurgency. Yet the problem was greatly expanded because the British had not consulted different ethnic groups within Malaya over the future status of their nation and made no effort to accommodate their differing concerns.[13] London failed to recognise the depth of the ethnic divide on the Malaya Peninsula or in the Borneo territories.[14]

The problems between the Malays and the ethnic Chinese were acute, and in the end the difficulties were overcome only by the remarkable leadership of Tunku Abdul Rahman as Prime Minister and Tan Siew Sin as Finance Minister. His father, Tan Cheng Lock, had also played a remarkable and responsible role as leader of the Malaysia Chinese Association, in helping a new Malaysia to be born. Both leaders knew there had to be an accommodation. The British had devised their plan for the decolonisation of Malaya, and for the creation for the broader Malaysia, in London. This was a common practice of the Colonial Office. The plan devised by the British had involved consultation only with the United Malays National Organisation (UMNO). The Chinese and other ethnic groups had been largely ignored, and certainly the British territories in Borneo had not been adequately consulted. This lack of a broad-based consultation, but especially lack of consultation with the Chinese community, which was quite large and well organised, was a major mistake. Britain's oversight fed the insurgency. It made it easier for the communists to find recruits, and it clearly prolonged the insurgency unnecessarily.

The British handling of Malayan independence had broader consequences for South-East Asia, feeding into Indonesian politics. Britain's errors made it possible for Sukarno to claim that the proposed model for the new Malaysian state was a British plan and not a local indigenous plan involving different groups within Malaya and Borneo. Nevertheless the British stuck to their plan and ultimately carried it through with significant help from Australia and New Zealand.

During this time Australia had a remarkable High Commissioner in Malaysia, Tom Critchley, who maintained an extraordinarily close relationship with the Malaysian leadership. His relations with Tunku were second to none and, through him, Australia was able to exercise some influence and some moderation at critical times.

Apart from our military contribution, which was considerable and included all three services, Australia made no contribution to the national framework nor the political developments that took place. This was a case of Britain unravelling her empire. Britain was going to make the decisions and did not want, nor did it solicit, advice from Australia. It was a question of Australia following Empire leadership yet again and copping Britain's long-standing penchant for poor to no consultation.

These events distinguished Australia's relationship with Malaysia from our relationship with Indonesia. While the British initially gave support to Holland, there was no British link to the Dutch East Indies, and the British had little influence there, playing a substantively neutral role after the withdrawal of its forces in 1946. Australia—Evatt in particular—mapped out a role that was independent and much more in tune with the time than would otherwise have been the case. Over Malaysia, Australia was reliant on the British Empire for the determination of policy. In the Netherlands East Indies, Australia forged an independent path.

One of the unfortunate consequences of the way in which the British had handled the problem of Malaysian independence was the offence it gave to the new Indonesia.[15] There was argument and dispute over the ownership of territories in Borneo. Rather than declaring war, President Sukarno invented Konfrontasi (Confrontation) in 1963. It was neither peace nor a fully-fledged war, but many believed it could have become war.[16]

Australia trod a fine line. We supported Malaysia and the position that the British had developed over the Borneo territories.[17] We had three company groups fighting in Borneo against Indonesians. One of the last military actions resulting from Confrontation was in Borneo and, over the last few weeks, three Australians died in conflict with the Indonesian Army. As Minister for the Army, I can remember visiting a forward command post then occupied by an Australian company, patrolling the border with Indonesia. The command post had been built originally by and for the Gurkhas. The dimensions were hardly large enough for the Australians.

During Konfrontasi, Australia demonstrated that its young Foreign Affairs department was capable of delivering good policy and effective relationships, distinguishing Australia from Britain at the time.

Mick Shann was a remarkable public servant and was Australia's Ambassador in Indonesia from 1962 to 1966, covering most of the period of Konfrontasi. He was indeed a great ambassador for Australia. He had filled many important roles. He had a laid-back and informal manner, but had impressed all those who came to know him. I first met Mick Shann when I visited Jakarta at the beginning of 1965 and stayed with him at the Australian Embassy. Shann went out of his way to expose me to a variety of Indonesian people. One night after dinner we visited two Indonesian Harvard-trained economists who were responsible for preparing Sukarno's budget. We asked how the processes were going. They giggled and said it would depend upon the imports. This confused us, so we asked them: what does it mean, it will depend upon the imports? We thought you wanted less imports. Well, they replied, our printing press is running twenty-four hours a day to meet our target of more than 900 per cent inflation. We need new printing presses that can print much more currency. Such was the state of the Indonesian economy.

Shann had access to Sukarno and maintained good relations with him, and was able to persuade many of Indonesia's leadership that Australia was acting independently, that it was not a lackey of the British Empire. Shann would use Australia's independent position to help persuade Indonesia to accept Malaysia as a future entity.

Shann also took me down to the kampungs, where I had four hours with Dipa Nusantara Aidit, a senior PKI (Communist Party of Indonesia) leader, only a few short months before the attempted PKI coup in 1965. Aidit was clearly well educated, very well informed and indeed extraordinarily bright. The attempted PKI coup was unsuccessful very largely because at the last minute General Nasution, the then Indonesian Defence Minister, had warning of his impending assassination and was able to escape and rally elements of the Indonesian army. He had no real wish for public office and, very shortly thereafter, General Suharto took over.

During the period of Konfrontasi the British Embassy was trashed and the British Ambassador ridiculed. The Australian Embassy and residence were properly guarded, and Mick Shann was held in high esteem and maintained access to Sukarno.[18] In an extraordinarily difficult environment, what greater accolade could any ambassador have? He gave Australia a linkage and access to the highest reaches of the Indonesian Government, which at times proved to be invaluable. The linkages Australia enjoyed at this time far exceed those of recent Australian governments. Australia proved that it could act on its own accord and develop rapport with a key neighbour—we did not need British guidance on conducting diplomatic affairs in our region.

Konfrontasi, as the result of British proposals for Malaysia, was not the only difficulty that we had with Indonesia. Because it was part of the former Dutch empire, Indonesia had claimed jurisdiction over what is now known as West Irian. There were fierce arguments before this occurred. Many in West New Guinea wanted their own independence, as they still do. There were many, especially in Australia, who wanted a genuine act of self-determination. In the end, the international community, particularly the United States, agreed to an act of self-determination, but it was designed in such a way that it would lead to the incorporation of West New Guinea in Indonesia. If Australia had pressed for a genuine expression of self-determination on the part of the West New Guineans, we would not have been successful. We would not have been supported by major powers. We had in fact gone some distance down that particular path and were extricated from an embarrassing situation only with difficulty by Sir Garfield Barwick, as Foreign Minister in 1961, who claimed that Australia had to face the 'hard facts of international life' as the government had been unable to sway the great powers to our way of thinking.[19] An independent West New Guinea would probably have been the best solution. That was not the outcome, as we all know. The United States, in particular, came down heavily on the side of Indonesia.[20]

This was not the only time when the United States acted in such a way. During Kontrontasi, Barwick told the press that Australian troops under attack in Borneo would have been covered by ANZUS.[21] The Americans were annoyed at this. There had been talks between Australia and the United States involving Under Secretary of State, Political Affairs, Averell Harriman in 1963, which initially caused Australians to believe that if there were a full, overt attack against Australian forces, America would come to Australia's assistance. However, in the discussion in the Cabinet room with Harriman, the Minister for Trade and Industry, John McEwen, who had a greater depth and perception than he is often given credit for, pressed Harriman more closely. McEwen pointed out that any attack on Australian forces would be likely to appear in the role of subversion, of infiltration, not an old-fashioned military invasion.[22] If it became clear that the Indonesians were fully involved in such tactics, what then would be America's response? Harriman was remarkably equivocal and said, in the short time available for the discussion, that he could not find the words necessary to give a sufficiently precise answer.[23] In other words, McEwen had gone to the nub of the matter, and there was a doubt about whether or not America would respond.

It is worth noting that, in 1963, a correspondent for *The Economist* had written that 'no Indonesian regime short of a blatantly communist one would earn active American hostility, no matter what harm it did to notional Australian interests'.[24] Putting it in plain terms, why would the United States choose Australia over and above 95 million people in Indonesia, the largest Islamic country in the entire world?

East Asia and South-East Asia was clearly an unsettled area. Overshadowing it all, however, was the possibility of war between China and the United States. America had built a special relationship with President Chiang Kai-shek, perhaps especially with his wife Soong Mei-ling, who had become very influential in Washington circles. Even after the victory of the communist Chinese in 1949, the United States signed a defence treaty with the Kuomintang relating to Taiwan. This was of course later abolished when the United States recognised the People's Republic of China.

As the communists were moving to victory in China itself, Chiang Kai-shek fled, with as much of his army as he could move, to Taiwan. They took with them many of the ancient and natural riches of China. The communist Chinese were not well equipped to pursue Chiang Kai-shek to Taiwan. If they had attempted to do so, the American Pacific Fleet would have stood between Taiwan and the mainland. That would have been effective at that time. One thing the mainland and Taiwan had in common was that they both claimed to be part of one China. They believed in one China and did not want it to be divided. It was then a question of who would be governing that one China. The flight of Chiang Kai-shek's forces across the Taiwan Straits had, of course, resolved the issue on the mainland. Taiwan was, many times through the next decades, a danger point that could have led to war between China and the United States.

For example, during 1954 and 1955, the Chinese decided to test American resolve by shelling Quemoy and Matsu, two islands in the Taiwan Straits. The United States Congress authorised Eisenhower to use American force to defend Taiwan against Chinese machinations; some in his administration even going so far as pushing for the use of nuclear weapons against mainland China. Indeed Secretary of State John Foster Dulles stated that the American policy 'will gradually include the use of atomic weapons as conventional weapons for tactical purposes'. Eisenhower did not follow through with the threat, but numerous American warships were moved into the straits.[25]

It is noteworthy that, even at this time, military experts in the United States were advising Eisenhower that, if there were a war with China, tactical nuclear weapons would have to be used.[26] Eisenhower ran a serious risk of isolating the United States on this issue. The British Prime Minister, Anthony Eden, supported by Australia's Foreign Minister Casey, were arguing that the offshore islands should be given up, that it would not be worth fighting for them. Menzies, in a meeting that took place in the United States, on 14 March 1955, sought to probe this issue and to tease out different elements of the dispute.[27] At one point, Menzies put the question whether, if he could persuade the British to agree on a commitment to defend Taiwan, would Eisenhower persuade the nationalists on Taiwan to give up Quemoy and Matsu? I do not believe that there was ever a serious attempt to persuade the British to accept this proposition, but Menzies was certainly arguing for a modification in American policy.

In addition, I had always understood that Menzies himself had informed Eisenhower that, if there were a war over Taiwan, Australia would not be a part of it. There is no official record for that view. When Allan Martin was writing Menzies' biography,[28] I checked this point with him, and he said he also had not been able to find any clear written evidence that that had occurred, but his understanding was the same as mine. At the very least, Australia was having negotiations at the highest level, to seek an accommodation that would avoid war.

The State Department papers themselves emphasised that Menzies believed the Americans should give greater attention to Chairman Mao's suggestion: that China should join the four-power meeting, at the very least for Asian affairs. Menzies suggested that if Chou En Lai's proposal were accepted, it might open the opportunity to explore a settlement, much wider than the offshore islands and Taiwan.[29] It is a matter of record that Chou En Lai's suggestion was not pursued by the United States.

We need to remind ourselves that from Federation to World War II Australia had relied on Britain for defence. We had believed in that strategic dependence. In the end, as we have seen, Britain was not able to help Australia. Prime Minister Curtin transferred our sense of dependence to the United States by his appeal to America for help. One might have thought that, after the war ended, Australia—with its new-found determination to build and expand, to broaden its population base, to take charge of its own foreign affairs, to establish its own foreign affairs department, to be actively involved in United Nations affairs—would want to be more independent than it had ever been. We certainly had legal authority—there was no longer any doubt about that—but did we have the will, the wish, the determination? Evatt, as Foreign Minister, showed more independence and significant strength of mind than any other Australian had to that point in dealing with other nations, especially with great powers.

Political leaders of both persuasions in the post-war years decided, however, that we should seek safety in America's shadow. That led us directly to the ANZUS Treaty. Australians often speak as though this treaty is special and unique to Australia. This view is encouraged by Americans who come here for ANZUS discussions. They are very good at flattering those whom they want to please for the moment. ANZUS was in fact one of a series of treaty arrangements made by the United States at the end of the Pacific War.

The most effective, the most committing, was the United States Treaty with Japan. That was regarded as a treaty to defend if Japan came under attack. In return, Japan undertook to restrict its military spending to 1 per cent of GDP and not seek to become a nuclear power. Although this figure is particularly low for an economy the size of Japan's, the nation undertakes a number of large expenditure programs that might have military application despite the fact that they do not appear on any military budget. I will return to Japan, its military expenditure and increasingly nationalistic policies later in the book.

Although we might be disappointed, we should not be surprised that Australia followed the road of strategic dependence. We had not become used to independence, with the certain exception of Evatt and, to an extent, of Spender and Barwick; we had not acted as an independent country. The world around us was not a benign place. We wanted the traditional security that we believed close relation-ships with a great power gave us. Events in Indonesia, the difficulties with Sukarno with Konfrontasi, the PKI attempt at a communist coup, the communist insurgency in Malaya, were all very close to Australia. We and others regarded the communist north in Vietnam and the recent war in Korea as events that justified the belief that communism was an outward-looking, thrusting, aggressive force, determined to expand wherever it could. There are many who believed that Australia was on the Soviet Union's list for communist takeover in the later 1940s. It is perfectly understandable how, in that world, Australian leaders should look for safety by establishing a close relationship with the United States.

This was a very different world from that which exists today. The communist insurgencies through South-East Asia, the Korean War and later the Vietnam War as well as communist victories in China, all pointed to an uncertain future. The Cold War was very much alive and well. Australia would have been bold and possibly foolish to go it alone. A close relationship with the United States was therefore a desirable and sensible national objective, despite the fact that, on the American side, it was never regarded as something that would lead to automatic support for Australia. ANZUS is primarily a treaty to consult, and we should never take for granted the provision of American military support should we get into difficulty.

It is worth noting that during this time, where Britain or its colonies were involved, as in the case of Malaysia, Australia tended to follow along and accept that Britain was virtually the sole determinant of policy. In other areas, however, in relation to the Japanese Peace Treaty, in relations with America, and concerning the independence of Indonesia, Australia was far more independent and pursued policies that Australia believed to be not only best for Australia but also best for a peaceful region. Australia was not always successful in winning an argument, but the fact that views were put, and put vigorously, was a significant advance from earlier times.

The Cold War had become a harsh reality. Problems in Europe and in East and South-East Asia attested to that. The communist victories in China in 1949 added to these concerns, and communism, as later events were to prove mistakenly, was regarded as a monolithic, worldwide and evil ideology. It is not surprising, against that background, that we should look for a new protector. Significant mistakes were made by Western strategists. The West, and, I believe, especially the United States, felt that communism was a monolithic world force, seeking world domination. We seriously underestimated the nationalist element in communist movements in a number of countries. This is certainly true in relation to Vietnam. An independent movement fighting against a colonial power would not generally have been able to get military or financial support from countries of the West. Therefore they would go where they could, to the communist countries, to the other world. That did not necessarily make them communists in Stalin's mould.

From my first visit to China in 1976, I realised there were very significant differences between Chinese attitudes and the attitude of the Soviet Union; a difference that led to my belief that this was a China with whom the West could work.

Unfortunately, I had previously accepted the general interpretation of communism in those years. I had believed that communism was an immense and oppressive force that was entirely dangerous. Few people had understood the extent to which communist parties in different countries were affected by their own sense of nationalism. If this had been widely understood in the West, much of the history of the last thirty or forty years would have been very different. Yet, as this chapter has shown, it was a complicated world in the decades following World War II. Australia, for the first time, showed some independent spirit. Yet the realities of the time consolidated our tradition of strategic dependence, albeit that dependence now resting with the United States.

7

The cost of strategic dependence

In the previous chapters I have focused on specific periods of history during which Australia's foreign policy, and the way we went about making it, were shaped. This chapter is different. I will focus solely on the Vietnam War, a conflict that became very divisive within Australian society. I want to focus on Vietnam because I believe it acts as a warning to Australia, a warning of the repercussions of inter-twining our foreign policy with that of a major power. Although in the previous chapter I acknowledged that the global realities of the decades after World War II meant that continuing our policy of strategic dependence made sense, this chapter highlights the implications of following through with such a policy. It is a case study of the perils of blind strategic dependence.

The decision-making at the highest levels of American government was dysfunctional and contributed in no small part to the disastrous failure of US foreign and security policy towards Indo-China. It should have been a lesson to Australian governments that came after—blindly following American foreign policy, a policy sometimes based on bad intelligence, bad judgement and multiple agendas, is a risky position to take. Sadly, the wars in Iraq and

Afghanistan suggest that it was a lesson not learnt. As all these wars seem to prove, strategic dependence involves blindly following great powers into war.

This chapter is clearly influenced by McNamara's book, *In Retrospect*, which was published in 1995. Robert McNamara was US Secretary of Defense between 1961 to 1968 and was intimately involved in the Vietnam War. Although I believe there are deficiencies in his book, and some of the quotations he uses are not quoted in full, he recognises that mistakes were made, particularly by the Johnson Administration. He recognised that there were major mistakes in the intelligence concerning Vietnam, coming from a variety of sources. Unfortunately, the Kennedy and Johnson administrations relied most heavily on intelligence that came through the US military and through the US Embassy in Saigon. There were CIA assessments that were always much more cautious, much more doubting and questioning than the optimistic reports upon which the Johnson Administration relied and on the basis of which the President made a decision to escalate the war dramatically. By 1965–66, McNamara, in the position of Secretary of State for Defense, had accepted the accuracy of CIA intelligence, which was much more circumspect, cautious and doubtful of the ultimate outcome than that emanating from military sources. Yet the United States was so caught up with opposition to the spread of world communism that it found it very difficult to accept any view that did not fit that preconceived analysis.

The major mistake made by the American Government was the assumption that Vietnamese communism was a part of a world movement towards global communist domination. The assumptions about the power of the US Army and Air Force and their capacity to impose a solution on Vietnam were also plainly wrong. They totally underestimated the consequences of an incompetent and corrupt South Vietnamese government. McNamara accepts his share of responsibility. One of the reasons for writing his book was not only to set the record straight but also the hope that future US administrations might learn lessons from Vietnam.[1] Unfortunately, as we can see from Iraq and Afghanistan, they have not done so.

At the end of World War II the French sought to re-establish their empire, including in Indo-China. General de Gaulle would push for the return of French colonial possessions after the war, exclaiming: 'The purposes of the civilizing efforts accomplished by France in the colonies rule out any idea of autonomy, any possibility of evolution outside the framework of the French empire …'[2] This comment harked back to old and outdated ideas. The desire to retain colonial possessions would ultimately be futile, but not before decolonisation struggles in North Africa, West Africa and Indo-China would contribute to the fall of the French Fourth Republic.

In Indo-China in 1945, the redoubtable nationalist leader Ho Chi Minh declared the Democratic Republic of Vietnam and that 'the whole Vietnamese people, animated by a common purpose, are determined to fight to the bitter end against any attempt by the French colonialists to reconquer the country'.[3] Up to this point, Ho Chi Minh's movement, the Vietminh, was largely a nationalist movement designed to establish the independence of Vietnam and remove the vestiges of French colonial authority.[4]

On behalf of the Vietminh, Ho Chi Minh had made the following announcement in September 1945: 'For these reasons, we, members of the Provisional Government, representing the whole Vietnamese people, declare that from now on we break off all relations of a colonial character with France; we repeal all the international obligation that France has so far subscribed to on behalf of Vietnam and we abolish all the special rights the French have unlawfully acquired in our Fatherland.'[5]

The French were going to have to fight to re-establish their empire. Although the Vietminh had received Allied support against the Japanese during World War II, the international political situation was rapidly changing.[6] By 1950 the Chinese communists had won, the Korean War had commenced and the Cold War had all of sudden become hot in East Asia. Regional conflicts were quickly classified as a part of the West's struggle against the global communist threat.

The French were therefore supported by the British and the United States both recognising the independence of the State of

Vietnam, under Bao Dai, within the French Union in February 1950.[7] Indeed, by 1953, 70 per cent of the financial cost of the Indo-China conflict was being carried by Washington.[8] The major influence of the State of Vietnam was in the south of the country.

According to the Pentagon Papers, on 6 March 1950, the Secretary of Defense, Louis Johnson, wrote to President Truman: 'The choice confronting the United States is to support the legal government in Indochina or to face the extension of communism over the remainder of the continental area of Southeast Asia and possibly westward …'[9] The domino theory of communist expansion had taken hold in Washington.[10]

Accordingly, the American attitude towards French colonialism changed since the anti-colonial sentiments expressed during the concluding days of the war. President Truman became far more concerned with the spectre of communism than with colonial issues.[11] Indeed, just before his death, President Roosevelt relaxed his staunchly anti-colonial position at the behest of Churchill and the British leader's concern for the British Empire.[12] The need to keep France firmly in the anti-communist camp and supportive of Washington's plans in Europe overcame any American concerns with becoming entangled in Indo-China. Hence, the Americans hoped that support for the French in Indo-China would translate into a more favourable French position on defence and security arrangements in Europe.[13]

By 1950, Ho Chi Minh's government, which in reality controlled much of the North, was recognised by both the Soviet Union and China. The major powers therefore had chosen different sides in the contest for Vietnam. That virtually guaranteed that the Vietminh—North Vietnam—would become closer to the communist bloc. The transition from an anti-colonial uprising to an ideological battle between the West and communism had been complete.[14] Ho Chi Minh was given considerable help from China and from the Soviet Union, where he had trained before the war. His movement was unified, it was well led, and it attracted widespread support across Vietnam. He was a most able strategist and tactician.

After long-drawn-out battles, in 1954 the French were defeated at Dien Bien Phu on 7 May. French forces had been besieged for fifty-five days. They had been caught by surprise. With extraordinary fortitude and ingenuity, Ho Chi Minh had been able to manoeuvre heavy guns to shell the French forces, which were out-generalled and out-gunned. A colonial mentality had given the French confidence in their ability to retake their Indo-China territories after World War II yet, in the end, they accepted that they had been militarily outmanoeuvred—only through negotiation would France extricate itself from the conflict it had in no small part brought upon itself.

The Geneva Accords were concluded in July 1954, calling for free elections to unite Vietnam. Such elections were to be held during 1956. Meanwhile, a dividing line was established between north and south at the seventeenth parallel with a small demilitarised zone north and south of that line. In the initial stages, there was to be free movement so that the Vietnamese could decide whether they wanted to live in the North or the South. It is suggested that 600,000 to one million people moved from the North to the South, about 78 per cent of whom were believed to be Catholics.[15]

Ho Chi Minh was the undisputed leader of what became North Vietnam. Ngo Dinh Diem, in the South, emerged as the strongest and most effective of the warlords broadly governing the region. He was a devout Catholic and was appointed Prime Minister of the State of Vietnam with the backing of the Eisenhower Administration when French control of the South was faltering. The French had considered Diem a less than reliable candidate, and the government he led was by no means democratic. (Indeed Diem consolidated power through a rigged referendum in October 1955, replacing Bao Dai as head of state and consolidating his power.) Quite soon after, Diem indicated that South Vietnam would not participate in elections as mandated by the Geneva Accords to achieve the unification of Vietnam.[16] He justified that statement by saying that there could be no free election north of the seventeenth parallel, defeating the point of having elections at all as the result would ultimately be compromised. From his own record, I doubt he wanted a free election either. It is worth noting that Diem himself had never won a free and open election.

In 1955 the United States began providing support to the South Vietnamese Government. It was argued at the time that the training of South Vietnamese forces would be required to preserve freedom south of the seventeenth parallel and contain the spread of communism.[17] The United States had never been impressed by earlier French attempts at training the Vietnamese forces and felt that a proficient native Vietnamese force was required to secure Washington's broader regional aims. Proponents of the domino theory feared that, should South Vietnam fall, it would result in inevitable communist domination and control of South-East Asia. As such, between 1955 and 1960, support valued at more than US$2 billion would be provided to South Vietnam by the American Government.[18]

In 1961 the newly elected President Kennedy said he was prepared to support South Vietnam with supplies, finance and advisers. Kennedy decided in late 1961 to send about 16,000 advisers to South Vietnam to help train the South Vietnamese Army. This decision came after sustained pressure from US military and political chiefs to shore up the government of South Vietnam and halt continuing communist military successes.[19]

Military reports were optimistic in the very early years. On 5 February 1962 the United States military reported: 'The actions which the South Vietnamese Government have taken to counter the very serious threat of subversion and aggression, covert aggression, in that nation, are beginning to be effective leading to an improvement in the situation, but it is far too early to predict the eventual outcome.'[20] By July 1962 the military were again advising that assistance to Vietnam was paying off, and the Kennedy Administration began to fashion an exit strategy for the US military advisers on the ground.[21] By October, the reports were even more optimistic.[22]

In the event, these reports proved to be grossly over-optimistic. Later, the Americans tended to blame the Vietnamese for providing information that they believed the Americans wanted to hear. McNamara argues that American military commanders viewed Vietnam through the prism of a military operation only, when in fact the conflict was a much more 'complex nationalistic and internecine struggle'.[23] He accepts the blame for letting this view prevail. This is a useful insight for contemporary American conflicts; how much consideration was given to possible nationalistic and ethnic struggles when regimes in Iraq and Afghanistan were removed? What real thought was given to the post-conflict nations the United States would be leaving behind?

In these early years, President Kennedy gave the impression that he did not want the United States to become involved in a major land war on Asian soil. Kennedy had stressed all along, and told Americans in Vietnam to emphasise to the South Vietnamese Government time and time again, that America could help but the Vietnamese had to organise their own defence and rely upon themselves.[24]

As a result of the optimism shown in the intelligence reports produced through 1962, McNamara had ordered long-range planning for a phased withdrawal of US advisers. This was based on the assumption that it would take three years to subdue the Vietcong and on the belief that the training of the South Vietnamese army would proceed effectively.[25] The Pentagon Papers make it quite clear that the expectation of a three-year time frame for subduing the Vietcong was completely unrealistic and was based on only the most Micawberesque predictions of success.[26]

Quite clearly, the assessments being given to him were at the very least wrong or, more disturbingly, completely misleading. At a later point in 1963 the CIA Director, John McCone, wrote:

Information furnished to us from MACV [Military Assistance Command Vietnam] and the Embassy concerning ... Viet Cong activities in a number of provinces and the relative position of the SVN (South Vietnam) Government vs the Viet Cong Forces was incorrect, due to the fact that the field officers ... had been grossly misinformed by the South Vietnamese province and district chiefs ... The province and district chiefs felt obliged to 'create statistics' which would meet the approbation of the Central Government.[27]

Was this entirely a fault of South Vietnam? Was it a fault of the relationship between the US officers and South Vietnam? Were the Americans themselves aware that the reporting was wrong? As one official would comment on the period in 1964: 'The more we learn about the situation today, the more obvious it becomes that the excessively mechanical system of statistical reporting which had been devised in Washington and applied in Saigon was giving us a grotesquely inaccurate picture. Once again it is the old problem of having people who are responsible for operations also responsible for evaluating the results.'[28] This lesson would be ignored in the years to come.

Through 1963 the equation was altered substantially when a political and religious crisis erupted across Vietnam. Buddhists, who constituted a majority in South Vietnam as they did in the North, had become angry at Diem's curb on religious freedom and launched violent protests that led to heavy-handed retaliation by the security forces.[29] The response was brutal, but it simply inspired more protests. There were self-immolations by Buddhist monks.[30] There were deep concerns for the stability of the Diem Government, with various Buddhist factions claiming to speak on behalf of the majority of the South Vietnamese people. The US Government was fearful of a coup or the collapse of the South Vietnam Government.[31]

Through the summer of 1963, conflicts smouldered between the government and the Buddhists. Nhu, Diem's brother, had become his most senior adviser. Martial law was declared, and he ordered military units to raid Buddhist pagodas in August.[32] Several hundred were jailed. The Buddhist protests had become more than a religious fight, evolving into 'widespread popular resentment of an arbitrary and often oppressive rule'.[33]

At this time, General de Gaulle made a suggestion that might well have resolved the issues if the United States had paid any attention to his views. He issued a call for Vietnam's unification and neutralisation in the struggle between East and West, between communism and democracy. Nhu was reported to have opened direct links with de Gaulle.[34] One of the most serious blunders of the US Administration at this time was that no effort was made to explore de Gaulle's options. If it had been pursued, it might have become an honourable way out for everyone concerned, not least for the people of both Vietnams.

Diem's assault on the Buddhists deeply concerned the Americans and reflected in the starkest fashion the fears they held over the stability and direction of the South Vietnamese Government. It changed the way Washington viewed the Vietnamese situation. It is worth noting two significant events here in detail—the planned removal of Diem and the military build-up from 1965—because they give an insight into the way in which Americans view the world. More particularly, they suggest that US administrations did not regard any action as being off limits, particularly if the administration thought America's interests were involved. (That attitude was repeated by President Bush Jnr in going into Iraq and Afghanistan. It was also clearly repeated by President Obama in his willingness to use drone attacks to kill American citizens outside the United States, such as Anwar al-Awlaki in Yemen, without charge, without arrest, without trial.)

During the raid on the Buddhist pagodas, nearly all the key decision-makers—the President, Secretary of State Dean Rusk, National Security Advisor McGeorge Bundy, CIA Director John McCone, and McNamara himself, Secretary of State for Defense—were all out of Washington at the same time.[35]

Without proper consideration, without participation by the senior people in charge, in the space of a day the United States took actions that ultimately resulted in a military coup and the assassination of Diem and Nhu. It was a time of tragic and serious mistakes that demonstrated the lack of coordination within the US Administration and a predilection to make the most serious decisions without proper examination. Indeed, decisions were made without the most senior people in government, those who are ultimately responsible, getting into one room and discussing the issues.

According to McNamara, Roger Hilsman Jr, who succeeded Averell Harriman as Assistant Secretary of State for Far Eastern Affairs, took the initiative to have Diem removed. Harriman sent a cable largely drafted by Hilsman to the new and inexperienced American Ambassador in Saigon, Henry Cabot Lodge, beginning with a stringent attack on Nhu and a condemnation of his actions. The cable made clear that Diem should be given an opportunity to get rid of Nhu. It was also made clear that if Diem was not prepared to take this path, he also should be removed and that the generals who so acted were promised direct support for any interim period while a new government was being established.[36] This cable was drafted without any broad or general discussion of the issues, without any examination of who might take Diem's place and without any real understanding of the consequences of that action. The similarities to the decision-making surrounding the second Iraq War is remarkable.

A number of people were involved in these discussions, whom at different periods after the events I came to know quite well. Harriman, a most senior American diplomat, at that time was influential and also wanted Diem gone.[37] Michael Forrestal, a young staffer in the White House, a protégé of Harriman, immediately sent the cable,[38] as far as I can tell on his own initiative, to President Kennedy. Forrestal reported to the President 'Clearances are being obtained from the Undersecretary of State George Ball and Defense … Suggest you let me know if you wish … to hold up action.'[39]

Ball, Undersecretary of State for Economic and Agricultural Affairs, was asked to call the President, and Kennedy advised that he would agree to the cable if his senior advisers all concurred. This comment by Kennedy was misinterpreted, perhaps deliberately. It meant exactly what it said: if all senior advisers agreed, Kennedy would go along with it. It did not mean, however, that Kennedy had approved the action and that his approval should be used to persuade others. Ball phoned Dean Rusk and told him that the President agreed. That was not true. Kennedy had agreed with a caveat: if all his senior advisers agreed, he would agree. So Ball, presumably as a sponsor of the cable, stretched the truth. Dean Rusk, because he had been told the President agreed, supported the cable but without any enthusiasm. The head of CIA was absent so Harriman sought approval from Richard Helms, Deputy Director for Plans. He also was reluctant to support it, but he too supported it because he had been told it had the President's endorsement.[40] So both Rusk and Helms were, in a sense, misled.

The cable was sent out on Saturday night, 24 August 1963. It authorised discussion with South Vietnamese generals about the certain removal of Nhu and the probable removal of Diem.

In McNamara's book, one thing struck me as giving a pointer to the character of American governments. It is a pointer that any ally would do well to note. Even Dean Rusk, whom I knew personally as an extraordinarily decent person, comes through this episode as indecisive and not having proper control over his department. I later got to know McNamara well. He had been a hardliner, but he was also thoughtful and prepared to ask questions. Nobody—not Rusk, not McNamara, not the CIA, not the President—not one of them asked whether the United States had the right to order the removal of the head of government and head of state of a country with whom they were an ally, fighting a difficult war. They implicitly assumed that they did. I am sure there are some who will believe that I am naive at my surprise at that admission. Maybe so, but it is an admission whose consequences, if we wish to deal with the United States, we need to understand.

General Max Taylor was the President's senior military adviser. The cable shocked him, especially the fact that it had already been sent and, as he knew, without adequate discussion. He would later say that '... a small group of anti-Diem activists picked this time to perpetrate an egregious "end run" in dispatching a cable of the utmost importance to Saigon without obtaining normal depart-mental clearances'.[41] Taylor could see that this decision represented a major change in American policy towards Vietnam. President Kennedy came to regard the cable as a major mistake.[42] Through all of this, de Gaulle's proposals for neutralisation of the whole of Vietnam were ignored.

Lodge was very much in favour of getting rid of Diem despite the fact that he had been in Vietnam only a few days himself. Lodge immediately called a meeting to consider how to organise a coup. He regarded that cable of 24 August as instructing him to achieve the removal of Diem from leadership in Vietnam. Not surprisingly, the CIA was used as the conduit to senior disaffected generals, Tran Thien Khiem in Saigon and Nguyen Khanh in Pleiku. The generals were told Nhu had to go but that Diem's position was up to them.[43]

In Washington, the President chaired a significant number of discussions, probing in detail to establish the best course of action. They did not seem to realise that the original cable had already determined the outcome. It is a little difficult to approach generals in the circumstances of South Vietnam and say, 'We want you to get rid of your leader' and then a day or two later to speak to them again and say, 'Oh no, we have changed our minds'. Reservations were surfacing about the path the Americans were following, and Kennedy cabled Lodge insisting that the Vietnamese generals be made aware of the President's 'contingent right to change course and reverse previous instructions'.[44] A pretty remarkable statement given that Kennedy had absolutely no jurisdiction over South Vietnam.

At one point, the President sent a long cable to Lodge that was meant to be the basis of a conversation with Diem, and which was also meant to be conciliatory, almost as though nobody had approached the generals, days before, to organise a coup.[45] How could the President believe that the United States could send such a message? How could people who are presumably intelligent, sensible, certainly holding high office, believe that they could send a message to discontented generals in a country like Vietnam and ask around: 'Who is willing to organise a coup?', then think you can withdraw?

It was, if you like, an attempt—and the most serious one the President had made—to withdraw from the first cable relating to a coup. Unknown to General Taylor and unknown to Secretary of Defence McNamara, Hilsman, Assistant Secretary of State for

Far Eastern Affairs, sent Lodge a letter, which, in the light of the President's cable, was almost treasonable. 'Dear Cabot, I am taking advantage of Mike Forrestal's safe hands to deliver this message ... I have the feeling that more and more of the town is coming around to our view (i.e. that Diem must be removed by a coup) and that if you in Saigon and we in the Department stick to our guns the rest will also come around. As Mike will tell you, a determined group here will back you all the way ...'[46]

President Kennedy had allowed a most vital decision to be made without full and proper examination and without the main players in the one room. He never acted with precision and determination. A much more vigorous discussion should have been held about whether they could or could not win with Diem. If the answer was in the negative, withdrawal should have been a considered option rather than assassination. None of the players asked themselves who in Vietnam could do the job better. Who would become leader if Diem is removed? Nobody asked whether Vietnam should be neutralised, as proposed by France, or whether they should just withdraw on the grounds that South Vietnam could not get its political situation in order in a civil war in which politics was just as important as, if not more important than, military operations. No one asked whether they even had the right to be involved at all.

Through all this time, there was inaccurate reporting of the military state of South Vietnam. Policy was not based on accurate reports. The Ambassador to South Vietnam before Lodge's appointment, Frederick Nolting, would write years later that in twenty-two years of public service, he never again saw anything 'resembling the confusion, vacillation and lack of coordination in the US Government' at that time.[47]

Lodge advised at the end of October that plotting among Vietnam's generals was now far advanced and that America should not thwart a coup. The faction that wanted to get rid of Diem had never stopped pushing and never stopped, if you like, undermining Kennedy. This is despite the President's October determination that America 'not take any initiative to encourage actively a change in government'.[48] Ultimately, his own indecisiveness probably made that easier than it should have been.

About 9.30am on 2 November, the President and his senior advisers were advised that Diem and his brother Nhu had committed suicide. General Duong Van Minh had given the order to capture Diem and Nhu. It was originally reported that they had committed suicide, yet that could not have happened because their hands were tied behind their backs. At a later point, General Minh said that if there was going to be a coup, both Diem and Nhu would have had to be killed.[49]

As events unfolded, no successor was able to gain control of the government of South Vietnam. There was a game of musical chairs between the generals. Between 1955 and 1975 there were eleven changes of government in South Vietnam. President Minh was technically in charge of the government on four separate occasions. There was no unity, no sense of purpose. It is no wonder the people of South Vietnam were overcome by the North. The inevitable end should have been evident to everyone.

Less than three weeks after the assassination of Diem and Nhu, President Kennedy himself was assassinated in Dallas. Kennedy's assassination changed America. He had inspired hope, had been a light on the hill. While Johnson implemented Kennedy's programs and talked of his great society, he was not able to inspire people as Kennedy had. The great expansion of the war in Vietnam began on Johnson's watch and prompts an unanswerable question: would that have happened if Kennedy had lived? Kennedy had emphasised several times that, although the United States could help in many ways, this was a fight the South Vietnamese had to win for themselves. He told a reporter during a TV interview: 'In the final analysis, it is their war. They are the ones who have to win it or lose it. We can help them, we can give them equipment, we can send our men out there as advisers, but they have to win it … All we can do is help.'[50] Kennedy made mistakes in relation to the early years of America's involvement in Vietnam, yet we will never know what would have happened if Kennedy had not been assassinated.

President Kennedy was known for having collected around him a group of young, highly intelligent and public-spirited young Americans, the best and the brightest. Such people filled the White House, but these advisers did not really know anything about due process, about the careful collection of facts and evidence that are essential if governments are to make good policy. They were very sure of themselves and were often praised in the media. Many of them were gung-ho about Vietnam. Their judgements and advice was not properly thought through and certainly not tested by rigid analysis. They did not really know how to test the validity of reports coming out of Vietnam. They contributed significantly to the divisive policy debates that were undertaken within the US Administration from 1965 onwards, when Secretary of State for Defense McNamara had come to rely more on CIA estimates and much less on military estimates from Vietnam.

The CIA analysts, the professionals, were much more sober in their views. They thought the United States would face enormous difficulty in Vietnam. CIA reports going back as far as 1945 indicated the overwhelming popularity of the Vietminh throughout the countryside. CIA officers had often been working on Asian or Vietnamese affairs much longer than military intelligence officers. Most of them would have begun their work in Vietnam with the build-up of advisers and those military forces who took over the war from the Vietnamese themselves. The CIA recognised that the Vietminh had significant advantages. The basic stimulus among the 'politically conscious Vietnamese' was nationalism, not communism. They had also been opposed to the Diem coup, arguing that the intelligence relied upon was shaky. The United States was becoming too involved in Vietnamese politics and it was likely to breed subsequent coups and produce governments with which Washington might not get along.[51]

Throughout the war, the CIA continued to be cautious. They advised that the Vietcong had great advantages, a great capacity for perseverance. They doubted whether the bombing of either the North or the Ho Chi Minh trails would diminish supplies to the Vietcong's southern frontier. They were correct. The bombing, which was massive and brutal, had very little effect on the activities of the Vietcong. It is an incredible outcome given that the 6,162,000 tonnes of bombs and ordnance dropped by the US military between 1964 and 1973 exceeded the amount dropped by the United States in both World War II and the Korean War combined. To put it another way, the amount of bombs dropped on Vietnam was equivalent to a hundred times the combined impact of the Hiroshima and Nagasaki atomic bombs.[52] It was an incredible display of firepower, particularly considering the lack of influence on the outcome of the war.

The US Administration was much more inclined to put the Vietnam War into the global Cold War context. It felt that communism was monolithic. The Vietnam conflict was part of an outward-looking, aggressive communism controlled from Moscow and Beijing, whose aim was world domination. If Vietnam fell, the rest of Indo-China would fall and, indeed, some suggested that there would be implications for such countries as the Philippines, Japan and even for Australia or New Zealand.[53] According to this view, the Vietnam contest was not just for Vietnam but also a vital chapter in a worldwide fight against communism. One cannot help but wonder whether current American views on global terrorism and the War on Terror also fail to consider the national politics and tensions within the countries involved. It is easy to get caught up in the global paradigm of the time and ignore the subtleties inherent in the domestic politics of every country. Be it communism or terrorism, getting blinded by the international context means mistakes will be made.

The CIA recognised that the argument that Vietnam was a major and important conflict within the fight against communism was not accurate. That nationalism played a very significant role in the motivation of the Vietminh was largely ignored or misunderstood. A lack of understanding of this issue clearly influenced Johnson's decision to embark on a massive expansion of American military forces in Vietnam, an expansion at great cost that did not alter the final outcome.[54] A proper understanding of the Vietminh would most likely have avoided such an expansion.

In addition to that, the administration did not recognise, as the CIA did, that the South Vietnamese entity was fragile, that it was weak, that there was no cohesive government, that corruption was widespread and that the regime was not effective enough to attract widespread loyalty throughout South Vietnam. In other words, it was no competitor for the Vietminh and the Vietcong.[55]

By 1965, McNamara himself began to lose heart. More and more he doubted the reports coming out of Vietnam. He thought they were misguided, and he turned more and more to relying on analysis from the CIA. One remarkable thing, however, is that, for two years after he had begun to demonstrate private doubts about the conduct of the war and its ultimate outcome, he maintained a strong public support for President Johnson's policies. In the end, McNamara and Johnson came to a parting of the ways in 1967. The escalation of hostilities over this period is the second Vietnam War incident that I want to discuss in detail.

McNamara had other arguments with President Johnson, not only over the interpretation of the war but also over the internal handling of issues inside the United States. McNamara claims that he believed that the Senate should be taken into the President's confidence, that it should be kept informed, that the President should carry the American public with him, but such behaviour was not in Johnson's nature. He was a consummate but secret politician who marched to his own political agenda. Years later when testifying before the Senate Foreign Relations Committee on the possible use of force before the first Gulf War, McNamara would say no president should take a nation to war without the popular consent of Congress. As it turned out, the first President Bush acknowledged that and achieved full support from Congress for the first Iraq War, but in Vietnam, President Johnson did not.[56]

In August 1964, North Vietnamese naval units were alleged to have engaged USS *Maddox*, one of two US Navy ships, close to but not in North Vietnamese waters. As a result, USS *Maddox* was fired upon, but no significant damage was done. There were South Vietnamese naval operations against North Vietnam at the time. The American ships were not part of it; they were in international waters and were, as you might say, almost hovering in the background.[57] The North Vietnamese could have believed that the American ships were part of one operation.

President Johnson manoeuvred a resolution through the Congress as a result of this incident. The Gulf of Tonkin Resolution gave the President full war powers in relation to Vietnam. Congress never for one moment believed that that could result in the expansion of 16,000 advisers to an army of 550,000. A key part of the Gulf of Tonkin war powers resolution went this way:

> Whereas naval units of North Vietnam ... in violation ... of international law, had deliberately and repeatedly attacked the United States Naval Vessels, lawfully present in international waters ... and whereas these attacks are part of a deliberate and systematic campaign of aggression ... against its neighbors ... the United States is therefore prepared as the President determines to take all necessary steps including the use of armed force to assist any member or prodigal state of the South Asia collective defence treaty requesting assistance in defence of its freedom.[58]

From what we do know of the Gulf of Tonkin incident, there is little doubt that President Johnson used it for his own political purposes and led people to believe that it was a much more significant event than in fact it was.

Senator Fulbright, one of the most respected United States senators, and who had presided over the hearing concerning this resolution, later came to believe he had been misled. Fulbright had been told that the President would not use the powers conferred by the resolution without full congressional consultation, but that consultation did not take place.[59]

There is much that will never be known definitively about the Gulf of Tonkin incident. It would not be beyond understanding to believe that the North Vietnamese felt that the American ships were also part of the South Vietnamese action against North Vietnam. There might be documents in Vietnam that can demonstrate whether that is true or false, although, given the conduct of this war, it would not be surprising. Critics would charge the Johnson Administration with deception over Tonkin to provide justification for war, yet McNamara maintains that this charge is unfounded.[60]

Further pushing the United States towards escalation was an attack in 1965 by the Vietcong at Pleiku where a number of Americans were killed and many more were wounded. McGeorge Bundy was in Vietnam at the time, and Kosygin was visiting Hanoi from the Soviet Union. Politicians in Washington and McGeorge Bundy himself put these factors together and came to the conclusion that this was world communism throwing down the gauntlet. With that interpretation, the American President had to respond vigorously.[61] The interpretation was not supported by CIA analysts. The three events were, if you like, an unfortunate combination of circumstances, which led to a major misunderstanding by the United States and to a massive escalation of the war; indeed, to the Americans taking over the war.

Shortly after Pleiku, the bombing program Rolling Thunder—the concentrated bombing of North Vietnam that would last between March 1965 and November 1968—began, as did the American troop build-up, culminating in 550,000 Americans fighting in the war. The Vietcong were able to match this escalation. From the earliest days the CIA, especially, had warned that the US Army would face enormous difficulties in Vietnam. The presence of a foreign army made it easier for the Vietcong to recruit. They made it easier to argue that their fight for their own independence must continue no matter what the cost. They could evoke images of French colonialism and claim that the Americans were no different.

The failure of the US Army in Vietnam and the failure of the bombing campaign over the North and through the Ho Chi Minh trails should be a stark reminder that reliance on military power to achieve political objectives can be dangerous and that there are very great limitations on the effectiveness of that military power. This was perhaps the starkest lesson of Vietnam, a lesson that America has still not learnt. A strong military does not by default equal power.

A foreign army cannot impose a system of government on a country by force. The same lesson has been taught in Iraq and is being taught in Afghanistan. Neither country will become a democratic government in America's image, which is really what America has wanted. The use of armies in such circumstances often makes an enemy of the people who belong to that country, and everyone ends up wanting the foreign army to leave. This is to say nothing of the national and cultural differences of any individual nation that must be considered when designing systems and institutions of good government—just because a system works well in one country does not mean that an identical system will work well, if at all, in another.

By July 1965, McNamara returning from Vietnam to Washington, was reporting to the President:

> The situation in South Vietnam is worse than a year ago (when it was worse than the year before that). After a few months of stalemate, the tempo of the war has quickened ... There are no signs that we have throttled the inflow of supplies of the VC or can throttle the flow while their material needs are as low as they are ... Nor have our air attacks on North Vietnam produced tangible evidence of the willingness on the part of Hanoi to come to the conference table in a reasonable mood. The DRV/ VC (Democratic Republic of North Vietnam/Viet Cong) seem to believe that South Vietnam is on the run and near collapse; they show no signs of settling for less than a complete takeover.[62]

McNamara concluded his report by saying there were only three options available to the United States at this time in the middle of 1965.[63] First, the United States could withdraw, accepting that withdrawal would really constitute unconditional surrender. Second, it could continue as is, which ultimately would lead to the same outcome as option one. Finally, the United States could expand its forces, consistent with the recommendation of General Westmoreland, while simultaneously launching vigorous efforts to open negotiations.[64]

McNamara said that this course would almost certainly stave off the possibility of medium-term defeat, but it would also increase the difficulty and cost of withdrawal at a later point. Nevertheless, McNamara says he was driven to option 3. McNamara claims that he thought an acceptable outcome could still be achieved under option 3, but he also says, in blunt terms, that later events proved that judgement to be totally wrong.[65]

The decision to instigate Rolling Thunder had been made after intense debate, yet sending in the marines in 1965 involved little discussion within the Johnson Administration. In June 1965, and after defeat at Ba Gia, General Westmoreland reported the need for greater US troop commitment, describing the South Vietnamese army as being near collapse and experiencing astronomically high rates of desertion.[66] Westmoreland requested forty-four battalions, nine of which were to be held in preparation. The troops would ensure success of a three-phase plan to destroy North Vietnamese forces.[67]

The scale of Westmoreland's request caused chaos in Washington— he was effectively proposing to take over the war from the South Vietnamese. Westmoreland pushed the view that there was only one course of action available, and American leaders, including McNamara, took this on face value.[68] On 28 July 1965, Johnson approved the deployment of troops outlined in the first phase of Westmoreland's plan. The illusion of a military victory was firmly in place. McNamara eventually accepted his mistake in not asking further questions or encouraging debate over options and the underpinning assumption of Westmoreland's plan. McNamara had built a career out of forcing organisations to consider consequences and alternative courses of action—he never understood why he did not push for this kind of rigour in 1965.[69]

The US involvement in Vietnam has to be judged an unmitigated failure; a failure almost guaranteed by an American interpretation of events, which led to the Americans believing that they were the ultimate determinant of what could or could not happen. There was no question of ethical decision-making. It was a question of what seemed to be expedient at the time, whether that was the assassination of Diem, the Gulf of Tonkin resolution, relying on intelligence that was politically expedient rather than accurate or President Johnson's refusal to take Congress—and thus the American people—fully into his confidence.

As a result of the divisions within the United States itself, President Johnson did not stand for re-election, and Nixon won under a commitment to get America out of Vietnam. When the Paris Accords were finally negotiated in 1973, Nixon claimed 'peace with honour'. We can see the same process happening in Afghanistan. The purpose was to build up and strengthen indigenous forces, so that the South Vietnamese could take over the total conduct of the war with enough strength to look after themselves. Those with any comprehension of Vietnam knew that this was a subterfuge, knew that it was not going to work, that its only purpose was to provide an excuse for the so-called honourable withdrawal.

What of Australia's role in all of this? How did our policy of strategic dependence contend with the Vietnam War?[70] In the 1960s Australia generally accepted the common view of communism: that it was monolithic, aggressive and dangerous. If Vietnam fell it would put other countries in Indo-China under increased threat of communist overthrow. Together with the US Administration we underestimated the strength of nationalism in Vietnam and regarded the conflict there as part of the communist thrust for worldwide domination. Yet whatever significance Australians may attach to our involvement in Vietnam, we do not rate a mention in McNamara's book.

Australia had recognised South Vietnam on the same day as the United States. Diem had visited Australia in 1957 as a guest of the government, but Australia was cautious in its initial approach to Vietnam. The number of advisers we sent was small. In 1964, which was after the assassination of both Diem and Kennedy, the Minister for Defence, Senator Paltridge, announced that the Australian Army Training Team Vietnam would be increased to eighty-three advisers.[71] It was still a small commitment. In 1964 Menzies announced that national service would be introduced to increase the army's strength from 22,750 to 37,500. This was a major expansion, a major preoccupation, and it was undertaken so that we could fulfil our obligations in Malaysia. We had a continuing commitment in Malaysia as a result of Australian help during the long-run communist insurgency and as a result of Konfrontasi with Indonesia. There is no doubt, on re-reading Menzies' speech to the Parliament, that the government was heavily influenced by the fear of communism as a monolithic, dangerous, aggressive force.[72] From today's perspective we need to put this fear in context. Communist insurgencies had occurred in Indonesia in 1965, in Malaya delaying independency for more than a decade, in Thailand as well. They were all potent reminders of then present dangers. National service also gave Australia potentially the capacity for a much more significant role in Vietnam. I was not a senior member of the government at the time and cannot say whether or not the expanded role was anticipated. It might well have been. In 1964 two hundred additional advisers were sent, still a modest number compared to the then American involvement.[73]

The government announced in the following year that, as a result of requests from both the United States and Vietnam itself, we would despatch an infantry battalion to South Vietnam with logistic support. In his speech to Parliament, Menzies clearly links the decision to send troops to the threat of worldwide communism: 'The takeover of South Vietnam would be a direct military threat to Australia and all the countries of South and South-East Asia. It must be seen as part of a thrust by Communist China between the Indian and Pacific Oceans.' Yet it was also congruent with the Australian policy of 'forward defence'; encouraging the United States to maintain a military presence in Asia was the cornerstone of this policy and an important part of strategic dependence.[74] 'Forward defence' was a policy designed to keep danger as far away from Australia as possible. It was under a policy of 'forward defence' that we had, with the United Kingdom and New Zealand forces, helped Malaya to overcome its insurgency. It was 'forward defence' that led us to support Malaysia against Konfrontasi with Indonesia. It was 'forward defence' that led us to the five-power defence arrangements negotiated a year or two later, under which we kept forces in Malaysia and Singapore for quite some time. With this policy in mind, Menzies would say that our commitment was due to a request from the South Vietnamese Government. Yet although a request was received, it came after the decision to send troops had been made, a decision based more on overtures from Washington than from Saigon.

In 1975 a report was tabled in the House of Representatives that examined government documents covering Australia's commitment of troops to Vietnam. The report was commissioned by Prime Minister Whitlam, but was compiled by R.G. Neale of the Department of Foreign Affairs, as it would rely on Cabinet documents from the previous government. The report found that, contrary to official statements, the Australian commitment of a battalion was not due to a request by Vietnam but rather a 'response to pressure from the United States seeking political support from "friends and allies"'.[75] Australian troops were not deployed to Vietnam in response to a request from South Vietnam, nor owing to our obligations under SEATO as was often mentioned, but rather as a result of American pressure.[76]

In 1966 Menzies resigned and Harold Holt became Prime Minister. Holt announced that Australia's commitment to South Vietnam would be increased to a full task force based on two battalions and that it would also include conscripts. There were two infantry battalions, an SAS squadron, combat and support logistic units and eight RAAF Iroquois helicopters. From the beginning of 1969 to mid-1970, more than a third of Australia's available combat strength was deployed in Vietnam.[77]

When Holt became Prime Minister, I was asked to join the ministry for the first time in my political career and was asked to be Minister for the Army. It filled me with no little trepidation. I had been too young to serve in World War II, and I strongly felt that Australians like myself owed an enormous debt to those who had served, sometimes in both World Wars I and II.

In the environment of the time, with the knowledge I then had, I fully supported the commitment in Vietnam. As was common in the West, I believed that communism was monolithic, that it was outward-thrusting, aggressive and a danger to democratic states.

The major decisions concerning force composition were made before I joined the government, but I was given the job of administering and overseeing the operation. Once a decision was made to establish a task force based on two battalions, Australia's operations were confined to Phuoc Tuy Province. This arrangement was negotiated by Lieutenant General Sir John Wilton, an extraordinarily able soldier and diplomat. The Australian Army, at the time, did not want an integrated operation with the Americans. Operating procedures were quite different. The army believed it was more concerned than the Americans to operate economically and to do more to save the lives of Australian soldiers. If the whole of Vietnam had operated the way the Australian Army operated in Phuoc Tuy Province, and if throughout South Vietnam the same effort had been made to improve the lot of people in the villagers through programs of civic action, the ultimate story in Vietnam might have been quite different. Australians who served there did so with high distinction. We should never forget that.

When I first visited Vietnam in 1966, as Minister for the Army, the briefings I was given from American sources were all highly optimistic. They were given by the military. In light of events of the previous two or three years, it is difficult to see how that level of optimism could be justified. These briefings presumably were a mirror image of those that McNamara himself had come to recognise were overly optimistic. I did not have access to CIA reports, which gave a different picture of events. McNamara had already come to believe that the situation had steadily deteriorated and that the Vietcong's capacity had increased markedly. Military optimism seemed to rely very heavily on body count numbers and on the belief that the Vietcong could not continue to recruit sufficiently to make up for the numbers that were alleged to have been killed. That was clearly a very crude analysis and basis on which to make any definitive judgement.

When Menzies made the decision to send the first Battalion Group to Vietnam, I was still only a private Member of Parliament. Later, when Holt expanded that first battalion to two and then three battalions, as Minister for the Army, I was pretty low in the pecking order of government. I do not believe, however, that the government had available to it the CIA assessments that were exhibiting a considerable degree of caution and scepticism about the military and political situation in Vietnam. It is my understanding that when the Australian Government made its decision, it was based on the undue optimism expressed by the US Army in Vietnam, by the State Department and by the White House.

About a month before the official decision, Air Chief Marshal Sir Frederick Scherger, who was also Chairman of the Chiefs of Staff Committee, led an Australian delegation to military talks in Honolulu. Before this delegation, Australian intelligence regarding American intentions in Vietnam was imprecise and reliant on reports from our Washington embassy. He was given a series of questions on which to seek clarification from the Americans. They were questions the Americans presumably could have answered. Despite his brief to seek clarification before Australia made firm commitments, Scherger was so eager to commit Australian forces that he did not pursue the brief that had been prepared for him by the Department of Defence. On his return to Australia he made the recommendation to send a battalion—his report made scant reference to the questions he had been sent to Honolulu to answer.[78]

Ascertaining exactly what Australia knew about the real situation in both Vietnam and Washington at the time is difficult, yet Neale's report mentions an official note that suggests 'that the relatively optimistic picture of the military situation given by the President in his message to the Prime Minister contrasted with our own military assessments and with some private United States assessments'.[79] At the political level at least, Australia was being told that circumstances in Vietnam were considerably better than they actually were.

There is no firm evidence that Australia was made aware of the bitter divisions that had taken hold in Washington.[80] Those, like President Johnson, and the people on board with him, who wished to press ahead at all costs, who believed that power and power alone could win, who could not conceive of American defeat, ultimately influenced Australia's decisions on Vietnam. Did we have any under-standing of the caution being expressed by the CIA and its analysts?

If we look at Menzies' statement in Parliament given on 29 April 1965, we can see that he believed success was not only possible but also almost certain. We accepted the global view of communism and the global view of the danger to the rest of South-East Asia, and even to ourselves, believing that fighting in Vietnam was a part of this struggle. We were not aware of McNamara's changing views and the cautious assessment continuing to come from the CIA. We had no comprehension of the intricacies of life in Vietnam, where nationalism was more important than communism, the Vietminh were popular and the South Vietnamese Government, regarded very largely as a creation of the French, was corrupt and had very little support. I doubt these elements were part of the Australian consid-eration. Yet it is part of the policy of strategic dependence. Much like our previous reliance on British diplomacy and intelligence, we were reliant on the information provided to us by the Americans to make an informed decision. The decisions we ultimately made were anything but informed.

As a private Member of Parliament, I had accepted this global interpretation and the views of the Americans. Although this was the overwhelming feeling at the time, it was of course wrong. Yet because of the view that Vietnam fitted into the Cold War paradigm, there was no real desire to look for other explanations. We accepted too easily that South Vietnam represented something that was good and that the Vietminh and North Vietnam represented something that was wrong, very much to be opposed. We cast the issue as a simple case of good and evil when, in reality, it was so much more complicated. If we look at what Australia has done since in Iraq and Afghanistan, it is not only America who has failed to learn lessons.

What was America telling the Australian Prime Minister at the time? We can be sure that President Johnson would not say to an Australian Prime Minister that which he was not prepared to say to the American Senate. He would not say to an Australian Prime Minister that, although the military are very confident about what is happening in Vietnam, the CIA was not. That would be beyond probability. He wanted Australia's commitment to be enlarged for political cover for himself. He wanted the burden shared. He wanted another allied flag flying on the battlefield. He was not going to express doubts. He was not going to share CIA assessments, which Johnson and his administration, with the exception of McNamara, were regularly ignoring. He wanted another banner next to America in an armed conflict against the spread of communism.

If Harold Holt had known of the doubt, he would never have said: 'And so, sir, in the lonelier and perhaps even more disheartening moments which come to any national leader, I hope there will be a corner of your mind and heart which takes cheer from the fact that you have an admiring friend, a staunch friend that will be all the way with LBJ.'[81] The phrase came to be accepted as saying that Australia would do whatever the Americans wanted. Sir John Bunting, who was present with Holt when he used those words, a most decent and honourable public servant and head of the Prime Minister's Department, told me that, in the context of his speech, the words did not carry the unfortunate implications that were generally later accepted in Australia. But they do fit well with the notion of strategic dependence: that Australia would do whatever its great and powerful friend required in order to court its favour and earn protection. We went along with bad decisions made by London and, as Vietnam shows, we were happy to go along with the bad decisions made by Washington. Sadly, we still are today.

Despite strategic dependence, I still find it impossible to believe that any Australian Government would have taken the course that we did take if they had been fully advised of the assessments McNamara was in fact making and giving to the President. This is regardless of our broader aims at the time of keeping the United States engaged in South-East Asia and adhering to our policy of forward defence and despite our deeply rooted fear of the communist threat. If we had known what the CIA and McNamara both believed at that time—that the cause for which America was fighting in Vietnam was hopeless, and that America in South Vietnam could not succeed—we would never have become so involved. There was information within the US Administration, although the White House was paying no attention to it, that should have been put before an ally.

The Vietnam conflict started with broad public support in Australia. It ended with the most terrible divisions, after very large casualties for Australia and for America. We sent almost sixty thousand Australians to Vietnam; 521 of them would never come home.[82] More than three thousand would be wounded, with many more suffering psychological and medical conditions for decades after. This is an astounding sacrifice to make in a war where our participation was predicated on grossly optimistic assessments of what was actually happening. At best, the Americans were derelict in their duty to inform us of the true situation in Vietnam; at worst, they were deceitful.

Whatever the result, we joined the ship of war in Vietnam when the war was already doomed. That is not a very comforting thought for the soldiers and families who served or who died in Vietnam.

There is one final point to make. The US Administration had reliable information, yet it did not use it. Even before the commitment of troops during Kennedy's time, when intelligence reports were saying the situation was deteriorating, the American Government relied on the far more positive military reports to direct their decision-making. It allowed domestic politics, as interpreted by President Johnson, particularly when viewed through the prism of the Cold War, to determine what happened. There was no idea of due process, which is not only a legal term but also a term important to government to make sure that facts are accurate, to make sure that information is properly processed, to guarantee that those with a real contribution to that process have an opportunity to make their points without fear or favour. Due process in government is critical to good government.[83]

America is not alone in totally lacking due process that can have serious implications on many areas of government policy. Prime Ministers in Australia who believe they should get their own way if they want it strongly enough also deny due process. When circumstances are not understood, when we look at issues through our own eyes alone, when we fail to understand people on the other side, who might or might not be enemies, we fall into error. If that is to be avoided, we need to have the capacity to understand the situation through the enemy's eyes, as well as through our own. If we do not, we will make misjudgements, miscalculations.

There was no doubt that the situation in Vietnam from the end of World War II right through to the fall of Saigon was complex—a milieu of anti-colonial, nationalistic and Cold War struggles. If this complexity had been realised by the Americans, then perhaps they might have been able to devise more constructive policy. The same could be said of the French. Lack of good process, which includes an understanding of cultural differences, led to the most grievous and horrible mistakes in Vietnam, mistakes that might have begun with a belief that communism was worldwide, monolithic and ended with America believing that it could impose its will on another society by force of arms alone.

The war in Vietnam did change American thinking and how the United States interacted with the world. It was weary from a conflict that had cost it dearly. In campaigning for the presidency in 1969, Richard Nixon outlined what would become known as the Nixon or Guam Doctrine:

> First, the United States will keep all of its treaty commitments.
>
> Second, we shall provide a shield if a nuclear power threatens the freedom of a nation allied with us or of a nation whose survival we consider vital to our security.
>
> Third, in cases involving other types of aggression, we shall furnish military and economic assistance when requested in accordance with our treaty commitments. But we shall look to the nation directly threatened to assume the primary responsibility of providing the manpower for its defense.[84]

Nixon claimed in his speech that US intervention 'Americanised the war in Vietnam' and that freedom was not just America's business but was also the entire world's business and, in particular, that of the nation whose freedom was under threat. Some commentators interpreted the doctrine to mean that 'no longer would Americans man the front lines against global communism'.[85]

The Guam Doctrine, according to Nixon, was meant to apply to American obligations worldwide. I took it at the time to mean that the President was trying to persuade allies to do more, but I doubt the doctrine made a great deal of difference to the way America would have behaved or the way allies would have behaved, although a great fuss was made about it at the time. I believed at the time and believe still that President Nixon's enunciation of the Guam Doctrine was part of his overall attempt to give credibility to the United States' withdrawal from Vietnam.

For Australia, the Guam Doctrine, however, did not alter our attitude much; it did not lead to a greater emphasis on our defence forces.[86] The policy of strategic dependence on which we had relied was strong, and political leaders at the time could not really conceive of a circumstance in which it would not be effective. We had by this time forgotten that that policy had failed during the 1930s and failed early in World War II because Britain was too weak to give effect to the policy. We had not taken those lessons to heart as we should have. We did not yet fully realise that strategic dependence was a large part of our role in Vietnam.

Regardless of Nixon's position, McNamara said that the United States had been so very wrong throughout this war. This is most true. Yet, on the issue of Diem, he also never questioned America's right to kill—in plain terms, to murder—the head of government of an ally with whom America was fighting a war. What faith can a nation have in an ally that believes it is within its right to remove that nation's head of state?

When a lesson has been learnt at such terrible cost, it would be good to think that they, and we, would change our behaviour as a result of such mistakes. This is not to say that the Americans would treat Australia the same as they did South Vietnam. The relationship is different; our democracy is robust, and the world is a changed place. Yet, more broadly, we have followed America into two more wars since Vietnam, which involved poor process, fabrication and reliance on over-inflated military information. Since the end of World War II, we have considered our strategic interests as being best served by following the American lead on major international conflicts. In Vietnam, our decision to follow has meant that young Australians paid the ultimate price. The same happened in Iraq. It continues to happen in Afghanistan. We do not want to follow them into another such conflict. Yet our policy of strategic dependence dictates that we must follow the lead of the Americans, to make sure that they know we are on their side. Vietnam should have been a warning to us, that although the context of the Cold War might have made strategic dependence a necessary policy, it would be at a cost. It came at a cost with the British, and so to it came at a cost with the Americans. The question Australia must ask itself is whether, if the global context does not dictate such a policy, as is now the case, is a cost such as that we bore in Vietnam worth it?

8

The 'grand bargain' out of time

I have argued that, although it is never ideal and can come at great cost, strategic dependence was a policy that Australian leaders had little choice but to adopt. It fitted the context of times. It was not perfect, but I believe it was inescapable. Vietnam provides the starkest example. Yet almost a century of strategic dependence has left an indelible mark on the Australian psyche—we almost crave a great and powerful friend; it is a part of who we are as a nation. As a young nation, this made some sense yet, as we matured and had international successes of our own, this feeling should have diminished and been slowly replaced with our own sense of identity and confidence in our diplomatic abilities. Yet it did not. Sure, we developed our own foreign policy and diplomatic infrastructure, but, with a few exceptions, it always acted within our policy of strategic dependence. In this chapter, I trace the final stages of the Cold War, from the thawing of relations between the United States and China, to the Soviet invasion of Afghanistan and finally the collapse of the Soviet Union. This is the last period in our history in which I believe strategic dependence was appropriate. It was the last time we could realistically argue that we needed a great and powerful friend. The world would soon change, and Australia would face decisions about the future direction of her foreign and defence policies.

After Vietnam, global opinions on the validity of the Domino Theory changed. Before the conflict and all the way through it, there were those who argued the validity of the Domino Theory, those who argued about the strategic importance of Vietnam to America or the West's wider interests in the fight against a monolithic communist movement. They were proven to be wrong, as were those who argued that it was in Australia's interests to become deeply involved. This included the Australian Government, of which I was a part. Many of the assumptions about global communism, and indeed those underpinning the Domino Theory, began to unravel in the mid-1970s. Other nations in South-East Asia were not consumed by the communist orbit after the fall of Saigon as had been predicted.

The reasons for this seem clear enough. The global interpretation of communism that provided much of the rationale for American and Australian involvement in Vietnam was plainly incorrect. This had been demonstrated by the divisions between the Soviet Union and China. In addition, it had become clear that the war in Vietnam was not part of a global thrust, designed to engulf the whole of East and South-East Asia. It was much more a fight for the independence of Vietnam. It is true that there had been insurgencies in Thailand and in Malaysia but, to the extent that communism was involved, it was exploiting local grievances rather than part of a deliberate global movement.

There is also another reason. South-East Asian countries, particularly members of ASEAN, had strengthened their own institutions and societal cohesion and were therefore in a much stronger position to resist or to overcome any external threat than in earlier decades. Prime Minister Lee Kuan Yew of Singapore privately used to support the Vietnam War on the basis that it bought more time for ASEAN to achieve these objectives.

Whitlam came into office a few months after Nixon's famous visit to China in 1972, which had been carefully orchestrated over the previous couple of years. Nixon's visit led to the Shanghai

Communiqué, which was a precursor to formal establishment of diplomatic relations between Washington and Beijing and the end of American diplomatic recognition of Taiwan seven years later in 1979, during the time I was Prime Minister.[1] The United States was recognising that the two parts of China are part of one China, but emphasised that reunification must take place peacefully.[2] This recognition was formalised in a joint communiqué in 1979.[3] On the Chinese side, there was, of course, a strong assertion that China and Taiwan were two parts of one country.

Despite it taking seven years to achieve diplomatic relations, the Shanghai Communiqué was indeed a historic moment. It opened the possibility of a different world. Recognition of China, and the growing understanding that Chinese communism was quite different from Soviet communism, helped to create a different political climate and gave some respectability to President Nixon's withdrawal from Vietnam. It also made it easier to develop a new relationship with China that could develop separately from the relationship with the Soviet Union. Nixon recognised that the world was more complex and that over-simplification can lead to serious errors and most tragic mistakes.

I have always wondered how much of this initiative belonged to Henry Kissinger, whom I knew well, or to the President himself. I can remember speaking to a young American Congressman who said that they would occasionally get a call to go over and speak with Nixon. They would talk after dinner and discuss the future, how to make the world a safer place. This would also be consistent with his approach to China and suggests that the initiative might have belonged just as much to Nixon as it did to Kissinger.

During my first visit to China in 1976, I noticed the gulf that had opened between the Soviet Union and the People's Republic of China. I also realised that Chinese and Soviet communism had clear and considerable differences. China was then quite consistently opposed to hegemony, whether by the Soviet Union or the United States. They opposed foreign troops in any country and were clearly concerned at the Soviet Union's policies. Knowing that I was to visit China, the Philippines wanted me to ask the Chinese which was most important: government-to-government relationships or party-to-party relationships. Until the early 1970s, with the history of the Malayan insurgency in mind as well that of the PKI coup in Indonesia and the continuing insurgency in the southern Philippines, there was a strong belief that China gave significant support to communist-led insurgent groups; in other words, to party organisations in different countries. Nixon's visit to China opened a different possibility.

Without any equivocation, Hua Guofeng, the Chinese Premier at the time, with whom I had eleven or twelve hours of discussions over two to three days, told me quite unequivocally that party-to-party relations would never be allowed to interfere with or to diminish the importance of government-to-government relations. This was interpreted as meaning that China would no longer support insurgency groups in other East or South-East Asia countries. When this was reported to the Philippines and others, it was regarded as a most important statement. It was the first time it had been said and, as the years passed, it was demonstrated to be accurate.

Such notions were captured in the Shanghai Communiqué. On the Chinese side, it was stated: 'China will never be a superpower and it opposes hegemony and power politics of any kind.'[4] It is worth noting that the most recent China Defence White Paper repeated a statement of that kind.[5] On the Chinese side, they affirmed that 'All foreign troops should be withdrawn to their own countries'.[6] They, of course, supported the independence of Vietnam, Laos and Cambodia. It opposed 'the revival and outward expansion of Japanese militarism', something that is also reflected in their current White Paper.[7]

On the American side, apart from the conventional attitudes expressed by both countries in terms of goodwill and progress and working for a prosperous peaceful world, it said:

> ... the two sides agreed that countries, regardless of their social
> systems, should conduct their relations on the principles of

respect for the sovereignty and territorial integrity of all states, non-aggression against other states, non-interference in the internal affairs of other states, equality and mutual benefit, and peaceful coexistence. International disputes should be settled on this basis, without resorting to the use or threat of force. The United States and the People's Republic of China are prepared to apply these principles to their mutual relations.[8]

The communiqué continued, once they had each expressed their own view, by expressing strong support for normalisation of relations between China and the United States, in the interest of not only themselves but also of the world. They jointly said: 'Neither should seek hegemony in the Asia–Pacific region and each is opposed to efforts by any other country or group of countries to establish such hegemony.'[9] It continued: '… it would be against the interests of the peoples of the world for any major country to collude with another against other countries, or for major countries to divide up the world into spheres of interest'.[10] This was something that the European powers had done for centuries.

The Chinese side affirmed the importance of the question of Taiwan and said that it was critical to 'the normalisation of relations between China and the United States'.[11] It reaffirmed that 'the People's Republic of China is the sole legal government of China; Taiwan is a province of China … the liberation of Taiwan is China's internal affair in which no other country has the right to interfere …'[12]

The US side declared that it 'acknowledges that all Chinese on either side of the Taiwan Strait maintain there is but one China and that Taiwan is a part of China. The United States Government does not challenge that position.' The United States emphasised the importance of 'a peaceful settlement' of the issue by the Chinese themselves and affirmed its own 'ultimate objective of withdrawal of all US forces and military installations from Taiwan. In the meantime, it will progressively reduce its forces and military installations on Taiwan …'[13]

These attitudes on both sides were impeccably expressed. It could be argued that China has done a better job than the United States in adhering to the basic principles contained within those statements. China has not, to this point, been an imperial power as Britain, France, Germany, Italy and earlier Spain and Portugal were imperial powers. (Whatever view one takes of the China–Tibetan relationship, it still does not fit the pattern of European colonisation and imperial ambition in South America, Africa and other parts of Asia.) The United States by contrast has been such a power, especially in relation to the Pacific and indeed in relation to China itself, at the time of the Boxer Rebellion, in concert with European powers. I use the word 'imperial' in the sense of a country pursuing either direct control of another nation's territory or imposing unequal treaties designed to gain significant economic or strategic advantage.[14]

We cannot ignore the fact that economic power alone gives a country influence. The most notable examples over the last couple of centuries have, of course, been Britain and the United States. There is no doubt that such powers use economic weight to gain an advantage for themselves and often to establish an unequal playing field for their own industries. China, as a result of its growing and enormously profitable economy, has started to develop economic and trade influence around the world. This is inevitable, but it is not to be confused with the old imperialism of the colonial powers.

Prime Minister Whitlam was ahead of the game on China because he had been to China, as Opposition Leader, in a ground-breaking visit the year before Nixon. His visit coincided with Kissinger's visit, and demonstrated quite clearly that a Whitlam Government was prepared to exercise greater independence in foreign affairs. It simulated in many ways principles first exhibited by Evatt as Minister for External Affairs. It also led to some concern in the United States about the reliability of Australia as an ally and about the status of joint bases in Australia.[15] This was particularly related to the fear that the Whitlam Government might reveal sensitive information regarding the base at Pine Gap, a fear that was heightened after the raid of ASIO's offices by the Attorney General, Lionel Murphy. Perhaps the

Americans were worried about an independent mind, reminiscent of Evatt, being in a key position.[16]

Little by little, those fears diminished in the American mind, because of the actions of the Minister for Defence, Lance Barnard, working very closely in tandem with Sir Arthur Tange, Secretary of the Department of Defence, whom I had appointed in 1970. Tange spoke to me about these events later on, after he had retired. He had great respect for Barnard, and believed he had done a first-class job in helping to maintain the strength of the alliance at that time.

Because of the Cold War, it was still a time to maintain close relationships with the United States, and I believe that, at heart, Whitlam would have recognised that. But Whitlam also knew that Australia should create space within that relationship to pursue its own interests.

The economic problems of the 1970s really absorbed Western countries. It was a period when the focus of many governments was inward rather than outward on foreign policy issues. When my government was in power (from November 1975 to March 1983), in the initial years, it was the economy that was paramount. I can remember on my fourth visit to Washington in 1979, inflation had started to come down in Australia, Treasury estimates were suggesting that we would achieve an inflation rate of less than 6 per cent by the middle of the year.[17] By the standards of those times, that was remarkably low. In a discussion on economic matters US President Carter said to me that more and more people were arguing that inflation was important and that he should do something about it. During 1979, inflation rose from 9 per cent to 13 per cent in America,[18] and Australia's inflation was heading towards 5 per cent, according to Treasury estimates.[19] The speech I gave to the Economic Club in New York in January 1979 was largely written by the Treasury. At that time, Treasury thought our economic policies were running well. Unfortunately, the second oil shock and later events in Australia guaranteed that those Treasury estimates would be quite wrong, with the Australian inflation rate higher than 10 per cent by the end of 1979.[20]

There was a second significant rise in world oil prices in April 1979 that affected the global economy, including Australia. The ACTU began a significant push, such as the 1978 National Wage Case, for increased wages and for a shorter working week. There was still a good deal of regulation in the labour market. My government tried to argue that industry should not discuss or negotiate on the question of reduced working hours. Reduced hours and higher wages together would add very significant costs. Australian industries had started to do well, and the metal trades especially were relatively easy prey to union demands. (The metal trades were also affected by discussions around the minimum rates of pay contained in the Metal Industries Award.)

Domestic economic issues took much time and energy of Western governments during this period, Australia and the United States included. Yet the international context did not remain static; it did not provide respite for leaders to focus solely on solving domestic economic troubles.

I was at Nareen, our property in Western Victoria, on 27 December 1979, when the head of the Prime Minister's Department rang me and said that the Soviet Union had invaded Afghanistan. The communist government in Afghanistan, led by Nur Muhammad Taraki, had been under pressure,[21] and had appealed succes- sively to the Soviet Union for help.[22] Leading up to the invasion, Soviet leaders had been reluctant to help, perhaps recognising the quagmire in which they could be involved by giving significant military support to Afghanistan. Perhaps the Soviet Union recog- nised that Afghanistan was not a cohesive nation but a nation of warlords whose reliability and support was determined solely by their own self-interest. In other words, they would switch sides with- out any restraint. There was no tradition of centralised authority and control.

Afghanistan, through much of the late twentieth and early twenty- first centuries, has had a confused and upsetting history.[23] There was competition originally between the United Kingdom and Russia, later the Soviet Union, for influence. The country is also ethnically divided between Pashtun, Tajik, Hazara, Uzbek, Aimaq and other smaller ethnic communities.

Since World War II, Afghan governments had, by and large, tried to maintain a balance between its relationship with the Soviet Union and the United States; perhaps wanting help from both, but not getting too close to either. Western policy unfortunately pushed Afghanistan closer to the Soviet orbit in 1953 and 1954, and then again in 1961. Afghan governments appealed to the United States for help, particularly around border issues with Pakistan and the establishment of 'Pushtanistan', but were ultimately rebuffed.[24] Later, in 1976, Afghani foreign and domestic policy decisions, aimed at moving Kabul away from Moscow's influence, received a very lukewarm response from Kissinger.[25]

Before the Soviet invasion, there was a weak pro-communist government in Kabul.[26] It never had much sway in the provinces, and the country was beset by significant ethnic disturbances. The government appealed more and more to the Soviet Union for help and, indeed, asked the Soviet Union to send troops to Afghanistan to help the government maintain authority. It was in Brezhnev's time that the fateful decision was made in December 1979 to invade Afghanistan.[27] That led to a long-drawn-out and costly war. The Soviet troops did not find support among the general population or the ethnic groups of Afghanistan. They were foreigners interfering in Afghani affairs. The Soviets found much the same reaction as the Americans had found in Vietnam. There was a second similarity. The Soviets were not able to establish a government with authority that had the respect of Afghanis and could govern the country effectively.

When Gorbachev came to power in 1985, he believed that the war in Afghanistan was bleeding the Soviet Union.[28] It was too costly, and the Soviet Union just had to withdraw. Yet just as the Americans did in Vietnam, Moscow had to put the best face on the withdrawal that they could. They trained an army in support of the government so that the government would be able to look after itself. When the Soviets did withdraw in 1989, unsurprisingly, the Afghan Government installed by Moscow could not support itself.[29]

The divisions remained; the government was unpopular and was ultimately overthrown by elements of the Mujahideen in 1992, some of whom had received money, arms and training from the United States during their conflict with the Soviets.[30]

The division between the warring Mujahideen warlords allowed the Taliban, then a student politico-religious movement in southern Afghanistan, to become influential. The Taliban, backed by Pakistani intelligence, continued to gain strength, ultimately taking Kabul and forming government in 1996.[31] The Taliban Government sought to establish a most extreme interpretation of Islam. It became a centre for terrorism, along with the tribal areas in Pakistan that gave support and provided a home for Osama bin Laden.

Reading about Soviet policy in Afghanistan, from this perspective, seems to be similar to American policy in Vietnam after President Johnson had decided to place an army of more than half a million men in Vietnam. The terrain and the geography were, of course, totally different but, that aside, there were similarities. Afghanis of whatever persuasion did not like domination by a foreign power any more than the Vietnamese had liked it. Soviet involvement tended to create enemies and strengthen resistance. The Soviets began a policy of training local people and, when they came to withdraw, they did so under the pretence that the Afghan Government, led by President Mohammad Najibullah, now had sufficient strength to defend itself—the same pretence that was undertaken by President Nixon, in relation to Vietnam. On both counts the pretence was wrong.

The Soviet invasion of Afghanistan, at the time, was taken as an example of Soviet aggression, of Soviet strength, or a desire to expand. It was once again slotted into the global communist paradigm. President Carter, when he first came to office, was not well versed in foreign affairs. He had been a Governor in Georgia between 1971 and 1975, relatively isolated from external influences. In his early years, he was naive in his attitudes and proposals. I can remember Australian Defence Department officials expressing considerable concern in the early days of the Carter Administration. For example, President

Carter had been talking about a treaty with the Soviet Union that sought to neutralise the Indian Ocean. Defence was concerned that a treaty with the Soviet Union of the kind being proposed might well diminish America's capacity to assist Australia under ANZUS, should we ever need it.[32] For that reason, I sought a meeting with President Carter early in his term of office to press these points on him. In the event, no treaty was negotiated with the Soviet Union, and Australia's concerns fell away. Just one more example of Australia's preoccupation with our dependence on a great power.

I can also remember an occasion when President Carter had been speaking with President Brezhnev, and he told me quite simply that President Brezhnev had lied to him during that conversation. I do not think he should have been particularly surprised, but he was. That had a significant effect on his attitude to the Soviet Union. As a result of such experiences, President Carter strongly believed that a firm response to Soviet aggression in Afghanistan was needed. Indeed, during his last eighteen months in office, he had begun to rearm and strengthen the US military because he had come to regard the Soviet Union as unreliable and untrustworthy. He never got much credit for this because of his earlier policies.

President Carter thought that, if there was not a strong response from the United States and from others, the Soviet Union could be encouraged to repeat its aggression. In a statement responding to the invasion of Afghanistan, he talks of the Soviet Union extending 'their control to adjacent countries, the stable, strategic, and peaceful balance of the entire world will be changed'. President Carter's speech was strong and motivated significantly by a concern that the Soviet Union was seeking to expand its influence throughout the whole region and, in particular, gain control of oil supplies. Perhaps rather presciently, Carter also stated: 'History teaches, perhaps, very few clear lessons. But surely one such lesson learned by the world at great cost is that aggression, unopposed, becomes a contagious disease.'[33] Those who came after President Carter had clearly forgotten any lessons learnt from the Soviet invasion when they made their own plans in 2001.

In a speech early in 1980, after the Soviet invasion of Afghanistan, I reviewed the situation in Parliament. I had made a major statement on foreign policy in June 1976, and in 1980 I quoted again some parts of that earlier statement:

> The Soviet Union has an immense responsibility before mankind—to use its power and influence to strengthen the fabric of international peace and security. It has an historic opportunity to use its position to help build a stable and humane international order and to end the arms build-up. It will be judged by the great majority of mankind against these standards.
>
> The time has come to expect a sign from the USSR that it understands this and that it is serious about reaching global accommodation with the West. A tangible signal is required from the USSR in the form of a restraint in its military expansion. The pace is being set by the USSR, not by the US.
>
> Mr Speaker, when that speech was given in 1976 there were many commentators throughout this nation who regarded it as a hard-line, Cold War statement. As events have sadly proved, it was all too accurate. The Soviet Union gave us a sign, but not the sign we wanted, not the sign honourable people would have prayed for. Instead, it has caused trouble in South-East Asia, in Africa through Cuban surrogates, in north-east Africa and now in south-west Asia. In all these circumstances it is the Soviet Union, not the United States and the United States' friends, that has given cause for concern, for fear in many places, and for heightened tensions.
>
> I think we need to understand why the invasion of Afghanistan is important ... The Union of Soviet Socialist Republics has invaded a non-aligned state, a member of the Non-Aligned Movement and the Islamic Conference. The most powerful and largest land army in the world has moved for the first time outside what had been accepted as the Soviet bloc, the Soviet power grouping. That places the

Soviet Union in the position potentially to exert pressure and influence, or even control, over the supplies of oil which are vital to countries such as Japan and European countries and which are of great importance to Australia and many other countries. That is a new element in Soviet moves that has not been present in previous crises. It is for that reason that we believe that this is potentially the most serious of all the crises since 1945.[34]

The Australian and American views were remarkably similar at that time.

Paul Dibb, head of the National Assessments Staff, National Intelligence Committee, recounted in a later article he wrote in 2010 that the Office of National Assessments, which was Australia's premier intelligence body, agreed with these 'deep-seated suspicions of Soviet intentions',[35] although there were some on the National Assessments Board who argued that the Soviet Union would have great difficulty carrying out its intentions in Afghanistan.

The reaction of Australia and America—and indeed the West generally—to the Soviet invasion of Afghanistan was clearly influenced by the perception of Soviet activities in far-flung parts of the world.[36] There are examples of Soviet expansion or intervention in Angola. They had transported Cuban combat troops there in 1975 and had expanded the USSR's military facilities in Somalia. Soviet expansion occurred not only into Angola and Somalia but also into Yemen and Ethiopia between 1975 and 1978; all of which preceded the invasion of Afghanistan.

In addition to that, the document 'Strategic Basis of Australia Defence Policy', published by the Department of Defence in 1973, claimed that 'it is a signal success for the USSR to have achieved equal status with the US and it will not lightly yield it or accept any US ascendancy'.[37] The next 'Strategic Basis of Defence Policy', dated October 1975, pointed to 'substantial and sustained growth of the USSR's military power and defence spending, and that if this trend were to continue unabated, "the USSR would be perceived internationally to be militarily stronger than the United States'".[38] This expansion ran a serious risk of creating much greater tension or confrontation.

It is worth recording that this major expansion of Soviet world-wide activities followed America's clear defeat in Vietnam and took place at a time when American confidence and morale was low and when America was perceived to have been beaten in war by a relatively small Asian country. These elements were all part of the equation when President Carter reacted very strongly to the invasion of Afghanistan and declared that the invasion was 'the greatest threat to peace since World War II'.[39]

As Dibb continued in his article, there was a widespread political belief in Washington that the invasion of Afghanistan was part of a grand Soviet strategic plan, which would go much further beyond Afghanistan and was squarely aimed at America.[40] The age of détente was clearly over. These factors would influence not only the United States but also clearly the Australian Government and the assessments made by the Office of National Assessments. The need for strategic dependence was still present.

Carter sought to lead worldwide sanctions against the Soviet Union, particularly on weapons and agricultural trade. When the Australian Government looked at the various proposals it wanted to make sure that it pursued policies that would achieve adequate public support and would prove sustainable.

These were years in which Cold War philosophies still dominated international thinking. They were years in which Australia still believed that a policy of strategic dependence was appropriate for the time. That meant reliance on a major power. That also meant that we needed to do what we could to support US policies and Western policies in general, especially in regard to what was accepted as blatant aggression by the Soviet Union against Afghanistan.

The invasion of Afghanistan had rekindled in the Western world memories of the monolithic and aggressive nature of communism and its determination to expand wherever it could. The lessons we had begun to learn, as a result of strategic differences between the Soviet Union and China, were pushed aside and the lessons of Vietnam came to be forgotten all too quickly.

The main lines of policy were commonly followed by major Western states. America, Europe, Australia and New Zealand broadly followed the issues outlined in Carter's speech.[41] For example, New Zealand imposed trade restrictions and downgraded its diplomatic relations with Moscow, and British Prime Minister Margaret Thatcher would push heavily for a boycott of the Moscow Olympics. Wheat sales were banned, a sanction that Australia supported with relative ease because we had a one-desk seller for all Australian wheat at the time.[42] President Reagan, before his election, had promised to lift wheat sanctions against the Soviet Union. The wheat embargo was therefore lifted in 1981.

It is worth making the point that, when this was announced, Doug Anthony, Leader of the National Party and Deputy Prime Minister, advised me that he had an agreement with the United States, with his counterpart, that when sanctions were ultimately lifted, as they would be, he would be notified as soon as the decision was made. He wanted to make sure that our Wheat Board sales-men could be in the Soviet Union as quickly as American salesmen. When we finally got word in 1981, as a result of President Reagan's election commitment, Anthony found that American salesmen had been in the Soviet Union six weeks earlier. Not quite a level playing field, but then trade with great powers never truly is.

Australia did not implement a ban on wool sales and, while this achieved a good deal of discussion and attack from the Opposition in Australia, the reasons were clear enough. Wool was sold by auction. We often did not know whom the end purchaser was as agents bought on behalf of others. Wool sales would have been impossible to police. Such a simple answer was hard to sell when there were a number of wool growers within the government itself.

More important was a decision to try to boycott the Olympic Games. This became a most divisive and unfair policy, placing a lot of responsibility on a few individuals, none of whom sought such responsibility. The government pursued it because, with our general attitude to the Soviet Union, we believed we should show a united position with other countries of the West.[43] I can remember one of our first discussions; we wanted policies that were sustainable and would carry public support. If there was difficulty or pain involved for the local community, it was important that it be seen to be equitable and not of a kind that would erode quickly.

I can remember speaking to Chancellor Helmut Schmidt during a visit to Germany in 1980 after I had visited the United States. This was after the Soviet invasion of Afghanistan. President Carter had announced that America was going to pursue a boycott of the Games in Moscow. Chancellor Schmidt advised me that, twenty-four hours before he saw the President announcing such a policy, the President personally assured the Chancellor in conversation that it was not on the American agenda. Schmidt asked me, instead of going straight home after Germany, if I could go by the United States and try to emphasise to the President the need for meaningful discussions and meaningful conversations with major European leaders on such a major issue. Chancellor Schmidt was extraordinarily frustrated by a lack of consultation between the United States and its allies, including important members of NATO. He was not used to being ignored. I told him it was a discussion he should have himself. He said that he had had too many discussions, and if he had another discussion he would not be able to stay even-minded and even-tempered, and that would do nobody any good. I thought about that for quite some time, then I said if the French President, Valéry Giscard d'Estaing, and the British agree, I would speak with Carter. I spoke to Lord Carrington, British Foreign Minister, about it and his view was that Britain would react somewhat differently, but he could see no harm in me trying to carry that message back to the United States. Schmidt told me he had spoken to d'Estaing, and he agreed that I should.

On my return through the United States, I again met President Carter. The outcome was another lesson in how unreceptive major powers can be to any real suggestions about the way they should or should not do business. They are always going to follow their own procedures, or lack of procedures, make up their own minds and then they will inform other people. Nothing was going to alter that. Not the Australian Prime Minister, not the German Chancellor.

On my return to Australia, we had lengthy discussions in Cabinet about whether or not to boycott the Olympic Games, or at least to try to persuade the Olympic Committee to boycott, because we were not prepared to take the step of denying passports to Australian sportsmen and women. The history is well known. It was totally divisive. The Olympic Committee decided, in a split vote, to attend the Games, but some sports decided to go, others decided to boycott.[44] Even within sports, some individuals made the decision for themselves. Some went, others did not. This policy defied one of the first principles that we had discussed when we were working out what we should do in support of the general Western position. It went against the question of sustainability and equity.

It is easy to see how divisive this policy would be and how support for such a boycott would be eroded as time passed. It was a belief that there ought to be solidarity among the reactions of Western powers to the Soviet invasion of Afghanistan that led to the government trying to persuade athletes not to go. We succeed in some cases, we failed in others, and left our sporting world extraordinarily divided. Not a good result by any means.

By 1985 all sanctions against the Soviet Union had been lifted except for trade in high technology. The Soviet Union's withdrawal from Afghanistan started in May 1988 and concluded in February 1989. The Soviet Union was in Afghanistan for the best part of a decade. The lessons they learnt were very similar to the lessons the Americans learnt in Vietnam. It was not part of a global thrust for expansion, but rather one to secure a friendly government in Afghanistan to avoid problems with Islamic Soviets on the southern Soviet Union border.

President Reagan came into office in 1981. He had great charm. In many ways he was a simple man; he had a great faith in America and America's strength. His great achievement was to rebuild America's pride and America's confidence in its abilities, which was important not only for America but also for the whole world. In 1985 President Gorbachev became the General Secretary of the Communist Party of the Soviet Union. At this time, significant problems within the Soviet Union began to become evident. President Reagan had really thrown down a challenge; he was going to rearm and strengthen America. He declared American military strength to be a 'pre-requisite to peace'.[45] He was going to make it very difficult or impossible for the Soviet Union to keep up. He wanted to place as much stress on the Soviet economy as he possibly could. There were already huge financial strains within the Soviet Union as military research had absorbed much of the Soviet Union's wealth. Consequently, other sectors of the economy were starved for resources and investment and fell way behind Western equivalents. This led to problems throughout the whole country, but especially in the rural and remote provinces.

President Gorbachev won an election in 1986 promising two policies, glasnost and perestroika. Glasnost was openness and freedom of speech, whereas perestroika was about promising to rebuild the economy. At that time, the Soviet economy was in a state of stagnation, and all sectors of society and economy, apart from the military, were subject to severe shortages. Severe economic and political troubles followed.

Perestroika saw the introduction of laws liberalising individual and family-based work, devolving greater autonomy to state enterprises and lowering restrictions on economic cooperatives, all of which were attempts at restructuring the Soviet economy.[46] It is doubtful whether Gorbachev ever undertook the full range of specific economic policies necessary to achieve a rebuilding of the economy. In any event, the result was failure, partly because of the tension between making the existing Soviet economy work more effectively and replacing it with a market-based economy that had an entirely different underpinning logic. He never introduced the reforms that would have enabled a market-based economy to be established with any strength. He was trying to improve the system as it was rather than replace it. Further, it would have involved a much greater squeeze on military expenditure than anything that Gorbachev was able to achieve in order to free resources for the non-military economy. By the end of the Gorbachev era, the Soviet economy was 'no longer a functioning command economy but not yet a market system'.[47]

He also did not understand how glasnost's freedom of speech would unleash political feelings that had been pent up for many decades in many parts of the Soviet Union, including Georgia, Armenia, Azerbaijan, Kazakhstan, Latvia and Lithuania.[48] The feelings of antagonism towards the Soviet Union, to the Soviet leadership and to Soviet policies had been kept on a leash for many decades. When these feelings were brought into the open, the ideas that came with them were powerful. They gathered strength and caused severe demonstrations, again especially throughout the provinces and the Warsaw Pact nations to Russia's east.

This disintegration began on the periphery. There was mass dissent in the Baltic region. In 1987 Estonia demanded its autonomy. Lithuania and Latvia were not far behind. More than two million Baltic citizens would join hands in a human chain, stretching from Tallinn to Vilnius, to demonstrate their desire for independence. The southern republics began to move in similar directions. There were massive demonstrations through the southern parts of the country. Gorbachev refused to allow any secession that was being demanded, and thus began a civil war which continued for many years.

President Gorbachev had opened a Pandora's box. Nationalist movements emerged in Georgia, Ukraine, Moldova, Belarus and the Central Asian Republics. The power and influence of the central government was seriously weakened. By 1991 the Soviet Union had fallen apart and fifteen separate countries emerged. Nobody had predicted this. As a result, the United States was left supreme. The collapse of the Soviet Union was to unleash significant changes of attitude in the United States—unfortunately, changes that have not been beneficial.

On later occasions, I met Gorbachev and had long discussions with him. Because of his role he had a very high reputation in the West, but I was left with the feeling that when he was President, he did not really know what he was doing. He did not understand what free speech would do in a country where pent-up bitterness, disappointments and even hatreds of the central government could suddenly be expressed publicly. In economic policy, his policies were not sufficiently specific and were not well thought through. If, under perestroika, he had wished to rebuild the Soviet economy in a way that was much more congruent with the market-based system of the West, he had no idea where to begin or what policies to put in place. In any case, President Gorbachev's policies, along with the pressure applied by President Reagan's rearmament, were two of the reasons for the collapse of the Soviet Union and for the end of the Cold War.

This changed the world in dramatic ways. The fall of the Soviet Union was significantly responsible for consequential changes within the United States. The United States was now supreme. The restraint necessarily imposed by a competitive superpower no longer existed—the world moved from a bipolar system to a unipolar one. The ideas of American exceptionalism and manifest destiny, as the nation almost chosen by God to lead and to be supreme, became more often enunciated. It had always been there under the surface. The idea of American unilateralism dominated administrations post Cold War and, particularly, after the attacks of 11 September 2001. When the Soviet Union existed, the United States felt impelled to consult other countries and at least provide a façade of consultation when working with the other nations—such are the requirements of world dominated by a bipolar system. America then had to recognise that it was one of two superpowers in the world. With the collapse of the Soviet Union, the United States was left standing on top of the mountain alone. The combination of such circumstances has resulted in the century in which we now live not being one of peace and progress and of advancement of human kind but a century of conflict, division and fear.

For Australia, we did not realise that this was a time when we could have—and should have—started to assert a real Australian independent foreign policy. The need for strategic dependence had ended. There was no longer a global threat that endangered

Australia's security and prosperity. There was justification for reliance on the British Empire in the days up to World War II, although that reliance was misplaced. There was greater justification for working within the American system and with other Western countries during the dangerous Cold War. Solidarity among liberal democracies was critical. After the break-up of the Soviet Union, once the threat of communism spreading throughout the world had subsided, Australia's foreign policy priorities towards the remaining superpower should have changed. There was no longer any fear of attack or any reason for Australia to make its own best interests, and the interests of the region in which we live, subservient to earning the goodwill of the United States.

We should have noted that Canada had not joined the United States in Vietnam or in Iraq. Although Canada has the advantage of being geographically alongside the United States and therefore inevitably under American protection, and we have no such luxury, they still exhibited a degree of independence, which we have not. I have always believed that the United States respects those of an independent mind, so long as they can produce valid reasons for their point of view, and that they do not really respect a country that follows their directions, even if it is congruent with their own interests. Canada has shown how it is possible to exercise a degree of independence in relation to America, and to maintain a good relationship. It would not be beyond our capacity if we had the courage, the determination and the vision to enunciate policies clearly, to do likewise.

Unfortunately, we have not yet learnt the lesson that a smaller power never buys the goodwill of a major power by just doing what that major power wants. A degree of independence goes to respect and to a country's pride. In many things, the national interest of Australia will coincide with the national interest of the United States. Yet, on occasions when our national interests do not align, Australia should tell the United States that we cannot support it. We should have said this in relation to Vietnam. We also should have said this in relation to Iraq and Afghanistan. As it is believed Menzies did to President Eisenhower over Taiwan in the 1950s, our leaders should not be afraid to put our national interests ahead of those of a great power. On the contrary, we have followed America into three wars—Vietnam, Iraq and Afghanistan—and, whatever was believed at the time, and although Afghanistan had the sanction of the United Nations, at least in the initial stages, those wars have been three major international mistakes.

The post–World War II era is largely described as one of peace. Yet, if we consider the conflicts Australia has been involved in since, excluding peace-keeping operations and the six years during the occupation of Japan after World War II, then we have been at peace for less than thirty years since 1945. In the sixty-seven years since the conclusion of World War II, Australian soldiers have been involved in conflict, in one way or another, for more than half the entire time. Another way of looking at this is that Australia has been fighting different wars, some of them admittedly contemporaneously, for more than forty-eight years in the post-war period.[49] In hindsight we claim to be a peace-loving nation yet, on this basis, we are a nation that has hardly ever been at peace. This should give us pause to question our policies, the way we have supported our values. Surely we should question ourselves ruthlessly and determine to do better in the future.

On the disintegration of the Soviet Union, the United States and Australia both lost opportunities to contribute greatly to a better world. While the first President George Bush understood the need for a multilateral world, understood the need to work through the United Nations and through coalitions of nations to achieve major objectives, his view did not long prevail. This was a period in which those who believed in American exceptionalism—that America alone should determine policy for the future—gained great power and influence and changed the United States, perhaps for all time. This was a period when the United Nations could have become a most effective instrument, but the United States became impatient with its procedures and wanted to do what the United States itself determined. This was, of course, a major mistake.

Australia made a different kind of mistake. There were reasons for working very closely with the United States during the period of the Cold War. The Soviet Union had been regarded as an outward-thrusting aggressive force. Free nations of the world needed to cooperate closely; therefore they all needed to give up some element of their own independence to achieve a cooperative approach in helping to contain the Soviet Union. This in reality often meant supporting that which America wanted to do.

Since the main danger had disappeared, had been taken off the table, Australia should have reassessed its priorities. We should have enthusiastically understood that there was a chance for real independence—the first real chance in our history as a nation, and as a series of colonies before Federation, to establish a foreign policy designed to suit Australia's interests, to work for peace, cooperation and trust among all the nations of the Western Pacific and of East Asia. There would, of course, still have been many things on which we would agree with the United States, especially a United States that was willing to work multilaterally with other nations. But we would accept that there would be other issues in which our own and regional interests would be paramount and we would work with regional partners and neighbours.

Part III

A time to end strategic dependence

'I believe America is exceptional'
BARACK OBAMA

9

The new unipolar world

With the break-up of the Soviet Union and the end of the communist threat, there was an unprecedented opportunity to work for a better world. A key part of how the new world order would be shaped rested with the United States as the only remaining superpower. As the remnants of the former Soviet Union formed independent republics across Europe and Asia, the vision for the world set by Washington was to be an important indication of how the post–Cold War era would be shaped. President George Bush Snr exemplified the possibilities of that world in a speech made to Congress on 6 March 1991.[1] He had a wide experience in international affairs. He knew what was necessary to calm old enmities but, perhaps more important, what was necessary to preserve and strengthen alliances and bring those former enemies into the community of nations.

Bush Snr started the post–Cold War era positively. If the hopes, ideals and pragmatism exhibited in that speech to Congress had still governed US policy, we would indeed be facing a different world today. I believe we would be part of a more cooperative and peaceful world. In his speech, given against the backdrop of the first Gulf War, President Bush Snr pointed out that the victory over Iraq was 'a victory for every country in the coalition … for unprecedented international cooperation and diplomacy … for the rule of law and for what is right'.[2] The victory of Desert Storm was a coalition effort in the best multilateral sense. It was a coalition that involved nations from every part of the world, but especially from the Middle East. It was not a Western war; it was an international effort. There were more than thirty countries in that coalition. It had the approval of the United Nations. It provides a stark contrast to the second Gulf War led by his son a decade later.

The purpose of his speech to Congress was to speak of the world after the break-up of the Soviet Union and after the first Gulf War. He wanted the world to know of a new international view in Washington. The issues in the conflict had been clear. Saddam Hussein had invaded and occupied Kuwait.

> Tonight, I come to this House to speak about the world—the world after war. The recent challenge could not have been clearer. Saddam Hussein was the villain; Kuwait, the victim. To the aid of this small country came nations from North America and Europe, from Asia and South America, from Africa and the Arab world, all united against aggression. Our uncommon coalition must now work in common purpose: to forge a future that should never again be held hostage to the darker side of human nature.[3]

President Bush Snr not only understood the necessity of military power, he also understood its limitations. The United Nations resolution legalising the war restricted itself to safeguarding Kuwait's independent future.[4] It did not mandate the occupation of Iraq; it did not mandate regime change. This was not accidental. President Bush Snr came under quite extensive criticism in the aftermath of the war for not marching on to Baghdad and destroying Saddam Hussein, but his reasons for not doing so were substantial, indeed overwhelming. Of particular importance was the need to keep the agreement his government made with the international community, thereby building trust in America's leadership and willingness to play by internationally acceptable rules and norms.[5]

The President understood the reality of Iraq. It was an uneasy combination of Kurds, Sunnis and Shias. The religious animosities between the religious factions had been kept in check by a ruthless and cruel dictator. It would have been easy to overthrow Saddam Hussein at that time but then, as we have learnt from the second Gulf War, the question of replacing him with a viable, peaceful, united government that represented all factions in Iraq and was able to maintain the peace has proved to be beyond the capacity of the United States and the Coalition of the Willing.

President Bush Snr understood that overwhelming military power would not create the peaceful and democratic substitute for Saddam Hussein. Tempting as it must have been, and despite the urgings of some considerable people, he refused to be seduced to an end that would only end in disaster, as it has ten years later, under President Bush Jnr.[6]

In his speech to Congress, President Bush Snr concentrated on the practical realities of creating a better world. He said:

> First, we must work together to create shared security arrange-
> ments in the region. Our friends and allies in the Middle East
> recognize that they will bear the bulk of the responsibility for
> regional security. But we want them to know that just as we stood
> with them to repel aggression, so now America stands ready to
> work with them to secure the peace. This does not mean station-
> ing US ground forces in the Arabian Peninsula, but it does mean
> American participation in joint exercises involving both air and
> ground forces. It means maintaining a capable US naval presence
> in the region, just as we have for over 40 years. Let it be clear:
> our vital national interests depend on a stable and secure Gulf.[7]

President Bush Snr spoke of the need to control the prolifera-
tion of weapons of mass destruction and missiles needed to deliver
them; the need to prevent, in the wake of the war, a new arms race;
the need for Iraq to convince the world of its peaceful intentions,
something which Saddam Hussein unfortunately failed to do. Bush
spoke also of the need to create a 'new momentum for peace'. He

understood that security does not depend upon military power alone. He spoke of the dispute between Israel and its neighbours, who 'for the first time found themselves confronting the same aggressor'.[8] He wanted to strengthen the United Nations; he wanted to work multi-laterally in partnership, in cooperation and remove the deadlocks that plagued the Security Council during the animosities of the Cold War. He was not frightened of American leadership where and when it was necessary, but did not want to work alone, unilaterally putting America above all others. He wanted a new world order.[9]

President Bush Snr understood the difference between power and strength. Power alone involves military capacity, technical and, in some cases, numerical superiority. Power is necessary for strength, but strength is much more than power. Strength comes from an attitude of mind: a sense of serious purpose and understanding that one must work with others through diplomacy and compromise. Understanding difference and working with that difference shows true strength. Power alone will seldom, if ever, achieve a political objective. The possession of strength in these terms is essential for world leadership. President Bush Snr showed a better understanding of the limitations of military power than many who had preceded him and his son, who later succeeded him.

As somebody who actively participated in World War II, President Bush Snr knew of the hopes that emerge at the end of conflict, the desire for enduring peace and the tragedy when that possibility proves beyond reach. With the end of the Soviet Union, the possibility for an enduring peace and cessation of ideological conflict was there once again. Bush had learnt much from his time as Vice President under Reagan about the role of power, particularly great power, and the responsibilities with which it comes. For example, at the beginning of the Falklands War in 1982, people like Jeane Kirkpatrick, US Ambassador to the United Nations, and Thomas Enders, Assistant Secretary for Latin American Affairs, were both arguing fiercely that the United States should preserve the purity of the Monroe Doctrine and support Argentina against America's strongest ally in Europe and strongest partner in NATO, the United

Kingdom. The British were 'apoplectic about the conduct of the Reagan Administration, particularly its Ambassador to the United Nations, Jeane Kirkpatrick, who made no secret of her sympathies for the Argentine regime—it was a "right-wing", not a "left-wing" dictatorship'.[10] Washington, and Kirkpatrick in particular, proved to be Britain's major obstacle to freeing the islanders.

There were many right-wing dictatorships that had been supported by the United States in Latin America, including Fulgencio Batista in Cuba and Augusto Pinochet in Chile. So, from that point of view, Kirkpatrick was not out of line.[11] More seriously, the British Ambassador to the United States during the crisis, Sir Nicholas Harrison, concluded that Kirkpatrick and the State Department had played 'an untoward role in helping to persuade the Argentine generals that they could get away with occupying the Falklands.'[12] According to this report, they were advising Argentina that Britain would not fight. Bush Snr saw the folly of such moves and made sure that Kirkpatrick lost the argument when the United States came to decide on the issue, ultimately agreeing to support the United Kingdom. Such debates cast doubt on the reliability of the United States as an ally.

Indeed, during Thatcher's time there were a number of disputes that could have led to a major rift between President Reagan and Prime Minister Thatcher. In addition to the Falklands, the President did not accept Thatcher's views of President Gorbachev or her views relating to a reduction of nuclear arms. Reagan's invasion of Grenada, a member of the British Commonwealth, without informing the British, could easily have burst into a major public dispute. This is not a good record for the special relationship.[13] If even during the tensions of the Cold War Britain and the special relationship were subject to the whims of American strategic objectives, what faith can Australia have in the United States choosing to side with us should the need arise? Would it choose us over Indonesia, for example? Do decades of close relations and historic similarities count for more than immediate strategic objectives? As the examples above and evidence I have pointed to in previous chapters indicate, I have serious concerns as to whether America would indeed side with Australia in an hour of need.

George Bush Snr learnt from these experiences and wanted to seize the moment and opportunity that the end of the Cold War gave the world. In the way he conducted the first Gulf War, he demonstrated the importance of the United Nations and of getting as large and as broadly based a coalition as possible in support of the war. This view was especially important in the Middle East. In his intervention in Somalia, he also made sure that there was appropriate UN support and the support of troops from other nations, including Australia.[14] On a broader understanding of events, his influence over the Falklands War was substantial. None of this should be surprising.[15] Bush focused on foreign policy that was designed to 'manage relationships between states' rather than one that sought 'to alter the nature of states' as his son did a decade later.[16] Perhaps the most important paragraph in his speech was one in which he said:

> Now, we can see a new world coming into view. A world in which there is the very real prospect of a new world order. In the words of Winston Churchill, a world order in which 'the principles of justice and fair play protect the weak against the strong' ... A world where the United Nations, freed from cold war stalemate, is poised to fulfil the historic vision of its founders. A world in which freedom and respect for human rights find a home among all nations. The Gulf war put this new world to its first test. And my fellow Americans, we passed that test.[17]

This was the America we all wanted to see, to hear. This is the America we wanted to see lead, in partnership with other nations, to move the world forward in peace, in a shared sense of security, providing greater opportunity for poorer nations to advance the prospects of their own people and to establish an effective and appropriate level of authority for the United Nations. It was the America the post–Cold War world needed yet, as the decade progressed, it was an America that the world would not get. The expansion of NATO is an example of how the post–Cold War world began to move away from the optimism and cooperative approach elucidated by Bush Snr and exemplified by the first Gulf War. The schism that expanding the alliance would have on West–Russian relations would become more manifest over the years and continues to this day with nations such as Georgia being courted for inclusion in NATO. The foundation for this conflict was formed during the 1990s.

In 1989, as the Berlin Wall came down, moves to unite East and West Germany were begun, and NATO itself started looking for a new role. With the disintegration of the Soviet Union, NATO's job was, in effect, accomplished—an enormous success. It had been established to prevent the spread of the Soviet Union into Western Europe as part of a major containment strategy. It worked beyond expectation. It had held together the nations of Western Europe, which had been combatants for centuries. Yet, after the fall of the Soviet Union, was NATO to have a role? Was it to disappear? Was there room for the alliance in this post–Cold War world? It was regarded as an important part of the North Atlantic diplomatic and security structure, in the great and successful experiment to help unify Europe and also to maintain the trans-atlantic alliance. For the European Union it was important that NATO be preserved. An important part of its fabric would have been destroyed if it were unwound. There were those who argued that NATO should develop a role to help preserve peace and to establish order beyond the boundaries of NATO. That alone would have been a useful function and should have contributed to cohesion in Europe. There were many, both within and outside NATO, who wanted more for the alliance.

There was also the question of Germany. West Germany was in NATO, East Germany a key part of the Warsaw Pact. West Germany was going to work for unification. It would be difficult, if not impossible, to have part of Germany in NATO and part not. Various compromises were discussed. The issues were difficult. Both sides of a unified Germany needed to be on an equal footing; otherwise division would remain.

Some of the former Warsaw Pact countries clamoured to join NATO, with such Eastern European leaders as Vaclav Havel and Lech

Walesa, presidents of the Czech Republic and Poland respectively, pushing Washington to expand the alliance.[18] There were those in the West, President Clinton especially, who pressed for the expansion of NATO.[19] His administration would claim that NATO expansion increased the security of European nations and made Russia a partner of the West.[20] Clinton would say that the 'grey zone of insecurity must not re-emerge in Europe'.[21] Further, the administration was concerned about instability in some of the embryonic states emancipated from the Warsaw Pact and that expansion would assist in the transition to pluralistic democracies. Although at that stage membership of the European Union would have been premature, membership of NATO seemed to be regarded as some kind of halfway house. The United States, and President Clinton especially, and many in Europe were pushing for the expansion of NATO eastward.

There were those who also argued that a movement east would assist the democratisation of Russia.[22] That shows the unreality, the naivety, of a number of those advising and forming United States and European Union policy. It is a little difficult to expect an organisation designed to defend Western Europe against a Soviet attack to become an instrument in the increasing democratisation of Russia. Indeed Russian President Putin himself said in 2008 that 'NATO is not a democratizer'.[23]

Henry Kissinger argued that a democratic Kremlin was far from assured and that 'though Russia might have lost its empire it did not lose its imperial ambition'.[24] The common view was that an enlarged NATO would become a protection against a resurgent Russia, thus giving weight to Russia's concerns. The inclusion of Ukraine and Georgia in expansion plans has caused particular consternation in Moscow, with President Putin telling NATO leaders at their 2008 conference that the 'appearance of a powerful military bloc on our borders will be taken by Russia as a direct threat to the security of our country'.[25]

As Putin's comments above indicate, the foundation of a major strategic mistake was being laid during the 1990s. Mary Elise Sarotte, professor of history and international relations at the University of

Southern California, describes in detail the diplomatic moves that were made at that time and the efforts to satisfy both Germany and Russia.[26] In the negotiations Gorbachev made mistakes and did not get written agreements to his central proposition that NATO should not move east. I can understand Gorbachev making that mistake; he was not good at tying down a point or following through to make sure that his understanding was shared.

President Clinton persuaded himself that expansion of NATO was not anti-Russian and that expansion would help Russia by 'stabilising a historically volatile region'.[27] That would not have been credible to Russia. This was pointed out in an open letter to President Clinton by a number of high-profile Americans, who argued: 'NATO expansion, which continues to be opposed across the entire political spectrum, will strengthen the non-democratic opposition, undercut those who favour reform and cooperation with the West, bring the Russians to question the entire post-Cold War settlement.'[28]

Perhaps President Clinton was ignorant of the history of Eastern Europe, ignorant of Russia's sphere of interest, going back for centuries before communist times. If Clinton had meant what he said—that it would help Russia manage that region—then why not include Russia itself in NATO, or reorganise the alliance to include Russia as a part of the North Atlantic security infrastructure? Such a concept was never addressed and, as far as I have been able to find, never raised.

Future Russian leaders would conclude that America would never regard Russia as a cooperative and collaborative partner in major international events; that America would always pursue its own advantage at the expense of any nation, including Russia. Russia therefore would have to rebuild its own strength and look out for its own interests. Under President Putin and under President Medvedev, this is certainly what has happened. The consequences have been to compound problems in the Middle East, particularly relationships with Syria and Iran. The consequences are continuing.

NATO should have enjoyed its victory, subdued and modest, not boastful and certainly not aggressively. The pact should have refashioned European security to include Russia, not continue to hedge against it by buttressing the Western European states with the newly formed republics in the east. It was not only decisions around NATO that would continue to have implications for American and Western foreign policy throughout the 1990s. Conflicts and humanitarian crises in Africa and the former Yugoslavia would have a considerable influence on how the United States viewed its role and the role of its allies, including NATO. It would affect the behaviour, particularly of Washington, in international events up to the attacks of September 11.

In December 1992 President Bush Snr undertook a major military humanitarian intervention in Somalia, the first of its kind. A number of countries participated, including Australia. It had the sanction and support of the United Nations.[29] The purpose of this intervention was simply to enable aid so desperately needed in Somalia to be delivered safely. Unfortunately, at the end of President Bush Snr's time and in the beginning of President Clinton's, the mission somehow went astray.

The American military commander had become the UN special envoy. However good they might have been at military affairs, they were not good at diplomacy and understanding the nature and the culture of Somalia. They had no capacity to try to reduce divisions between the three warring factions, especially after a US helicopter was shot down over Mogadishu and eighteen American soldiers were humiliated and killed. The mission changed. It was no longer a mission to enable aid to be distributed safely; it became a mission to hunt General Aidid, which was ultimately unsuccessful. This led to a crisis of confidence in the mission as a whole, leading to considerable loss of life and to the ultimate withdrawal of the US-led UN mission in March 1995. Yet it also had a flow-on effect, which influenced American confidence in conducting other humanitarian and peace-keeping missions in the future.[30]

President Clinton had come into office in January 1993. President Clinton was from a different background and a different mould from the President he replaced. He was outgoing and certainly had

great charm, but he was much more of a domestic American politician with little knowledge of broader international events. He was,
however, a quick learner, but he made some terrible mistakes, some
of which he has admitted. For example, it was on his watch that
the genocide in Rwanda occurred, an occurrence of gross proportions made possible by a failure to act by both the United States
and the broader international community. Clinton would later
take responsibility for it, saying: 'I blew it ... I feel terrible about
it, and all I can ever do is tell them truth ... and try to make it
up to them.'[31]

Perhaps Clinton's attention was never really focused on Africa.[32]
Certainly the genocide in Rwanda could have been prevented if
action had been taken either by the United States or by the European
Union or, for that matter, by the United Nations. Ignorance was no
defence. The United States knew what was happening, and briefings
from the CIA would have emphasised the point.[33] That tragic inaction led to up to one million being killed, up to 250,000 women
being raped[34] and tens of thousands dying from cholera as refugees fled to camps near Goma, in the Democratic Republic of the
Congo.[35] This was also during a time when both the United States
and the European Union were coming to be heavily involved in
discussion concerning the future of Europe and the future of NATO.
Their attention was diverted from Africa, exacerbated by its lack of
strategic importance in the post–Cold War era.

It was not just African concerns that faced the Clinton Administration. In 1998 the Kosovo War was a major event on the new
NATO's agenda. It was a war that created deep divisions within
Europe itself. It was nevertheless giving birth to a new role for
NATO,[36] one that could have been a constructive force in peace-
keeping or even in peace-making, supplanting perhaps the national
forces from individual member states in different parts of the world.
If that had been NATO's role with its original membership, that
would have been understandable, it would have been sensible and
productive, but for many that was not enough as we have seen in
NATO's own expansion east.

The Kosovo War demonstrated deep divisions in Europe, including among the members of NATO.[37] Many, Germany in particular, including Helmut Schmidt, former Chancellor, believed the mission to be totally wrong. The main driver had been British Prime Minister Tony Blair, who had adopted missionary zeal in efforts to bring President Clinton alongside, so that America would take a leadership role in the fight against Serbia.[38] Certainly Serbia had lost respect and support as a result of the massacres at Srebrenica of Bosnian Muslims. The atrocities committed by Belgrade were abhorrent. But that does not excuse the partisanship of subsequent actions by the United States and NATO.

In 1998 the US State Department removed the Kosovo Liberation Army (KLA) from its list of terrorist organisations. It had to do so because of the support the United States was giving to the KLA. The *Wall Street Journal* reported that in January 1998 the US Special Envoy to Bosnia, Robert Gelbard, said, 'The Kosovo Liberation Army is an Islamic terrorist organisation. We strongly condemn terrorist actions in Kosovo, the UCK (KLA) is without any question a terrorist group.'[39] The KLA was in fact closely allied to the Albanians. Albania was the main route for running drugs into Europe.[40] There was no doubt that the KLA financed a significant part of its operations as a result of the drug trade.

In addition, during the Bosnian War, according to William Shawcross in *Deliver Us From Evil*, the United States not only condoned but also encouraged Croatian ethnic cleansing of Serbs from the Krajina, some of whom had been there as farmers for hundreds of years.[41] The largest ethnic cleansing, involving the displacement of more than 250,000 people and which actually took place in the Balkans, was hardly mentioned and never condemned by NATO or the West. Partiality and special pleading dominated the conflict.

These Serbian refugees were the people whom CARE International and CARE Australia were assisting as a result of events during the Bosnian war. CARE's job was to provide heating oil and what food it could. Ethnic cleansing by the Croatians received no notice, no criticism.[42]

Madeleine Albright, as US Secretary of State, seemed to be a perfect instrument in the manipulation of such policies. She organised a conference at Rambouillet that was meant to avoid war and come to a settlement. In reality, the Rambouillet conference was designed by Albright to give the United States and NATO an opportunity to start bombing Serbia. She is reported to have believed that four or five days bombing would bring Milosevic to heel. But the campaign went on for seventy-eight days; some suburbs were flattened. The terms at Rambouillet were so harsh that no Serbian leader could have accepted them. They were much harsher than the terms ultimately agreed at the end of the war. If the final settlement terms had been presented to Milosevic at Rambouillet, he might well have accepted them.

Henry Kissinger, former United States Secretary of State, was reported in London's *Daily Telegraph* on 28 June 1999 in this way: 'The Rambouillet text, which called on Serbia to admit NATO troops throughout Yugoslavia, was a provocation, an excuse to start bombing. Rambouillet is not a document that an angelic Serb could have accepted. It was a terrible diplomatic document that should never have been presented in that form.'[43]

Throughout the Kosovo campaign, NATO and the West showed a partisanship in relation to the Kosovo War that did not bode well for future peace-keeping operations. The claim that the Kosovo War was a humanitarian operation cannot be sustained. In his book, William Shawcross details the partisanship and the complicity of NATO and the United States in these terrible conflicts.[44]

This brief mention of the Kosovo War is relevant to this book because it is one example of the way in which great power relationships play themselves out. Great powers, by virtue of being a great power, do not have to be in the right and, in many cases, are not. They can be motivated by expediency, prejudice and special pleading. We should not want our foreign policy to be too heavily influenced by such powers. They can outline great and wonderful ideals for the world, much like Bush Snr did as the Berlin Wall came crashing down. Yet they can also bend principles and lean on allies to suit their immediate—and sometimes erroneous—strategic needs. Although the errors of the 1990s were serious, the United States after 9/11 and the Bush Jnr Administration once and for all quashed any hope of a post–Cold War order based on cooperation, understanding and compromise.

When President Bush Jnr came into office in 2001, about twenty neo-conservative members of the American Enterprise Institute went to work in the White House. His administration included senior neo-conservative people elevated to high office, such as Dick Cheney as Vice President, Donald Rumsfeld as Secretary of Defense, and Paul Wolfowitz as Deputy Secretary of Defense. It was a high point of neo-conservatism control over key offices of government. They were deeply imbued with the ideas of American exceptionalism and the use of American power and the determination to make America secure for the future. They believed that the world needed to be changed, in America's image. It would seem the world had to change but America would not.

The United States was caught unaware by the attacks of 9/11. The world was stunned. There was still great goodwill towards America as a result of its leadership role in the first Gulf War and as a result of the end of the Cold War, despite the happenings of the 1990s as discussed above. Worldwide sympathy for America was substantial. The attacks were bound to change, profoundly and deeply, the way the United States would respond to international events.

President Bush Jnr announced the War on Terror. For some time the United States had worldwide support as a consequence of 9/11. Perhaps that began to change because of the manner of President Bush Jnr's response. His famous comment: 'Either you are with us, or you are with the terrorists', left no room for discussion concerning the best way to overcome fundamentalist terrorism. Indeed the subsequent line of Bush's speech read: 'From this day forward, any nation that continues to harbour or support terrorism will be regarded by the United States as a hostile regime.'[45] This speech made a fundamentally grey and complex issue black and white, delineating good from evil. Such comment jarred in many quarters around the world.

Al Qaeda were believed to be hiding out in Afghanistan; President Bush Jnr demanded that they be handed over. The Taliban Government refused, so a war against Afghanistan, sanctioned by the United Nations, began. There is no doubt that, whether sanctioned by the United Nations or not, America would have gone to war against the Taliban. The Taliban Government was fairly quickly defeated. Afghanistan was heavily bombed. After about three weeks, Secretary of Defense Rumsfeld said there were no more targets to attack.[46] Only after twelve years is the war winding down.

The hunt for Al Qaeda and the global effort against Islamic terrorism were seriously weakened when the Bush Administration decided it was going to invade Iraq; the first regime change of the three rogue states nominated by President Bush Jnr, the others being Iran and North Korea. From this time onwards there is little doubt about the direction of American policy and its impact on the so-called Axis of Evil; a policy made all the more likely given the deep wounds inflicted on the American psyche by 9/11.

To show the gulf between that philosophy and that of President Bush Snr, former Secretaries of State James Baker and Larry Eagleburger and former National Security Advisor Brent Scowcroft all counselled President Bush Jnr, in the days before he went to war, that it was not a war America should start.[47] James Baker, in particular, was concerned that America should not go to war in Iraq alone. He wanted a broadly based coalition. Baker used these words: 'The costs in all areas will be much greater, as will the political risks, both domestic and international, if we end up going it alone or with only one or two countries.'[48] Brent Scowcroft, with wide experience in national security affairs had this to say: 'Our pre-eminent security priority—underscored repeatedly by the President—is the war on terrorism. An attack on Iraq at this time would seriously jeopardize, if not destroy, the global counterterrorist campaign we have undertaken.'[49] Both comments were prophetic. The loyalty of these men to President George H. Bush was absolute. Not one of them would have made the statement if they had not had clearance from the President, if he had not agreed that the statements should be made.

There has been much speculation about the cause of that war, about the actual reasons for it. It was a known diversion from the War on Terror, which President Bush Jnr had earlier announced and which led to the invasion of Afghanistan. It was known that the idea of weapons of mass destruction was, in large part, a fabrication. The United States was not getting the information it wanted from its usual intelligence sources and therefore Donald Rumsfeld established a special unit in the Defense Department designed to cherry-pick intelligence to provide what the Bush Administration wanted.[50] Douglas Feith was appointed to achieve this purpose.

Douglas Feith, former Undersecretary of Defense for Policy, was a close associate of other neo-conservatives, including Richard Perle and Paul Wolfowitz. He had been appointed as Undersecretary of Defense for Policy in 2001. Supervising the Pentagon Office of Special Plans, his office 'was predisposed to finding a significant relationship between Iraq and al Qaeda' and 'drew conclusions that were not fully supported by the available intelligence'.[51] The Office of Special Plans was dismantled and criticised by Congress and the media, with 'General Tommy Franks, who led both the 2001 invasion of Afghanistan and the Iraq War, once call[ing] Feith "the dumbest fucking guy on the planet"'.[52]

The United States, the United Kingdom and Australia would only have had to wait two or three months for the end of the Blix enquiry to have the absence of weapons of mass destruction con-firmed.[53] Although there are views that Iraq was invaded for oil, or to complete a half-finished job, it is more credible that President Bush Jnr went to war to advance the principles enunciated in 1997 by the neo-conservatives: to promote democracy by force of arms in Iraq. And this leads to a second change in strategic context in the post–Cold War era: changes in the domestic political make-up of the United States. Coupled with a changed American international out-look brought about by the attacks of September 11 and the ensuing War on Terror, the rise of neo-conservatism and the growing influ-ence of American exceptionalism have changed America as a nation and, importantly for Australia, as an ally.

The changes in the global context since the end of the Cold War have been profound, both in terms of the missed opportunities first elucidated by Bush Snr and in terms of the role the United States has adopted since the fall of the twin towers. The end of the communist threat should have changed the world for the better—it has not. Although the ideological struggles of the twentieth century might have ended, atrocities in Africa and Yugoslavia were allowed to happen, Russia was not brought into the fold and religious animosities have been fed by the War on Terror. In this context, Australia needs to consider whether its position is best suited by continuing its policy of strategic dependence, particularly given that the United States shoulders much, not all, but much of the blame for how the new international order the world hoped for in 1990 has been derailed.

10

In God we trust

The foreign policy history of the United States is one of extremes, oscillating between distant isolationism and extreme interventionism. For example, when President Wilson, the reluctant entrant into the Great War, went into the post–World War I discussions, idealistically arguing for the League of Nations, the American Congress turned its back on that high ideal. Members of Congress did not want to have any part in world affairs, especially if European states were involved. This was the period of isolation, of withdrawal. During this period the United States had no aspirations for any kind of world leadership and little interest in affairs outside its own region of influence.

World War II, however, led to great changes. This was a period in which the United States amassed enormous wealth and power. America was certainly the wealthiest nation in the world and, on some counts, the most powerful, but that judgement had to be made with caution because the Soviet Union also had very significant military and strategic power. The two superpowers competed for influence, for authority and for ideological ascendency. Neither wanted a nuclear war, and therefore both powers were careful not to tread too strongly in areas where the other might have a significant national interest. There were occasional lapses from that degree of restraint, but the desire to avoid a nuclear war prevented those lapses turning into a disaster.

Despite great power, the United States was, in this period, restrained by the presence and power of the Soviet Union. The fall of the Soviet Union led to a very significant change as, for the first time, America was supreme, economically and militarily, and without strategic competition. There were no challengers, no rivals; no other nation came close to the military, economic and, indeed, cultural power of the United States. It was in this period that we began to see America for what America is today.

The impact of September 11 on the United States has been profound. Yet other fundamental changes were emerging, particularly in the domestic make-up of American society and, as a result, in American political discourse before those atrocious attacks. The United States since the early 1990s has become a different country. Although American exceptionalism has been ever present through its history, the idea has become more dominant in US politics. It is based on a belief that the United States was predestined to expand democracy, if possible, worldwide. To those who subscribe to the view of exceptionalism, the United States remains 'the beacon of light in the darkness and the defender of the rights of man as long as the nation exists … America and Americans are exceptional because they are charged with saving the world from itself.'[1] During the Cold War this sentiment was kept in check by the Soviet Union; before it by the European powers. Since the 1990s, however, there has been no strategic counterbalance to US power and therefore no one keeping a lid on America's belief in its own exceptionalism.

In tandem with growing sentiments about American exceptionalism, the policies of the neo-conservatives, based in no small part on the notion of manifest destiny, began to gain influence during this period.[2] The idea that worldwide democracy is needed to make America safe from challenge or attack has taken hold in the United States. Since it has become the only superpower, the United States has also been infected by a sense of triumphalism, of superiority and of righteous destiny. It is no longer the same America from which Australia sought protection and friendship during World War II and throughout the Cold War.

It is not surprising that Australian leaders did not realise this in the early 1990s. Nonetheless, the changes in the United States have made it not only desirable but also critically important for us to establish a greater degree of strategic independence. This would not involve the denial of ANZUS; it would involve calling ANZUS back to its original meaning, to its original intent.

There are too many who have probably not read the ANZUS Treaty and are unaware of the spirit in which it was concluded. It is a treaty to consult if there should be an attack on the territory or forces of the United States or of Australia in the Pacific. Following consultation, it is possible that military support could follow. It is not automatic that America would come to our aid. It is not inevitable and, on America's side, it may require the passing of a War Powers Act through Congress. We have never fought a war with America that has been covered by the terms of the ANZUS Treaty. If we had, then surely the treaty would have been invoked. We need to advise the United States that we will no longer automatically follow it into the wars that it pursues; in other words, it no longer has our *carte blanche* support. We need the chance to decide, for ourselves, whether a proposed US course of action is in the best interests of Australia.

At the time the first President Bush was outlining his view of the post–Cold War order, I thought that his objectives were so obvious that nobody could oppose them. They were so obvious that experienced diplomats and political leaders would have the good sense to grasp the possibilities and not squander or destroy them by mistaken and foolish decisions. Perhaps such hopes represented a naive idealism on my behalf. Yet these possibilities were destroyed as a result of foolish policy decisions, some of which I have outlined above in regard to NATO, Africa and the War on Terror. Although these decisions were undoubtedly influenced by the global context, they were as much a result of the philosophy and attitudes of those who believed in American exceptionalism and manifest destiny; by those who believe, almost fanatically, that the United States is a unique nation, quite literally chosen by God to create the world in its image. Such sentiments have been expressed by American leaders in the past. For example President Reagan spoke of a 'divine plan' for America, quoting Pope Pius XII in saying: 'Into the hands of America God has placed the destinies of an afflicted mankind.'[3] President Bush Jnr also referred to a divine mission, stating: 'We have a calling from beyond the stars to stand for freedom.'[4]

Such political leaders become missionaries for a cause. They cease to look at the facts of a situation; they believe their own instincts, and that conversations with God give them an absolute right to do what they think best, because what America thinks best is indeed best by definition. Such views, together with the emergence of neo-conservatives, destroyed the dream elucidated by Bush Snr and which I had hoped would become reality.

American exceptionalism is not a new thing. Alexis de Tocqueville was writing about the position of Americans 'as quite exceptional' in 1840.[5] As a broad notion, it has existed throughout most of America's history in one form or another. It is a motivating force in American political affairs that has done enormous damage to the United States and, indeed, to the entire world.

Morton Abramowitz, US Ambassador for Turkey and Thailand, and one of the founders of the International Crisis Group, wrote in 2012 that American exceptionalism, the belief that the United States is a uniquely virtuous country—indeed, the greatest force for good—'dooms United States foreign policy'.[6] Abramowitz wrote that the United States constantly reminds many countries, particularly China, that if they wish to be part of the international community they must play by the rules. He wrote: 'China, the greatest rule breaker in the US rule book, has not invaded any country since 1978, and then it was for three weeks. It is hard to remember all the times we have invaded countries—or just bombarded or attacked them incessantly with drones—covertly or overtly, without any international benediction. The United States is allowed to violate its own rules, as long as it serves our security and other interests as every administration defines them.'[7] In other words, America's sense of exceptionalism and manifest destiny puts it apart from other states.

In a similar vein on American exceptionalism, Paul Pillar, a twenty-eight-year veteran of the CIA, wrote:

> It encourages the mistaken belief that American values and political institutions, because they are deemed superior to anyone else's, will be readily accepted and understood by non-Americans. It makes it difficult for Americans to see the negative sides of what many non-Americans see, fairly or unfairly, in the United States. It thus is difficult for Americans to understand anti-Americanism. It encourages inconsistent one-way application of principles, which often provide another source of resentment of the United States. Americans see nothing wrong, for example, with rejecting having the International Criminal Court exercise jurisdiction over US citizens while the United States asserts its own extraterritorial jurisdiction over many crimes that occur in other countries. It leads to the mistaken belief the principles of international relations do not apply to the United States as they apply to other countries.[8]

In particular, however, it inhibits any understanding on the part of American leaders of the limitations of what America can achieve in foreign policy. Vietnam, Afghanistan and the second Iraq war are all strong examples of this—military power alone cannot create a benign democracy in America's image, but it can incur an immense human cost. Systems and institutions that work in America will not automatically work in other nations by virtue of the fact that they are American systems and institutions. The idiosyncrasies of each individual country differ and need to be taken into account when considering how a nation's society and polity are structured. American leaders, particularly since the War on Terror was announced, have been unable to grasp this fact. They have often acted with little knowledge of, or scant regard for, the history and culture of other nations.

One of the reasons for American exceptionalism is that the United States shares a fault found in many nations, including in Australia. It is often very hard for a country to look at its own history the way others see it. A lack of critical self-reflection and awareness can be a dangerous thing for any nation, but can be dangerous for many more nations when it relates to a superpower.

If we wish to make progress with other nations, if we really want to win the diplomatic argument where we think we are right, it is necessary to be able to do two things. The first is to really try to understand the nature and facts of a dispute and, in particular, the person with whom you are negotiating; to ask what will they regard as reasonable, or possible. What will they be able to accept, so that they return to their own country with head held high? It is necessary to understand the causes of the argument and how it arose from the other person's point of view as well as from your own. If we do not have this understanding, and a sense of the limits of what we can ask or what we can demand of others, we will never make progress. Second, it is equally important to be able to see, in unvarnished terms, how other countries see us, to see what they expect of us. When we are heavily influenced by our own myths, by our own national interpretations of ourselves, it is often very difficult to make these distinctions. It is particularly difficult for the most powerful nation in the world.

For example, the attitude of President Reagan and Prime Minister Thatcher to South Africa represents a case in point. To both of them, the African National Congress was composed of terrorists and communists. Indeed, Thatcher claimed that the 'ANC is a typical terrorist organisation ... anyone who thinks it is going to run the government in South Africa is living in cloud-cuckoo land.'[9] For Reagan and Thatcher, the ANC was dangerous. As a consequence, without avowedly saying so, they both did what they could to support the Afrikaner government, particularly through the Reagan Administration's policy of constructive engagement. When the US Congress passed the Comprehensive Anti-Apartheid Act of 1986, a sanctions bill, President Reagan, vetoed it.[10] This was one of the very rare occasions when Congress mustered the overwhelming numbers needed to override a presidential veto.[11] Neither Thatcher nor Reagan understood the nature of the ANC, or the problem.[12]

During the 1980s I had a CIA report on the ANC in which the CIA itself made it clear that the ANC were nationalists, not communists. The report noted that, since they could get no support from the United States or the United Kingdom, they went to communist countries for support. The CIA was firmly of the view that it was a nationalist organisation, fighting for equality.

I have heard many Americans, active in public life, say that the United States has never gone to war except to fight for the freedom of others. How many Americans are aware that there are many examples of American aggression throughout history? As long-time editor of *The National Interest* Owen Harries points out, hard-headed realism is also very much part of the American character. Throughout American history, this realism has led to the use of force against the American Indians, the Mexicans in Texas and California and the Spanish in the Philippines.[13] Harries could also have suggested the African Americans, many of whom had joined the fight to end slavery. American leaders need to reflect on this past when deciding to militarise an argument in the present and ask whether they are making the same mistakes they made previously.

Perhaps the American campaign in relation to the Philippines had a touch both of realism and of American exceptionalism. 'President McKinley said that the decision to take the Philippines came to him one night when he got down on his knees and prayed, and God told him to take the Philippines.'[14] None of this sits well with the idea of going to war only to fight for the freedom of others. We need to be suspicious of those who claim to have advice from God. To claim God is on your side is no guarantee of virtue.

The idea of American exceptionalism, which has, in one form or another, existed since the birth of America with Jefferson, through Woodrow Wilson to the present, has never excluded the most ruthless acts. Those ordering and involved in these ruthless acts have not seen any contradiction in their actions, even if they mimic the actions of an enemy that American finds immoral or bellicose. Just as past great powers have done before it, America has convinced itself that it is different and better than the rest. It is allowed to operate using a different set of rules from the rest of the world. Yet, ultimately, 'the United States has behaved like all the rest, pursuing its own self-interest first and foremost, seeking to improve its relative position overtime, and devoting relatively little blood or treasure to purely idealistic pursuits'.[15]

The notion of exceptionalism through this history is also tied to a sense of justice and how to achieve it. A noticeable example of the difference between Americans and other nations is found in comparing the acceptability of the use of force to obtain justice. In repeated surveys, the German Marshall Fund has found a divergence between American and European Union citizens on this measure, with the latest survey indicating that 74 per cent of Americans thought it acceptable to use force, as opposed to 34 per cent of European Union citizens.[16] This is a stark comparison.

Understanding American exceptionalism, which goes to the heart, to the belief, to the spirit of America as a nation, is essential to the management of Australia's own affairs, about which I will write more later.

Against the background of that sense of superiority and of perfection, what chance is there of an American president and a governing class emerging, which really believes that the world must be a cooperative multilateral place—that the most powerful nation cannot merely dictate, that it must work with and understand other nations? President Bush Snr did understand the need for a cooperative world. He was an avowed internationalist; he wanted to work with, and strengthen the United Nations. He wanted to work with and through coalitions, to a much greater extent than many presidents were prepared to accept. He would never have said, 'You're either with us or against us'.[17] To a significant extent, he might have been an exception from the generality of United States presidents, who have, in most cases, been notoriously difficult to influence or

to persuade to modify policy. In this age of unchecked exceptionalism, can we realistically expect an avid internationalist in the White
House again?

On a purely pragmatic basis, there is an argument at the end of
George F. Kennan's 'Long Telegram' from Moscow that said that the
Soviet leaders believed that their systems would be safe only when
democracy had been destroyed.[18] This was one of the motivating
factors that caused the non-communist world to be most concerned
about communist expansion and communist aggression. Ironically,
the neo-conservatives at the end of the twentieth century turned
that argument on its head and virtually proclaimed that America
would be secure only when the world was a democracy in America's
image. Belief in such an argument provides America with a worldwide mission, to be accomplished if possible by persuasion, if not,
then by force of arms. This might well have been, apart from the
desire to secure Iraqi oil supplies, the main motivating force of the
second Gulf War.

The neo-conservative movement goes hand in hand with sentiments of American exceptionalism. In 1997 the Project for the New
American Century wrote of the philosophy and the motivation that
was to guide neo-conservatives and their formulation of foreign
policy. They issued a Statement of Principles, in which the signatories
had this to say: 'Having led the West to victory in the Cold War,
America faces an opportunity and a challenge: does the United States
have the vision to build upon the achievements of past decades?
Does the United States have the resolve to shape a new century
favourable to American principles and interests?'[19]

The statement talks of America's vital role in maintaining
peace and security, virtually worldwide. If America does not do
that, America will attract challengers to its fundamental interests.
America's purpose was to work with democratic allies and to challenge regimes hostile to American interests and values. That in one
sentence is really saying that if you are not a democracy, you must
be hostile to America. It is value laden foreign policy writ large. It
conveniently ignores the fact that the United States has often made

allies of the most barbarous dictators. It, once again, paints the world as black and white, good and bad.

The actions of President Bush Jnr in particular have been reinforced by belief in the idea of American exceptionalism, by the God-given duty to advance democracy, if necessary by force. His action over Iraq speaks to this argument. The misguided belief that America could successfully establish a benign democracy in Iraq and that democracy would spread throughout the Middle East was due to confidence in America's democratic example and the pervasiveness of its influence, a belief that the American system had universal applicability and it was his duty to apply it. That is, philosophically, a consistent reason, founded in American exceptionalism and neo-conservative philosophy. It provides the most coherent explanation for the war in Iraq: self-belief bordering on complete self-delusion.

Weapons of mass destruction were publicly mooted as the main reasons for going to war because, as Wolfowitz said, 'The truth is that for reasons that have a lot to do with the US government bureaucracy we settled on the one issue that everyone could agree on, which was weapons of mass destruction, as the core reason.'[20] This is duplicitous not only to the American public that funded a war to rid the world of supposed weapons of mass destruction but also to the international community that put faith in what Washington was claiming.

Deceit aside, the extraordinary thing about the war is that a number of highly educated and talented people could go to war and for some, endorse a war, with such a dismal and obvious ignorance of the country they were attacking. How could you have believed that the Kurds, the Sunnis and the Shias would enable one all-embracing democratic government to be established? How could you believe that the religious jealousies and rivalries, spanning centuries, would not arise once Saddam Hussein's iron fist had been removed?

The societal impact on Iraq of such ignorance has been immense. The medical journal, the *Lancet*, estimated that civilian casualties totalled 600,000 as a direct result of violence.[21] The United States does not keep figures of civilian deaths of collateral damage. I do know that Iraq very quickly went from being the safest country in the world for non-government organisations to work in to being the most dangerous. That was CARE Australia's experience. CARE Australia ceased to work in Iraq.

What has happened since the withdrawal of troops of the Coalition of the Willing, which of course included Australia, is plain for everyone to see. We are reminded almost daily, but certainly weekly, of the chaotic state of the country, with more bombings and more casualties as time passes. There is no suggestion that an end is in sight. There was no discussion about the responsibility the Coalition of the Willing bears for the ongoing turmoil. There is no real evidence that America and its allies have learnt from this mistake; no real appreciation of the horror the innocent Iraqi people have had to endure.

The justifications given for the Iraq War are not the only example of political change within America since the Cold War. One of the most significant developments began very early in the first term of President Bush Jnr. It was a change to redefine what the Americans would classify as acceptable behaviour, to achieve their strategic objectives. We have seen how this Bush Administration from the very beginning was trying to find a justification for a regime change in Iraq.[22] Yet other, perhaps more insidious, changes were underway. Cheney and Rumsfeld, in particular, were impatient with the operation of the CIA—Rumsfeld particularly wanted to end the CIA's near monopoly on human intelligence.[23] Congressional supervision and oversight limited the extent and the nature of the operations that they could undertake. There were certain procedures that had to be pursued, involving the chain of military command, which also limited the possibility of direct executive action. Rumsfeld set about turning the Joint Strategic Operations Command (JSOC) into a new, highly trained and expert secret army, which could undertake special operations in almost any part of the world.[24]

JSOC had been established in 1980 and was originally a training and coordinating organisation. It has grown from around 1800 troops before the attacks of September 11 to as many as 25,000, depending on mission requirements. Cheney turned it into a lethal organisation under the direct control of the White House and subject to presidential direction and tasking. It has its own drones, reconnaissance planes and dedicated satellites.[25] It is this organisation that conducts most of the drone attacks and targeted assassinations and numerous other operations, which have been described by author Jeremy Scahill in a book called *Dirty Wars*.

During the Bush Jnr era it would have been Rumsfeld and Cheney who were most involved with JSOC. The only legal justification for such a private army is a single paragraph of authorisation, which really says that the President might use any means to pursue the War on Terror anywhere in the world. The paragraph is a follows:

SEC. 2. AUTHORIZATION FOR USE OF UNITED STATES ARMED FORCES

(a) IN GENERAL.—That the President is authorized to use all necessary and appropriate force against those nations, organizations, or persons he determines planned, authorized, committed, or aided the terrorist attacks that occurred on September 11, 2001, or harbored such organizations or persons, in order to prevent any future acts of international terrorism against the United States by such nations, organizations or persons.[26]

It is significant that, unlike other war powers authorisations, there is no geographic limit to the presidential power. There is no time limit, no sunset clause. For the first time, the power was directed not at nations but specific organisations or persons. The President himself is the sole arbiter: 'he determines'. The power is unending because it involves the prevention of future attacks. One can only say that, while President Bush Jnr, Cheney and Rumsfeld used this power to great, if illicit, effect, President Obama has used it more extensively—particularly in legitimising drone strikes—magnifying danger to American democracy.

The use of such powers, without any basic legal authorisation, beyond the reach of any present congressional law, is the antithesis of democracy. This is emphasised by the fact that drone killings are now used against specific targets, individuals or organisations, whom the White House believes are a danger to the United States. The United States has published an alleged factsheet of the principles and standards used before drone strikes are undertaken. The standards have already been breached. The document says, 'Finally, whenever the United States uses force in foreign territories, international legal principles, including respect for sovereignty and the law of armed conflict, impose important constraints on the ability of the United States to act unilaterally—and on the way in which the United States can use force. The United States respects national sovereignty and international law.'[27] Bluntly, it does not.

The new Prime Minister of Pakistan, Nawaz Sharif, has said that 'US drone strikes are an "unacceptable" violation of his country's sovereignty and demanded an end to these missions'. In addition, Hamid Karzai, President of Afghanistan, has condemned US drone strikes against militants in Pakistan.[28] Statements by the head of state of Afghanistan and the head of government in Pakistan seem to have been totally ignored. How does that stand with respect for sovereignty?

Other aspects of the principles set out in the White House paper have also arguably been breached, too much is a matter of assessment and not of fact. The White House is strangely silent about the number of civilian casualties caused by drone strikes. There have been reports of civilians being killed at weddings, at meetings. One report suggests that fifty civilians are killed for every terrorist.[29] That might be extreme, but other authoritative reports repeatedly suggest a figure of sixteen to twenty civilian casualties for every strike—the Bureau of Investigative Journalism has done a significant amount of work in this area.[30]

A process of profiling organisations and individuals has also begun.[31] If there is to be a meeting and those attending the meeting have an appropriate profile—they are young, they are male, they are like others against whom there might have been some direct evidence—such profiled groups are also targeted. These signature strikes target anonymous suspected militants 'that bear the characteristics of

Qaeda or Taliban leaders on the run'.[32] In the case of Yemen, this 'in effect counts all military-age males in a strike zone as combatants ... unless there is explicit intelligence posthumously proving them innocent'.[33] Hardly a benchmark for justice.

These processes, which seem to be a permanent part of White House power, say a great deal about the extent to which America, once the world's greatest democracy, has been prepared to forgo its own value system in the fight against terrorists. It defines the extent to which terrorists have won because the world's most powerful democracy is now using the weapons of terrorists. Clearly, America has judged that weapons compatible with its own principles and the standards of basic justice are no longer by themselves sufficient to defend democracy.

It is no accident that the growing feeling of American exceptionalism, of manifest destiny, began to have a much greater influence in American affairs after 1990. It is also no accident that the neo-conservatives, through the Project for the New American Century, developed their Statement of Principles, setting out America's obligations and duty for the century in which we now live. It was designed to be a century in which America would be, and would remain, supreme and unchallenged. Because the United States regards itself as an exceptional nation, it sought, and seeks to play, a major role in determining how other countries may live. It is impatient of systems of government unlike its own. It lectures other states and tells them what they should or must do. Being exceptional, America is not bound by the rules that are made for lesser states. Russian President Putin made this point in response to comments by President Obama that US policy makes America different, makes America 'exceptional'. Putin said: 'It is extremely dangerous to encourage people to see themselves as exceptional, whatever the motivation. There are big countries and small countries, rich and poor ... We are all different, but when we ask for the Lord's blessings, we must not forget that God created us equal.'[34]

Through this chapter I have traced the influence of the sense of American exceptionalism and of the neo-conservatives and their current domination of American policy.[35] We need to understand these changes because they vitally affect our own relationship with the United States. We need to be conscious that today's America has changed substantially. Are we now seeing the real America, evolving since 1990? Must we accept that the kind of action begun by President Bush Jnr and, in too many ways, amplified by President Obama as the norm for American behaviour?

The philosophy of American exceptionalism and the rise of the neo-conservatives through the ranks of think tanks like the Heritage Foundation and the American Enterprise Institute represent a major part of the betrayal of the aspirations enunciated in President Bush Snr's speech in Congress in March 1991 and the hopes of the international community for a new post–Cold War world order. The historic view of American exceptionalism and God-given duty, coupled with the philosophy and attitudes of the neo-conservatives, which gathered great strength in the late 1990s, spelled an end to that cooperative America.

America and those who have supported its adventures, especially the United Kingdom and Australia, have learnt at terrible cost that there are limits to the exercise of military power. It is a lesson that has been learnt time and time again from Vietnam onwards. Your forces can be infinitely superior to those of your enemy, but that is no guarantee of victory. If a war becomes a guerrilla operation, if it turns to terrorist-style attacks, if you are part of an alien army operating in a country whose culture and past are very different from your own, a culture and past that you do not understand and probably do not believe are particularly important, then winning the war can become an impossibility. In these circumstances the exercise of military power is of little assistance in establishing the political solution you hope for. It cannot overcome a great gulf between cultures.

Belief that you are an exceptional nation with a worldwide destiny can become an impediment when others see it differently. The United States should have learnt twice—and so should have we—that overwhelming military power will not enable you to achieve political objectives. The first lesson was Vietnam, the second was Iraq and a third has unfolded in Afghanistan. Yet history suggests that America will not heed these lessons and that Australia will once again step into line with America when we are called to do so as an ever-dutiful ally.

There is a huge gulf in our value systems. While Australians believe that, for Australians, this is the best country in the world, we do not proclaim exceptional privilege and virtue for ourselves. We do not claim that we are endowed by God to bring justice and peace to the world. We do not automatically assume that what works in Australia will work elsewhere, or that the way we do things cannot be improved by learning from other nations. Although our political culture displays elements of the extreme, on both sides of the political equation, the pervasiveness and influence of a movement like the neo-conservative movement has not yet taken root in the Australian polity.

This 'values divide' is a problem for our ongoing strategic dependence on the United States and is a problem that looms large, given that the region in which we live is growing in importance, both economically and politically. The fact that we have a common language with the United States masks the depth of the divide between our value systems. This makes continuing a policy of strategic dependence a fraught prospect.

11

The changing Asia–Pacific

As outlined earlier in the book, Asia has fulfilled a significant role in embedding the need for strategic dependence in the Australian psyche. Fear from the north loomed large over policy-makers during the first decades after Federation. In the early post-war years, East and South-East Asia went through an unsettled period, much of which involved Australia. The period is important because, through it all and underneath the alarms of daily events, a slow steadfastness of purpose was developing in a number of South-East Asian countries to take greater control of their own affairs. Over time, such attitudes contributed to the progress of East and South-East Asia and have helped to maintain peace and stability across the region. Such progress slowly changed the perspective of Australian leaders, shifting from being fearful of our northern neighbours to seeing the opportunities inherent in establishing strong and cooperative relationships with them. Understanding the transition is important in comprehending the current state of affairs in our region and strategic considerations Australia needs to tackle. Along with the changes in the global and American domestic contexts outlined in the previous two chapters, changes in our region point to strategic dependence no longer being in Australia's best interests.

We should remember that in those early years one of the important nations in South-East Asia, if not the most important, Indonesia, was a non-aligned country. Indonesia sought to maintain good relationships not only with the United States but also with the Soviet Union, although Jakarta and Moscow were less close after the demise of the PKI. They made it very clear, however, in a quiet way, that they did not want to see great power rivalry take place within South-East Asia. Indonesia, particularly Suharto, saw ASEAN solidarity as a mechanism to achieve this by putting forth a united front to thwart any external attempts to intervene in the region.[1] A solid and united core would allow South-East Asia to withstand more effectively the divisions caused by the Cold War. It was a view also expressed by the then Indonesian Foreign Minister, Adam Malik, who stated that ASEAN would inspire 'a region which can stand on its own feet, strong enough to defend itself against any negative influence from outside the region'.[2] I believe that wish was, by and large, respected by both superpowers, allowing the foundation nations of ASEAN, particularly Indonesia, to focus on significant domestic issues.

The initiative to form ASEAN came about while Thailand was brokering a reconciliation between Indonesia, the Philippines and Malaysia. Thanat Khoman, Thai Foreign Minister at the time, recalls that all four countries realised that the only way to avoid future confrontations was through regional cooperation.[3] ASEAN was formed in 1967 at a meeting between the foreign ministers of Indonesia, Malaysia, Philippines, Singapore and Thailand, who signed the Bangkok Declaration. The foundation nations declared that 'the collective will of the nations of Southeast Asia to bind themselves together in friendship and cooperation and, through joint efforts and sacrifices, secure for their peoples and for posterity the blessings of peace, freedom and prosperity'.[4]

This was a significant achievement as it relied on both Indonesia, as the dominant power, to exercise future self-restraint from any future Konfrontasi-style aggression and not only to accept the external security arrangements of other partner nations[5] but also the other nations accepting Indonesia's commitment to regional cohesion and stability.[6]

Since then ASEAN has grown to include Brunei, Myanmar, Cambodia, Laos and Vietnam. The growth of ASEAN has occurred without great fanfare. Its development has been steady and co-operative. It was an organisation that showed that the South-East Asian nations were far-sighted and determined to take control of their own future. Their capacity to move forward and the influence of ASEAN as it grew were underestimated by the West. There is no doubt that ASEAN and its members have been significantly respon-sible, in the years since, for the peaceful development and economic progress of South-East Asia. As it grew in confidence, its scope, its ambitions, grew to be even more effective in advancing relationships between the countries of East and South-East Asia and in developing linkages with other countries and regions around the world.

The quiet development among South-East Asian nations was, in large measure, successful in achieving friendship and cooperation between states that had had fractious and extraordinarily difficult relationships.

Where there have been problems, for example between the Philippines and Malaysia over the sovereignty of eastern Sabah, they have been contained. Indeed some disputes, such as border disagree-ments between Thailand and Cambodia, have gone as far as the International Court of Justice. Yet, despite these problems, ASEAN remains intact and the region devoid of interstate armed conflict.

The founding of ASEAN, and the progress it has helped facilitate, should not cloud the historic achievements of the region before European colonisation. For example, I can remember a visit to Vietnam in 1996 when I was vice-president of CARE International, and the international board of CARE was meeting in Hanoi. Australia ran a mission in Hanoi on behalf of the entire CARE family. A government minister gave a reception for the board members of CARE and the senior staff. In his opening remarks welcoming us, the Vietnamese minister said he had chosen this location quite deliberately because this reception was being held among buildings that were part of the first university established in Vietnam in 1076, hundreds of years before Oxford or Cambridge were dreamt of.

Australians should always remember that we are not necessarily the educated elite, bringing intelligence and competence to Asia. We can learn much from our neighbours, who have a long history of achievement in many areas of human endeavour. We can learn much from the way they conduct themselves, quietly, steadfastly, overcoming problems, which on occasion have been acute, making friends of enemies so that they could work together peacefully.

Australia has had a long relationship with ASEAN. We were its first dialogue partner in 1974, and we have been involved ever since. I believe our contribution to the discussions has helped in the expansion, growth and strength of ASEAN. We signed the ASEAN–Australia Comprehensive Partnership in 2007, formalising the desire to increase political, security, economic, cultural and development cooperation between Australian and all ten ASEAN member nations.[7] Significantly, Australia, along with New Zealand, signed a free trade agreement with ASEAN in 2009, arguably Australia's most ambitious trade agreement to date.[8] Our relationship with ASEAN continues to deepen and should be a priority for the current and all future Australian governments.

ASEAN has also expanded its international relationships and forms the key foundation of broader regional groupings. It now has ten dialogue partners, including Canada, China, the European Union, India, Japan, New Zealand, Republic of Korea, Russia and the United States. These meetings have now developed into an annual ASEAN regional forum that draws together twenty-seven countries concerned for the security of the Asia–Pacific region.

Indonesia, in particular, should be given credit for its growth, for its development and for its success. ASEAN has been significant in encouraging progress and development in Cambodia and Myanmar. Indonesia has played a leadership role in the region, despite not always receiving encouragement and support from the West. For example, during the 1997 Asian financial crisis, international financial institutions such as the IMF and the World Bank were trying to micro-manage the Indonesian economy in a totally offensive and unrealistic fashion. These international institutions, in fact, acted far too slowly to this Asian crisis. If a similar situation had arisen in South America, I have no doubt that the United States would have prompted the World Bank and the IMF to move swiftly, speedily and immediately to provide assistance and to shore up their economies. The Asian Tigers, the swiftly growing economies, had often been spoken of as ultimate competitors to the United States, and it might well be that the United States did not mind some halt to that progress.

The underlying strength of Asian economies was demonstrated in particular by Malaysia. Prime Minister Mahathir Mohamad had regarded the IMF and World Bank decisions as totally intrusive and unrealistic, and made it clear that Malaysia would make its own decisions. Although many of Mahathir's decisions were also based on domestic political considerations, particularly concerning his deputy Anwar Ibrahim, his actions 'helped discredit the IMF's austerity fix, the one-size-fits-all solution that the fund misguidedly—and arrogantly—tried to impose in East Asia'.[9] So he introduced measures that resulted in a revival of the Malaysian economy, and possibly more quickly than that of other countries of the region. Yet, despite the hiccups of the 1997 crisis, the ASEAN nations, both Indonesia and Malaysia included, have continued along the path of economic progress, so far avoiding any major confrontation of the sort that so often plagued their early relationships.

Australia has also played a key part in creating multilateral architecture for the Asia–Pacific region. I can remember discussions with Prime Minister Masayoshi Ohira of Japan, in 1980, in Melbourne. We both wanted a more all-embracing and wider association of East and South-East Asian nations and one that would pay particular attention to economic progress, to trade, to development and to open markets. We were aware, at the time, that Indonesia had reservations about any new organisation. Indonesia was concerned that a new organisation might undercut ASEAN and damage ASEAN's own development. We nevertheless felt that a broader economic grouping was important, and we looked for ways to make a start without arousing the concerns of Indonesia or of other ASEAN partners.

We established in the first instance an organisation that was called the 'Pacific Community Seminar'. Very shortly the name was changed to the Pacific Economic Cooperation Council (PECC). It was not a government organisation. It was promoted initially by universities, by academia, but it also involved business leaders and government officials. The first meeting of this organisation was held in 1980, in Australia. Eleven countries were involved in the first meeting. Sir John Crawford, at that time Vice Chancellor of the Australian National University, was the first chairman. Later meetings were held in Thailand in 1982 and Indonesia in 1983, indicating a welcome degree of support for PECC.

These meetings achieved the purpose that Prime Minister Ohira and I had wanted. Countries across the region understood the need for stronger economic cooperation across East and South-East Asia. That made it possible for APEC to be formed in 1989, again on the proposal of Australia. APEC now has twenty-one Pacific Rim country members, and an annual leaders meeting is held. Members of ASEAN were enthusiastic supporters.

Local political architecture was again strengthened in 2005, when the East Asia Summit was established. The ten ASEAN countries, along with Australia, China, India, Japan, New Zealand, Republic of Korea, Russia and the United States, were founding members. The centrepiece is an annual leaders summit usually held back to back with an annual ASEAN leaders meeting. This is a far cry from the East and South-East Asia of a few decades ago when Malaysia was fighting for survival, when Konfrontasi raged, when Indonesia itself was subject to a PKI coup. It is a far cry from the problems that developed over Timor Leste.

Through this process, Indonesia and other countries of the region are really saying that, left to themselves, they have a way of resolving problems of overcoming difficulties with patience, diplomacy and respect, leading to cooperation and agreement. There will always be differences between the nations of the region, but strong institutions and a desire for peaceful resolution will guide negotiation.

The way ASEAN and its constituent nations have gone about their diplomacy is very different from tactics employed by Australia, the United Kingdom or America. We tend to speak too often, publicly and loudly, about what other countries should do. That is not necessarily the best way to overcome problems between nations, especially when we apply a double standard and ignore our own domestic problems.

At the IISS Asia Security Summit (the Shangri-La Dialogue) in June 2012, the President of Indonesia, Dr Susilo Bambang Yudhoyono, gave a keynote address that emphasised the progress that had been made and how much more could be achieved.[10] He believed that Indonesia's lessons during its transition to democracy would be relevant to Myanmar and believed that process would strengthen ASEAN as a whole. This is important because originally Vietnam, Cambodia, Laos and Myanmar looked upon ASEAN with some suspicion. Through time, trust was built. They are now equal members of the association.

Dr Yudhoyono's address also drew attention to the fact that Timor Leste is still not part of ASEAN. He clearly looked forward to the day in which Timor Leste would be a full member, a thought that would have been impossible fifteen years ago. The process of joining is moving forward positively, with Timor Leste officially applying for ASEAN membership in 2011 when ASEAN was chaired by Indonesia.[11]

Clearly, the President believed that processes that have been put in place by a number of South-East Asian and Asian countries have much to offer a peaceful world. If the same attitude is undertaken, he is optimistic that much progress can be made. He is not blind to the possibility of renewed rivalry between major powers. That would clearly be a backward step. He emphasised that all the countries of the region would want to have good relationships with both China and the United States. They certainly would not want to choose, or be asked to choose, between them.

The President clearly believed that Asian achievements should be used as an example for others to follow. He pointed to eighteen leaders at the East Asia Summit in Bali in 2011 agreeing to a set of morally binding principles,[12] which would promote peace in the region. He pointed clearly to cooperation that had occurred, especially in response to natural disasters, and emphasised the co-operation of many countries with Indonesia, after the tragic tsunami in Aceh, in 2004.

What the President was talking about clearly requires, in his terms, 'leadership', 'creativity' and 'courage', especially when countries have to be led away from a traditional mindset. He did not shirk talking about the South China Sea. In his view, sometimes progress was too slow. It took ten years to finally agree on guidelines for the Code of Conduct in the South China Sea, and he looked for faster progress in achieving agreement within the ASEAN–China Working Group, so that the Code would be embraced by all countries involved. In the President's terms, the geopolitics of conflict, consultation and rivalry should be replaced by the geopolitics of cooperation. He recog-nised that that would involve breaking away from a mindset deeply ingrained in certain countries.[13]

These themes were re-emphasised a year later by the Indonesian Minister for Foreign Affairs, Dr Marty Natalegawa, at a conference on Indonesia, held in Washington in May 2013.[14] The Foreign Minister again referred to the Code of Conduct in relation to the South China Sea. Indeed, if such a code can be established and firmly agreed by all parties, it would do much to relieve a potential dif-ficulty. It could indeed form the framework to resolve other disputes, such as between China and Japan over the Senkaku/Diaoyu Islands. He spoke of the need for trust between states. He again returned to the theme that problems in the East and the South China Sea do not have to lead to conflict. He believed such matters could be resolved, but he also emphasised that if that were to happen peacefully, it 'requires a commitment from parties to a territorial dispute to respect a certain code of behaviour or conduct'. He again pointed to the fact that, '[i]n the South China Sea context, this has meant the drawing up of a regional code of conduct between ASEAN and China'.[15]

If such a Code of Conduct can be finally agreed and given legal force, it would be a major achievement. Such an agreement would take time; it should not be rushed. It is better for it to be thorough, to make sure all options are covered. It is not necessary that a settlement of all territorial disputes be undertaken to achieve that. If the Code of Conduct can describe and agree to that which is acceptable, and that which is not, then that could be sufficient. The Code could even borrow from an example, in the Antarctic Treaty, where all the parties agreed that they would not press territorial claims. They do not withdraw them, if you like, but they put their territorial claims on hold. That enables nations to cooperate on other matters that can ensure peaceful cooperation and development. The same principle could well be relevant in the context of the South China Sea.

The very considerable progress achieved by ASEAN and other Asian forums has been achieved without Western intervention, in particular, with little or no involvement from the United States. The evolving strategic environment within the Asia–Pacific, and in South-East Asia in particular, has occurred primarily as a result of the determination of Asian nations. Asian nations have taken it upon themselves to establish regional infrastructure, such as ASEAN, conducive to peaceful coexistence and economic development. These efforts are not without areas of concern, but the way in which they have been developed and the underpinning rationale for their existence is commendable.

The progress that has been made, with Indonesia often playing a leading role, should raise questions in the minds of Australia, the United States and of other Western countries involved in the Western Pacific. How can we change our own diplomatic behaviour to work with regional partners more effectively? Can the success of ASEAN be applied to solving other global issues? So often Western intervention has appeared to make problems worse, rather than better. It is difficult to claim progress, for example in Iraq, Afghanistan or in countries across North Africa and indeed at present in Syria, as a result of Western diplomacy. Given the success of institution-building in Asia, particularly South-East Asia, it is a policy of engagement rather than intervention that should be pursued. Such determination by Asian nations is something Australia should acknowledge and realise that it has ultimately made our own security more assured and increased our own economic opportunity. It has not weakened our prospects in the region, unlike our endeavours in Iraq and Afghanistan, which have incurred a huge cost in Australian lives, resources and reputation.

It is against this background that we need to look at the US 'pivot' towards the Western Pacific and the two-track policy that the United States is adopting in its relations with China. One track represents dialogue, cooperation and understanding; the other a much more dangerous policy of containment and antagonism towards China. Former Secretary of State Hillary Clinton provides a good example of operating on the first track, pursuing diplomacy, engagement and dialogue with China.

For example, when I was in Beijing in May 2012, Clinton led the fourth round of the Strategic and Economic Dialogue with China.[16] These discussions have taken place over the last four years. They seem to have gone well. They have been constructive, including the July 2013 discussions between Obama and President Xi in Washington.[17] If such engagement continues to be pursued, the Dialogue could well lead to a much better relationship and to the beginning of trust between the United States and China. There was much discussion of the peaceful resolution of disputes not only between the nations but also around the world. There was an emphasis on the two countries getting to know each other better and discussion on what policies need to be implemented to achieve a deeper relationship. There was discussion of what processes were needed to enable the two countries to work through their differences. Such an approach was impeccable and, if pursued vigorously in future years, could build upon the dynamic that President Yudhoyono spoke of when he described how many problems have been overcome by consensus, patience and understanding.

The approach underscored by the Dialogue should be commended and both America and China encouraged to continue along the path of engagement. It is in the best interests of both nations and, as China's power increases, all nations around the world, particularly those in the Asia–Pacific. Yet, unfortunately, there is another side to American policy in relation to China; a second track to Washington's approach to Beijing. The way a nation describes its own policies might not be the way other nations interpret or understand those same policies. Perception can become reality when aims and intentions are not made explicit. If there is a basic misunderstanding of a policy and its aims, especially if caused by lack of transparency or attempts to cover a motive or a purpose, then trust between nations is next to impossible. There is a real risk of this occurring between America and China.

For example, we could argue whether the US pivot is simply a refocusing of resources or a military build-up in the Western Pacific. Further, we could argue that the pivot does or does not constitute a policy of 'containment' against a growing China. In either event, America needs to be explicit as to what the pivot entails and how it relates to China. The policy is open to different interpretations and clearly fuels a lack of trust between China and the United States. If Washington is to continue with the pivot then it needs to explain—and explain in unambiguous language—why the sudden change in policy.

This military and strategic expansion is the second track of United States policy towards China. Many people believe that it does constitute 'containment'. Many in South-East Asia are wary of the pivot, and China certainly believes it is a policy of 'containment'. As one Chinese professor put it, 'The pivot is a very stupid choice … the United States has achieved nothing and only annoyed China. China can't be contained.'[18] There are many in Australia who believe it to be 'containment'. American representatives saying otherwise will not help to change these regional perspectives.

Towards the end of 2012, Joseph Nye visited Beijing and wrote shortly afterwards an article published in the *New York Times*, 'Work with China, don't contain it'. Nye had earlier strongly supported America's reinforcement of its military in the Western Pacific, and

I imagine he still does. He wrote this article because, he said, 'I was struck by how many Chinese officials believe such a policy ("containment") is already in place and is the central purpose of President Obama's "pivot" toward Asia.'[19] Nye has an intuitive understanding of foreign policy. He has been a strong advocate of diplomacy of 'soft power' and has criticised the United States for relying too much on the military, on 'hard power', in past years.[20] Given Nye's credentials, scholarship and the offices he has held, both in government and academia, it is astounding that such a person was unaware that China believes that a policy of 'containment' is being implemented.

If American political leaders keep denying that 'containment' is in place and that any effort to rebalance US forces strategically in the region is simply fulfilling obligations to allies, then China's leadership can hardly be blamed for not accepting that explanation. Chinese people have often said to me: which America do we believe—the one pursuing discussion and consultation through the Strategic and Economic Dialogue, or the one pushing for 'containment' via a military build-up? At some point, Australia is going to have to decide which of these two options it supports. Supporting both will become increasingly difficult, if not impossible.

In a speech given in Tianjin, China, in May 2012, involving people from around 20 countries, former Prime Minister Goh Chok Tong of Singapore said, 'Any rhetoric of "containment" is dangerous. My view is that any attempt by the US to contain China will not work, nor will countries in the region want to take sides on this.'[21] Singaporeans are notoriously reticent in relation to critical comments about the United States. These words were strongly stated, strongly based and, quite obviously, strongly felt.

Despite their denials of 'containment', there are many statements by American leaders that lend support to the Chinese perception that a policy of 'containment' is not only in place but also is being reinforced. Statements by successive secretaries of state, although never mentioning 'containment', provide a strong factual basis for this conclusion.[22] I suggest therefore that, if the United States is to have an open and transparent relationship with China, it should not continue to say that 'containment' is not 'containment' as it will only lead to more confusion and more suspicion. Washington should have greater confidence in its own diplomatic skills, rely on diplomacy and put continued military expansion ('containment') aside.

Chuck Hagel, US Secretary of Defense, gave a pretty good summary of how the policy of 'containment' is progressing in a speech given at the beginning of June 2013.[23] He spoke of the US investments in the Pacific and, in particular, of the 'rebalancing' of America's military forces into the Pacific, how the marines and army would be strengthened since the war in Iraq is over and America is drawing down from Afghanistan. Hagel noted that Washington intends to have 60 per cent of its naval assets in the Pacific by 2020. This is in addition to the US Air Force also maintaining 60 per cent of its overseas-based assets in the region, including the stationing of tactical aircraft and bomber forces currently based in the continental United States.[24] He referred again to the Marine Air-Ground Task Force, stationed in Darwin. The first of four Littoral Combat Ships was already deployed to Singapore. Deployments through the Philippines have also been strengthened, with joint training exercises as well as the United States negotiating to station equipment there and rotate through personnel.[25] The last US military base in the Philippines was Subic Bay. It caused such ill feeling that it was closed in 1992. The policy of 'rotating through' is clearly developed to give America the military reach it desires, without the public and political consternation that the term 'base' has raised in the past. Further, more modern aircraft have been deployed to Japan, and a fourth fast-attack submarine will be placed in Guam.[26] Stealth bombers had earlier been deployed to Guam.[27] It is a considerable addition to the massive power that the United States already deploys, especially through its carrier task forces.[28]

Strengthening arrangements with existing defence partners, such as encouraging tripartite security cooperation between America, Australia and Japan, is only part of Washington's policy. Developing new relationships with nations in the region has also been on America's agenda. For example, in a visit to Vietnam's Cam Ranh

Bay in 2010, Secretary of Defense Leon Panetta said, 'Access for United States naval ships into this facility is a key component of this relationship and we see a tremendous potential here.'[29] I believe the Vietnamese are astute enough not to be drawn into a highly provocative move against their neighbour, China. Most American naval ships are nuclear weapons capable. Strategic discussions are also being held with Thailand and with India. The United States claims that these activities will add to peace and security, to freedom of the seas throughout the Western Pacific, but where are the threats to such freedom?

The region is clearly not without strategic concerns, some of which are most serious and dangerous in nature. The situation on the Korean Peninsula is a clear example of an issue confronting the region, made even more serious by the North's successful development of nuclear weapons. North Korea is well known for being unpredictable and reclusive, and has made it very difficult for any efforts by South Korea to achieve a sustained improvement in relations between Seoul and Pyongyang; an improvement that I am sure many people from both North and South would want to achieve.

The United States has not always made this process easy. When President Bush Jnr named Iraq, Iran and North Korea in his 'axis of evil', he also spoke of regime change. Initially, those states might have believed it to be merely rhetoric, but when he turned rhetoric into reality by going to war with Iraq, the seriousness of Washington's intent was hammered home to Tehran and Pyongyang. Such threats are hardly conducive to closing nuclear programs. This involves arguments over the Non-Proliferation Treaty (NPT), which gives all ratifying states the right to establish enrichment facilities. Apart from the original nuclear states, other states, although allowed to move to enrichment, are banned from producing nuclear weapons. The United States has been quite relaxed about states regarded as friendly pursuing nuclear programs. It has been totally hostile to countries regarded as unfriendly to the United States—notably Iran and North Korea—pursuing enrichment. How much of this dispute relates to the desire of the United States and the West to deny to certain states rights accepted under the NPT? The partisanship of this attitude is underlined by the failure of the original five nuclear armed states to pursue adequately the provisions of Article 6 concerning the abolition of nuclear weapons.[30]

In more recent times, the United States has stopped talking about regime change in relation to Iran or North Korea. Does North Korea really believe that the change is real? America could contribute to the resolution of difficulties in the Korean Peninsula by really making it plain that regime change is not only off the table but also is not under the table, waiting to be resurrected. Certainly, the North Korean Government is paranoiac and unpredictable. The movement of US ships and missiles into the region does nothing to reduce tension. Both South Korea and Japan have undertaken similar activities, but the US moves would obviously be the most significant. Restraint on behalf of the United States, even in response to provocation, might help to diffuse the tension and indicate to the North that bellicosity will not receive a response. Only engagement and adherence to international expectations will receive a response. If that change could occur, it might make it possible for China to exercise more influence on North Korea and help make substantial progress in resolving problems on the Peninsula. Although Pyongyang's recalcitrance and disregard for the welfare of its own people does nothing to help the situation, restraint, maturity and diplomatic leadership from the United States is the only way the situation will be resolved peacefully. If the United States wants to demonstrate to the world some of the idealism exhibited in President Bush Snr's speech on the post–Cold War era, then here is an opportunity for it to do so.

Further, the US military build-up in the Western Pacific through the 'pivot' should not be cast as necessary because of the situation on the Korean Peninsula—such force simply is not required. Why the build-up is occurring needs to be better explained, particularly if it is in relation to China.

The Strategic and Economic Dialogue that the United States instituted with China should make the military build-up unnecessary. We are entitled to ask: what is the purpose of that military expansion? What are the dangers, what are the threats? The presence of US military forces, enhanced or otherwise, is not a precondition for achieving a successful resolution to a difficult issue. Asian states have accomplished so much in their own right. Does America claim to have been the major influence in maintaining the peace?

The United States would say that it has brought a major benefit to the Western Pacific by establishing a period of peace during which countries could develop their own institutions and strengthen their governance. This assisted greatly in development of the whole region. There is an element of truth in this, and I will give credit where credit is due. As part of the Cold War dialectic, there is no doubt that the efforts of the United States and of European powers, through NATO, prevented the further expansion of the Soviet Union. This benefited the whole world, including Asia. One could even argue, as former Prime Minister Lee Kuan Yew did, that by its involvement in the Vietnam War, for all its misadventure, America assisted other Asian countries by buying them valuable time, which they might otherwise not have had. In hindsight, I doubt that argument is credible because it could carry weight only if communism had in fact been monolithic, with Soviet, Chinese and Vietnamese communism being one and the same. Although Western leaders felt this to be the case through much of the Cold War, it ignores nationalism. As the CIA recognised in Vietnam, from the outset, nationalism was a major influencing factor in the war, with communism, in many respects, being the rhetorical vehicle for change.

The Western Pacific, benefiting from America and the West's general opposition to the expansion of the Soviet Union, is of a different order from actions that the United States might have taken specifically to advance progress and stability of countries in the Western Pacific. At this time, the United States was not undertaking actions specific to the Western Pacific. This distinction is important and needs to be understood in discussing the future of the region. 'Containment' in the Cold War was a necessary and effective policy, yet it is an unnecessary and dangerous policy to pursue in relation to China.

It is also difficult to see how the American military build-up is relevant to the problems of the East and the South China Seas. The United States talks of territorial disputes and of the need to solve them. In the example of Asia's diplomatic progress led by ASEAN, American involvement could be an impediment rather than a benefit. ASEAN's leadership in diffusing South China Sea problems is testimony to the region's ability to handle its own problems. Although progress remains slow, there is a shared desire to achieve resolution. Vice-President Joe Biden's public intervention in August 2013, on this issue, is certainly counterproductive.[31] Quiet diplomacy, out of the public eye, could have been useful.

The United States already has considerable power in the Western Pacific and the capacity to project power into any part of the entire region. Nobody is suggesting that the United States should leave. Even senior Chinese themselves have said to me, 'We don't want America to go. We know our size makes some of our neighbours nervous. If America departed, they would be even more nervous.' There is a big difference, however, between maintaining a long-standing presence and expanding that presence, as is currently being proposed by Obama's 'pivot'. Only one conclusion can be drawn, and that is that the build-up is directed at 'containing' or 'balancing' China's growing power.

It could be argued that the expansion of America's military facilities in the Western Pacific is a response to China's own military expansion. Yet that argument needs careful analysis. China's military expenditure is often taken out of context by the West. Beijing has numerous powerful neighbours, some of them unstable, and, like Russia, it shares land borders with more nations than most others. Unpredictable North Korea is a problem I have already discussed. A well-armed Russia, historically competing for territory with China, but with which most territorial disputes have in recent years been resolved without conflict, borders China's north. India, with which China has had quite recent wars, is a strategic competitor in the region. Pakistan, unstable and fragile, faces significant and destabilising domestic challenges. Of course both India and Pakistan are nuclear-armed and maintain significant standing armed forces. China also shares borders with Afghanistan and many Central Asian republics. Iran is reasonably close. If the United States were surrounded by a band of such countries, the American people would be paranoiac with concern. So of course, and not unreasonably, China wishes to strengthen its military and its ability to protect its borders.

Chinese defence expenditure began from a fairly low base but, because its economy has grown so rapidly and so effectively, its defence expenditure has also grown substantially. To compare the increases in China's military expenditure with those of Japan or the United States is totally misleading. To extrapolate that forward, as though that rate of increase will continue in the future, is even more misleading.

What we do know is that the United States spent more than $700 billion on defence, in 2011, or 41 per cent of the world's total, which was 4.7 per cent of American GDP. Japan spent just under $60 billion, or 3.5 per cent of the world's total,[32] a significant amount for a country that is meant to be pacifist and which, under its constitution, is not allowed to go to war.[33] China spent $146 billion, a little more than 8 per cent of the world's total and 2 per cent of China's GDP.[34] To put this into perspective, the United Kingdom spent $60 billion, Germany $48 billion, France a little over $60 billion, Britain and France both spent 3.6 per cent of GDP. For completeness, Australia spent a little more than $26 billion in 2011 or 1.5 per cent of GDP.[35]

If we look at it another way, US defence expenditure is about 11 per cent of total government expenditure. The United Kingdom about 5 per cent, Australia under 5 per cent, China 8 per cent, France around 4 per cent.[36] What emerges from these figures, above all, is the massive expenditure of the United States on defence, unequalled by any other country, not even approached by any other country.

It is unsurprising for any great power that has to protect a long sea boundary to develop a blue-water navy. Here, again, reporting of the developments of the Chinese Navy almost suggests that such actions are illicit and duplicitous. Why would China want a navy? For what purpose? It must be aggressive; it must be to close the East and South China Seas, to take control of those waters. Of course, the probability is that the development of China's navy is none of those things. Why would China want to disturb the peace of the Western Pacific? Particularly when that peace has allowed Beijing to focus on trade and economic initiatives that have facilitated spectacular economic growth over the past two decades. It is not reasonable to expect a great power like China to commit to being a land power alone. We also ought to note that China has about 250 nuclear intercontinental weapons whereas the United States has about 7700 warheads.[37] It is an unbalanced strategic relationship and one that is still firmly tipped on the side of the Americans.

Is America prepared to allow China space? Space is going to be essential for peace in the Western Pacific. Hugh White, Professor of Strategic Studies at the ANU, has argued for a group of powers to form a concert of Asia.[38] It might be easier, however, for China and America alone to set out procedures for close consultation and discussion of matters in the Western Pacific and to reach an accommodation between them. White also suggests that it should be a major element of Australian policy to try to persuade America to such a course. Such a suggestion has much merit, but can the United States really be persuaded? I doubt it. It is supreme, the major superpower, still economically the most powerful, but not for long. The conclusion that must be drawn from all the evidence since the fall of the Soviet Union in 1991, the statements of American exceptionalism, the ideas of the neo-conservatives, the policies of Bush Jnr and Obama, suggest that not only is America taking those actions necessary to maintain American supremacy but also it is determined to do so. If this conclusion is correct, it will clearly lead to difficulties between China and the United States at some point.

Does the United States really believe, given the current military imbalance and trade imperative between the two nations, that China offers a military threat either to the United States or to countries of the Western Pacific? A major war would disrupt the whole region and damage China and the United States. It is clearly a war that would be in nobody's interest. Leaving aside the rest of the world, the Chinese and American economies are now so closely connected by investment, by financial markets, by trade, by China buying US treasuries to sustain a continuing and growing US debt. Both countries would lose massively from war. America might have less capacity to withstand the loss than China. China would be operating much closer to home than the United States. The US lines of communication would be long. The biggest factor would be China's capacity to endure hardship, equivalent to that endured by the Vietminh in the Vietnamese War. The United States would have no such capacity.

We should also remember that the Soviet Union was an expansionist power and sought to bring more countries within the communist empire. It also talked of the need to destroy democracy and said that only the end of democracy would make the Soviet system safe. China is not an imperial power, in the sense that the Soviet Union was an imperial power, or in the sense that major European states and indeed, the United States, have been imperial powers.[39] On the contrary, China has been totally consistent in condemning hegemony. China opposes powers that seek to dominate or unduly influence the policies or attitudes of other states. It was the Soviet Union's pursuit of hegemony that led to the major break between the Soviet Union and China. Today, China would regard the United States as a hegemonic power, as the one who seeks to determine rules that others should follow. This is a major difference between the Soviet Union and China. It is also one of the reasons why policies of 'containment' are utterly inappropriate in relation to China.

China must know that the second track of US policy is aimed at it. Too many US representatives talk of America's defence reorganisation within the Pacific and South-East Asia, indicating the extent to which countries of the region will also be supported by the United States. The Secretary of Defense makes no secret of it. When senior figures in the Obama Administration make it clear that the policy is directed at China's rise, how can Chinese leaders consider it anything less than 'containment' and an effort to prevent China's rise?

American strategies and policies are deeply rooted in outdated, balance-of-power, Cold War philosophies. Maybe it is even, in part, caused by the policy influence of the military–industrial complex in the United States. President Eisenhower warned in 1961 of the unhealthy influence that could have on American policy: 'In the council of governments, we must guard against the acquisition of unwarranted influence, whether sought or unsought, by the military industrial complex. The potential for the disastrous rise of misplaced power exists and will persist.'[40] The threat of such insidious power from the military–industrial complex would be no less in America today than in President Eisenhower's time. To what extent does it influence contemporary American policy?

Sometimes, American policy in the region is defended by high-lighting Asia's economic strength, and America's involvement in that needs to be protected. Is a major military expansion really necessary for that purpose? Who or what country would challenge America's participation in economic development? The Western Pacific and China depend on markets in America and America itself depends on markets throughout the region. America needs to realise that China will continue to grow irrespective of whether Washington attempts to contain it—the increasing demand from a growing Chinese middle class will continue to feed economic expansion.

The United States talks as though China might wish to curtail freedom of the seas in the East and South China Sea. That is an absurd allegation. It is an important waterway for trade that involves many countries. A significant portion of China's own trade goes through the East and South China Sea, much of it in foreign-registered ships. China and the United States have an equal interest in preserving freedom of the seas. It also worth recalling that China has ratified the United Nations Convention on the Law of the Sea (UNCLOS) whereas the United States has not.[41] UNCLOS Articles 19, 20 and 21 are relevant to 'Innocent Passage'. A plain reading of those sec-tions suggests that the exact scope and juridical nature of the 'Right of Innocent Passage' appears to be far from certain when viewed in light of contemporary state practice. Many states adopt treaties and normally consider such treaties as binding, but it is not uncommon for these same states to derogate from the treaty provisions when it is in their interest to do so.

Despite both President Bush Jnr and President Obama seeking ratification, the Senate has so far refused to act. That is one impediment to a common interpretation of the right to innocent passage. I doubt any difficulty would arise in relation to merchant ships. Difficulties would come with the movement of naval vessels between the 12-mile limit out to the edge of the Exclusive Economic Zone (EEZ), where its naval movements cease to be innocent passage and start to be a nuance or provocation.

There are precedents for progressing this matter and for avoiding difficulties. In 1989 a joint statement between the United States and the Soviet Union issued an agreed uniform interpretation of rules of international law governing innocent passage. It became known as the Treaty of Wyoming.[42] The treaty was designed to prevent misunderstanding and differences of interpretation, relating to the EEZ bordering Soviet Union and the United States. A similar treaty should be negotiated with China. It would be critical for Chinese–American relations. It should remove possible points of misinterpretation and misunderstanding. Such an agreement between China and the United States would complement a Code of Conduct for activities in the East and South China Seas, if they can also be brought to a successful conclusion.

If China and the United States could enter in good faith into consultation that does establish a precedent that could usefully be followed, it would have to be based on reciprocity. What the United States was able to do outside the 12-mile limit off Shanghai the Chinese should be able to do outside the 12-mile limit off Los Angeles or New York.

Another element to the China–US relationship is Japan and how Tokyo's strategic interests are interpreted and achieved. Japan's influence throughout the Western Pacific is substantial. To this point, their strategic posture has been subdued owing to its pacifist post–World War II constitution. As the third largest economy, 1 per cent of its gross domestic product represents a substantial sum.[43] Japan's defence forces are wide-ranging, well equipped and effective. Tokyo's submarine capacity, at sixteen vessels, is particularly significant.[44]

Japan has only one or two gaps in its armoury before it would represent a fully rounded military power—the Japanese Constitution prohibits long-range ships, such as aircraft carriers, and long-range aircraft, such as strategic bombers or ballistic missiles. That might now be less important owing to the remarkable development of Japan's missile technology. Japan's space program, conducted by the Japan Aerospace Exploration Agency, had new legislation passed by the Diet in 2012 allowing for the potential development of space-based military applications, particularly missile defence.[45] Indeed, Japan's missile program is already technically advanced and compatible with American missile defence programs, with sea- and land-based missile defence systems deployed.

In recent times, Japan has been participating in strategic exercises with the United States and with Australia, and has become much more nationalistic in its attitudes. Although there is still a strong liberal base within Japan, the government is more nationalist and the country, as a whole, is accepting a more assertive approach. The tsunami disaster and ensuing nuclear incident at Fukushima in 2011, along with decades of stagnant economic and population growth, have in part inspired the Japanese to reflect on their nation's politics and where the country is heading.

Foreign affairs commentator Gideon Rachman wrote on 14 August 2012 in the *Financial Times*, 'A gaffe-prone Japan is a danger to peace in the Pacific'.[46] More and more Japanese ministers seem to be undertaking actions that would have been regarded as normal in the 1930s but not in the cooperative and internationally focused Tokyo of the post-war decades.

The major dispute between China and Japan now focuses on what the Japanese call the Senkaku Islands but which the Chinese call the Diaoyu Islands. The Japanese have controlled the islands since the conclusion of the first Sino-Japanese war. The Boxer Rebellion took place in 1900 just a few years later. On that occasion, countries from the Eight-Nation Alliance, including the United States, Japan, the United Kingdom, Russia and France, marched to Peking and forced unequal treaties on the Chinese. The humiliations experienced by China as a result of these unequal treaties have, of course, been long redressed. The recent history of militarism by Japan towards China is something Beijing has not forgotten.

The Japanese were expelled from Taiwan and other Pacific Islands, as a result of World War II. Taiwan had always been regarded as part of China. Chiang Kai-shek fled to Taiwan after his defeat by Chairman Mao on the mainland. Chiang Kai-shek, who had a very close relationship with Washington, was able to maintain Taiwan's separation from the mainland.

One of the problems in the relationship between China and Japan relates not only to Japan's invasion of China during World War II but also to the atrocities committed by Japanese troops. Three hundred thousand Chinese civilians were killed during the Rape of Nanking in 1937–38. Japan has never overtly and clearly apologised for that atrocity. Continual visits by Japanese leaders to the Yasukuni Shrine commemorating Japanese war dead upset both China and South Korea. If Tokyo admitted what occurred during the war, it might provide a basis from which a better relationship could be established. Yet presently Japan is not in the mood to admit guilt on that issue or to apologise for its wartime atrocities.

The growing militarism in Japan, however, might represent a dangerous factor in future years. Hugh White wrote in December 2012 that a war between China and Japan over the East China Sea islands could be possible and could have taken place during 2013.[47] The status of the Diaoyu/Senkaku Islands could indeed become a major point of conflict between China and Japan. Nicholas Kristof, US journalist, had this to say in the *New York Times* on 19 September 2012: 'I find the evidence for Chinese sovereignty quite compelling. The most interesting evidence is emerging from old Japanese government documents and suggests that Japan in effect stole the islands from China in 1895 as booty of war.'[48]

In Deng Xiaoping's time, it was agreed that the ultimate status of the islands would be deferred for future generations, so that the peace treaty between China and Japan could be concluded in 1978.[49] Under that basic agreement, neither side was to press its claim, nor to press for resolution of the issue, until it became more propitious to do so.

It would seem that Japan started the latest round of escalation, by buying the islands and making them government property. Japan would argue that the government was trying to avoid a more volatile situation, which was threatened by the militarist right-wing Governor Ishihara of Tokyo, who also wanted to purchase the disputed territory.[50] According to Kristof, Japan was trying to calm waters rather than to inflame them, but China did not accept it that way.[51] The status quo, as it had existed for a considerable time, had been disturbed, in the first instance by Japan. As a consequence, China has reacted, sailing ships through the area, and the dispute has become difficult. The anti-Japanese violence in China is unacceptable but has to be understood against the wide knowledge of Japanese atrocities in China during World War II. The situation is not helped by Japan's absurd claim that there is no dispute. The islands, according to Tokyo, belong to Japan.[52] There is clearly a dispute. There is historical evidence that the islands were taken as booty of war in 1895. European powers, and indeed America, have recognised that the treaties forced on China around that period were unequal treaties that needed to be redressed.[53] The fact that Japan relies on that particular treaty for ownership weakens its claim significantly.

The real danger of this issue, of course, revolves around the Defence Treaty between Japan and the United States. There is little doubt that the new, more assertive government in Japan would feel reinforced by that Defence Treaty. The United States officially claims to be neutral in relation to the conflict but, as Kristof writes, '… it seems clear to me that it de facto sides with Japan.'[54] The United States would be obliged, under the terms of its defence treaty with Japan, to intervene on the side of Tokyo in any armed dispute over the islands.

In recent matters, China has reported its view of these issues to the United Nations through the Commission on the Limits of the Continental Shelf.[55] Japan has responded, of course, rejecting the Chinese view.[56] I cannot see a UN process that is likely to lead to a resolution. If conflict is to be avoided, somehow or other, both sides need to return to the informal agreement that existed before the Governor of Tokyo stirred the issue. If this could be formalised, it would be even better. There could be a Code of Conduct for the East China Sea, whereby claimants to territories did not press their claims but did not withdraw them either, shelving them for the time being. If they were then prepared to cooperate, in maintaining the peace, in patrolling, in development—especially if possible—of oil and gas reserves, that would be the best that could be hoped for. Yet, it might be too much to hope for.

The questions between China and Japan are not helped by the expansion of the armed forces of both countries. The Japanese insist that their strategic situation has not altered but, at the same time, a recent review of their defence capabilities has recommended increasing Japan's surveillance capabilities and boosting its marine force and missile capabilities.[57] The attitude of Prime Minister Shinzō Abe, as leader of a more nationalist, more assertive Japan, is unlikely to make resolution of these issues easier.

One of the issues confusing and compounding relations between China, Japan and the United States, in particular, is the way issues between China and the rest of the world are reported in the media; by the way in which US representatives, whether they be the President, Secretary of Defense, Secretary of State or military officers, describe China's actions and attitudes.

As an example, a US Navy captain, James Fanell, Deputy Chief of Staff for Intelligence and Information Operations for the Pacific Fleet, described as a 'top US Navy intelligence officer', was in Australia in February 2013. Fanell warned Australia that China is a bully on the high seas and that it wants to sink American warships and seize control of waters from its neighbours. He also accused China of fabricating history, to establish claims to disputed islands in the South and East China Seas.[58] He clearly described China as the principal threat. He is one of a string of American representatives who have come to Australia indicating what America is doing to reinforce allies in the region, to combat such threats, to expand its military forces, to build a defensive network from Japan, through the Philippines to Australia and through Singapore to India.

On another occasion, Bonnie Glaser, from the Center for Strategic and International Studies, spoke at the Sydney Institute on 24 May 2013.[59] Her approach was much more nuanced, less combative, and I have no doubt she thought she was being tactful. Her remarks were riddled with the implication that China is the bad boy of the region and other countries have something to fear, and the American military build-up is therefore necessary. In relation to the Philippines, for example, she was encouraging the Philippines and leading them to believe that America would come down on their side over problems in the South China Sea. She showed absolutely no understanding of the progress that has been made by ASEAN and in other regional forums to take charge of East and South-East Asia's own affairs and of the mechanisms that these countries are developing to handle their own problems. Even so, as an American assessment, it was probably much more balanced than most.

It needs to be understood that there seems to be a deliberate act of policy on the part of the United States. Representatives are sent from the State Department or the military, such as James Fanell, or from think-tanks like the Center for Strategic and International Studies, to put the American point of view and to disparage China. Such propaganda is almost always based on a falsehood, or on the US interpretation of circumstances, which is often partisan. If US perceptions are taken as reality, then there will be trouble between China and the United States.

If this attitude persists, there will indeed be trouble between China and the United States. The situation is made more serious by America's defence relationship with the Philippines and Japan. Both countries could, as a consequence, become more assertive in their own right, believing that the United States would stand behind them, no matter what they did, or no matter what the consequences. Another issue on the sidelines of these relationships is of course the unresolved issue surrounding the status of Taiwan.

Although there have been tense periods that could have led to war between China and Taiwan, involving the United States, this has not happened, and is now less likely than before. I believe it is less likely given the huge amount of cross-strait trade—valued at $110 billion in 2010[60]—and the increasing number of people movements between the two territories. Indeed, in 2012, more than 2.5 million Chinese residents travelled to Taiwan and more than 3 million Taiwanese residents to mainland China.[61] These figures indicate that those who live on both sides of the strait, and those who have money to invest, believe that the problem of Taiwan's future will be handled peacefully.

The issue could only become difficult if, as a result of elections in Taiwan, a pro-independence president was elected. However, as a result of developments in Taiwan itself, and on the mainland, that is most unlikely. Both China and Taiwan want a peaceful resolution, which is within their grasp. This is important because it should remove Taiwan from America's list of concerns about the Western Pacific.

While some people hold a contrary view on this issue, the 2009 Australian Defence White Paper was moderate in tone, saying little more than that 'Taiwan will remain a source of potential strategic miscalculation, and all parties will need to work hard to ensure that developments in relation to Taiwan over the years ahead are peaceful ones'.[62] Overall, and on the basis of the increases in trade and the cross-straits movement of people, I remain optimistic.

The United States tends to look at issues merely through American eyes. It is their view, their understanding of history, their interpretation of how people will react. The United States needs to ask itself how China views these events. What influences and motivates China? China is a great, proud and ancient nation. China's history began not with the communist party but thousands of years before that. China's achievements, through the millennia, have been substantial, and all of this is part of modern China. China would recall the humiliations of the 1890s and 1900s, the period of the Boxer Rebellion. They would recall the actions of the European powers, along with America and Japan, who marched to Peking, and the troops who scraped the gold veneer off urns in the Forbidden City. These humiliations influenced China not to be rash, not to be premature, but to be totally determined in redressing the indignities then experienced. If the United States cannot understand this, then it will miscalculate with the probability of serious consequences.

The United States has to be given credit for the outcome of the Cold War. That ended with the break-up of the Soviet Union and the end of the communist threat. The US role in that cannot be underestimated. It was enormously important to the entire world.

Since the end of the Cold War, however, we need to question much more closely the consequences of the growing strength of American exceptionalism and the policies of the neo-conservatives. We, who live in this region, especially need to question seriously what additional benefits an expanded American role brings. We know the region benefited from American success through the Cold War but what specific Western Pacific event has America been involved in that has added value to that broad context?

One of the things that makes me fearful of America's deployment is that where it has become heavily involved, whether it be Vietnam in earlier years, the Middle East, Iraq or Afghanistan, US interventions seem to leave behind continuing chaos. Where can America point to real progress or real peace as a result of American military intervention? Is its history of failure in the Middle East and in South-East Asia to be replicated in the Western Pacific?

The Asia–Pacific region has worked very hard to establish a region that is, by and large, devoid of major conflict between the states. Many issues remain that could flare up: the South and East China Sea dispute and North Korea, to name but two. However, regional architecture is being established to try to avoid problems in the South China Sea. Similar processes could be put in place in relation to the East China Sea. The nations of the region have shown themselves to be capable of resolving their own problems in a manner conducive to a mutually agreeable settlement; resolutions sympathetic to their political, historical and cultural make-up and not imposed on them by third parties believing they know best.

The region that Australia feared and looked first to Britain, then to America for protection from has changed. It has matured as a region, and the nations within it have developed and grown. Australia needs to change too, to reflect the new realities of our geographic home. In order to truly do so, our policy of strategic dependence needs to end. Yet, sadly, we have not done so and have continued to follow our historic pattern of dependence and acquiescence. Indeed, I would go so far as to say that we are now more heavily aligned with the United States than at any time in our history. The post–Cold War era has been one of missed opportunities for Australia to end strategic dependence.

12

Missed opportunities

Given our history, perhaps it was too hopeful to believe our leaders would realise, let alone grasp, the opportunities for a more independent Australian foreign policy provided by the end of the Cold War. The end of the communist threat, an increasingly stable and prosperous Asia–Pacific region and an Australian government that had Asian engagement firmly on its policy agenda boded well for Australia's foreign policy development. Yet, much like the dreams and aspirations for a new global order that faded away as the 1990s progressed, the possibility of a more independent Australian foreign policy began to disappear as well. Instead, we now find ourselves as dependent on America as before, if not more so, with our military and intelligence capabilities ensconced within the US military infrastructure to such a point the two have become blurred. In the space of twenty-three years, we have become so enmeshed with America's strategic aims that we jeopardise our own future security and important bilateral relationships in the region. With both major political parties providing continued and steadfast bipartisan support for the relationship with Washington, I remain pessimistic about the chances of our political leaders acknowledging these risks, let alone acting on them. It is important to understand how Australia came to be in this position.

Paul Keating was a controversial Australian Prime Minister. People were either strongly, even fanatically, on his side or highly critical of him. He had been a good Treasurer in the Hawke years and had followed through on a number of reforms of lasting benefit for Australia. He had a sense of Australian identity and of Australian purpose. One of the main points of contention was that he believed it necessary to reduce the emphasis on ties with Britain, and especially the monarchy, in whatever way he could. This was not done merely for his own sake, but because Keating believed that our ties with Asia should be greatly strengthened, especially with Indonesia. His government would further develop the foreign policy work of the Hawke Government, continuing the policy objectives outlined in the Fitzgerald report on immigration and the Garnaut report on relations with North Asia.[1] He saw Australia playing a more significant role in the affairs of East and South-East Asia, deepening a policy of Asian engagement for Australia. He was the first Australian Prime Minister operating entirely after the end of the Cold War. This opened the possibility for greater strategic independence on Australia's part.

During Prime Minister Bob Hawke's time, Australia–Pacific Economic Cooperation (APEC) finally came to fruition. The idea of an organisation representing countries of East and South-East Asia had first been mentioned in consultations with Australia in Prime Minister Ohira's time. The initial reluctance of Indonesia, which wanted to give priority to ASEAN, had first to be overcome, but the Hawke and Keating Governments advanced the concept and made it reality. These actions represented Australian initiatives. It was a constructive contribution to establishing regional infrastructure.

Consistent with his effort to give greater attention to countries of the region, Keating wanted APEC also to be a forum for a regular leaders meeting. He lobbied hard for that point of view and ultimately persuaded US President Clinton that it should be supported. This led to some arguments with Malaysian Prime Minister Mahathir and, as a consequence, relations between Malaysia and Australia were frosty. Keating's wish for a leaders meeting as part of the APEC meeting was ultimately consummated in 1993.

During this period, Australian Foreign Minister Gareth Evans, working with the United Nations, was largely responsible for the most effective peace-making, peace-keeping and democratic settlement with which the United Nations has been involved. He worked tirelessly to bring Cambodia in from the cold.[2] He worked with a small group of nations under the heading 'Friends of Cambodia' and achieved great things. The military operation, which was the largest single UN military operation, was under the control of Lieutenant General John Sanderson from Australia and on the civilian side by a quite remarkable Japanese, Yasushi Akashi. Sanderson and Akashi worked very closely together. It was a classic example of how to bring peace to a region that had been torn by internal conflict and war. Evans worked particularly well with the United Nations. He achieved considerable international support. It would not have happened without his drive and his energy. It is an example of the fine international work Australia can do on its own accord, without the need for guidance from an ally or protector. It was reminiscent of Evatt's role with the United Nations.

Australia's foreign policy during Howard's years as Prime Minister demonstrated a total belief in American power and that Australia would therefore be most secure the closer it came to the United States. Subsequent governments have reinforced this trend.

Prime Minister Howard did not believe that relationships with Indonesia or any part of Asia should be allowed to prejudice or diminish our relationships with the United Kingdom. He would have wanted to maintain the full strength of our relationship with Britain and did not recognise that, as time passed, the strength of the British relationship was bound to diminish. Australia was a different country from the nation that had for so many years pledged loyalty to the crown and Empire. He also did not support Keating's priority of working much harder at expanding and building relationships with Indonesia and other countries through East and South-East Asia, particularly through multilateral mechanisms. Howard's relationship with the United States was particularly close, especially after the commencement of the Bush Administration. Initially, the Howard Government was able to establish better relationships with Mahathir and undo some of the damage caused by unwise remarks from Keating. This changed when Mahathir heavily criticised Australia's role in Iraq and in Timor Leste.

Howard maintained good relationships with the United Kingdom, the United States and China. He was understood and respected internationally. His government played a constructive role during the 1997 Asian financial crisis, particularly with the affected nations in South-East Asia. For the first time, Australia contributed additional funds to those of the IMF, along with Japan, to assist countries damaged by the collapse. Australia, in particular, played a role in assisting Indonesia when the World Bank and the IMF sought to impose intrusive and unrealistic conditions on Indonesia.

The problems of Timor Leste continued to bedevil relationships between Indonesia and Australia. The time has long past when Australia or any other country was concerned that Timor Leste could become a communist enclave. Communism, as a world force, no longer existed. President B. J. Habibie, whom I got to know well in later times, was struggling with the problem of Timorese independence and suggested that Timor Leste received special autonomy within the Indonesian Republic. He offered that as part of a UN-mediated negotiation process between Indonesia and the country's former colonial master, Portugal.

Australia's policy at this point changed, without too much discussion, with no Cabinet decision. Prime Minister Howard and Foreign Minister Alexander Downer changed the policy. The Prime Minister wrote a letter to President Habibie proposing that there be a referendum within ten years on whether or not Timor Leste should stay within Indonesia or move to independence. If that proposal had been discussed in Cabinet, if it had received the full advice of the appropriate federal government departments, it might never have been made. That referendum would have been hanging over Timor

Leste for a decade, clouding Timor Leste–Indonesia relations and therefore Australia–Indonesia relations. There would have been ten years of campaigning, those for and those against. It would have been an unsettled and possibly a dangerous period. President Habibie understood this; he saw the writing on the wall, however, and saw that a decision involving the possibility of independence would have to be part of an ultimate solution, but he wanted to get it done with and out of the way. So, in January 1999, President Habibie said he was going to hold a UN-sponsored referendum in six months.

This prompted violent opposition from pro-integration groups within Timor Leste. There was considerable violence. That ended with an overwhelming vote in favour of independence, but it was also necessary to establish a UN peace-keeping force, which Australia led. While the United States ultimately provided logistic support for that force, initially they had been unwilling and not particularly cooperative. This was indeed an independent action by Australia and, in the final result, would be regarded as one of Prime Minister Howard's significant achievements. This would have been regarded as looking after our own region, rather than demonstrating a move towards a more strategically independent foreign policy.

In Howard's time, Australia made it quite clear that we supported American unilateralism, the US willingness to ignore the United Nations and the US willingness to use military pre-emption as important principles in Australian foreign policy. Indeed, in a television interview, Howard made the comment that Australia itself would consider a policy of pre-emption: 'I think any Australian Prime Minister would … It stands to reason that if you believed that somebody was going to launch an attack again your country … and you had the capacity to stop it and there was no alternative … then, of course, you would have to use it.'[3] The region was not impressed, with Malaysia's Mahathir stating that Howard was behaving like 'the white-man sheriff in some black country'. The Philippines called the remarks 'arrogant'.[4]

President Bush Jnr said that Australia was regarded rather as a good sheriff in our own part of the world, upgrading Howard's earlier description of Australia as a deputy sheriff in the region.[5] We certainly gave that appearance, an aspect of policy that does not serve Australia well in East and South-East Asia. There are many who would prefer us to be more independent, to make up our own mind and not merely to reflect US views. This is particularly important because much of the thrust of this book demonstrates that you do not create a bank of goodwill with great powers on which you can necessarily and inevitably draw at a time of your choosing. Great powers do what is in their best interests and not that of their allies, no matter how close.

Britain should have learnt that lesson from its humiliation over Suez, at the hands of the United States, but has not. The 'special relationship' remains a principal policy objective. Australia too should have learnt that goodwill is not guaranteed by the marginal support provided by the United States during the East Timor crisis. In earlier times, the United States has stood back and thereby indicated support for Indonesia rather than for Australia.

When Downer, speaking from China, suggested that we might not inevitably follow the United States if there was a war with China over Taiwan,[6] the Prime Minister was reported as assuring President Bush that Australia would of course remain a loyal ally.[7] A nice comparison, a quite different emphasis from that held by the Menzies Government, when there were real alarms over the offshore islands in Taiwan in the mid-1950s.

It was the Howard period that consummated an even greater strategic dependence upon the United States than we had during the Cold War. Our defence forces are so closely intertwined with those of the United States that that in itself impinges on our strategic independence and, indeed, on our sovereignty.

Although great power policies and actions can be based on principle, very often they are not; they are based on expediency that will preserve their power and influence. Considerations for their allies are, at the very best, secondary. Events in Asia, Eastern Europe and in the Middle East have shown that the United States has often acted with a most imperfect understanding of the problems it was confronting.

That has caused much loss of life and contributed to instability; in the common jargon of today, to collateral damage, measured in tens upon tens of thousands of civilians killed. Does Australia want to be tied to a power that can involve itself in such actions, or do we want to establish sufficient strategic independence for us to make up our own minds in our own time? We need to decide how best to secure Australia's future and peace for the region in which we live.

For those who want Australian independence, who are proud of this nation's achievements and who recognise the difference in values and purposes of the United States and of Australia, it represents a problem that is not written about, not spoken about, but which must be addressed if Australia is to stand proud as an independent nation. There is bipartisan failure to understand that our position is so close to the United States that our own sovereignty and strategic independence, our capacity to make separate decisions, is now heavily circumscribed.

As a result of the changing and dynamic background in East Asia and the Western Pacific, Australia needs to examine the totality of its relationship with the United States. The ANZUS Treaty is a commitment to consult. If Australia were under attack the US Congress might need to pass a war powers resolution before any military help could be provided. ANZUS was designed to give Australia assurance about its own security at the end of World War II. It has become a treaty through which successive governments have made Australia subordinate to American wishes and to carry out American foreign policy. This subordination has been made in the belief that America would respond to a call for help and has been made without really considering what the Treaty actually obliges Washington to do—nothing but consult.

Today, we are so heavily enmeshed in American military and strategic affairs, in interoperability and in the use of military hardware, that it is difficult to distinguish a separate military or strategic identity. If we had the capacity to influence American policy objectives as an entirely separate sovereign nation, with Washington regarding us as an equal partner, then the relationship would have relevance.

Yet Australia and other, much larger and more powerful countries have found it extraordinarily hard, if not impossible, to influence US policy. Washington's general practice has been and remains one whereby America decides what it wants to do, and only after that is America prepared to have discussions with other countries. Ex-post negotiation is not negotiation at all.

When I was a young and raw Minister for the Army, I was given the job of overseeing the Australian Army's deployment of a task force to South Vietnam. At a meeting with the Military Board, I can remember asking, in my innocence, whether this should be an integrated operation or whether Australia should be allocated a separate piece of territory to look after. I was told, in no uncertain terms, that an integrated operation was most inadvisable. It would lead to friction because the two countries' operating procedures and concern for the well-being of troops was so different. It was graphically described to me that, if we had an integrated operation, Australians would be shooting Americans and Americans shooting Australians within a few weeks. Those days are now gone. We have interoperability, close coordination of strategic weapons and plans, and probably a greatly reduced capacity to operate on our own account, unless we have America's approval for what we want to do.

The support we give to American hard power is one part of this unequal relationship. President Obama and Prime Minister Julia Gillard announced a rotation of a Marine Air-Ground Task Force of 2500 troops through Darwin in November 2011.[8] We were also told at that time that there would be an increase in the deployment of US aircraft and related use of Australian airfields and aircraft facilities. It is reasonable to assume that US Marine air force deployments would be used to round out the Marine Air-Ground Task Force, so that it becomes a fully-fledged fighting force.[9]

Secretary of Defense Leon Panetta in June 2012 had this to say: 'A critical component of that effort is the agreement announced last fall for a rotational Marine Corps presence and aircraft deployments in northern Australia.' He went on: 'The first detachment of Marines arrived in April [2012], and this Marine Air-Ground Task

Force will be capable of rapidly deploying across the Asia–Pacific region, thereby enabling us to work more effectively with partners in Southeast Asia and the Indian Ocean and tackle common challenges such as natural disasters and maritime security.'[10] These words clearly point to an effective battle-ready task force, with a balanced air force or Marine Air Wing and naval forces also deployed in the region.

Darwin will become a fully operational US base, which will be able to deploy significant power anywhere throughout the region. The suggestions implicit in the original remarks by Prime Minister Gillard and President Obama—that this is much more of a training operation than anything else—is clearly a gloss on the real purpose of the deployments. In fact the base commits us firmly to being the southern linchpin of America's policy of 'containment'.

Discussions have occurred with Australia concerning the use by the US Navy of HMAS *Stirling* in Western Australia and of Cocos Island for the use of unmanned aircraft.[11] These additional deployments are obviously going to cost a great deal, although I have no doubt the United States will try to get its allies to foot at least a part of the bill. The Australian Government has been singularly silent concerning the cost to Australia of these US deployments.[12]

Other factors, which are hardly known in Australia, are also relevant. On 21 August 2012 the British edition of the *Guardian* reported that 'Major General Richard Burr of the Australian Defence Force would direct training and supervise the Pacific command's efforts'[13] in the Western Pacific. He would in fact become the Deputy Commander of the US Army Pacific, which oversees more than 60,000 American soldiers in the Asia–Pacific region. This appointment, for two and a half years, was announced not by the Australian Defence Minister or the Department of Defence, but by the United States Secretary of Army, John McHugh.

It is surely a significant appointment. It is possible to regard it as an indication of the high regard in which America holds Australia, and indeed Major General Burr, but it is also possible to regard it as one more indicator of the way in which Australia is complicit in, and party to, US military plans in the Western Pacific.

If the United States were to undertake a military operation with which the Australian Government disapproved—and I can envisage circumstances in which that would happen—it would be a brave Australian government that withdrew the second in command of US Army forces in the Pacific. If you can conceive of no circumstances in which our interests and the interests of the United States can diverge, then you will see little problem with such cooperation. If there are circumstances, however, in which our national interests and those of the United States might well diverge, then this appointment could become more than an embarrassment to both nations. The fact that the appointment, which was clearly an important one, was not announced by the Australian minister, or at least by the Department of Defence in Australia, only compounds the extent of our subservience to America.

This involvement is deepened by the fact that an Australian guided-missile frigate, HMAS *Sydney*, was deployed with the US Navy's 7th Fleet George Washington Carrier Strike Group, which is stationed at Yokosuku, Japan, until 13 September 2013.[14] It is the intention to repeat that deployment in 2014.[15] If the United States chooses to exhibit a show of power in relation to North Korea or in relation to China in the East or South China Sea, through the deployment of the carrier strike group, then an Australian ship is one of the escorts. By default, we are again complicit in their policy and in their actions. I have no doubt our navy regards it as a compliment, but it is a compliment that pays scant regard to any thought of Australian strategic independence. It is a compliment that could again become a significant embarrassment if Australia's national interest diverges from that of the United States. Such a ship could obviously only be withdrawn with extreme difficulty and against massive pressure from the United States, if we wanted Australia to be disengaged from a particular American operation.

The deployment of an Australian ship as part of the George Washington Carrier Strike Group is not an exercise; it is an active military deployment. The appointment of Major General Burr as second in charge of the US Army is not an exercise; it is an active military deployment. Obviously, there is no problem with military exercises. It would be much better if such exercises could include not only the Japanese but also forces from other countries in the region, including China.

These factors would become even more relevant if Australia were to accept America's proposal that we should operate ten or twelve Virginia-class nuclear submarines.[16] The suggestion, apparently, involves Australia getting the submarines at a particularly good price in return for which we would man them, run them and pay for them, and also undertake considerable patrolling that otherwise the United States would undertake on its own account. The submarines would, of course, fill Australian purposes in addition. If these submarines end up being the replacement for the Collins-class submarines, our armed forces would be integrated ever more closely with that of the United States. We would become even more dependent upon the United States for continuing operations and for maintenance.

I am not entering the argument as to whether Australia should have conventional or nuclear submarines, but I am opposed to any suggestion that would end up with Australia becoming even more dependent on the United States, for the operations of our military forces. This particular proposal would certainly result in greater strategic dependence. One might even ask, is that why the United States proposes it?

There are a number of significant facilities in Australia, of great importance to America's future plans. In part, the purpose of these facilities is to gather intelligence; to be able to see into the farthest places of the earth and know the communications that are being passed around, to know what is being said or planned. The facilities gather intelligence; information that is important in maintaining a peaceful world. Other aspects of these facilities can be used to support offensive military operations, and there is no way the United States is going to ask us for permission before using facilities in such a manner.

Pine Gap is one of the oldest intelligence-gathering establishments in Australia. It was, in the first instance, an information-gathering operation. It initially had no other capacity. Nurrungar, established close to Pine Gap, had a specific purpose of monitoring and tracking any missile that was launched over a large part of the Earth's surface. As a consequence, America knew what country had missiles, whether they were reliable and accurate, and how far they could go; clearly, information of great strategic importance, particularly in the context of the Cold War.

During missile tests, information on the performance of various parts of the missile in flight is sent by radio signal to the test base. US satellites in geo-stationary orbit sitting above the Earth intercepted this missile telemetry, and downlinked the data to Pine Gap and other ground stations, where it was then processed into usable signals intelligence about the performance and capacities of new Soviet missiles. Pine Gap continues this activity today, monitoring the testing of missiles by a wide variety of countries, including North Korea.

I have no concern with such operations continuing as they were originally intended, but as Pine Gap's facilities have been greatly expanded from the original surveillance operation at its inception, and it now not only gathers intelligence but also is integral to the conduct of modern warfare, I have grave concerns over its continued operation.[17] It can now be used to target drone killings, whether to take out a single person or to destroy some other target. It could be used to provide information essential in the launching of a missile attack. Such involvement in offensive operations is not necessarily in Australia's interest. Such purposes would make it a prime target for attack if there were ever a significant war involving the United States and China. The real question for Australia is whether we want to be involved if there ever were a major war between China and the United States.

Pine Gap is the most important US-operated base in Australia. About eight hundred people work there; that is, about twice the number of two decades ago.[18] Employment numbers reflect the changed purposes and changed use of the base. It is commanded by an American officer; the deputy is an Australian. The primary contractors at the base are American.

Former Defence Minister Robert Hill said a decade ago: 'The work done at the joint facility indicates how countries are complying with agreements not to proliferate weapons systems and capabilities, or showing when they are working against such agreements.' Recently, the previous Defence Minister Stephen Smith emphasised that '… intelligence collected at Pine Gap contributes to the verification of arms control and disarmament agreements'. Smith continued: 'As a nation that prides itself on playing an active role in the counter-proliferation of nuclear weapons, the value of the data obtained from Pine Gap cannot be underestimated.'[19]

I have no doubt that those statements were, and are, correct, but the base has significant additional functions. The base is now used to pinpoint targets in real time, to facilitate targeted assassinations or drone killings. It is the development of new weapons systems that enables the base's technology to be used in new and aggressive ways. There is a great deal of difference between the collection of information for defensive purposes and collecting information that is part of an offensive war machine.

In congressional testimony in 2000, the then director of the National Reconnaissance Office, Keith Hall, said: 'In the future, US forces will rely upon space systems for global awareness of threats, swift orchestration of military operations, and precision use of smart weapons.' Read that as providing precise targets for drone killings. He went on to say that the aim was to enable US military forces to deliver 'precise military firepower anywhere in the world, day or night, in all weather'.[20] Pine Gap is now one of the facilities that supplements such capabilities.

Thus Pine Gap in Central Australia is now directly linked 'on a minute-by-minute basis, to US and allied military operations in Afghanistan and, indeed, anywhere else across the eastern hemisphere'.[21] It is clear that Australian personnel are involved in drone attacks, in assassination. This has happened in Pakistan and probably Afghanistan and maybe Yemen, and it could happen in future on the Korean Peninsula or, much more significantly for Australia, in the Taiwan Straits, in the East and South China Seas.

Smith said in a recent statement that Pine Gap operates with the 'full knowledge and concurrence' of the Australian Government. Later, however, he tried to modify this statement by saying that 'concurrence … does not mean that Australia approves every activity or tasking undertaken'.[22] The words 'full knowledge' and 'concurrence' means that we approve the use of Pine Gap for targeting American drone killings. How can we argue otherwise? What nation would allow a base on its territory to conduct missions about which it has full knowledge, but of which it does not approve? It is simply an impossible scenario, a contradiction in policy.

Is this done under the original Pine Gap agreement, or under a subsequent agreement? There is certainly no law of the Commonwealth that would legitimise Australians participating in what could be regarded as the murder of citizens of a country with which we are not at war. If we are at war with a country, the use of drones could be a legitimate weapon, like any other, against the military of that country, in that country. For Australians to participate in the killing of citizens who have not been charged or brought before any court of law, where evidence is given in secret and cannot be challenged and tested, is quite another matter. Such people can be targeted in a third country, meant to be a friendly country, with which we are not at war. No Australian Government should approve such processes and actions.

Unlike in Australia, the Americans have provided a legislative basis for undertaking such killings. The paragraph entitled 'Authorization for use of United States Armed Forces' (see chapter 10) is the alleged legal basis for American operations, such as drone killings, including killing of Americans. The words 'in order to prevent any future acts of international terrorism against the United States' leave the current powers, used first by President Bush Jnr and second by President Obama, intact, in perpetuity.[23] No sunset clause is included.

A sixteen-page memorandum, a 'Department of Justice White Paper', sets out the Justice Department's interpretation of the powers available to the White House, as a result of that congressional resolution.[24] How much credibility should be given to that Justice

Department White Paper, prepared during the Bush Jnr era, is open to serious question. We already know the extent to which Justice Department lawyers undermined the integrity of their profession, in justifying torture at Abu Ghraib and Guantanamo Bay. For what it is worth, the White Paper says, first, that an informed 'high-level' official of the United States Government has determined that the targeted individual poses an 'imminent' threat of violent attacks against the United States. Yet no definition is given for 'high-level official'. Who decides what level of seniority is classified as 'high'? It is extraordinarily vague for a document covering such an important piece of legislation. The word 'imminent' is not defined. We know one of the persons killed in a drone attack was a 16-year-old son searching for his father in Yemen, who was also on the list for assassination.[25] Did an unnamed high-level official deem this 16-year-old boy to be an imminent threat of violent attack? Was he identified through intelligence gathered from Pine Gap or some other facility?

The Justice Department White Paper says that if capture is not possible, then the operation should be conducted in the manner consistent with applicable 'law of war principles'. Later in the White Paper, the 'law on war principles' are defined as the principles of 'necessity', 'distinction', 'proportionality' and 'humanity'.

The unending war powers resolution passed through Congress immediately after 9/11,[26] and the Justice Department White Paper[27] are not the only legal basis of drone killings. There is the 16 September 2003 Executive Order, signed by Secretary of Defense Rumsfeld, that establishes JSOC as the principal counter-terrorist force of the United States and which preauthorised fifteen countries where counter-terrorist action could be taken, irrespective of whether or not the United States was at war with those countries. Further, there is the 2004 Executive Order also signed by Rumsfeld,[28] known as the Al Qaeda Network Executive Order or AQN Exord, that provides the legal basis for JSOC's operations. They allow JSOC to operate anywhere in the world. They have been used to establish a secret army sidelining congressional supervision and the normal procedures of military command, and they give direct authority to the White

House. It establishes, if you like, a secret executive army, unchecked, unchallenged, targeted in secret and used in secret. Authority for these exords rests entirely on the single paragraph war powers resolution passed after 9/11.

Although the rules and procedures for this secret offensive special force were established under President Bush, it has been used more extensively by President Obama, by a president who spoke against such processes as a presidential candidate. As a result of President Obama's actions, we can take these processes as a continuing part of presidential authority and power. This represents a significant change to an earlier, more lawful America. It is relevant to our own relationship with the United States. How can we allow Pine Gap, which is now at the very heart of our relationship with America, to be used in such a fashion? Australians working there are not covered by US law or by any Australian law. Indeed, as a signatory to the International Criminal Court (ICC), the killings of civilians may make them liable for prosecution under the ICC.

The next significant base established here was North West Cape, Naval Communication Station Harold E Holt, named after the former Prime Minister. Its initial, major purpose was to communicate with nuclear submarines patrolling in the Indian Ocean. Then, for various reasons, it became less important to America's strategic plans and, in 1982, the United States passed control of the base entirely to Australia. The United States was still able to use the communication systems.

In 2008, however, the joint status was formally resumed, allowing the United States 'all necessary rights of access to and use of the station'. It is a facility of significant strategic importance to the United States. Australian Senator Scott Ludlam recently put it this way: 'North West Cape continues to facilitate, enable and support nuclear armed submarines, offensive attack weapons platforms, thereby legitimising the retention and deployment of nuclear weapons.'[29]

This base now has a significantly expanded role. The United States wants not only to know everything that happens in space but also to dominate space. These new activities were agreed, and

255

a statement was issued on 15 November 2012 by the Minister for Defence: 'Defence space cooperation—space situational awareness',[30] which defined the details of a new agreement with the United States. This objective would seem to abrogate the 1967 treaty concerning activities in space, which outlaws the use of space for military purposes.[31] The treaty is clear; it is comprehensive; it has been ratified by 102 states. Space was to be used to improve the lot of mankind. Knowledge of space was to be shared. There was to be freedom of scientific investigation, including the moon and other celestial bodies. It is not to be subject to national appropriation. Weapons of mass destruction were banned, and space was to be used exclusively for peaceful purposes. It is difficult to believe that the United States' current actions in space are consistent with the 1967 treaty.

There are other bases of significant importance and which rely on American facilities. Headquarters Joint Operations Command, the command and control facility for our forces fighting in Iraq or Afghanistan, for example, is located close to Bungendore, outside Canberra. It relies on American satellites, on American facilities, for the capacity to communicate. That reliance by Australia on the United States for military communications in reality means that we cannot conduct operations unless the United States approves of them. That is a derogation of sovereignty. For our own communications, we have paid $900 million for access to a satellite which America still owns and therefore presumably controls, but which we can use for our military communications.[32]

On 2 August 2012 Stephen Smith said that there are no American bases in Australia. He used these words at a press conference: 'We don't have United States military bases in Australia and we are not proposing to. What we have talked about in terms of either increased aerial access or naval access is precisely that—greater access to our facilities.'[33] He implied that all the joint bases are Australian, and Americans just have access to our facilities. If only it were true, but it is not. Whatever the technical ownership of the base may be, whatever the agreement describes, if the United States has full access to the base it is an American base. If it serves US purposes, collecting information, which they might or might not share with us, it is an American base. If it is used to issue commands to American forces in far parts of the world and it is clearly serving American purposes then, once again, it is an American base.

We have significantly diminished our capacity to act as a separate sovereign nation by the way in which we have committed ourselves to American purposes.

When Prime Minister Whitlam came into office in 1972, he renegotiated the terms of the agreement in relation to North West Cape. The letters 'US' were taken out of the name of the facility. That was nothing more than changing the façade. It made no difference to the way in which the base was used. It was still an American base.

There is one other point in relation to US bases both in Australia and in the region. The United States has, with its allies, developed new language. In older times, what the Americans are doing in Darwin, what they are doing in Singapore, and what they are looking to do again in the Philippines, the word 'base' would clearly have been used. Now they use the term 'rotating through', which is designed to give the impression that the deployment is temporary, or that it is for training purposes and not part of an offensive strategic deployment. The words 'rotating through' tend to hide the true purpose of a deployment. As the *Washington Post* points out: 'Such arrangements are seen by defense leaders as a way to project American power at a lower cost and impose a lighter American footprint in countries where more permanent methods, such as a US military base, would not be welcome.'[34]

It is against this backdrop that Australia must decide on its future foreign policy direction. Do we continue to tether ourselves to American aims and policy in the region or do we, for the first time in our history, decide to carve out our own role in the region? Do we work constructively with our near neighbours to create a regional response to regional problems?

I believe our relationship with the United States has become a paradox. Our leaders argue we need to keep our alliance with the United States strong in order to ensure our defence in the event of an aggressive foe. Yet the most likely reason Australia would need to confront an aggressive foe is our strong alliance with the United States. We need America for defence from an attacker who is likely to attack us because we use America for defence. It is not a sustainable policy.

The world changed at the conclusion of the Cold War. The international context changed, moving from a bipolar to a unipolar world, in which the United States, and the West more broadly, failed to establish a new, cooperative and understanding world order. Change also occurred domestically in America, where unchecked exceptionalism and neo-conservative tendencies have undermined the integrity of the United States, making acceptable behaviour and conduct that previously would have been considered shameful. Simultaneously, the Asia–Pacific, the region we call home, has changed, too. It has established a series of institutions and norms that have facilitated rapid economic growth and, by and large, co-operation among the nations of the region. Yet strategic challenges remain, and these challenges are such that Australia might be forced to choose on which side of the argument we sit.

Conclusion

Australia needs to decide which direction it is to take into the future: are we to continue to follow our policy of strategic dependence or will we, for the first time in our history, move towards a more strategically independent foreign policy?

A major part of this question concerns our relationship with the United States and what it will constitute in the future. In some ways this debate has already begun. This is particularly so in terms of America's ongoing role in the Asia–Pacific and its ability to manage its relationship with a growing China—a major issue in determining the future of Australia's policy of strategic dependence. Indeed, it is a concern over the future of China that motivates many to want to continue our policy of strategic dependence on the United States, regardless of the consequences. Hugh White's recent book, *The China Choice*, made a substantial contribution to this debate. White argues that the United States has three choices: to withdraw from Asia; to push back against China in order to maintain US supremacy; or to seek agreement on a new order for the Pacific, conceding China a bigger role where 'America and China would share power in Asia as equal partners in a joint regional leadership'.[1] These alternatives, although not the only possibilities for the United States, make it possible to focus the debate and ultimately to define options available to Australia. Australia must consider the relationship between America and China as a key part of its future thinking regarding foreign and security policy footings. As such, it is worth examining the issue of a rising China in greater depth.

Many writers, especially from America, but also from Australia, claim that China is becoming increasingly assertive and, indeed, aggressive in the conduct of foreign relations, especially with its neighbours. I am not sure that this is so. From the beginning of the twentieth century, China was weak and was subject to many unequal treaties, designed to give strategic advantages to other powers. Through most of the twentieth century, China's influence remained dormant. Internal arguments, a powerless central government, the Japanese invasion and the fight to establish a communist state (albeit with Chinese characteristics) all took much of China's energy. It was clearly a period of relative withdrawal from wider international affairs. It is a period that should not necessarily be regarded as a norm, or something to which China should be expected to return.

During the last quarter of the last century, China has emerged as a most powerful economy and, indeed, is now the largest economy in Asia. This growth has also resulted in China becoming a growing military power. China is perhaps doing little more than returning to a place of historic influence that it had enjoyed through many previous centuries. Other powers need to understand this change and that the time of Chinese isolation from broader international affairs has ended.

China's economic success has served the Asia–Pacific well, with many nations, Australia included, sharing in the economic prosperity a growing China has underpinned. Beijing is the largest trading partner of every country in the Western Pacific. During the Global Financial Crisis China's continued growth, stability and adjustment of domestic policies to meet changing circumstances did much to assist all the countries of this region, including Australia. There should have been a feeling of gratitude to China as a consequence. If China had gone the way of the United States, we all would have been facing very high levels of unemployment, equivalent to that which has been experienced in Europe.

It was also during this time that allegations of Chinese aggression and assertiveness have come to the fore. Many leading Americans have delivered speeches on this topic. For example, such speakers as General Herbert Carlisle, US Navy Captain James Fanell and Bonnie Glaser, from the Center for Strategic and International Studies, have all spoken in Australia.[2] There are variations on a theme; they often tend to lack detail, but what they have said represents a concerted American point of view on how the power relationships in the region should play out. America is clearly showing a determination not only to remain in the region but also to increase its role. Washington expects Beijing to accept this without objection.

Although I have examined America's actions at some length, China's actions also need to be analysed carefully. I have asked a number of people to describe in what way China is being aggressive. The ready answer is in relation to Japan, in particular, the Diaoyu/Senkaku Islands dispute. The point remains that although the United States does not claim to adjudicate in relation to that dispute or indeed, to any of the disputes in the East or South China Seas, it by default falls on the side of the Japanese.

One of the unusual aspects of the Chinese–Japanese relationship is that Japan seems to behave as though it is the aggrieved party. On the historical record, that is just not true. It is Japan that invaded China. It was Japan that committed atrocities in China. It was Japan that took the Diaoyu/Senkaku Islands from China in 1895. Before that militarist period, Japan had shown little interest in the islands. Only in quite recent times has Japan paid any substantial attention to the Diaoyu/Senkaku Islands.

Through history, countries have won or lost territory as a result of war. The indignities inflicted on China during China's period of maximum weakness fall into a somewhat different category today. Above all, China, as appropriate for any great power, demands respect, especially from those nations from Europe and the United States and Japan that exploited China's weakness in times past. This needs to be understood as an inviolate part of China's attitude. It will influence China's future actions.

The most balanced description of the Chinese–Japanese dispute over the Diaoyu/Senkaku Islands, a dispute that Japan absurdly denies, comes from the reporting of Nicholas Kristof in the *New York Times*. A thoughtful piece by Han-Yi Shaw from Taiwan, along with Kristof's reporting, puts the dispute over these islands into an international context.[3] It demonstrates that while Japan claims ownership of the island, documents from the Japanese National Archives, the Diplomatic Records Office and the National Institute for Defense Studies Library clearly show that the Meiji Government acknowledged Chinese ownership of the islands in 1885. The islands were in fact incorporated into Japan, following a Cabinet decision early in 1895, in the era of Japan's colonisation of Taiwan and Korea.

Other claims of Chinese assertiveness relate to border issues with India, problems in Tibet and in Xinjiang Province. The border issue with India could be resolved in a manner similar to that which resolved border issues between China and Russia. These questions are important, especially in relation to Tibet, but the issues they raise are not relevant to Australia's policy of strategic dependence on the United States. They are not part of the equation that could lead to conflict between the United States and China.

There are also questions regarding China's assertiveness in relation to the South China Sea, where many countries have competing claims of territorial ownership and maritime access. Yet a concerted, patient and consultative approach by ASEAN, in discussions with China, continues to give hope that sensible rules can be established for a Code of Conduct in the South China Sea.

Nonetheless, in discussing alternatives for the future of the Pacific, it is critical to understand the issues involving China and China's motivations regarding these issues. What we describe as aggressive might well, in China's perception, be seeking to redress injustice or territory lost in a war to a hostile Japan. Australia and the United States, in particular, need to have the breadth of understanding of these issues and be able to put events in the Asia–Pacific into the perspective of other regional nations—China included. By appreciating how other nations comprehend important and potentially destabilising issues, we can make a first but important step in attempting to seek a resolution.

This provokes the question of what options are realistically available to the United States in the Asia–Pacific. Washington is certainly not going to withdraw, and why should it? America does have long-standing interests in the Asia–Pacific. I have already discussed the role played by the United States in the region during the Cold War, but in contemporary times the important part of those interests relate to trade, investment and the interplay of capital markets. It is hard to see how a greatly expanded military force, seeking to contain China, is relevant to the maintenance of those interests.

The United States claims that the military build-up is necessary, in part, to maintain freedom of the seas in the East and South China Seas and freedom of access for commercial vessels. China is equally dependent on these same sea lanes, and has a comparable commercial interest in maintaining international access. Increasing naval forces will only add to the existing difficulties between Washington and Beijing around Freedom of the Seas—an escalation in naval movements increases the chances of a misunderstanding over innocent passage. It would undermine the chances of establishing an equivalent of the Treaty of Wyoming between America and China.

Washington also believes it is essential to maintaining a stabilising role, in a region that Washington has always considered critical to its own strategic interests. Yet the United States is seriously and dangerously mistaken in the view that a military build-up is necessary for this purpose. Washington also underestimates the advances made by ASEAN in overcoming past enmities and establishing a constructive, cohesive entity without Washington's involvement. There are other ways to advance reasonable relationships in all of these areas, to come to a consensus that both sides can agree to and implement. One is already being pursued by ASEAN, seeking to establish a Code of Conduct for the South China Sea. China is being encouraged to help draft such a code and to accept it. I am sure it will not happen quickly but, once agreed, it would be a significant advance.

It should be noted that such a code does not have to resolve territorial disputes. Today's players should have the foresight to put the territorial claims aside, as Deng Xiaoping did regarding the Senkaku/Diaoyu Islands many long years ago.[4] This attitude enabled the issue of ownership to be set aside for many years. If a Code of Conduct can be more formally established in today's world, then a build-up of American naval forces in the region ceases to be relevant. It is a question of diplomacy, of soft power, of tact, of a capacity to understand and bring together differing points of view, rather than a display of military might that will resolve the issues of the South China Sea. This is something that has been one of the great achievements of the ASEAN countries and one they should continue to drive in the case of potential maritime disputes in South-East Asia.

Although America claims that China has become assertive and aggressive, the Chinese point of view would be markedly different. Which comes first? In 2009 there was a major incident when USNS *Impeccable* was operating south-west of Hainan in the South China Sea, in China's Exclusive Economic Zone.[5] The United States Navy has admitted that the ship was conducting submarine surveillance, but also asserted that it required no permission from China. The Chinese claimed that the operations were much too close to the Chinese coast.

The *Impeccable* was surveilling waters just off China's new Hainan naval base for its nuclear submarines at Yulin, on the south coast of Hainan.[6] If China had a surveillance ship anchored just outside the territorial waters, off America's navy base at Norfolk, Virginia, I have no doubt America would want that spy ship removed. Such incidents could easily become volatile and dangerous, and emphasise the need for both sides to follow the precedents established between the Soviet Union and the United States in the Treaty of Wyoming.

The announcement of a military hotline between the People's Liberation Army and the Pentagon in late 2008 was a welcome first step, but it seems not to have been taken further. It falls far short of the hotline established between the USSR and the United States, after the Cuban Missile Crisis in 1962. Other positive steps need to be taken to avoid friction in the territorial waters or the Extended Economic Zone of both countries.[7]

In these circumstances, however, it is not reasonable to claim that China's pursuit of a blue-water navy, of a capacity to protect its own direct interests, is aggressive or assertive. It is a position that any major power would have taken. Indeed, US commentators welcomed the deployment of Chinese Navy ships to the international anti-piracy task force in the Gulf of Aden—the biggest naval operation by China in more than six hundred years—as a contribution to the global public good.[8]

Another potential flash point that is often raised by analysts, and one in which China is painted as the aggressive party, is Taiwan. I doubt that conflict will erupt over Taiwan. If an independent-minded person were ever elected president of Taiwan, that could certainly cause significant difficulties between Taipei and Beijing—we have seen this in the past. Yet the chances of a truly independent Taiwanese president taking office, fully committed to independence, is becoming more and more remote. Both sides simply have too much to lose through a potential conflict. If the issue is left to China and Taiwan alone, the problem will be resolved peacefully. One day, we will find that there is another one China, where a two-system solution has been put in place, much like the arrangements in Hong Kong or Macau.

So this leaves few areas that realistically represent major points of potential conflict. Given the relative lack of flash points, America would have been better advised to maintain the status quo in the Asia–Pacific rather than enunciate the so-called pivot towards Asia. The current forces in place are substantial, effective and more than sufficient for current strategic requirements. They could easily be expanded if an unforeseen need arose but where can one see the necessity for that expansion? The expansion of the United States forces in the Western Pacific can itself be the cause of friction and of danger. The Americans should have maintained the status quo, rather than try to alter the equation.

America maintaining the substantial forces that it has had in place over a long time is quite a different proposition from an America substantially increasing those forces and seeking to contain China as a consequence. Maintaining the status quo by keeping US military deployment as it is would give smaller countries on China's periphery a sense of comfort and confidence in the relationship between Beijing and Washington going forward. Yet, by unnecessarily increasing military power, that sense of confidence could easily evaporate if America's apparent policy of containment causes friction between China and the United States.

In more general terms, it is important to make assessments about China's future policies. In one sense, during China's period of almost complete internal preoccupation, the world has developed around it and rules have been established for the behaviour of states. China did not fully participate in that process. Fitting China into the international system more fully is not merely a question of getting China to obey pre-established rules. Rather, it is about listening to China's concerns and, where possible, seeking to accommodate them. That is, of course, not to say that the world should acquiesce to all of China's demands—Beijing is far from perfect—but at the very least the international community needs to listen to, and attempt to, accommodate a Chinese view on major global issues and the rules underpinning the international system. China's future course will be a reflection of, or a reaction to, the policies of the United States and major European countries and the international system these states have established over the last sixty years.

China certainly—and I am sure the United States also—would not want a war or a conflict to develop between the two. However, if the United States tries to maintain its position as number one and the world's hegemonic superpower, then problems could well arise. Australia's policy should be directed to try to drive America off that course, to try to persuade America to seek a new agreement in relation to Asia, to share power rather than seek to assert its own supremacy. The problem is that America is not in a mood to move in that direction. Its objective is the maintenance of American supremacy, driven by American exceptionalism and neo-conservative philosophy. Sharing power with China is not in Washington's strategic thinking. Developments since 1990 provide strong evidence to support this contention. Nonetheless, Australia should try to persuade America to a different path; it remains in our best interest to try. In doing so, however, we need to remember that on such issues America is not easily persuaded.

An examination of these issues points overwhelmingly to the need for cooperative and respectful bilateral discussions between China and the United States concerning dispositions in the Asia–Pacific. It is noteworthy that the United States and the Soviet Union took steps designed to reduce friction and avoid tension, steps that should be replicated in the relationship between the United States and China. That this has not happened should cause concern. Despite potential flash points, there is the argument that a war between China and the United States will never arise because their economies are so closely connected by capital markets, by commerce, by trade, by self-interest, that the two would never allow a situation to develop into a real war. Such a view has been commonplace throughout history, often leading to the most severe conflicts.

When Archduke Franz Ferdinand was shot in Sarajevo in 1914, few believed that his assassination would lead to a war in which more than 15 million people would be killed. War often starts from small and insignificant events. An open Chinese invasion across the Taiwan Straits, taking Taiwan by force, would be a major event, but that is not going to happen. Small events that touch on pride, esteem, that promote misjudgement, miscalculation can all eventually lead to war. Each side believes the other will hold back or will not act because the event is so trivial. Yet in so many cases they do act, resulting in escalation that promotes further reaction. Such a situation can easily spiral out of control.

If America were to lose a war with China, in military terms at least, America could withdraw to the western hemisphere. Australia cannot withdraw anywhere. We would remain here, geographically part of the Asia–Pacific, but also a defeated ally of a defeated superpower. That would raise issues of some complexity and of some danger for Australia. It is not a position that any Australian government would want to be in. That is the worst case consequence of a continuation of the policies and approaches adopted by Australia, especially since 1996.

Despite the many practical things that China and America have in common, and which should well create a positive framework for peace, that is not what it is all about. America is economically and militarily number one and wishes to remain so. That means asserting power and influence over other states in a way that could be unacceptable to a growing and strengthening China. That is the equation we need to be concerned about: a rising China and an America in fear of being pushed off the top of the greasy pole.

Hugh White has suggested that if America cannot be persuaded to share power, there could well be a conflict involving China and the United States, and he concluded that America might well lose. This should come as no surprise as America has already participated in three wars, including Vietnam, in which military battles might have been won but the political battles have been lost. The United States would lack the fortitude to be successful in a war with China.[9]

Direct competition between the United States and China aside, the most likely trigger for such a calamity would be an assertive and increasingly militaristic Japan. Japan has its China relationship upside down. China should be the aggrieved power, not Japan.

If a war between China and the United States was to occur with a continuation of current policies, it would be very hard, if not impossible, for Australia not to be involved.

There are other aspects that cannot be ignored in determining Australia's future course. One major aspect is the moral dilemma in which we find ourselves on account of our intelligence-sharing arrangements with the United States. Significant numbers of civilians have been killed as a result of drone attacks in countries with whom neither the United States nor we are at war.[10] These civilian deaths raise serious questions of the possible perpetration of war crimes and/or crimes against humanity. The United States would claim that the single-paragraph war powers resolution passed by Congress after 9/11, and various executive orders emanating from the White House since, provide the necessary legal authorisation. Since significant numbers of civilians have at times been killed, and especially in countries with whom the United States is not at war, this authority would be tenuous at best, and US personnel could be vulnerable before the International Criminal Court. Australians operating at Pine Gap are doing so without any authority and could be equally liable. Some difficult issues could arise if Pakistan takes us to the International Criminal Court, for example, despite the fact that Pakistan is not a State Party to the Rome Statute. Pakistan has arguments against Australia because of Australia's participation in drone strikes in Pakistan.

Quite apart from these technicalities, by far the most important point is one of ethics and of due process. Over hundreds of years, advocates for a fair justice system argued against 'Star Chamber' techniques, in which those in authority used secret evidence that could not be tested or cross-examined, in which the prisoner was given no opportunity to answer, or to conduct any reasonable defence. For drone killings, somebody in the White House, or with authority delegated from the White House, has returned to using the same techniques as the Star Chamber of old. We have overthrown the progress of hundreds of years and reverted to secret accusations and secret indictments. Indeed, today's practice is worse than in the times of the Star Chamber. In those days, it was only the prisoner who would be killed. Today, collateral damage involves untold numbers of civilians, including women and children. This is the measure of today's civilisation. It is the measure of the terrorists' victory.

Quite apart from potential illegalities, the strongest argument against the continued use of Pine Gap for such purposes is a practical one. If a number of countries start to follow US practice in developing offensive drones, and use them for the same purposes as the United States is now using them, the world would become even more unstable, more dangerous and more unpredictable.[11]

We should not participate in such a course. Philip Alston, the United Nations Special Rapporteur on extrajudicial, summary or arbitrary executions, put it this way: 'If other states were to claim the broad-based authority that the United States does, to kill people anywhere, anytime, the result would be chaos.'[12]

The issues facing the Asia–Pacific, the US–China relationship and our practical and moral dilemmas around the use of intelligence gathered at Pine Gap are major strategic issues for our nation. Australia's decisions must be made in a highly complex world and a world that is rapidly changing. As I see it, Australia has three options available to it, in attempting to contend with these challenges.

Australia's first option would be to continue with the steady development of the current relationship. In effect, this would mean to continue our historic policy of strategic dependence on a great and powerful friend. It would also be the easiest, politically at least, but it has a number of problems associated with it. Being seen to be a surrogate of the United States, almost as Washington's deputy sheriff in this part of the world, is not good for relationships in East and South-East Asia. It also, more importantly, involves following US decisions in foreign and security policy issues, irrespective of whether these decisions relate to a part of the world important to us or to our national interests.

At its core, maintaining or expanding our current relationship involves making judgements about Australia's security needs and whether these needs are reflected by American interests. It blurs and makes it very difficult for us to discern our own national good over what we believe America would want us to rate as important. It would involve submerging our own identity, going along with American objectives, and being prepared to fight in America's wars.

It would involve going along with drone killings in Pakistan or other countries. Drone killings in Pakistan have been undertaken against the repeated opposition of the government of Pakistan, not least the current government of Prime Minister Nawaz Sharif. Also, Pakistan's Peshawar High Court has determined that such attacks are illegal and a violation of Pakistani sovereignty.[13]

Continuing as we are would also involve increased pressure from the United States to establish a more formal and all-encompassing defence relationship with Japan; a relationship that would make it much harder, if not impossible, for us to avoid being involved in any conflict between China and Japan.

So continuing our American relationship as it has evolved to this point, and expanding it even further, as we would be pressed to do, carries implications for Australia that should cause us much concern. It is not only wrong but also contrary to any rational analysis of Australia's own national interest to be bound by American decisions to go to war, when America wants us to go to war or to condone unethical killing when the Americans deem it necessary. This option leaves the United States in charge of Australia's future. It continues the policy of strategic dependence and, as this book has shown, such a continuation will undoubtedly come at a significant cost. Yet, unlike in previous times, it comes with very little benefit.

A second option might involve trying to have it both ways: an attempt to assert our independence while allowing the relationship to continue. Theoretically, we could tell the United States we would not automatically follow it into its wars. It could not expect us to do so any more than it could expect Canada automatically to follow it into wars.

We need to remember that Canada did not support the United States in the earlier war in Vietnam, did not support the United States in relation to Iraq and has on a number of issues, especially in relation to Cuba, differed sharply from American policy. America has respected that independence, and it has not diminished Canada's relationship with the United States. If Canada has been able to achieve a degree of strategic independence, geographically close to both the United States and a potential adversary in Russia, why should Australia, in a more geographically advantageous position, not be able to do likewise?

In addition, we have an example much closer to home. New Zealand, some time ago, made a stand on principle in relation to nuclear-powered ships as well as ships and aircraft carrying nuclear weapons.[14] Although I might have regretted New Zealand's position at the time, it was in fact far-sighted and correct.

However, times have changed, and Australia has allowed itself to become very tightly enmeshed in America's strategic affairs. We are strategically more important to America than New Zealand ever was, so asserting our independence within existing arrangements could prove significantly more difficult. If we now try to assert a degree of strategic independence and leave other matters untouched, we will find ourselves left with some very difficult questions and hard problems to solve.

What happens if the United States uses that Marine Air-Ground Task Force in Darwin against countries with whom we wish to maintain friendship? We cannot host that task force and pretend that what it does and who it might attack has nothing to do with us when we provide the infrastructure to support its existence in the region. By hosting that task force, we are making American military actions much easier and more effective throughout South-East Asia and the Western Pacific. We cannot avoid complicity in what America does by just saying that we are not involved and we are not going to add forces of our own.

To avoid complicity in a possible American offensive use of that Marine Air-Ground Task Force, supplemented by offensive naval units, would involve asking the marines to be 'rotated through' some-where other than Australia. I suspect the United States would find the proposition that the task force should now be moved difficult to accept, and persuading Washington to do so would require diplomatic and political prowess on our behalf. Yet it would not be impossible. Unfortunately, other issues of even greater strategic importance make this second option impossible for Australian leaders to pursue.

Chief among these other issues is the current operations at Pine Gap. If Australia wanted to establish some element of strategic independence within the alliance, the capabilities of Pine Gap, and America's strategic thinking relating to its use, will cause the greatest difficulty. When it was first established in 1966, Australia never envisaged that Pine Gap would develop far beyond its original purpose of collecting information on the testing of Soviet missiles. However, in the period since it was built, Pine Gap and systems related to it have undergone extraordinary technical development, greatly increasing the sensitivity and breadth of its signals intelligence capacities—most notably in the interception of cell phones and satellite communications. This has provided the technical basis for Pine Gap to provide data enabling the targeting of illegal US drone attacks, in countries with which neither the United States nor Australia are at war, including Pakistan, Yemen and Somalia.[15] The fact that the information gathered in outback Australia can now be used, almost in real time, by weapons such as drones has increased the importance of Pine Gap in American strategic thinking; hence the difficulty.

In the beginning, Pine Gap was defensive in character. The new uses to which the information it gathers can be put transforms Pine Gap into a critical part of an offensive weapons system. Australia should not be a part of it.

This further aspect of Pine Gap's activities, which also was never envisaged by the government that allowed its establishment, might be even more dangerous to hopes for peace in our region. Following the closure of the US base at Nurrungar in 1999, Pine Gap has hosted a remote ground station for several generations of US early warning satellites. Powerful infrared telescopes on geo-stationary satellites detect the thermal signature of ballistic missile launches. Today, this technology, originally aimed at providing early warning of possible attack on the United States, has been extended to contribute to the rapidly evolving US and Japanese missile defence systems on land and sea, aimed at defeating a North Korean missile attack.

Most Australians would think that this is a reasonable contribution for Australia to make to the defence of the United States and Japan—it is, after all, missile defence. Yet Australians would be more concerned if they realised the way in which this nominally defensive system interacts with the deadly logic of deterrence in a world with thousands of nuclear weapons. China has long been concerned that the object of US and Japanese missile defence is not only North Korea but also China itself, and that it has a highly offensive role that dramatically undermines what little strategic stability there is, in the always dangerous world of nuclear deterrence.

Ever since China exploded its first nuclear weapon in 1964, China's leaders have been adamant that they would not join the nuclear arms race that saw the United States and the Soviet Union expanding their already huge nuclear arsenals in lock-step in an insane parody of 'balance'. Today, a quarter of a century after the fall of the Berlin Wall, the United States possesses 7,700 strategic nuclear warheads whereas China has maintained strict limits on its nuclear arsenal, which now contains about 250 strategic nuclear warheads. The Chinese describe this small arsenal as 'the minimal means of retaliation', and have pledged never to be the first to use nuclear weapons in war. The Chinese leadership has long believed that a small stock of nuclear weapons will be enough to make a nuclear-armed adversary—even the United States—think twice about an attack on China, even if it means China inevitably suffering huge casualties from a nuclear first strike.

The great problem for Australia today is that the Chinese leadership fears, with some justification, that US and Japanese missile defence that depends on Pine Gap might be able to destroy most, if not all, of China's nuclear missiles in flight, thereby vitiating China's nuclear deterrent force and leaving the country vulnerable to nuclear blackmail. By hosting Pine Gap, Australia is contributing to the undermining of China's long-standing minimalist nuclear deterrent, destabilising the precarious strategic fundamentals in East Asia.[16]

If America is involved in military operations anywhere in the Western Pacific or in the East or South China Seas, then Pine Gap would be highly relevant to those operations. We cannot deny the facility's existence; neither could we dictate to the Americans that the information it gathers must not be used for the targeting of their weapons. We can hardly say to our neighbours that we are not complicit in American drone killings when the real-time information our facility collects is used for that purpose. In practical terms, it is not realistic to say that Pine Gap information can be used for one purpose but not for others. That is beyond our power.

The Marine Air-Ground Task Force and Pine Gap are the two elements that bind us most closely to America's military posture and to any offensive operations in which America may be involved, in years ahead. We would be faced with a dire situation if a dispute involving Japan and China also involved the United States and we found that a variety of weapons were being targeted using information gathered at Pine Gap, or the Marine Air-Ground Task Force was used for offensive operations. We would not be believed if we tried to assert that we were not playing a role in such a conflict. China and other regional nations would be right for not believing us, for we would be playing a role, and a major one.

In addition to these two elements, the three-month deployment of HMAS *Sydney*, a guided missile frigate, as part of the 7th Fleet of USS *Washington*, adds to our complicity in America's military affairs. This deployment is to be repeated in 2014.[17] The appointment of Major General Burr, an active Australian major general, as second in command of the US Army in the Western Pacific, further adds to that complicity. If we were to purchase and operate US *Virginia*-class nuclear-powered submarines, as has been suggested, that would only add to our integration with America's armed forces.[18] We would be even more subject to America's policies.

To try to continue the relationship as it is, but to say to America that we are not going to follow it into wars of no direct concern to Australia, and which are not technically covered under ANZUS, becomes more than problematic.

Although the purposes of the Marine Air-Ground Task Force and the potential purposes of Pine Gap are enormously important to America's offensive capabilities, some people might believe that Australia could merely pretend that these facilities are not relevant for some future conflict. The Australian Government could not dictate which conflict those forces could be used in and which they could not. We would need to understand that positioning of US forces could result in Darwin being attacked or, much more likely,

Pine Gap itself being directly targeted. These factors would involve Australia, whether we like it or not, whether the conflict had anything to do with us or not. Australia would be dragged into the war regardless of our views. Australia's fate would depend upon the outcome of the contest between China and the United States, a contest that no matter who was the winner would exact a heavy toll on the region, us included.

This analysis shows us clearly that the second option is no option at all. It provides no escape from our dilemma and no real ability to chart a course any different from continued strategic dependence— the ability to pick and choose the elements of our alliance that we want, and discard those we do not, simply is not possible. We are too closely intertwined with US strategies and plans. Australian facilities are too heavily involved.

We must turn therefore to the third option, an option of strategic independence to avoid complicity in America's future military operations and secure a future that best serves Australia's interests. Strategic dependence might have fulfilled this role in decades past, but its usefulness as a platform for Australia's foreign and security priorities has ended.

These are some features of the alliance, as presently constituted, that have us caught in a vice. To avoid complicity in America's future military operations, the Marine Air-Ground Task Force would be asked to leave. The deployment of our frigate, as part of that carrier strike group, would cease and Major General Burr would be replaced, presumably by an American. These three actions could be undertaken relatively easily and quickly, without too much disruption. Pine Gap is another matter. The balance of benefits and dangers to Australia from hosting both the signals intelligence and missile defence activities at Pine Gap has clearly shifted to the negative. However, the facility is a huge one, of great importance to the United States, and replacing it will take time—perhaps four to five years. To shut the facility down forthwith would leave a gap in America's strategic capabilities, which would be much more than an annoyance to the United States, but a requirement to close it within five years would be reasonable.[19]

A government determined to recapture Australian sovereignty would, however, need to make it plain that, over a period, such facilities would have to be replaced. A courageous Australian government, with concern for the integrity of this nation, would follow the path to strategic independence.

There is no doubt that the United States would take the strongest possible exception to such moves. Every pressure would be exercised on an Australian government so that the United States would maintain strategic control. We would need to resist such pressures and make it clear that, in our view, the risks of a strategic alliance with the United States, of being forced into a war that was not in our interest, were so great that we had to cut the ties.

We need to look carefully at the risks, the costs and the benefits of a policy of strategic independence. There is no worldwide global threat as there was during the Cold War. As I have discussed, some point to China, to China's size, to China's strength. There are Australians who are afraid of China. It has been our DNA to be afraid of external threats, but we need to evaluate those dangers to see whether they are real. For China to be a danger, China would have to act out of character, contrary to all the traditions of its past. If China were to be a danger, it would also signal a total failure of Australian diplomacy. China does not represent a threat to the integrity of an independent Australia. We would earn greater respect as a consequence of such a policy.

Indonesia's population is approaching 300 million people. The most productive islands of this archipelago nation are overcrowded. There might be some who fear Indonesia and some who believe that we need the protection of America. This is misguided. If Indonesia were to become an enemy, it would be a consequence again of the total failure of Australian diplomacy. We need to have more confidence in ourselves. In the past, we have deluded ourselves if we believe that the United States would protect us against Indonesia. The *Economist* summed it up best in 1963 when it said: 'No Indonesian regime short of a blatantly communist one would earn active American hostility, no matter what harm it did to national

Australian interests.'[20] The United States would support Indonesia over Australia because it is the largest, most populist Islamic state in the world. On the question of Indonesia, we have relied on our own resources in the past, and we can do so in the future.

I discount direct threats to Australia as a result of strategic independence. It is strategic dependence that provides the greatest problem to our future in the region. Indeed, the current interpretation of ANZUS by Australian leaders is paradoxical—it might be the biggest threat to our own security despite it being presented as the guarantor of our security. Strategic independence would provide us with the motivation to look to the future, to ask ourselves what must we do to secure a future that best serves our needs and priorities, along with those of our region.[21]

First, we would need to drive an Australian agenda to really build and develop Australia, with a passion and zeal similar to that which was shown by our leaders in the early days after World War II. If we set a target for a population 40 or 45 million, that would be a lesser burden on today's Australians than the burden accepted by 7 million Australians after World War II. We would need to accept that we cannot enjoy all the riches of Australia for today's consumption; that we must invest in the future to a much greater extent than we have in the last twenty or thirty years. A greater number of people would require renewed investment in basic infrastructure, in the preservation and consolidation of water supplies, for the protection of the environment. Although these are costs, they are also benefits. We would end with a greater country, a better country; a country that was respected for what it is, and how it uses precious resources.

Second, we would be in a much stronger position to develop cooperative relationships with countries of East and South-East Asia. We would have demonstrated a sense of independence in the most categoric fashion. We would be well placed to be a more effective partner in South-East Asian affairs, to cooperate more fully with ASEAN. We could be considered a true partner in the region with our own views and not a set of opinions reflecting those of an assumed protector. An Australia motivated by such objectives and such purposes could well be able to play a more constructive role in maintaining peace throughout our region than an Australia that is a compliant partner, a strategic captive of the United States.

Third, in the broader international context, we could play a more effective role and seek constructive coalitions of other middle-ranking powers. As one of the temporary members of the Security Council, we could be more independent and more effective. We could be more forthright in helping to make the United Nations a more constructive and more effective force. We could play a leading role to see how major international organisations, organs of the United Nations, were fulfilling their tasks in today's world. The United Nations High Commissioner for Refugees is one organisation that needs reinvigorating with a new worldwide commitment to do something about refugees, not just within our own region but also worldwide. There are initiatives waiting to be taken by an Australia that is more independent, more forthright and more cooperative than we have been in the past.

Clearly, strategic independence would bring some advantages, quite apart from material change, to Australia. We would have a sense of motivation, a sense of purpose, a belief in the future of this country, a belief that the future rested in our hands. We would be in a good position not only to protect but also to advance the egalitarian values of our early leaders.

While these are considerable benefits for Australia, there are still dangers for the Western Pacific. As a strategically independent country, we could do much to lessen those dangers. As a strategic captive of the United States, we cannot even contribute usefully to the debate, and we would be drawn into any war that involved the United States. Let me consider the possibilities. Many would point to China as the source of future danger, but I do not believe that to be accurate, unless China was provoked, unreasonably. Such provocation could come from the United States, from Japan or, much less likely, from a flare-up in the South China Sea. It would be a major advantage not to be tied to the United States in such circumstances.

An independent Australia could act much more effectively in concert with other Western Pacific countries, on the one hand to avoid flashpoints and points of danger, and on the other to promote initiatives that would do much to maintain continuing peace throughout the region. Yet, as part of the American network, we would not be able to take such action. We would merely be regarded as a surrogate voice of America and therefore wield no true influence.

China has options concerning the way in which it responds to the US policy of containment. One option could be to increase China's own military strength, which indeed is happening, as it develops greater naval capacity, but it would also be possible for China to concentrate on a non-military response and almost to ignore American military activities. A more independent Australia would be in a better position to encourage China to focus on non-military responses. An Australian position that is not interpreted by China and other nations in Asia as automatically representing the view of Washington can only enhance our diplomatic standing and ability to influence regional policy.

There has been surprise at the speed and pace of China's progress, at the extent of China's rising economic influence and growing military power. There are many in China who believe that China's rise will continue, although at a somewhat slower pace. It is also believed that China will be able to handle future challenges and maintain stability in its own affairs, as it has over the last several decades. As China's economy grows, its investment in Africa and South America will grow, as indeed it has been doing. Beijing's economic influence and trading prowess will be greater than any other nation, precipitating a greater influence worldwide, one that might eventually outmatch that of the United States.

As a result of growing economic power, China would in effect be able to sideline US military power, almost to ignore it, and not respond to provocation. This would in effect make the policy of military containment irrelevant.

China might well show such restraint and patience if America or Japan pushed in ways that could otherwise lead to a military contest. If China continues to progress in the coming decades, as it has over the last thirty years, the policy of containment cannot succeed. China can well demonstrate that trade and economy can win over armies and war. This is an option for China that might avoid the consequences of war and the dangers of a major conflict between China and the United States. China could indeed have the diplomatic skills to pursue such a course.

Whichever way the dice fall, whether a conflict or war occurs between China and the United States or whether peace is maintained, Australia is better off being strategically independent. Certainly, if war occurs, we will then not be part of another American war with potentially disastrous consequences. That perhaps is the strongest reason for us to pursue strategic independence. The overall benefits that would flow from strategic independence are great, and could result in the making of Australia.

The most effective diplomacy is undertaken quietly, often behind closed doors, while people are seeking agreement and working to create a more secure world. The example of ASEAN, in particular, gives us grounds for optimism. Progress has been made; more progress will be made. The more countries that quietly participate in this process, the better it will be. The West has never truly recognised the progress, the advancement, the contribution, to security and safety throughout the region that ASEAN countries have themselves achieved without Western intervention or support. As a more independent country, we can help build on that. As a lackey of America's, it will be hard for others to take Australia seriously.

Pursuing strategic independence would not be easy, and it would obviously carry risks and costs. There would be direct military costs. We would not get the same access to American military equipment. The United States might indeed say that it will not sell to us at all. That is doubtful, because the financial advantage to the United States of military sales generally is substantial. We would not become a potential foe, just a more independent nation that still shares many of the goals America has, for a peaceful and prosperous world. This is important; strategic independence does not mean turning our backs on goals and priorities that we share with America. Much could still be achieved by a cooperative relationship, but a relationship in which we have the final say over our decisions.

Regardless, many countries in Europe could supply equipment of high quality and which would probably serve our interests just as well as American equipment. The great pressure to buy from America in recent years has come about because of America's desire for interoperability, for our forces really to be an extension of their own, with the same equipment, procedures and communications. It should be noted that many NATO countries do have their own equipment and military–industrial capacities, and clearly they do not regard that as inhibiting country cooperation and the development of joint plans.

We would clearly have to spend more money on defence. At the moment we spend 1.7 per cent of GDP, which is extraordinarily low by international standards. The Americans have always spent a high amount of 4.4 per cent, Britain about 2.5 per cent and France 2.3 per cent.[22]

American claims that we have been freeloading on them in recent years is correct.[23] As a middle-ranking power, standing on our own feet, we would clearly need to spend more. We are in a position to do so.

Defence signals might represent a more difficult problem. Under the UKUSA Agreement, there is a five-power arrangement between the United States, Britain, Canada, New Zealand and ourselves. We would still be able to operate our part of this arrangement. That being said, recent events regarding intelligence collecting in Indonesia raise further questions. The idea that we are spying for, and on behalf of, the United States, that we in fact are their agent, that we use our embassies in neighbouring countries, is not helpful to establishing good relations with Indonesia and with other countries in our own region. This will be just one more factor that tends to make America's enemies our enemies. Events in late 2013 point to the need for a serious examination of past policy. The maintenance of that network might not be in Australia's interests. Regardless, we could not rule out the fact that cutting ourselves free from the Marine Air-Ground Task Force and Pine Gap might cause the Americans to exclude us from this arrangement. It is noteworthy that New Zealand maintained its role after nuclear ships were denied access to New Zealand harbours. Canada is still involved, despite not participating in various US conflicts. The situation would be open to negotiation.

Nonetheless, through the seven and a half years in which I was Prime Minister, I cannot recall a single decision of government that was significantly influenced or altered as a result of defence signals intelligence. At the interoperable service-to-service level, it might well have had some influence, but at the level of high policy, virtually none. Further, Pine Gap's complex mix of activities requires a judgement of the positives and negatives for Australia, and on that basis the time has come to close Pine Gap.

There are clear costs to strategic independence. We should, however, be prepared to bear those costs, to make our own way in cooperation with other countries in the region in which we live. By doing so, we would be able to contribute in the best possible way to the security of our own region and, importantly, to secure Australia's future. In any event, I believe that these costs are insignificant compared to the potential costs involved in continuing our policy of strategic dependence, in an era in which it is no longer contextually appropriate. In the current political climate, having a public debate on any area of public policy is difficult, let alone one regarding the future of our relationship with the United States. Yet it is a debate we need to have.

Strategic independence does not mean ending our relationship with America and cutting our ties. It does mean having a different relationship, a more equal one in which we can feel free to say no or offer a differing opinion. Similarly, strategic independence should not mean acquiescing to all the demands of a growing China, ignoring such issues as human rights. It does mean needing to appreciate and accept that China will increasingly seek out a new role for itself, as its power continues to grow. Strategic independence would allow Australia to agree and disagree with both Washington and Beijing, as it suits our interests. We should not be afraid to express our views and stick to our beliefs.

We have seen therefore that the first option carries very significant risks for Australia and would ill serve our future. The second option would lead to the same result and be impossible to implement. In both circumstances, we would be pre-committed to follow wherever America required and, more likely than not, to put Australia in a position of considerable danger. The third option is one that we should pursue. It offers the best hope for the development of Australia as a nation, and the best possibilities for Australia playing a positive role in the region in which we live.

Notes

Introduction

1 John Latham, Attorney General and Minister for External Affairs under Prime Minister Joseph Lyons, opposed ratifying the statute. Lewis claimed Latham felt that 'the blood ties between the Dominions was [*sic*] not something that could be legislated and formalised, and that certain parties, for their own ends, could use the Statute to ruin the Empire' (quoted in Lewis, 'John Latham and the Statute of Westminster').

2 A number of US Government reports point to this conclusion. For example, a 2007 report commissioned by the United States Joint Forces Command, and conducted by the Institute for Defense Analyses, examined captured official Iraqi documents post-invasion and found that, although Saddam's regime had supported a variety of 'revolutionary, liberation, nationalist, and Islamic terrorist organizations', there was 'no "smoking gun" [i.e. a direct connection] between Saddam's Iraq and al Qaeda' (*Iraqi Perspectives Project*, p. ES-1). Similarly, a 2004 Senate Select Committee report on pre-war intelligence also found that although intelligence pointed to some contact between Saddam's Iraq and Al Qaeda, the CIA found that there was 'no evidence providing Iraqi complicity or assistance in an al-Qaida attack' (*US Intelligence Community's Pre-War Intelligence Assessments on Iraq*, p. 347). See also Senate Report on Intelligence Activities Relating to Iraq Conducted by the Policy of Counterterrorism Evaluation Group and the Office of Special Plans Within the Office of the Undersecretary of Defense Policy, which also points to intelligence failures in this area.

1 Colonial foundations of strategic dependence

1 Such sentiment was expressed by Australia's first Prime Minister, Edmund Barton, who proclaimed to the Australian Parliament in 1903: 'Let us call ourselves Britons. In using the term Britons in Australia, I wish it to be as

clear as possible that, in my belief, we have not forfeited, by our emigration, or by that of our fathers, any of the rights of Britishers at home, or any of our share in either the glory or the material prosperity of the Empire. We are Britons of Empire …' (extract from Barton, Speech by the Prime Minister and Minister for External Affairs in the House of Representatives, 7 July 1903, in Greenwood & Grimshaw (eds), *Documents on Australian International Relations 1901–1918*, pp. 43–4).

2 Hudson & Sharp, *Australian Independence*, p. 19.
3 Western Australia was in a somewhat different position and was accorded status of a self-governing colony much later than other states because there was a deep suspicion by the Colonial Office of the way in which locally made decisions would affect Aboriginal welfare. Yet, even when Western Australia was accorded self-government in 1890, powers over Indigenous people were reserved for the Colonial Office and transferred to Western Australia only in 1897 because Federation was clearly in sight.
4 *New South Wales Constitution Act 1855*.
5 Cochrane, 'British–Australian relations'.
6 Ibid.
7 Dependence on Empire was widespread and well accepted by early Australians, with Hudson and Sharp arguing that 'in the 1860s virtually all the colonists wanted dependence on the United Kingdom to continue on indefinitely' (Hudson & Sharp, *Australian Independence*, p. 10).
8 Bennett, *The Making of the Commonwealth*, p. 28.
9 Ibid.
10 See for example Benians, 'The Western Pacific, 1788–1885'; Casey, 'Australia's voice in imperial affairs'; Bennett, *The Making of the Commonwealth*.
11 Casey, 'Australia's voice in imperial affairs', p. 37.
12 Ibid., p. 38.
13 The Convention between Great Britain and France, signed on 16 November 1887, stated: 'A Joint Naval Commission shall be immediately constituted, composed of British and French naval officers on the Pacific State, charged with the duty of maintaining and protecting the lives and property of British subjects and French citizens in the New Hebrides.'
14 Hudson argues that even as late as 1911, Britain was not consulting Dominions on treaty matters that directly affected their interests. See Hudson, *Towards a Foreign Policy, 1914–1941*, p. 15.
15 Benians, 'The Western Pacific, 1788–1885', p. 352.
16 Kimberley wrote to the New South Wales Government that 'it is principally on account of the Australian colonies … that the affairs of the Fiji Islands are a matter of concern to this country'. Great Britain clearly had no direct desire to annex the islands and was only concerned with their status as a result of Australian interests (quoted in Benians, 'The Western Pacific, 1788–1885', p. 352).

17 This was welcomed by the Australian colonies. Benians argues that annexation was not for the purpose of colonisation, but rather London was concerned with the protection of Britain's colonies and of the indigenous population (through the Pacific Islanders Protection Act). See Benians, 'The Western Pacific, 1788–1885', p. 353.

18 See Grey, 'Defence'.

19 Parkes was particularly conscious of the need for a friendly power in control of New Guinea, given its importance 'owing to its size, supposed mineral wealth and proximity to Australia' (see Benians, 'The Western Pacific, 1788–1885', p. 355. This is also discussed by Grattan, 'Australia and the Pacific', p. 145). The issue of cost was made starkly by R.W.G. Herbert, Permanent Under-Secretary of the Colonial Office, who stated that 'if the Australian colonies desire such a step as the annexation of New Guinea it will be for them to provide the funds'; the colonies baulked at the cost (quoted in Bennett, *The Making of the Commonwealth*, p. 33).

20 Queensland took possession on 4 April 1883 after reports of German plans for New Guinea in the *Allgemeine Zeitung*. See Thomas McIlwraith, Queensland Colonial Secretary, letter, to Sir A.E. Kennedy, Governor of Queensland, 26 February 1883 (listed in Meaney, *Australia and the World*, pp. 54–7).

21 This is a quote of Lord Derby, Secretary of State for the Colonies, who argued that there were no signs that a foreign power was about to establish a colony over the unclaimed area of New Guinea (quoted in Grattan, 'Australia and the Pacific', p. 145. See also Lord Derby, British Colonial Secretary, despatch, to Officer Administering the Government of Queensland, 11 July 1883, in Meaney, *Australia and the World*, pp. 60–2).

22 Benians, 'The Western Pacific, 1788–1885', p. 360.

23 Ibid., p. 351.

24 Ibid., p. 359. See also a memo from Victorian Premier James Service to the Victorian Governor, which covers that colony's response to the German annexation of New Guinea, highlighting the disappointment Melbourne felt towards a perceived lack of interest on behalf of London.

25 Further discussion of this vulnerability and colonial responses to it can be found in Bennett, *The Making of the Commonwealth*, p. 34.

26 Ibid., p. 44. MacIver was a soldier of fortune who in 1883 raised a company of troops for the British colonisation of New Guinea. The company was ultimately abandoned after failing to receive the approval of Lord Derby.

27 Quoted in Murdoch, *Alfred Deakin*, p. 112.

28 See Murdoch, *Alfred Deakin*, pp. 114–16, for the speech Deakin gave at the 1887 Colonial Conference on which this passage is based.

29 Ibid., p. 115.

30 Some in the British press felt that as 'vigorous and pointed as that speech was, [it] was considered quite out of place by several of the other delegates' (see ibid., p. 116).

31 Hudson & Sharp, *Australian Independence*, p. 22.

32 Odgers, *100 Years of Australians at War*.

33 For example, Western Australian Agent General Walter James clearly linked the Boer War to the notion of protecting the British race, stating: 'The Boer War appealed to the Australian as involving the Empire and therefore the race. It excited the racial loyalty of the Southern Hemisphere, and became our quarrel just as much as yours. It is to the Empire as representing the race that our attachment clings, and so long as England maintains that leadership and defends race interests, we shall march side by side with her and all other portions of the Empire' (extracts from a paper read by Mr Walter James, 10 April 1906, Proceedings of the Royal Colonial Institute, vol. 37, 1905–06, pp. 228–30, listed in Greenwood & Grimshaw (eds), *Documents on Australian International Relations 1901–1918*, p. 46).

34 See Casey, 'Australia's voice in imperial affairs', pp. 39–40. A similar view regarding the patriotism displayed by the colonials was put by Frank Wilkinson, a wartime news correspondent, who remarked that an 'epidemic of war fever set in' when the troops departed and that it was a 'time of unprecedented enthusiasm, when public speeches teamed with patriotic promises, when public streets waved bunting from every other window, and when private subscriptions poured into patriotic funds' (Wilkinson, *Australia at the Front*, pp. 2, 64).

35 Norris, *The Emergent Commonwealth*, p. 123.

36 Odgers, *100 Years of Australians at War*, p. 30.

37 Wilkinson made a useful observation of Chamberlain's response, noting the lukewarm nature of the Colonial Secretary's feelings towards colonial troops: 'Thanks very much. You may send a few—not too many, because this is a serious business and we have no time to look after a lot of untrained men just now. However, we must give some of your people a chance of seeing active service. It will strengthen "those silken bonds" ...' (Wilkinson, *Australia at the Front*, p. 1).

38 Chamberlain asked the South Australian Governor to dispatch Britain's request to the colonies, saying: 'The Admiralty states that additional ships of light draught capable of navigating the Yangtze Kiang and other rivers are urgently required in China ... Her Majesty's government would be glad, therefore, if your responsible advisers would consent to the immediate dispatch to China of three vessels from the Australasian Squadron ...' (quoted in Nicholls, *Bluejackets and Boxers*, p. 22).

39 Ibid., p. 22.

40 Norris, *The Emergent Commonwealth*, p. 117. Leaders of Queensland, South Australia and Tasmania were favourably disposed towards Edwards' review (see Reynolds, *Edmund Barton*, p. 97).

41 See the Report of Major General Edwards published in the *Argus*, 15 October 1889.

42 For more on the Federal Council see Hirst, 'Federal Council of Australasia'; Hirst, *The Sentimental Nation*; and Reynolds, *Edmund Barton*.

43 The Tenterfield oration was published in the *Sydney Morning Herald*, 25 October 1889 and is also accessible in Parkes, *The Federal Government of Australasia: Speeches Delivered on Various Occasions*.

44 Henry Parkes, 3 March 1891, Sydney. See *Official Record of the Debates of the Australasian Federal Convention*.

45 See for example Benians, 'The Western Pacific, 1788–1885', p. 351; Casey, 'Australia's voice in imperial affairs', pp. 37–8; Bennett, *The Making of the Commonwealth*.

46 See for example Bennett, *The Making of the Commonwealth*, p. 31; Reynolds, *Edmund Barton*.

47 Garran, 'The federation movement and the founding of the Commonwealth', p. 433.

48 Barton, Edmund, 9 September 1897, Sydney. See *Official Record of the Debates of the Australasian Federal Convention*. See also Hudson & Sharp, *Australian Independence*, p. 32.

49 See Deakin, *The Federal Story*, pp. 178–9.

50 For example, New South Wales Premier George Reid told the 1897 convention on Australian federation in Sydney that a treaty-making power with foreign nations, such as that in the United States Constitution, was not appropriate for 'the constitution of a colony within the empire' (quoted in Hudson & Sharp, *Australian Independence*, p. 32).

51 This was pushed for by Joseph Chamberlain, Secretary for the Colonies. See Hirst, *The Sentimental Nation*, pp. 237–42.

52 Former Chief Justice of the High Court Murray Gleeson notes, on the role of the Privy Council, that there 'were to be no appeals from the High Court to the Privy Council on any question as to the limits *inter se* of the constitutional powers of the Commonwealth and the States, or as to the limits *inter se* of the constitutional powers of the States, unless the High Court should certify that the question was one that ought to be determined by the Privy Council. Subject to that exception, there was to be a right of appeal by special leave from the High Court to the Privy Council, but the Commonwealth Parliament was to have power to make laws limiting the matters in which such leave might be sought.' See Gleeson, 'The birth, life and death of section 74'.

53 Constitutional cases involving private interests could still be appealed to the Privy Council (Hirst, *The Sentimental Nation*, p. 242).

54 High Court of Australia, 'History of the High Court'.

55 Deakin said specifically on this matter: 'The governments from which we take the powers with which the federation is to be endowed are without exception less liberal than the government provided in this constitution.' See Deakin, *The Federal Story*, p. 178.

56 Quoted in Thompson, 'First steps in diplomacy', p. 5.
57 Quoted in Odgers, *100 Years of Australians at War*, p. 35.

2 Strategic independence consolidated

1 Stretton, 'Indigenous Australians and the vote'.
2 Chesterman, 'An unheard of piece of savagery', pp. 16–27, and Grimshaw, 'White women as nation builders', p. 16.
3 Section 41—Right of electors of States: 'No adult person who has or acquires a right to vote at elections for the more numerous House of the Parliament of a State shall, while the right continues, be prevented by any law of the Commonwealth from voting at elections for either House of the Parliament of the Commonwealth.'
4 Grimshaw, 'White women as nation builders', pp. 13–15.
5 Established by the *Conciliation and Arbitration Act 1904*.
6 The judgement can be seen at <http://www.aph.gov.au/binaries/library/intguide/law/harvester.pdf> (retrieved 24 October 2013).
7 The United Kingdom established the Trades Board Act in 1909, which founded four trade boards to set minimum wages in their relevant industries. The United States was even less advanced in this area, with statutory minimum wages not being introduced until 1938 with the passing of the Fair Labor Standards Act.
8 The provinces of Canada had a large say in minimum wage debates and passed their own legislation, such as the Men's Minimum Wage Act in British Columbia in 1925.
9 *Invalid and Old Age Pension Act 1908*. This replaced similar Acts in New South Wales (1900), Victoria (1900) and Queensland (1908).
10 For example, both Barton and Forrest, Australia's representatives at the conference, resisted Canadian pressure to establish Dominion navies, arguing instead to pay for an improved squadron of the Royal Navy to be based in Australian waters. They felt the time was not right for an independent Australian navy. See Reynolds, *Edmund Barton*, p. 200.
11 Grey, 'Defence'.
12 Stark, *The ANZUS Treaty Alliance*, p. 346.
13 DFAT, 'History of the Department of Foreign Affairs and Trade'.
14 Ibid.
15 The state agents-general represented the Federal Government in the years between Federation and 1906 before a Commonwealth appointment. See DFAT, 'History of Australia House'.
16 Reynolds, *Edmund Barton*, p. 200.
17 Deakin, in particular, pushed for a more consultative arrangement, arguing for 'a partnership of free nations, equal in status, organised for their common welfare'. See Murdoch, *Alfred Deakin*, pp. 241–2.
18 See ibid., p. 242.

19 Hudson & Sharp, *Australian Independence*, p. 47. Deakin did win some conces-
    sions from Britain at the conference, including getting the Admiralty to yield
    on the naval subsidy system and obtain agreement to found the Australian
    Navy. Further, idea of a 'planning body designed to assist cooperation between
    the military forces of the dominions and Britain in defence of the empire'
    was floated, culminating in the formation of the Australian general staff in
    early 1909. See McKernan & Browne, *Australia*, pp. 129–32, for discussion
    of both issues.

20 Hudson & Sharp, *Australian Independence*, p. 48.

21 McKernan & Browne, *Australia*, p. 135.

22 Reynolds, *Edmund Barton*, p. 200.

23 Norris, *The Emergent Commonwealth*, p. 132.

24 Reynolds, *Edmund Barton*, p. 200.

25 McKernan & Browne, *Australia*, p. 132.

26 Ibid., p. 134.

27 As Grey points out, 'In 1901 the Commonwealth had possessed no armed
    forces worthy of the name; numbered few among its citizens with any great
    experience of modern war; and had inherited a tiny defence administrative
    machine from the government of the colony of Victoria, the only Australian
    colonial government to create a separate defence ministry' ('Defending the
    Dominion, 1901–18').

28 Hudson & Sharp, *Australian Independence*, p. 44.

29 Ibid., p. 45. Also discussed by Bell, *Dependent Ally*, p. 10.

30 McKernan & Browne, *Australia*, p. 132.

31 Ibid.

32 See Nish, 'Australia and the Anglo-Japanese alliance, 1901–1911'.

33 Both Articles I and II of the Anglo-Japanese Alliance cover this point. Main
    points of the Alliance can be seen at <http://www.firstworldwar.com/source/
    anglojapanesealliance1902.htm> (retrieved 24 October 2013).

34 Both Articles III and IV of the amended Alliance cover this point.

35 See Nish, Steeds & Ayako, 'Anglo-Japanese alliance'.

36 This was particularly so around the area of immigration, with Australia impos-
    ing restrictions on Japanese immigrants there were at odds with British policy
    and objectives. For discussion, see Nish, 'Australia and the Anglo-Japanese
    Alliance, 1901–1911'.

37 For a history of the genesis of the Alliance, see Nish, Steeds & Ayako, 'Anglo-
    Japanese Alliance'.

38 Governor General to the Secretary of State for the Colonies, telegram,
    received 3 August 1914, in Greenwood & Grimshaw (eds), *Documents on
    Australian International Relations 1901–1918*, p. 561.

39 Odgers, *100 Years of Australians at War*, p. 41.

40 McKernan & Browne, *Australia*, p. 158.

41 Quoted in ibid., p. 161.

42 Australian War Memorial, 'Australian fatalities at Gallipoli'.

43 Quoted in Hudson & Sharp, *Australian Independence*, p. 49.

44 Louis, 'Australia and the German colonies in the Pacific, 1914–1919', p. 412.

45 Ibid., p. 412.

46 Ibid., pp. 413–14.

47 National Archives of Australia, 'Conscription referendums, 1916 and 1917—Fact sheet 161'.

48 Quoted in the *Argus* (Melbourne), 18 September 1916.

49 National Archives of Australia, 'Conscription referendums, 1916 and 1917—Fact sheet 161'.

50 Kildea, 'Australian Catholics and conscription in the Great War'. Kildea also talks of Sydney Archbishop Kelly, who, although initially not opposing conscription, became very influential behind the scenes in explaining to his congregations the risk conscription posed to the Church.

51 According to Casey, the aim was to 'recognise the right of the Dominions to an adequate voice in foreign policy and in foreign relations, and should provide effective arrangements for continuous consultation in all important matters of common Imperial concern' (Casey, 'Australia's voice in imperial affairs', p. 44).

52 This point is made by Hudson and Sharp, who argue that while conscription and casualties 'reinforced the devotion of some to the old empire and to the United Kingdom but inclined most to a more questioning attitude and some to want, if not outright independence, a degree of isolationism which might keep Australia out of wars' (*Australian Independence*, p. 52).

53 Ibid., p. 52.

54 In *Towards a Foreign Policy, 1914–1941*, Hudson highlights this point with the example of Hughes, who 'made his demands as a British imperialist as well as an Australian nationalist' (p. 9). See also Hudson, *Billy Hughes in Paris*.

55 Bridge, *William Hughes*, p. 54.

56 Hughes said the 'British Embassy of course acts for us in a casual sort of way, but you know what Englishmen are. They haven't the remotest idea of what Australia is like nor of its importance, and even with the best of intentions they are unsatisfactory. The only British representative here [in New York] is the Consul General. He is positively too dreadful for words' (quoted in Bridge, *William Hughes*, p. 56).

57 Ibid., p. 10.

58 Ibid., p. 60.

59 The Dominions went to the conference with a dual status—they were part of the British delegation but will 'have the same powers as, and be on an equal footing at the Conference with, Belgium and other smaller Allied States' (Hudson, *Billy Hughes in Paris*, p. 9). In *The Splendid Adventure*, Hughes himself would pen a more idealised version of this interpretation, arguing that although 'technically the status of the Dominions and India was no

higher than the status of the score of smaller nations which waited about with little information and even less influence while the four or five Great Powers decided, in actual fact they were included in the deciding Powers, for, by virtue of their membership of the British delegation, they formulated the policy which their spokesman, the Prime Minister of the United Kingdom, advocated in the Council of Four' (p. 237; see also Bridge, *William Hughes*, pp. 76–7).

60 Bridge, *William Hughes*, p. 66. Hughes also sent a cable to Watt on the matter—see W.M. Hughes, Prime Minister, to W.A. Watt, Acting Prime Minister, telegram, 11 November 1918 (in Meaney, *Australia and the World*, pp. 259–61). See also an account in the London *Times* of Hughes' objections: 'An Armistice that does less than justice to Australia and the British Empire' (*Times*, 8 November 1918, in Meaney, *Australia and the World*, pp. 256–9).

61 Bridge, *William Hughes*, p. 60. Hughes would later claim with respect to the League of Nations—although perhaps oddly, given Australia's position within the Empire—that 'no country would allow its vital interests to be decided by anyone except itself' (ibid., p. 66).

62 Ibid., p. 69. Lloyd George replied to Hughes' concern that the Anglo-Japanese Alliance granted Japan rights over islands north of the Equator and that Australia had been notified of this some years earlier. See David Lloyd George, British Prime Minister, to W.H. Hughes, Prime Minister, letter, 31 December 1918 (in Meaney, *Australia and the World*, pp. 263–4).

63 Indeed the issue of racial equality in the new world order dominated Japanese domestic politics at the conclusion of the war. See Lake & Reynolds, *Drawing the Global Colour Line*, p. 285, and Shimazu, *Japan, Race and Equality*, p. 51.

64 Hughes vehemently opposed it, at one point stating: 'The Japanese want to insert the proposed amendment into the Preamble. It may be all right. But sooner than agree to it I would rather walk into the Seine—or the Folies Bergères [—] with my clothes off' (Bridge, *William Hughes*, p. 85).

65 See ibid., p. 84, and Lake & Reynolds, *Drawing the Global Colour Line*, p. 292.

66 Indeed Hughes would undermine every attempt by the Japanese to pose a solution to the impasse, with Hughes 'morning, noon and night bellow[ing] at poor Lloyd George that if race equality is recognised in the preamble or any of the articles of the Covenant, he and his people will leave the Conference bag and baggage' (quoted in Lake & Reynolds, *Drawing the Global Colour Line*, p. 293).

67 Indeed Lord Robert Cecil, a member of the British delegation, replied to the Japanese after their repeated requests to intervene with Dominion opposition to the preamble that 'the question was essentially an Australian one' (Shimazu, *Japan, Race and Equality*, p. 125).

68 For example, Deputy Prime Minister Watt cabled Hughes reaffirming the Prime Minister's view that 'neither people nor Parliament of Australia could

agree to principles of racial equality' (quoted in Lake & Reynolds, *Drawing the Global Colour Line*, p. 294).

69 Maloney & Grosz, 'Billy Hughes and Woodrow Wilson'.

70 Fitzhardinge, 'Hughes, William Morris (Billy) (1869–1952)'. Fitzhardinge also wrote a more detailed account of Hughes; see Fitzhardinge, *William Morris Hughes: A Political Biography*.

71 Maloney & Grosz, 'Billy Hughes and Woodrow Wilson'.

72 Louis, 'Australia and the German colonies in the Pacific, 1914–1919', p. 417.

73 This was clearly the view of both the Japanese delegation and, more broadly, the Japanese public (see Shimazu, *Japan, Race and Equality*, p. 57).

3 Hanging on too long

1 Eggleston notes a number of issues around which consultation was poor or non-existent, such as increases in Dominion naval funding, negotiations concerning the League of Nations, participation at conferences such as Lausanne, which dealt with post-war Turkey and the recognition of the Soviet Union ('Australia and the Empire, 1855–1921', pp. 542–3).

2 Rhodes, *The Ango-American Winter War with Russia, 1918–1919*.

3 Ibid., p. 5.

4 At the very least this was the aim of Churchill, who had come to believe that Bolshevism was the worst tyranny in history, even exceeding that of German atrocities. According to Lloyd George, Churchill had 'Bolshevism on the brain … he is mad for operations in Russia' (Challinger, *ANZACS in Arkhangel*, p. 69).

5 Muirden, *The Diggers Who Signed on for More*, p. 80.

6 Grey, '"A pathetic sideshow"'.

7 Challinger, *ANZACS in Arkhangel*, pp. 69–71.

8 For further summary see Sales, 'W.M. Hughes and the Chanak Crisis of 1922'.

9 Ibid, p. 392.

10 Winston Churchill, British Colonial Secretary, to Lord Forster, Governor General, cablegram (secret), 16 September 1922 (in Meaney, *Australia and the World*, pp. 330–1).

11 Sales, 'W.M. Hughes and the Chanak Crisis of 1922', p. 394.

12 Lloyd George's cable evoked the following: 'Apart altogether from the vital Imperial and world-wide interests involved in the freedom of the Straits for which such immense sacrifices were made in the war, we cannot forget that the Gallipoli Peninsula contains over twenty thousand British and Anzac graves and that these should fall into the ruthless hands of the Kemalists would be an abiding source of grief to the Empire' (ibid., pp. 393–4). See also Winston Churchill, British Colonial Secretary, to Lord Forster, Governor General, cablegram (secret), 16 September 1922 (in Meaney, *Australia and the World*, pp. 330–1).

13 Sales, 'W.M. Hughes and the Chanak Crisis of 1922', p. 394.

NOTES

14 Hughes announced to the Australian public that 'Australia will join in whatever action is necessary, including the sending of a contingent, to ensure the
sanctity of Gallipoli' (Sales, 'W.M. Hughes and the Chanak Crisis of 1922',
p. 395).

15 Hughes cabled Lloyd George: '[Australia] should not be asked to join in an
unjust or unnecessary war. No one can say where this war once begun will
end. We are a peace loving democracy; we have been through a dreadful ordeal
in which we hope you and the world will agree we played our part worthily.
We are quite ready to fight in our own defence and in that of the Empire.
But we must know where we are going. In a good cause we are prepared to
venture our all; in a bad one, not a single man' (Sales, 'W.M. Hughes and the
Chanak Crisis of 1922', p. 397). See also W.M. Hughes, Prime Minister, to
David Lloyd George, British Prime Minister, cablegram, in Official Secretary
to Governor General to Secretary, Prime Minister's Department, letter,
20 September 1922 (in Meaney, *Australia and the World*, pp. 334–7).

16 Quoted in Sales, 'W.M. Hughes and the Chanak Crisis of 1922', pp. 403–4.

17 Grey, *A Military History of Australia*, p. 127. Further, the proceedings of the
1921 Imperial Conference reported: 'It was unanimously felt that the policy
of the British Empire could not be adequately representative of democratic
opinion through its people unless representatives of the Dominions and
of India were frequently associated with those of the United Kingdom in
considering and determining the course to be pursued' (Casey, 'Australia's
voice in imperial affairs', p. 45). Clearly this failed over Chanak.

18 See Hudson, *Towards a Foreign Policy, 1914–1941*, and Vinson, 'The Imperial
Conference of 1921 and the Anglo-Japanese Alliance', p. 264.

19 Vinson, 'The Imperial Conference of 1921 and the Anglo-Japanese Alliance',
pp. 262–5.

20 Ibid., pp. 257–8, and Hudson, *Towards a Foreign Policy, 1914–1941*, p. 53.

21 Vinson, 'The Imperial Conference of 1921 and the Anglo-Japanese Alliance',
p. 266. A useful summary of the Four Power Treaty and other treaties agreed
to at the Washington Naval Conference can be found at <http://history.state
.gov/milestones/1929-1936/NavalConference> (retrieved 25 October 2013).

22 Vinson, 'The Imperial Conference of 1921 and the Anglo-Japanese Alliance',
p. 266.

23 The fact that the Dominions had failed to gain direct representation at the
Conference was seen as 'an unnecessary slight [and] an unfortunate precedent'
for the developing post-war inter-imperial relationship (Hudson, *Towards a
Foreign Policy, 1914–1941*, p. 52).

24 Casey, 'Australia's voice in imperial affairs', p. 45.

25 Ibid., p. 46.

26 Grey, *A Military History of Australia*, p. 127.

27 Hudson, *Australian Diplomacy*, p. 20. Bruce would also note that every delegate
at the 1923 conference 'took the view that Empire defence was a task for the

Empire as a whole, and not for the individual nations comprising the Empire' (Cumpston, *History of Australian Foreign Policy 1901–1991*, p. 7).

28 Quoted in Hudson & Sharp, *Australian Independence*, p. 77.

29 Ibid., p. 115.

30 Indeed both Bruce and Hughes 'felt that Australia's advantage rested not with rigid demarcation of rights already enjoyed in everyday fact, but with a united Imperial diplomacy in which Australia could somehow participate' (Hudson, *Australian Diplomacy*, p. 19).

31 As Hudson and Sharp point out, Canada, South Africa and Ireland believed membership of the British Empire 'did not mean a single super-state ruled by London; it did not mean a mammoth federation ruled through new imperial organs from London; it did not mean a collection of semi-independent states still subject to external controls'. Great Britain, New Zealand and Australia held a countering view (*Australian Independence*, pp. 115–16). See also Marshall, 'The Balfour Formula and the evolution of the Commonwealth', p. 542.

32 Balfour Declaration, p. 2.

33 Ibid.

34 Indeed there remained some acceptance that Britain would continue to shoulder the responsibility for foreign affairs, recognising that imperial foreign policy would still be dominated by the British Foreign Office (Hudson, *Towards a Foreign Policy, 1914–1941*, p. 31).

35 Balfour Declaration, p. 2.

36 Ibid., p. 6.

37 As Hudson notes, 'As late as 1929, it was authoritatively argued that the dominions' status as League members depends on British grace and not on an extra-imperial body, on an initial request by His Majesty's government in Britain and not on dominion initiative' (*Australian Diplomacy*, p. 17).

38 This viewpoint was particularly pushed by Attorney General John Latham, who would fight the Statute of Westminster (the legislative manifestation of the Balfour Declaration) by arguing that 'the blood ties between the Dominions was not something that could be legislated and formalised, and that certain parties, for their own ends, could use the Statute to ruin the Empire' (Lewis, 'John Latham and the Statute of Westminster').

39 'No Act of Parliament of the United Kingdom passed after the commencement of this Act shall extend or be deemed to extend, to a Dominion as part of the law of that Dominion, unless it is expressly declared in that Act that that Dominion has requested, and consented to, the enactment thereof' (Statute of Westminster).

40 See Lewis, 'John Latham and the Statute of Westminster'.

41 Indeed, in 1935, the Lyons Government again separated external affairs from the Department of Prime Minister and provided the new agency with a modest staff of twelve public servants (Hudson, *Towards a Foreign Policy, 1914–1941*, p. 38).

42 The Mukden Incident was an attack staged by elements of the Japanese military on a Japanese-owned railway near Mukden, or modern-day Shenyang, a city in the north-eastern Chinese region of Manchuria. Despite failing to cause significant damage, the attack was used as a pretext for the full invasion of Manchuria by Japanese military forces in 1931.

43 Bruce stated that he 'was not quite as clear as I should like to be as to how the protection of Singapore is to be assured, I am clear on this point, that apparently it can be done' (quoted in Grey, *A Military History of Australia*, p. 128).

44 While he did not specify Japan as a potential aggressor, Lyons summarised this basic strategy in a speech to the House of Representatives (Prime Minister Lyons in the House of Representatives, *Commonwealth Parliamentary Debates*, 1937 Session, vol. 154, pp. 22–31, 24 August 1937, in Meaney, *Australia and the World*, pp. 428–33).

45 One criticism was that the defence of Singapore was based on the automatic transfer of the British fleet in the event of a conflict in the Far East—a situation deemed impossible if there should simultaneously be a conflict in Europe, which, of course, is exactly what occurred during World War II (Grey, *A Military History of Australia*, and Bell, *Dependent Ally*, p. 17).

46 Indeed delays in constructing the Singapore base led to Australia announcing a five-year naval construction plan, resulting in the contribution of ships to the strategy over additional funds (Grey, *A Military History of Australia*, p. 129).

47 See Grey, *The Australian Army*.

48 Grey, *A Military History of Australia*, p. 129.

49 Hudson, *Towards a Foreign Policy, 1914–1941*, p. 70.

50 The viewpoints of these Pacific powers are expressed in Hudson, *Towards a Foreign Policy, 1914–1941*, pp. 70–3.

51 Waters, *Australia and Appeasement*, pp. 21–2. *Anschluss* was the political union of Nazi Germany and Austria in 1938.

52 Ibid., p. 23.

53 Ibid., p. 27.

54 P. Liesching, British High Commissioner to Australia, to Lord Stanley, British Secretary for Dominion Affairs, cable, 31 August 1938 (in Meaney, *Australia and the World*, pp. 439–40).

55 Andrews, *Isolationism and Appeasement in Australia*, p. 23.

56 Bridge, *William Hughes*, p. 375.

57 Watt, *The Evolution of Australian Foreign Policy 1938–1965*, p. 24.

58 Ibid., p. 31.

59 Many of these letters and other correspondence between key officials of the Menzies Government, including Casey, can be found at <http://www.info.dfat.gov.au/Info/Historical/histdocs.nsf/vWeb?OpenView> (retrieved 15 November 2013).

60 The full transcript of Menzies' announcement can be seen at <http://www.awm.gov.au/encyclopedia/prime_ministers/menzies/> (retrieved 25 October 2013).
61 See for example Bell, *Dependent Ally*, p. 15.
62 Watt, *The Evolution of Australian Foreign Policy 1938–1965*, p. 29.
63 In his own memoirs, Menzies outlines three reasons for Australia immediately joining the war: the sentiments of the majority of Australians would have been shocked by delays, the need to assist Great Britain as quickly as possible, and Australia's allegiance to the crown (Menzies, *Afternoon Light*, pp. 16–17). On this last point, Menzies would also describe the possibility of Australia not being at war at a time when the King was at war as 'a metaphysical notion that quite eludes me' (Hasluck, *The Government and the People 1939–1941*, p. 155).
64 Andrews, *Isolationism and Appeasement in Australia*, p. 27.
65 Day, *The Great Betrayal*, p. 22.
66 Ibid., pp. 23–33.
67 Horner, *Inside the War Cabinet*, p. 7. It was thought that 'Japan would sit on the fence as far as the European war' and that, should Tokyo become a belligerent power, it would require a least 50,000 troops and four months to dislodge the British from Singapore (ibid., p. 12). Hasluck makes similar suggestions in *The Government and the People 1939–1941* (pp. 167–8), as does Martin in *Robert Menzies* (p. 316). See also R.G. Casey, Minister for Supply and Development, to Mr R.G. Menzies, Prime Minister, cablegram, 17 November 1939 (in Meaney, *Australia and the World*, p. 465).
68 Horner, *Inside the War Cabinet*, p. 7.
69 Day, *The Great Betrayal*, p. 34.
70 Bell notes in *Dependent Ally* that this is an interesting point when considering the notion of strategic dependence, given that Menzies' decision implies that 'what might be done in London (as a member of the War Cabinet) was more vital than what had to be done in Canberra' (p. 18).
71 Martin, *Robert Menzies*, p. 317.
72 Menzies to Bruce, letter, 22 February 1940, <http://www.dfat.gov.au/publications/historical/volume-03/historical-document-03-71.html> (retrieved 25 October 2013).
73 Lee, *John Curtin*, p. 98.
74 Ibid., p. 99.
75 Ibid., pp. 99–100.
76 Waters, *Australia and Appeasement*, p. 2.
77 Dowsing, *Curtin of Australia*, p. 97.
78 Quoted in Lee, *John Curtin*, p. 94.
79 Quoted in ibid., p. 95.
80 Dowsing, *Curtin of Australia*, p. 107.
81 Curtin, *Herald*, Melbourne, 27 December 1941, <http://www.ww2australia.gov.au/japadvance/austous.html> (retrieved 25 October 2010).

82 Day, *The Great Betrayal*, p. 229.
83 Quoted in Dowsing, *Curtin of Australia*, pp. 110–11.
84 Ibid., pp. 112–13.
85 Lee, *John Curtin*, p. 100. Mr Winston Churchill, UK Prime Minister (in the United States), to Mr John Curtin, Prime Minister, cable, <http://www.dfat.gov.au/publications/historical/volume-05/historical-document-05-271.html> (retrieved 25 October 2013).
86 Quoted in Freudenberg, *Churchill and Australia*, p. 354. Also Mr Winston Churchill, UK Prime Minister (in the United States), to Mr John Curtin, Prime Minister, cable, <http://www.dfat.gov.au/publications/historical/volume-05/historical-document-05-271.html> (retrieved 25 October 2013).
87 Freudenberg, *Churchill and Australia*, p. 354.
88 Lee, *John Curtin*, p. 102.
89 Churchill, *The Hinge of Fate*, p. 88. See also Curran, *Curtin's Empire*, p. 86.
90 Menzies, *Afternoon Light*, p. 92.
91 Churchill would write in his history of World War II of 'a painful episode in our relations with the Australian Government and their refusal of our requests for aid'. For his version of this episode involving Curtin, see Churchill, *The Hinge of Fate*, pp. 136–8.
92 Ibid., p. 139.
93 Lee, *John Curtin*, p. 106. This topic is also discussed in Bell, *Dependent Ally*, p. 26. After returning to Australia, many troops of the 6th and 7th Divisions would go on to fight against the Japanese in New Guinea, Borneo and Sri Lanka.
94 Lee, *John Curtin*, p. 106.
95 Crowley, *Modern Australia in Documents*, pp. 61–2, quoting *Sydney Morning Herald*, 19 March 1942.
96 Lebra, *Japan's Greater East Asia Co-Prosperity Sphere in World War II*, p. xiii.

4 Securing post-war Australia

1 The Australian War Memorial lists a number of accounts of the war worth pursuing (http://www.awm.gov.au/atwar/ww2/), including Dennis et al., *Oxford Companion to Australian Military History*, 2nd edn; Long, *The Six Years War*; Robertson, *1939–1945*.
2 See Statement of Immigration by the Minister for Immigration and Information the Hon. Arthur A. Calwell—Commonwealth Parliament, 9 August 1946, <http://www.immi.gov.au/media/history/post-war-immigration/_pdf/19460809_ministerial_statement.pdf> (retrieved 12 October 2013). Further statements by Calwell on immigration are available at <http://www.immi.gov.au/media/history/post-war-immigration/policy.htm> (retrieved 15 November 2013).
3 Price, 'Post-war migration: 1947–98', p. 116. See also Department of Immigration and Border Protection, 'Immigration to Australia during the 20th century'.

4 Statement of Immigration by the Minister for Immigration and Information the Hon. Arthur A. Calwell—Commonwealth Parliament, 9 August 1946, p. 25.

5 Price, 'Post-war migration: 1947–98', p. 121.

6 *Examiner* (Launceston), 21 February 1950.

7 The purpose of the council was to advise the government on community problems with the settlement process. See Department of Immigration and Citizenship, 'Immigration history 1945–1955'.

8 Commonwealth Bureau of Census and Statistics, *Official Book of the Commonwealth of Australia No. 58*, 1972, p. 156.

9 See *Sydney Morning Herald*, 'Mrs O'Keefe to stay, Gamboa allowed to come here', 17 February 1950, and *Sydney Morning Herald*, 'US Army problem now for Gamboa', 18 February 1950, for further information. The case of Mrs Annie O'Keeffe is another example; see Brawley, 'Mrs O'Keefe and the battle for White Australia'.

10 Menzies said, 'We will continue to maintain Australia's settled immigration policy, known as the White Australia policy, well justified as it is on the grounds of national homogeneity and economic standards. At the same time we believe in human and common-sense administration. All cases of aliens resident in Australia should be considered, not as if the law allowed no human discretion but in the light of the circumstances of each case. Nothing has done both the White Australia policy and our relations with Asiatic countries more harm than some of the stupid and provocative decisions of the Chifley Government' (*Examiner*, Launceston, 21 February 1950).

11 In their entry regarding post-war reconstruction, Dennis et al. note that it was argued the war was only worth fighting if life after it was better. As such, the Department of Post-War Reconstruction was established to coordinate 'the commitment to full employment and a range of practical social welfare measures such as widows' pensions, maternity allowances, unemployment and sickness benefits, the establishment of the Commonwealth Employment Services', along with many agreements with states covering housing, hospitals and education. See Dennis et al., 'Postwar reconstruction', *Oxford Companion to Australian Military History*, 2nd edn.

12 See for example Murray, *The Ironworkers*, and Fitzpatrick, *The Seamen's Union of Australia, 1872–1972*.

13 Australian Bureau of Statistics (ABS), 'A century of change in the Australian labour market'.

14 Ibid.

15 ABS, 'Employee earnings, benefits and trade union membership, Australia, August 2012'.

16 Dennis et al., 'Demobilisation', *Oxford Companion to Australian Military History*, 2nd edn.

17 For example, Chifley attacked the mining union and jailed its communist official during a dispute over restraining post-war reconstruction wages in 1949. See Sheridan, *Division of Labour*.

18 Australian Labor Party (ALP), *Official Report of Proceedings of the 18th Commonwealth Triennial Conference*, 27 September 1948, p. 52; and ALP, *Official Report of the Proceedings of the 19th Commonwealth Triennial Conference*, 1 March 1951, p. 53.

19 The Act can be seen at <http://www.austlii.edu.au/au/legis/cth/num_act/ba1947570l1947118/> (retrieved 15 November 2013). Clause 3 states some objectives of the Act, including 'the taking over by the Commonwealth Bank of the banking business in Australia of private banks'.

20 In *Bank of New South Wales v Commonwealth* (1948) (the Bank Nationalisation Case), eleven private banks and the governments of South Australia, Victoria and Western Australia challenged the *Banking Act 1947* (Cwlth) in the High Court. Judgement can be seen at <http://www.austlii.edu.au/au/cases/cth/HCA/1948/7.html> (retrieved 27 October 2013).

21 Bell, *Unequal Allies*, p. 175.

22 Ibid., pp. 174–5. The United States was aware, however, that Britain's economic and military decline in the region had to be balanced on account of the Soviet Union's rising strength.

23 Harper, *A Great and Powerful Friend*, pp. 182–3.

24 Meaney, 'Look back in fear', p. 401.

25 Ibid., p. 401.

26 Harper, *A Great and Powerful Friend*, p. 192.

27 Meaney notes that this was done not only with a more congenial disposition to the Americans but also with a greater focus on communism ('Look back in fear', p. 401).

28 Spender would say on the matter: 'We do not desire to prevent the Japanese people from winning their way back to the comity of nations. We know that the time must arrive sooner or later when the military occupation of Japan will come to an end ... Australia sees great danger to its own peace in a peace treaty which does not provide adequate safeguards against the revival of an armed and aggressive Japan, or any treaty which imposes no limitation upon Japan's ability to rearm. It is asking too much of us to believe that the forces of militarism in Japan are completely dead ... we are not satisfied that Japan can be trusted with military power without reasonable controls imposed by the countries who suffered so grievously at her hands' (quoted in Holding, Johnson & Andre, *Documents on Australian Foreign Policy: The ANZUS Treaty 1951* [hereafter *The ANZUS Treaty 1951*], p. 43. Also see Bell, *Dependent Ally*, p. 75, and Meaney, 'Look back in fear', p. 400).

29 The British also felt that Australia's fears of Japan were overstated. See Harper, *A Great and Powerful Friend*, p. 196.

30 Bell, *Dependent Ally*, p. 75, and Harper, *A Great and Powerful Friend*, p. 196.

31 Evatt had pushed for a broad-ranging security arrangement in the Pacific as early as 1946, with Chifley publicly canvassing the idea in 1949, given the development of NATO in Europe, although his proposal was initially focused on Britain and the Commonwealth, with the United States to be asked to join at a later date. See Holding, Johnson & Andre, *The ANZUS Treaty 1951*, pp. xxviii & 4.

32 Menzies and Spender would differ over the concept of a Pacific pact, with the Prime Minister stating that 'the Pacific Pact is not at present on the map because the Americans are uneasy about the stability of most Asiatic countries. We do not need a pact with America. They are already overwhelmingly friendly to us' (Holding, Johnson & Andre, *The ANZUS Treaty 1951*, p. 19).

33 Reece, *Australia, New Zealand, and the United States*, p. 127.

34 Holding, Johnson & Andre, *The ANZUS Treaty 1951*, p. xxvii.

35 As Harper notes, lenient terms with Japan and the Colombo Plan were both 'tactical weapons in the ideological battle' (*A Great and Powerful Friend*, p. 196).

36 Indeed Spender knew the writing was on the wall in respect of hard terms of peace, cabling Menzies: 'As we may well fail to secure general acceptance of our policy on Japanese re-armament, it is all the more important that we endeavour to obtain from the United States some kind of guarantee of our security. It is my understanding of the London talks that the direct defence of Australia has, by implication, been left to the United States' (Holding, Johnson & Andre, *The ANZUS Treaty 1951*, p. 53).

37 Churchward, *Australia and America, 1789–1972*, p. 163.

38 Spender cabled the following to Menzies, suggesting the need to make sure Australia's decision was seen as separate from Britain's: 'If the United Kingdom had announced its decision before Australia, I feel you would agree ... that it would be used against us politically. It would have been suggested that we could not make up our own minds until the United Kingdom gave the lead and as well we would have failed to obtain the favourable reactions from the United States which are so important for our relations with them' (quoted in Holding, Johnson & Andre, *The ANZUS Treaty 1951*, p. 18).

39 Spender said, 'It would be politically impossible for any Australian government to enter into a "liberal" Japanese peace treaty without firm guarantees against Japanese aggression' (quoted in Harper, *A Great and Powerful Friend*, p. 197).

40 The terms and relevant documents relating to ANZUS have been compiled into a useful volume (see Burnett, Young & Wilson, *The ANZUS Documents*).

41 DFAT's assessment notes the difference between the two, 'with Menzies prepared to take the United States on trust by settling for a Presidential state-ment of support for Australia and New Zealand, and Spender, who thought that a Presidential declaration might prove temporary and in any case would lack any accompanying planning machinery, determined to obtain a binding treating' (Holding, Johnson & Andre, *The ANZUS Treaty 1951*, p. xxxiv).

5 Dr H.V. Evatt

1 Crockett, *Evatt*, p. 187.
2 See for example Buckley, Dale & Reynolds, *Doc Evatt*, and Renouf, *Let Justice Be Done.*
3 Crockett, *Evatt*, p. 185.
4 Ibid., p. 212. As Bell writes, 'Evatt's attitudes as a maker of foreign policy included a passionate (even raucous) attachment to the Australian national interest, and considerable faith (perhaps excessive faith) in the virtues of international organisation and international law as the primary instruments for controlling conflict among nations' (*Dependent Ally*, p. 23).
5 Ibid., p. 214.
6 Three concerns discussed in ibid., p. 215.
7 Tennant, *Evatt*, p. 168.
8 Crockett, *Evatt*, p. 215, and Tennant, *Evatt*, p. 165.
9 Tennant, *Evatt*, pp. 166, 167.
10 Crockett, *Evatt*, p. 217.
11 Tennant, *Evatt*, pp. 173–4; see also Crockett, *Evatt*, p. 217.
12 Tennant, *Evatt*, p. 174.

6 Strategic dependence through the Cold War prism

1 Plokhy, *Yalta*, p. xxiv. This text provides an in-depth review of Yalta.
2 Czechoslovakia had been relatively stable, with de-Stalinisation and liberalisation processes not materialising as they did in other Warsaw Pact nations, notably Hungary and Poland. However, the 1960s economic slowdown caused a breakdown in consensus between leaders and workers, with the government instituting a series of economic reforms in response (US Department of State—Office of the Historian, 'Soviet invasion of Czechoslovakia, 1968').
3 Quoted in 'Policy review of Voice for Free Hungary programming, October 23—November 23, 1956', 5 December 1956, <http://www2.gwu.edu/~nsarchiv/NSAEBB/NSAEBB76/doc10.pdf> (retrieved 27 October 2013).
4 Ibid.
5 Kennan, 'The chargé in the Soviet Union (Kennan) to the Secretary of State' ('Long telegram'), 22 February 1946, <http://www2.gwu.edu/~nsarchiv/coldwar/documents/episode-1/kennan.htm> (retrieved 24 October 2013).
6 Evatt told his department that 'Australia has a vital interest in the preservation of the wartime friendship with the Dutch in relation to the NEI. At the same time, it is important to do everything to establish good relations with the Indonesians and others moving towards self-government. Australian policy is aimed at discouraging provocation and violence' (quoted in Tennant, *Evatt*, pp. 185–6).
7 Taylor, *Indonesian Independence and the United Nations*, pp. 7–8.
8 Tennant, *Evatt*, p. 169.

9 Menzies, in drawing parallels between Evatt's position and that of wharf labourers who were boycotting Dutch shipping in support of Indonesian sovereignty, stated: 'The very arguments used by those in charge of Australian foreign policy—I refer to the waterside workers—for throwing the Dutch out of the East Indies are the arguments that would be used for throwing the British out of the Malay peninsula and out of Burma and India, and for throwing Australia out of New Guinea and Papua' (quoted in Tennant, *Evatt*, p. 184). For more on the wharf boycotts, see Goodall, 'Port politics'.

10 Hudson, *Towards a Foreign Policy, 1914–1941*, p. 237.

11 Menzies stated: 'The Dutch, our friendly allies, have already been treated in a most offensive manner by the Australian Government. Millions of Australians feel bitterly ashamed at the feeble manner in which the Government had accepted dictation from a handful of Communist wharf-labourers. From the standpoints of both defence and trade, it is suicidal for the Government to continue an attitude which allows the Australians and the Dutch to be at cross purposes' (quoted in Tennant, *Evatt*, p. 185).

12 Dennis & Grey, *Emergency and Confrontation*, p. 5.

13 Edwards, *Crises and Commitments*, pp. 27–9.

14 Dennis et al., 'Malayan Emergency', *Oxford Companion to Australian Military History*, 2nd edn.

15 Sukarno would claim that a British proposal for Brunei to join other British territories in Borneo as part of the Malaysian Federation was neo-colonial, feeding in this his desire to be portrayed as a leader of the world's 'newly emerging forces', assisting his domestic political needs (Edwards, *Crises and Commitments*, p. 257).

16 Indeed the definition of Konfrontasi was usefully ambiguous for the Indonesian leadership. 'The ambiguities inherent in the term allowed President Sukarno considerable room to manoeuvre as he pursued both a diplomatic and a military offensive against Malaysia, and the whole process of Confrontation was intimately tied to domestic politics in Jakarta' (Dennis & Grey, *Emergency and Confrontation*, pp. 171–2).

17 Australia shared Britain's aim but, in the initial period, was also fearful that increased Indonesian activity might spill over into action against Papua New Guinea or, indeed, result in the break-up of Indonesia itself (Dennis & Grey, *Emergency and Confrontation*, p. 172). Further, the Australian leadership was wary of becoming a 'standing adversary' to Jakarta (Edwards, *Crises and Commitments*, p. 259).

18 Dennis & Grey, *Emergency and Confrontation*, p. 320. See also Woodard, 'Best practice in Australia's foreign policy', p. 85.

19 Weisbrod, 'Sir Garfield Barwick and Dutch New Guinea', p. 31.

20 The British provided only lukewarm support to the initial Australian position as well, stating that they would only support the Australian Government in the United Nations (ibid., p. 26).

21 This was based on an assurance he had been given by Rusk (Marr, *Barwick*, pp. 195–6).

22 'Report of meeting with Mr Averell Harriman in Canberra', NAA 7/6/63, A4940/C3812/1338485, p. 6.

23 Harriman's response to McEwen was that 'a reply ... would require a careful choice of words which he would not wish to attempt on the instant. However, he felt that the United States attitude would be much affected by the seriousness with which Australia itself was taking the situation. The United States had assumed extensive obligations abroad and had not yet turned away from an appeal by its friends. If there were a commitment on Australia's part, he did not think that the United States would let Australia down but he could make no commitments. This was a grey area between the two countries. Australia's other activities in South-East Asia would also influence the United States' (ibid., p. 6).

24 *Economist*, 'Canberra looks out', 12 January 1963, p. 103.

25 Pixley, 'Eisenhower's strategy in the Taiwan Strait', p. 12; Tucker, *Dangerous Strait*; Studeman, 'Thorns in the dragon's side'.

26 Eisenhower is quoted as saying, when asked about the appropriateness of using nuclear weapons should communist forces invade the offshore islands being shelled, 'In any combat where these things can be used on strictly military targets and for strictly military purposes, I can see no reason why they shouldn't be used just exactly as you would use a bullet or anything else ... Yes, of course they would be used' (quoted in Pixley, 'Eisenhower's strategy in the Taiwan Strait', p. 12).

27 Those present at the meeting were Menzies, Spender as Ambassador to the United States, Arthur Tange as Secretary of the Department of External Affairs, John Foster Dulles, Secretary of State, Herbert Hoover Jnr, Undersecretary of State, Livingston Merchant, Assistant Secretary for European Affairs, and Walter Roberts, Assistant Secretary for Eastern Affairs. 'Memorandum of a Conversation, Washington, March 14, 1955', US Department of State, Conference Files: Lot 60 D 627, CF 439, <http://history.state.gov/historicaldocuments/frus1955-57v02/d154> (retrieved 23 October 2013).

28 Martin, *Robert Menzies*.

29 Telegram from the Secretary of State to the Embassy in Australia, Washington, April 30, Department of State, Central Files, 793.00/055, <http://history.state.gov/historicaldocuments/frus1957v02/d233> (retrieved 27 October 2013).

7   The cost of strategic dependence

1 McNamara, *In Retrospect*, pp. xvi–xvii.

2 Quoted in Betts, *France and Decolonisation 1900–1960*, p. 60.

3 Ho Chi Minh, 'Declaration of independence', 2 September 1945.

4 A thoughtful overview of Vietnamese nationalism and Ho's early years is provided by Karnow, *Vietnam*, pp. 89–127.

5 Ibid.

6 Indeed Roosevelt initially was opposed to the French reassuming control over Vietnam yet, by the end of the war, Truman 'and other American officials were more concerned with restoring French power as an ally against the Soviet Union and opposed Ho's communist beliefs' (Hall, *The Vietnam War*, pp. 5–6).

7 This drew criticism from the Vietminh and other nationalists, who claim that Dai merely accepted the French position and control (Hall, *The Vietnam War*, p. 7).

8 Betts, *France and Decolonisation 1900–1960*, p. 89.

9 Pentagon Papers, *Aid for France in Indochina*, p. i.

10 Hall, *The Vietnam War*, p. 7, Kolko, *Anatomy of a War*, pp. 75–7, and Pentagon Papers, *Aid for France in Indochina*, pp. 2–5.

11 Betts, *France and Decolonisation 1900–1960*, p. 81, and Hall, *The Vietnam War*, pp. 5–6.

12 Betts, *France and Decolonisation 1900–1960*, pp. 79–80.

13 Ibid., p. 86, and Kolko, *Anatomy of a War*, p. 79, who makes the point that Vietnam was linked to so many international questions confronting the United States, including the role of France in Europe. That being said, the United States refused French requests for assistance before the Geneva Conference as the preconditions Eisenhower had put on such intervention (action by an international coalition, French consent to establish an independent Vietnam and approval of congress) had not been met (Hall, *The Vietnam War*, p. 8).

14 Betts, *France and Decolonisation 1900–1960*, pp. 85–6.

15 Hall, *The Vietnam War*, p. 9, and Tran, 'The Catholic question', p. 431.

16 Hall, *The Vietnam War*, p. 10.

17 Pentagon Papers, *Evolution of the War: Training of Vietnamese National Army, 1954–59*, p. 4.

18 Ibid., p. 1.1.

19 Ford, *CIA and the Vietnam Policymakers: Three Episodes 1969–1968*; see Episode 1, 1969–1963: 'Distortions of intelligence'.

20 Quoted in McNamara, *In Retrospect*, p. 46.

21 Ford, *CIA and the Vietnam Policymakers*.

22 McNamara, *In Retrospect*, pp. 46–7.

23 Ibid., pp. 47–8.

24 Ibid., p. 48, and Ford, *CIA and the Vietnam Policymakers*.

25 McNamara, *In Retrospect*, p. 47; Pentagon Papers, *Counterinsurgency*, Part IV B 4, pp. 1–4.

26 Pentagon Papers, *Counterinsurgency*, p. v, and Ford, *CIA and the Vietnam Policymakers*.

27 McNamara, *In Retrospect*, p. 48

28 Michael Forrestal, quoted in Ford, *CIA and the Vietnam Policymakers*.

29 Hall, *The Vietnam War*, p. 14.

30 McNamara, *In Retrospect*, p. 49.

31 Pentagon Papers, *Counterinsurgency*, p. 30.

32 Ibid., p. 17.

33 Pentagon Papers, *Counterinsurgency*, Part IV B 5, p. ii.

34 McNamara, *In Retrospect*, pp. 51–2.

35 Ibid., p. 52.

36 Ibid., pp. 52–3.

37 Ibid., p. 53.

38 State Department Telegram 243, Ball to Lodge, 24 August 1963, FRUS, 1961–63, vol. 3, pp. 628–9.

39 McNamara, *In Retrospect*, p. 53.

40 Ibid., p. 53.

41 Quoted in Ford, *CIA and the Vietnam Policymakers*; see Episode 2: 1963–1965: 'CIA judgments on President Johnson's decision to "go big" in Vietnam'.

42 McNamara, *In Retrospect*, p. 54.

43 Ibid., p. 56.

44 Ibid., pp. 60–1.

45 Ibid., p. 60.

46 Ibid., p. 70.

47 Quoted in Ford, *CIA and the Vietnam Policymakers*.

48 McNamara, *In Retrospect*, p. 81.

49 Ibid., pp. 83–4.

50 Quoted in ibid., pp. 61–2.

51 Ford, *CIA and the Vietnam Policymakers*.

52 Miguel & Rowland, *The Long Run Impact of Bombing Vietnam*, p. 2.

53 Ford, *CIA and the Vietnam Policymakers*.

54 Ford, 'Unpopular pessimism'.

55 Ibid.

56 McNamara, *In Retrospect*, pp. 142–3.

57 Hall argues that before the attack the *Maddox*, along with USS *C. Turner Joy*, had been conducting electronic intelligence-gathering in the Gulf of Tonkin (Hall, *The Vietnam War*, pp. 17–18).

58 McNamara, *In Retrospect*, p. 138.

59 Ibid., p. 141.

60 Ibid., p. 139.

61 Ibid., pp. 170–2.

62 Ibid, pp. 203–4.

63 Ibid., p. 204, and Pentagon Papers, *Direct Action*, Part IV, C 5, p. 4.

64 McNamara, *In Retrospect*, p. 204; see also Pentagon Papers, *Direct Action*, p. 4.

65 McNamara, *In Retrospect*, p. 204.

66 McNamara, Blight & Brigham, *Argument Without End*, pp. 348–9, 350.

67 See Pentagon Papers, *Direct Action*, for detailed explanation of the phases, including outlines of Westmoreland's requests.

68 McNamara, Blight & Brigham, *Argument Without End*, pp. 351–2.

69 McNamara, *In Retrospect*, p. 203.

70 For an excellent analysis of the decision-making leading up to Australia's commitment to Vietnam, based on a thorough examination of historical official documents, former Australian Ambassador Garry Woodard's *Asian Alternatives* is well worth a read.

71 The initial deployment of thirty military advisers was announced on 24 May 1962; see Dennis et al., 'Australian Army Training Team Vietnam', *Oxford Companion to Australian Military History*.

72 Menzies, Speech to the House of Representatives, 29 April 1965.

73 Neale, 'Australia's military commitment to South Vietnam', p. 11.

74 Ibid., p. 3.

75 Ekins, *Fighting to the Finish*, p. 2.

76 Ibid., p. 690, and Neale, 'Australia's military commitment to South Vietnam', p. 2.

77 Ekins, 'Overview of Australian military involvement in the Vietnam War, 1962–1975'.

78 Ekins, *Fighting to the Finish*, p. 690. Stephens argues that Scherger's 'attitude and comments implied that the despatch of Australian forces was not a matter of if, but rather of when. There is no doubt that he exceeded his authority to an extent that might be described as reckless' (Stephens, 'Scherger, Sir Frederick Rudolph (1904–1984)').

79 Neale, 'Australia's military commitment to South Vietnam', p. 32.

80 Searches of collections maintained by the Australian War Memorial, the National Archives of Australia and various American sources have not produced any documentary evidence to suggest Australia was aware of the divisions in Washington.

81 For the full text of Holt's speech, see Johnson, 'Remarks of welcome to Prime Minister Holt of Australia on the South Lawn at the White House'.

82 Australian War Memorial, 'Vietnam War 1965'.

83 I define 'due process in government' as meaning that governments act having taken full advice from those trained and equipped to give advice. So far as military involvement is concerned, it should take place only after the Defence Committee, which includes the Department of Defence, Foreign Affairs, Treasury and the intelligence services, have all had an opportunity to place their information and their views before the government. It also involves full and open consideration by ministers formally sitting together in the Cabinet. If we compare that definition with the processes that operated in the Kennedy and Johnson administrations, we can see that the American position was disorganised and denied the Americans any possibility of making properly informed and wise decisions.

84 Nixon, 'Vietnamization', speech, 3 November 1969.

85 Beinart, 'Return of the Nixon Doctrine'.

86 Indeed Bell notes that the Guam doctrine received hardly any attention at the time in Australia, as leading writers 'brushed it aside as a sort of presidential public relations exercise' (*Dependent Ally*, p. 104).

8 The 'grand bargain' out of time

1 Joint Communiqué of the United States of America and the People's Republic of China ('Shanghai Communiqué'), 28 February 1972, <http://www.taiwandocuments.org/communique01.htm> (retrieved 27 October 2013).

2 Clause 12 of the communiqué says that the United States acknowledges 'that all Chinese on either side of the Taiwan Strait maintain there is but one China and that Taiwan is a part of China. The United States Government does not challenge that position. It reaffirms its interest in a peaceful settlement of the Taiwan question by the Chinese themselves. With this prospect in mind, it affirms the ultimate objective of the withdrawal of all US forces and military installations from Taiwan.'

3 Joint Communiqué of the United States of America and the People's Republic of China ('Joint communiqué on the establishment of diplomatic relations'), 1 January 1979, <http://www.taiwandocuments.org/communique02.htm> (retrieved 27 October 2013).

4 Clause 6 of the Shanghai Communiqué.

5 The White Paper notes: 'China opposes any form of hegemonism or power politics, and does not interfere in the internal affairs of other countries. China will never seek hegemony or behave in a hegemonic manner, nor will it engage in military expansion. China advocates a new security concept featuring mutual trust, mutual benefit, equality and coordination, and pursues comprehensive security, common security and cooperative security' (Information Office of the State Council, 'The diversified employment of China's armed forces', p. 1).

6 Clause 6 of the Shanghai Communiqué.

7 Ibid. The White Paper notes China's dispute with Japan over the Senkaku/Diaoyou Islands, stating: 'On the issues concerning China's territorial sovereignty and maritime rights and interests, some neighboring countries are taking actions that complicate or exacerbate the situation, and Japan is making trouble over the issue of the Diaoyu Islands. The threats posed by "three forces", namely, terrorism, separatism and extremism, are on the rise' (Information Office of the State Council, 'The diversified employment of China's armed forces', p. 1).

8 Clause 8 of the Shanghai Communiqué.

9 Clause 9 of the Shanghai Communiqué.

10 Clause 10 of the Shanghai Communiqué.

11 Clause 11 of the Shanghai Communiqué.

12 Clause 12 of the Shanghai Communiqué.

13 Ibid.

14 Such treaties included the Treaty of Nanking, the Convention of Peking and the Boxer Protocol.
15 See for example former Secretary of Defence Arthur Tange's memoirs, Tange, *Defence Policy-making*, pp. 69–71.
16 This connection is also made by Bell, *Dependent Ally*, p. 22.
17 Fraser, 'Australia and some world economic issues'.
18 'American inflation rate history—1970 to 1980', 17 September 2013.
19 Fraser, 'Australia and some world economic issues', p. 3.
20 'Australian inflation rate history—1970 to 1980', 23 October 2013.
21 The Taraki Government had announced significant policy with respect to land redistribution, the status of women and the prevailing Afghani social order, resulting in little popular support and an armed resistance (see Dibb, 'The Soviet experience in Afghanistan', p. 496).
22 The Afghans made more than twenty requests for military assistance between April and December 1979 (Galeotti, *Afghanistan*, p. 8).
23 A good overview of the political and ethnic history of Afghanistan is provided in the introductory chapter of Kakar, *Afghanistan*, pp. 1–10. See also Galeotti, *Afghanistan*, pp. 3–10.
24 A key element of this rebuff was that the Americans believed Afghanistan to be less strategically important than Pakistan and Iran (see Saikal, 'Afghanistan during the Cold War', pp. 60–1). Kakar also points out that the tension between Pakistan and Afghanistan over Pushtanistan was in part responsible for Kabul seeking Soviet commercial assistance. Further, Dulles told Afghanistan to resolve its dispute with Pakistan and refused to sell Kabul military equipment, stating: 'After careful consideration, extending military aid to Afghanistan would create problems not offset by the strength it would generate' (see Kakar, *Afghanistan*, pp. 7 & 9).
25 Saikal, 'Afghanistan during the Cold War', p. 64.
26 Ibid., p. 64, and Kakar, *Afghanistan*, p. 15.
27 Galeotti, *Afghanistan*, pp. 7, 10. Galeotti argues that the final political decision to invade was made on 24 December in Brezhnev's office.
28 Saikal, 'Afghanistan during the Cold War', p. 68. See also Dibb, 'The Soviet experience in Afghanistan', pp. 497–8.
29 Saikal, 'Afghanistan during the Cold War', p. 68.
30 For a discussion on US and Pakistani assistance to Soviet resistance, see ibid., pp. 66–8.
31 Ibid., p. 69.
32 Tange, *Defence Policy-making*, pp. 105–6.
33 Carter, Jimmy, 'Address to the nation on the Soviet invasion of Afghanistan', 4 January 1980, <http://www.presidency.ucsb.edu/ws/?pid=32911#axzz2hevxVlUm> (retrieved 23 October 2013).
34 Fraser, speech to House of Representatives, 22 May 1980.

35 Dibb, 'The Soviet experience in Afghanistan', p. 496.

36 The example that follows taken from ibid., pp. 502–3.

37 The document is contained in an edited version published by the Department of Defence. See Frühling, *A History of Australian Strategic Policy Since 1945*, p. 445.

38 Ibid., p. 446.

39 Dobrynin, *In Confidence*, p. 443. Also quoted in Dibb, 'The Soviet experience in Afghanistan', p. 503.

40 Dibb, 'The Soviet experience in Afghanistan', p. 503. See also Dobrynin, *In Confidence*, pp. 447–8.

41 In his speech, Carter recalled the US Ambassador, halted trade in high-technology and strategic items, curtailed fishing privileges in US waters and declared that 17 million tonnes of grain ordered by the USSR would not be delivered. See Carter, 'Address to the nation on the Soviet invasion of Afghanistan', 4 January 1980.

42 See, for the wheat decision and other considerations, Cabinet Decision 10552, 'Australian response to Soviet intervention in Afghanistan', 9 January 1980, NAA: A13075, 10552, <http://www.naa.gov.au/Images/1980-FA-Afghanistan-Soviet-Olympics-boycott_tcm16-45335.pdf> (retrieved 23 October 2013).

43 In Cabinet Decision 10552, it was decided that a final decision not be made until a 'close examination of the various issues including an assessment of the views of other countries' had been conducted.

44 The Australian Olympic Committee notes: 'There was intense pressure from the national government and many sporting administrators and commentators to boycott the Games. Ultimately, the AOC decided in a split vote to attend the Games, but some sport federations and athletes were pressured into boycotting the Games of their own volition' (see Australian Olympic Committee, 'Moscow 1980'). The vote to send a team was six to five (see Fraser & Simons, *Malcolm Fraser*, pp. 477–8).

45 Reagan, 'Evil Empire' speech to the House of Commons, London, 8 June 1982.

46 The respective laws covering these areas were the Law on Individual Economic Activity, the Law on the State Enterprise and the Law on Cooperatives (see Brown, 'The Gorbachev era', pp. 331–4).

47 Ibid., p. 335.

48 Ibid., pp. 344–6.

49 Australian troops were active in Korea (1950–53), Malaya (1950–60), Konfrontasi (1963–66), Vietnam (1962–75), First Gulf War (1990–91), Afghanistan (2001–present) and the Second Gulf War (2003–09). For more information see Australian War Memorial, 'Australians at war', <http://www.awm.gov.au/atwar/> (retrieved 28 October 2013).

9   The new unipolar world

1 Bush, George Snr, 'Address before a joint session of the Congress on the cessation of the Persian Gulf crisis'.

2 Ibid.

3 Ibid.

4 Resolution 678 (1990) Adopted by the UN Security Council at its 2963rd meeting on 29 November 1990.

5 As Puchala points out, 'The United Nations [was] one of the instruments selected by the Bush Administration for the promotion and concretion of a normative vision of a preferred post-Cold War world' (Puchala, 'The President, the Persian Gulf War, and the United Nations', p. 223).

6 Richard Haas, a Special Assistant to President Bush, argues Bush felt that to go any further than they did would break the trust of international community, shattering the coalition, and would cost lives for no real political or strategic gain (see Haas, *War of Necessity War of Choice*, pp. 129–32).

7 Bush, George Snr, 'Address before a joint session of the Congress on the cessation of the Persian Gulf crisis'.

8 Ibid.

9 Puchala notes that the foreign policy vision of Bush assumed 'one world of compatible social, political, and economic values; that promotes democracy, open-market economics, international law, and international organisation; and that insists upon US leadership' because 'our moral principles and our material interests make us a leader'. The United Nations played a central role in this vision because, as Richard Baker reckoned, 'never in its existence has the potential of the UN as a force for peace and stability been clearer' (see Puchala, 'The President, the Persian Gulf War, and the United Nations', p. 224).

10 Heilbrunn, 'Refighting the Falklands War'. See also Gover, 'Britain scorned White House "fools" and "fascists" over Falklands War'.

11 As Argentina was a right-wing dictatorship and not a left-wing one, it 'fell under the rubric of her famous distinction between the two, with the latter supposedly being impervious to reform or collapse, which meant that the capital of the free world couldn't be too choosy about the reactionary, anti-communist dictatorships it chose to back' (Heilbrunn, 'Refighting the Falklands War').

12 Ibid.

13 The relationship between Thatcher and Reagan is discussed at length in Aldous, *Reagan and Thatcher*.

14 For further information see United Nations, 'Somalia – UNOSOM I: Background'.

15 Bush Snr had a background that instilled in him a broad view of international affairs. For example, he volunteered at an early age for World War II, in which he served as a naval pilot and was shot down and miraculously rescued by a submarine. After the war he completed his education before seeking to enter

public service. He had been Ambassador to the United Nations, head of the CIA and chief of the United States Liaison Office in the People's Republic of China.

16 Haas, *War of Necessity War of Choice*, pp. 11–12.

17 Bush, George Snr, 'Address before a joint session of the Congress on the cessation of the Persian Gulf crisis'.

18 Waller & McAllister, 'How Clinton decided on NATO expansion'.

19 The Bush Administration also recognised the need to reshape itself from a mechanism for containing Russia to one that could contend with emerging security challenges in the North Atlantic region (Grayson, *Strange Bedfellows*, p. 66).

20 Nelan & Branegan, 'NATO plus three'.

21 Mitchell, 'Clinton urges NATO expansion in 1999'.

22 These arguments are outlined in Barany, *The Future of NATO Expansion*.

23 Quoted in Alison & Neuger, 'Putin says NATO expansion is direct threat to Russia'.

24 Barany, *The Future of NATO Expansion*, p. 16.

25 Quoted in Alison & Neuger, 'Putin says NATO expansion is direct threat to Russia'. Former President Boris Yeltsin made similar comments in negotiations with President Clinton during 1997, despite ultimately signing an agreement with NATO (see Lippman, 'Clinton, Yeltsin agree on arms cuts and NATO').

26 Sarotte, 'Not one inch eastward?'

27 Barany, *The Future of NATO Expansion*, p. 15.

28 Open letter to President Clinton, 26 June 1997, signed by, among others, Owen Harries, Robert McNamara and Paul Nitze.

29 UN Resolution No. 794 (1992).

30 This point is made by Palmer, who argues that Somalia influenced Clinton and his advisers, who feared a repeat of events should peacekeepers be sent into Rwanda (see Palmer, 'What might have been', p. 47).

31 Remnick, 'The wanderer'.

32 Palmer points out that Clinton claims his administration did not appropriately attend to the Rwandan genocide on account of their focus being on the Bosnian crisis (see Palmer, 'What might have been', p. 47).

33 Palmer also notes that the Clinton Administration knew of the events in Rwanda as they were happening and received reports for the two full months during which the genocide occurred (see ibid. See also Halberstam, *War in a Time of Peace*).

34 The exact statistics on the casualties of the genocide are unknown and still bitterly debated. These figures are taken from the Outreach Programme on the Rwanda Genocide and the United Nations, 'Rwanda: A brief history of the country'.

35 For graphs of mortalities see Roberts & Toole, 'Cholera deaths in Goma'.

36 NATO's response to the earlier issues in the former Yugoslavia that led to the Kosovo crisis were seen as a test of NATO's credibility in the post–Cold War era (Bert, *The Reluctant Superpower*, p. 246). An excellent account of these events preceding the Kosovo Crisis is provided by Holbrooke, *To End a War*.

37 Norris, *Collision Course*, p. 9.

38 Norris notes 'British Prime Minister Tony Blair, enjoying a comfortable parliamentary majority, was the most resolute of the Alliance's political leaders, and he repeatedly maintained that thwarting Milosevic was a fundamental test for Europe. This led wags in the Clinton Administration to joke that Blair was 'willing to fight to the last American solider' (ibid., p. 9).

39 *Wall Street Journal*, 11 January 2001. Also reported in *Agence France Presse*, 23 February 1998.

40 For example, in congressional hearings, one US official stated: 'What was largely hidden from public view was the fact that the KLA raised part of their funds from the sale of narcotics. Albania and Kosovo lie at the heart of the "Balkan Route" that links the "Golden Crescent" of Afghanistan and Pakistan to the drug markets of Europe. This route is worth an estimated $400 billion a year and handles 80 per cent of heroin destined for Europe' (US Congress, Testimony of Frank J. Cilluffo, Deputy Director of the Global Organized Crime Program, to the House Judiciary Committee, Washington DC, 13 December 2000).

41 Shawcross, *Deliver Us From Evil*, p. 178.

42 Ibid.

43 Kissinger, *Daily Telegraph*, 28 June 1999.

44 Shawcross, *Deliver Us From Evil*.

45 Bush, George W., 'Address to the joint session of the 107th Congress', 20 September 2001.

46 Rumsfeld, Department of Defense news briefing, 9 October 2001.

47 Borger, 'Daggers drawn in the house of Bush'.

48 *Economist*, 'The hawks strike back'.

49 Scowcroft, 'Don't attack Saddam'.

50 See Levin, *Report of an Inquiry into the Alternative Analysis of the Issue of an Iraq-al Qaeda Relationship*.

51 See Pincus & Smith, 'Official's key report on Iraq is faulted', and Roth, '10 years later'.

52 Roth, '10 years later'.

53 Blix's briefing to the Security Council can be found at <http://www.theguardian.com/world/2003/feb/14/iraq.unitednations1> (retrieved 28 October 2013). Further documents on the United Nation's inspections of Iraqi weapons of mass destruction capabilities can be found at the United Nations Monitoring, Verification and Inspection Commission website, <http://www.unmovic.org/> (retrieved 28 October 2013).

10 In God we trust

1 Weiss & Edwards, 'Introduction: American exceptionalism's champions and challengers', p. 1. For a review of American exceptionalism, see Lipset, *American Exceptionalism*.

2 In their book *Manifest Destiny*, Heidler and Heidler examine the historical roots of the notion of manifest destiny in America's westward expansion.

3 Quoted in Walt, 'The myth of American exceptionalism'.

4 Bush, George W., 'Remarks accepting the presidential nomination at the Republican National Convention in New York City', 2 September 2004.

5 De Tocqueville wrote, 'The position of the Americans is therefore quite exceptional, and it may be believed that no democratic people will ever be placed in a similar one' (De Tocqueville, *Democracy in America*, pp. 36–7).

6 Abramowitz, 'How American exceptionalism dooms US foreign policy'.

7 Ibid. Abramowitz talks of rule-based foreign policy, and notes: 'The United States constantly reminds many countries, particularly China, that if they want to be part of the international community they must play by the rules. These are norms that we have largely formulated and instituted. Indeed, they are usually good rules. Still, only one country—the United States—can be exempt from the rules because of its virtue.'

8 Pillar, 'The errors of exceptionalism'.

9 Bevins, 'From "terrorist" to tea with the Queen'.

10 For discussion of the rationale for Reagan's opposition to the bill, see Redden, 'The US Comprehensive Anti-Apartheid Act of 1986'.

11 The vote was split 313 to 83 in the House of Representatives and 78 to 21 in the Senate.

12 Redden suggests that much of the Reagan Administration's objection to the Act—and that of US conservatives more broadly—was based on ANC links to communism and associated fears for US security. Yet this argument ignored the historical realities of South African politics, particularly as a result of apartheid. The position of Reagan—and, in many ways, the Act post-amendments demanded by the conservatives—placed the issue of South African self-determination on the 'back burner', replaced by an ideologically driven perceived threat to American national security that was deemed more important (see Redden, 'The US Comprehensive Anti-Apartheid Act of 1986', p. 605).

13 Harries, *Understanding America*, p. 20.

14 Zinn, 'The power and the glory'.

15 Walt, 'The myth of American exceptionalism'.

16 The only nation with comparable results in the survey was the United Kingdom, where 64 per cent of participants felt force was acceptable in some cases (see *German Marshall Fund*, Trans-Atlantic Trends). A discussion of these results and previous surveys is also undertaken in Leiber, *Power and Willpower in the American Future*.

17 Bush, George W., joint news conference with French President, Washington, 6 November 2001.

18 'In summary, we have here a political force committed fanatically to the belief that with US there can be no permanent modus vivendi that it is desirable and necessary that the internal harmony of our society be disrupted, our traditional way of life be destroyed, the international authority of our state be broken, if Soviet power is to be secure' (Kennan, 'Long Telegram').

19 Project for the New American Century, 'Statement of Principles'.

20 US Department of Defense, 'Deputy Secretary Wolfowitz interview with Sam Tannenhaus, *Vanity Fair*'.

21 Burnham et al., 'Mortality after the 2003 invasion of Iraq'.

22 See Levin, *Report of an Inquiry into the Alternative Analysis of the Issue of an Iraq–al Qaeda Relationship*, Senate Armed Services Committee, and 'Review of pre-Iraqi War activities of the Office of the Undersecretary of Defense for Policy', Department of Defense Office of Inspector General.

23 Investigative journalism conducted by the *Washington Post* uncovered Rumsfeld's reorganisation of American intelligence-gathering infrastructure. Rumsfeld established the Strategic Support Branch to provide himself with 'independent tools' for human intelligence-gathering. For an analysis of Rumsfeld's move, including increasing his own oversight of intelligence by strengthening the role of the Department of Defense in intelligence-gathering, see Gellman, 'Secret unit expands Rumsfeld's domain'.

24 Schmitt & Mazzetti, 'Secret order let US raid Al Qaeda'.

25 Priest & Arkin, '"Top Secret America"'.

26 'Joint resolution', Public Law 107–40, 107th Congress, <http://www.gpo.gov/fdsys/pkg/PLAW-107publ40/pdf/PLAW-107publ40.pdf> (retrieved 6 November 2013).

27 Office of the Press Secretary, White House, 'Fact sheet US policy standard and procedures for the use of force in counterterrorism operations outside the United States and areas of active hostilities'.

28 Trofimov, 'Karzai condemns US drone strikes in Pakistan'.

29 Kilcullen & Exum, 'Death from above, outrage down below'.

30 See Bureau of Investigative Journalism, 'Get the data: Drone wars'; also Elliott, 'Obama Administration's drone death figures don't add up'.

31 Entous, Gorman & Barnes, 'US relaxes drone rules'.

32 Zenko, *Reforming US Drone Strike Policies*, p. 12, and Entous, Gorman & Barnes, 'US relaxes drone rules'.

33 Zenko, *Reforming US Drone Strike Policies*, p. 12, and Elliott, 'Obama Administration's drone death figures don't add up'.

34 Putin, 'A plea for caution from Russia'.

35 For further reading on the rise of the neo-conservatives and their views on American foreign policy, see Halper & Clarke, *America Alone*.

11 The changing Asia–Pacific

1 Elson, *Suharto*, p. 181.
2 ASEAN, 'History: The founding of ASEAN'.
3 ASEAN, 'ASEAN at 30'.
4 ASEAN, 'History: The founding of ASEAN'.
5 Such as the Five Power Defence Arrangements,which included Malaysia and Singapore, along with the United Kingdom, Australia and New Zealand.
6 Tan, 'Herding cats'.
7 Copy of the partnership's declaration is available at <http://www.dfat.gov.au/asean/joint_dec_2007.html> (retrieved 23 October 2013).
8 For more information on this AANZFTA, see <http://www.dfat.gov.au/fta/aanzfta/> (retrieved 23 October 2013).
9 Wain, *Malaysian Maverick*, p. 109.
10 Yudhoyono, 'Keynote speech at the 11th IISS Asia Security Summit'.
11 Saragih, 'RI brings Timor Leste a step closer to ASEAN membership'.
12 'Declaration of the East Asia Summit on the principles for mutually beneficial relations, Bali', 19 November 2011.
13 Yudhoyono, 'Keynote speech at the 11th IISS Asia Security Summit'.
14 Natalegawa, 'An Indonesian perspective on the Indo-Pacific'.
15 Ibid.
16 The Strategic and Economic Dialogue was established in 2009 by President Barack Obama and former President Hu Jintao with the aim of allowing high-level discussions on important economic, political and strategic issues between the two powers.
17 For an overview of the items discussed and resolutions agreed to at the July 2013 talks, see Office of the Spokesperson, 'Department of State, US–China strategic and economic dialogue outcomes of the strategic track'.
18 Quoted in Nye, 'Work with China, don't contain it'.
19 Ibid.
20 See for example Nye, 'Soft power'.
21 Goh, 'Present state of the world'.
22 For example, when visiting Manila in 2011 and discussing the issue of territorial dispute in the South China Sea, Secretary Clinton stated, 'Any nation with a claim has a right to exert it … but they do not have a right to pursue it through intimidation or coercion … the United States will always be in the corner of the Philippines and we will stand and fight with you' (see Carpenter, 'Washington's clumsy China "containment" policy'). Further, Clinton's predecessor, Condoleezza Rice, stated before a visit to Australia in conjunction with Japanese defence officials: '… I think all of us in the region, particularly those of us who are long-standing allies, have a joint responsibility and obligation to try and produce conditions in which the rise of China will be a positive force in international politics, not a negative force' (see Lim & Yeo, 'Trilateral congregation').

23   Hagel, speech, International Institute for Strategic Studies, Singapore.

24   Ibid.

25   See Whaley, 'US seeks expanded role for military in Philippines'.

26   For Guam attack submarine decision see Dumat-ol Daleno, 'Deputy SecDef:
4th submarine to be deployed to Guam'.

27   This was part of a deployment to ensure continuous US bomber presence in
the Western Pacific and became worldwide news when one of the aircraft
crashed at Andersen Air Force Base (see Associated Press, 'Stealth bomber
crashes in Guam').

28   Hagel, speech, International Institute for Strategic Studies, Singapore.

29   Wan, 'Defense Secretary Leo Panetta highlights US ties to Vietnam during
visit'.

30   For a copy of the treaty, see United Nations Office for Disarmament Affairs,
'Treaty on the non-proliferation of nuclear weapons'. The DPRK ratified the
NPT in December 1985 but withdrew in January 2003 (effective April 2013).
It was the first state ever to withdraw from the NPT. Iran has signed the NPT
and is still a party to it, but has been found by the IAEA to have breached it
on numerous occasions.

31   See Amin & Chen, 'Biden says US to push China for South China Sea code'.

32   Stockholm International Peace Research Institute, *SIPRI Yearbook 2012*.

33   Article 9 of the Japanese Constitution states: 'Aspiring sincerely to an international peace based on justice and order, the Japanese people forever renounce
war as a sovereign right of the nation and the threat or use of force as means
of settling international disputes. (2) To accomplish the aim of the preceding
paragraph, land, sea, and air forces, as well as other war potential, will never
be maintained. The right of belligerency of the state will not be recognized.'

34   *SIPRI Yearbook 2012* and SIPRI Military Expenditure Database 1998–2012.

35   Ibid.

36   Ibid., and International Monetary Fund, *World Economic Outlook*.

37   Stockholm International Peace Research Institute, 'Nuclear forces
development'.

38   See White, *The China Choice*.

39   Indeed Henry Kissinger argues that military imperialism is not in the Chinese
style: 'China seeks its objectives by careful study, patience and the accumula-
tion of nuances—only rarely does China risk a winner-take-all showdown'
(Kissinger, 'China: Containment won't work').

40   Eisenhower, 'Military–industrial complex speech'.

41   United Nations, United Nations Convention on the Law of the Sea, <http://
www.un.org/depts/los/convention_agreements/texts/unclos/unclos_e.pdf>
(retrieved 24 October 2013).

42   See '1989 USA–USSR: Joint statement with attached uniform interpretation
of rules of international law governing innocent passage, adopted at Wyoming,
USA on 23 September, 1989'.

43 See World Bank, 'Military expenditure (% of GDP)', and Central Intelligence Agency, 'Country comparison: Military expenditures'. Also Bloomberg reports the budget in 2013 to be $US51.7 billion (Reynolds, 'Japan defense budget to increase for first time in 11 years').

44 See Global Security, 'JMSDF [Japan Maritime Self Defence Force] ships'.

45 Kallender-Umezu, 'Japan passes law permitting military space development'.

46 Rachman, 'Gaffe-prone Japan is a danger to peace in the Pacific'.

47 White, 'Caught in a bind that threatens an Asian war nobody wants'.

48 This issue is explored more fully in an article published through Nicholas Kristof: Shaw, 'The inconvenient truth behind the Diaoyu/Senkaku Islands'.

49 See Ministry of Foreign Affairs of Japan, 'Treaty of Peace and Friendship Between Japan and the People's Republic of China' and Kristof, 'China's new leader, and the islands dispute'.

50 See Ryall, 'Japan agrees to buy disputed Senkaku islands': 'The islands were formally annexed by Japan in January 1895 … Three of the uninhabited islands were sold in the 1970s to the Kurihara family, with the remaining isles remaining the property of the national government.'

51 Kristof, 'China's new leader, and the islands dispute'.

52 For a basic overview of the Japanese position, including interpretations of the Treaty of Shimonoseki, see Ministry of Foreign Affairs of Japan, 'The Basic View on the Sovereignty of the Senkaku Islands'.

53 Such treaties included the Treaty of Nanking, the Convention of Peking and the Boxer Protocol.

54 Kristof, 'China's new leader, and the islands dispute'.

55 See United Nations, 'Submission by the People's Republic of China concerning the outer limits of the continental shelf beyond 200 nautical miles in part of the East China Sea to the Commission on the Limits of the Continental Shelf'.

56 Response by the Japanese, <http://www.un.org/depts/los/clcs_new/submissions_files/submission_chn_63_2012.htm> (retrieved 28 October 2013).

57 See BBC, 'Japan military "needs marines and drones"'. The Japanese Ministry of Defense produces an annual White Paper, *Defense of Japan*, which provides an overview of Japanese military and strategic thinking. The latest paper, along with all papers back to 2005, can be retrieved at <http://www.mod.go.jp/e/publ/w_paper/index.html>.

58 See *Lowy Interpreter*, 'Blunt words on China from US Navy'.

59 Glaser, 'US policy priorities and the "rebalance" to the Asia–Pacific'.

60 This figure excludes trade with Hong Kong, which, when added, increased cross-strait trade to $152 billion in 2010 (see Ministry of Economic Affairs, 'The bilateral trade between Taiwan and Mainland China').

61 An additional three million travellers crossed the strait if Hong Kong and Macau are included in the figures. See Taiwanese Tourism Bureau, 'Yearly statistics'.

62 Department of Defence, 'Defence White Paper 2009', p. 34.

12 Missed opportunities

1 See Fitzgerald, *Immigration: A Commitment to Australia*, and Garnaut, *Australia and the Northeast Asian Ascendancy.*

2 See Gyngell & Wesley, *Making Australian Foreign Policy*, pp. 51–6.

3 Howard, John, television interview with Laurie Oakes, *Sunday*, Nine Network, 1 December 2002. Also quoted in Siracusa, 'John Howard, Australia and the Coalition of the Willing'.

4 Forbes, 'Downer bid to calm Asia fury'. Mahathir was also quoted in Siracusa, 'John Howard, Australia and the Coalition of the Willing'.

5 Grubel, 'Bush's "sheriff" comment causes a stir'.

6 Downer made the following remark: 'Well, the ANZUS Treaty is a treaty which of course is symbolic of the Australian alliance relationship with United States, but the ANZUS Treaty is invoked in the event of one of our two countries, Australia or the United States, being attacked. So some other military activity elsewhere in the world, be it in Iraq or anywhere else for that matter, does not automatically invoke the ANZUS Treaty' (see Downer, media conference, Beijing, 17 August 2004).

7 See for example Forbes, 'Howard assures US of loyalty'.

8 See ABC, 'Gillard, Obama detail US troop deployment'.

9 For those who wish to pursue the technical details of this question and to understand the intricacies of modern defence language, the report 'The "Joint Facilities" revisited—Desmond Ball, democratic debate on security and the human interest', by Richard Tanter of the Nautilus Institute, is well worth a close study.

10 Panetta, 'Shangri-La Security Dialogue'.

11 Woodley, 'Smith rejects proposal for US carrier base', and O'Malley, Garnaut & Welch, 'US eyes Perth naval base'.

12 See for example Nicholson, 'Marines lodging bill to hit $1.6bn'.

13 *Guardian*, 'Australian general to help lead US military push into Pacific'.

14 McDuling, 'Tri-nation naval exercise Pacific Bond kicks off'.

15 Horton, Department of Defence, email, 14 October 2013.

16 *Australian Financial Review*, 'US leaves door ajar on nuke subs'.

17 See Dorling, 'Pine Gap drives US drone kills'.

18 The Department of Defence, usually reluctant to provide any information regarding Pine Gap, provided Fairfax Media with the staffing figure of eight hundred. See ibid.

19 Quoted in Dorling, 'Desert secrets'.

20 Hall, 'Presentation to the Committee on Armed Services Subcommittee on Strategic Forces United States Senate on Space Policy, Programs, and Operations'.

21 Dorling, 'Desert secrets'.

22 Dorling, 'Pine Gap drives US drone kills'.

23 'Joint resolution', Public Law 107–40, 107th Congress, <http://www.gpo
    .gov/fdsys/pkg/PLAW-107publ40/pdf/PLAW-107publ40.pdf> (retrieved
    6 November 2013).
24 US Department of Justice, 'Lawfulness of a lethal operation directed against a US
    citizen who is a senior operational leader of Al-Qa'ida or an associated force'.
25 al-Awlaki, 'The drone that killed my grandson'.
26 'Joint resolution', Public Law 107–40, 107th Congress.
27 US Department of Justice, 'Lawfulness of a lethal operation directed
    against a US citizen who is a senior operational leader of Al-Qa'ida or an
    associated force'.
28 Schmitt & Mazzetti, 'Secret order let US raid Al Qaeda'.
29 Tanter, 'After Obama—The new joint facilities'.
30 Johnston, 'Minister for Defence—Defence space cooperation—space
    situational awareness'.
31 Department of Foreign Affairs and Trade, 'Treaty on principles governing
    the activities of states in the exploration and use of outer space, including the
    moon and other celestial bodies'.
32 Wroe, 'Military ties benefit from sixth satellite'.
33 Woodley, 'Smith rejects proposal for US carrier base'.
34 Wan, 'Defense Secretary Leo Panetta highlights US ties to Vietnam during
    visit'.

Conclusion

 1 White, *The China Choice*, p. 180.
 2 Diola, 'US commander; China's aggression leads to US, allies' closer ties'.
 3 See Shaw, 'The inconvenient truth behind the Diaoyu/Senkaku Islands', and
    Kristof, 'China's new leader, and the islands dispute'.
 4 Kristof, 'China's new leader, and the islands dispute'.
 5 Rosenberg, 'Contested borderlands of the South China Sea'.
 6 Ibid. For information on the Yulin base, see Kristensen, 'New Chinese SSBN
    deploys to Hainan Island'.
 7 Jeremy Patterson, 'Hotline to link US–China militaries', April 2008, Arms
    Control Association.
 8 Branigan, 'China sends naval fleet to Somalia to battle pirates', and *Economist*,
    'Cash and carry—A hijack dilemma for China'.
 9 This idea and the potential conflict scenarios between China and the United
    States are discussed in depth in White, *The China Choice*.
10 Bureau of Investigative Journalism, 'Get the data: Drone wars'.
11 See Rogers, 'Drone wars', and Wolverton, 'As drone tech improves, blowback
    from drone-targeted nations worsens'.
12 Quoted in Masters, 'Targeted killings'.
13 For analysis and a copy of the judgement see Ross, 'Pakistani court rules CIA
    drone strikes are illegal'.

14 Tanter, 'Standing upright there'.
15 Tanter, 'The "Joint Facilities" revisited', pp. 22, 39.
16 Ibid., pp. 22, 39.
17 Horton, Department of Defence, email, 14 October 2013.
18 *Australian Financial Review*, 'US leaves door ajar on nuke subs'.
19 Tanter, 'The "Joint Facilities" revisited', pp. 22, 39.
20 *Economist*, 'Canberra looks out', p. 103.
21 Grant, although more sympathetic to keeping the ANZUS arrangements, also notes: 'The alliance is in danger of becoming not just a security arrangement between two countries but a test of how as Australians we see ourselves, the world and the future' (*Fatal Attraction*, pp. 163–4).
22 SIPRI Military Expenditure Database 1998–2012.
23 See quote by former Deputy Secretary of State Richard Armitage in Joye, 'Free ride on US defence must stop'.

Bibliography

Secondary sources

ABC, 'Gillard, Obama detail US troop deployment', 26 April 2013, <http://www.abc.net.au/news/2011-11-16/gillard2c-obama-announce-darwin-troop-deployment/3675596> (retrieved 22 October 2013).

Abramowitz, Morton, 'How American exceptionalism dooms US foreign policy', *National Interest*, 22 October 2012, <http://nationalinterest.org/commentary/how-american-exceptionalism-dooms-us-foreign-policy-7640> (retrieved 21 October 2013).

al-Awlaki, Nasser, 'The drone that killed my grandson', *New York Times*, 17 July 2013, <http://www.nytimes.com/2013/07/18/opinion/the-drone-that-killed-my-grandson.html?_r=0> (retrieved 22 October 2013).

Aldous, Richard, *Reagan and Thatcher: The Difficult Relationship*, W.W. Norton & Co., New York, 2012.

Alison, Sebastian, & Neuger, James, 'Putin says NATO expansion is direct threat to Russia', Bloomberg, 4 April 2008, <http://www.bloomberg.com/apps/news?pid=newsarchive&sid=aq34xuTFCvx0> (retrieved 15 October 2013).

Amin, Haslinda, & Chen, Sharon, 'Biden says US to push China for South China Sea code', Bloomberg, 29 July 2013, <http://www.bloomberg.com/news/2013-07-28/u-s-to-push-china-for-south-china-sea-conduct-code-biden-says.html> (retrieved 16 October 2013).

Andrews, Eric Montgomery, *Isolationism and Appeasement in Australia: Reactions to the European Crises, 1935–1939*, Australian National University Press, Canberra, 1970.

Associated Press, 'Stealth bomber crashes in Guam', *New York Times*, 24 February 2008, <http://www.nytimes.com/2008/02/24/us/24crash.html> (retrieved 22 October 2013).

Australian Financial Review, 'US leaves door ajar on nuke subs', 10 October 2013, <http://www.afr.com/p/national/us_leaves_door_ajar_on_nuke_subs_iaX01mzsiLud6MWgnDG7bO> (retrieved 22 October 2013).

Barany, Zoltan D., *The Future of NATO Expansion: Four Case Studies*, Cambridge University Press, Cambridge, 2003.

BBC, 'Japan military "needs marines and drones"', 26 July 2013, <http://www .bbc.co.uk/news/world-asia-23433070> (retrieved 22 October 2013).

Beinart, Peter, 'Return of the Nixon Doctrine', *Time Magazine*, 4 January 2007.

Bell, Coral, *Dependent Ally: A Study in Australian Foreign Policy*, Oxford University Press, Melbourne, 1988.

Bell, Roger J., *Unequal Allies: Australia–American Relations and the Pacific War*, Melbourne University Press, Carlton, 1977.

Benians, E.A., 'The Western Pacific, 1788–1885', in *Australia*, vol. 7, part 1, *Cambridge History of the British Empire*, ed. J. Holland Rose et al., Cambridge University Press, Cambridge, 1933.

Bennett, Scott (ed.), *The Making of the Commonwealth*, Cassell Australia, Melbourne, 1971.

Bert, Wayne, *The Reluctant Superpower: United States Policy in Bosnia, 1991–1995*, Macmillan Press, Houndmills, UK, 1997.

Betts, Raymond F., *France and Decolonisation 1900–1960*, St Martin's Press, New York, 1991.

Bevins, Anthony, 'From "terrorist" to tea with the Queen', *Independent*, 9 July 1996.

Borger, Julian, 'Daggers drawn in the house of Bush', *Guardian*, 28 August 2002, <http://www.theguardian.com/world/2002/aug/28/iraq.usa> (retrieved 22 October 2013).

Branigan, Tania, 'China sends naval fleet to Somalia to battle pirates', *Guardian*, 18 December 2008, <http://www.theguardian.com/world/2008/dec/18/ piracy-china-navy> (retrieved 22 October 2013).

Brawley, Sean, 'Mrs O'Keefe and the battle for White Australia', public lecture for the National Archives of Australia, Canberra, 1 June 2006.

Bridge, Carl, *William Hughes: Australia*, Haus Publishing, London, 2011.

Brown, Archie, 'The Gorbachev era', in *The Cambridge History of Russia*, (ed.) Ronald Grigor Suny, Cambridge University Press, Cambridge, 2006.

Buckley, Ken, Dale, Barbara & Reynolds, Wayne, *Doc Evatt: Patriot, Internationalist, Fighter and Scholar*, Longman Cheshire, Melbourne, 1994.

Burnett, Alan, Young, Thomas-Durell & Wilson, Christine, *The ANZUS Documents*, Department of International Relations, Research School of Pacific Studies, Australian National University, Canberra, 1991.

Burnham, Gilbert, Lafta, Riyadh, Doocy, Shannon & Roberts, Les, 'Mortality after the 2003 invasion of Iraq: A cross-sectional cluster sample survey', *Lancet*, vol. 368, no. 9545, 21 October 2006, pp. 1421–8.

Carpenter, Ted Galen, 'Washington's clumsy China "containment" policy', *National Interest*, 30 November 2011, <http://nationalinterest.org/blog/ the-skeptics/washington%E2%80%99s-clumsy-china-containment-policy-6202> (retrieved 21 October 2013).

Casey, R.G., 'Australia's voice in imperial affairs', in *Australia's Foreign Policy*, ed. W.G.K. Duncan, Angus & Robertson, & Australian Institute of Political Science, Sydney, 1938.

Challinger, Michael, *Anzacs in Arkhangel: The Untold Story of Australia and the Invasion of Russia 1918–19*, Hardie Grant Books, Melbourne, 2010.

Chesterman, John, 'An unheard of piece of savagery: Indigenous Australians and the federal vote', in *Selective Democracy: Race, Gender and the Australian Voice*, ed. John Chesterman & David Philips, Melbourne Publishing Group, Melbourne, 2003.

Churchill, Winston, *The Second World War*, vol. 4: *The Hinge of Fate*, Cassell & Co., London, 1951.

Churchward, Lloyd Gordon, *Australia and America, 1789–1972: An Alternative History*, Alternative Publishing, Chippendale, NSW, 1979.

Cochrane, Peter, 'British–Australian relations', in *Oxford Companion to Australian History*, ed. Graeme Davison, John Hirst & Stuart Macintyre, Oxford University Press, South Melbourne, 2001.

Crockett, Peter, *Evatt: A Life*, Oxford University Press, South Melbourne, 1993.

Crowley, Francis, *Modern Australia in Documents*, Wren, Melbourne, 1973.

Cumptson, Ina Mary, *History of Australian Foreign Policy 1901–1991*, I.M. Cumpston, Canberra, 1995.

Curran, James, *Curtin's Empire*, Cambridge University Press, Melbourne, 2011.

Day, David, *The Great Betrayal: Britain, Australia and the Onset of the Pacific War 1939–42*, Angus & Robertson, Sydney, 1988.

——*Menzies and Churchill at War*, Oxford University Press, South Melbourne, 1993.

Deakin, Alfred, *The Federal Story: The Inner History of the Federal Cause, 1880–1900*, Melbourne University Press, Parkville, Vic, 1963.

Dennis, Peter, & Grey, Jeffrey, *Emergency and Confrontation: Australian Military Operations in Malaya and Borneo 1950–66*, Allen & Unwin, Sydney, & Australian War Memorial, 1996.

Dennis, Peter, Grey, Jeffery, Morris, Ewan, et al., *Oxford Companion to Australian Military History*, 2nd edn, Oxford University Press, South Melbourne, 2008.

De Tocqueville, Alexis, *Democracy in America: Part the Second: The Social Influence of Democracy*, vol. 2, J. & H.G. Langley, Philadelphia, 1840.

Dibb, Paul, 'The Soviet experience in Afghanistan: Lessons to be learned?', *Australian Journal of International Affairs*, vol. 64, no. 5, 2010, pp. 495–509.

Diola, Camille, 'US commander: China's aggression leads to US, allies' closer ties', *Philippine Star*, 30 July 2013, <http://www.philstar.com/headlines/2013/07/30/1030981/us-commander-chinas-aggression-leads-us-allies-closer-ties> (retrieved 21 October 2013).

Dobrynin, Antoliy, *In Confidence: Moscow's Ambassador to America's Six Cold War Presidents (1962–1986)*, Times Books, Random House, New York, 1995.

Dorling, Philip, 'Desert secrets', *Age*, 21 July 2013, <http://www.theage
.com.au/technology/technology-news/desert-secrets-20130720-2qb5c
.html#ixzz2bQfUJOxH> (retrieved 16 October 2013).

——'Pine Gap drives US drone kills', *Age*, 21 July 2013, <http://www.theage.
com.au/national/pine-gap-drives-us-drone-kills-20130720-2qbsa.html>
(retrieved 22 October 2013).

Dowsing, Irene, *Curtin of Australia*, Acacia Press, Blackburn, Vic, 1949.

Dumat-ol Daleno, Gaynor, 'Deputy SecDef: 4th submarine to be deployed
to Guam', *Navy Times*, 10 April 2013, <http://www.navytimes.com/
article/20130410/NEWS/304100029/Deputy-SecDef-4th-submarine-
deployed-Guam> (retrieved 22 October 2013).

Economist, 'Canberra looks out', 12 January 1963.

——'Cash and carry: A hijack dilemma for China', 29 October 2009, <http://
www.economist.com/node/14745027> (retrieved 22 October 2013).

——'The hawks strike back', 28 August 2002, <http://www.economist.com/
node/1301365> (retrieved 22 October 2013).

Edwards, P., *Crises and Commitments: The Politics and Diplomacy of Australia's Involvement in Southeast Asian Conflicts 1948–1965*, Allen & Unwin, Sydney, 1992.

Eggleston, F.W., 'Australia and the Empire, 1855–1921', *Australia*, vol. 7, part 1,
Cambridge History of the British Empire, ed. J. Holland Rose et al., Cambridge
University Press, Cambridge, 1933.

Ekins, Ashley, *Fighting to the Finish: The Australian Army and the Vietnam War,
1968–1975*, Allen & Unwin, Sydney, 2012.

——'Impressions: Australians in Vietnam—Overview of Australian military
involvement in the Vietnam War, 1962–1975', Australian War Memorial,
Canberra, <https://www.awm.gov.au/exhibitions/impressions/impressions.
asp> (retrieved 22 October 2013).

Elliott, Justin, 'Obama Administration's drone death figures don't add up',
ProPublica, 18 June 2012, <http://www.propublica.org/article/obama-
drone-death-figures-dont-add-up> (retrieved 22 October 2013).

Elson, R.E., *Suharto: A Political Biography*, Cambridge University Press, Melbourne,
2001.

Entous, Adam, Gorman, Siobhan, & Barnes, Julian E., 'US relaxes drone rules –
Obama gives CIA, military greater leeway in use against militants in Yemen',
Wall Street Journal, 26 April 2012, <http://online.wsj.com/article/SB10001
424052702304723304577366251852418174.html> (retrieved 22 October
2013).

Fitzhardinge, L.F., 'Hughes, William Morris (Billy) (1862–1952)', *Australian
Dictionary of Biography*, Melbourne University Press, Carlton, Vic, 1983,
<http://adb.anu.edu.au/biography/hughes-william-morris-billy-6761>
(retrieved 22 October 2013).

——*William Morris Hughes: A Political Biography*, vol. 1: *That Fiery Particle 1862–
1914*, Angus & Robertson, Sydney, 1964.

Fitzpatrick, Brian, *The Seamen's Union of Australia, 1872–1972: A history*, Seamen's Union of Australia, Sydney, 1981.

Forbes, Mark, 'Downer bid to calm Asia fury', *Age*, 5 December 2002, <http://www.theage.com.au/articles/2002/12/05/1038950101707.html> (retrieved 22 October 2013).

——'Howard assures US of loyalty', *Age*, 21 August 2004, <http://www.theage.com.au/articles/2004/08/20/1092972750685.html> (retrieved 22 October 2013).

Ford, Harold P., *CIA and the Vietnam Policymakers: Three Episodes 1962–1968*, Central Intelligence Agency, Langley, VA, 1998, <https://www.cia.gov/library/center-for-the-study-of-intelligence/csi-publications/books-and-monographs/cia-and-the-vietnam-policymakers-three-episodes-1962-1968> (retrieved 22 October 2013).

——'Why CIA analysts were so doubtful about Vietnam: Unpopular pessimism', *Studies in Intelligence*, no. 1, 1997, <https://www.cia.gov/library/center-for-the-study-of-intelligence/csi-publications/csi-studies/studies/97unclass/vietnam.html> (retrieved 22 October 2013).

Fraser, Malcolm, & Simons, Margaret, *Malcolm Fraser: The Political Memoirs*, Miegunyah Press, Carlton, Vic, 2010.

Freudenberg, Graham, *Churchill and Australia*, Macmillan, Sydney, 2008.

Frühling, Stephan, *A History of Australian Strategic Policy Since 1945*, Defence Publishing Service, Department of Defence, Canberra, 2009.

Galeotti, Mark, *Afghanistan: The Soviet Union's Last War*, Frank Cass, London, 1995.

Garran, Robert, 'The federation movement and the founding of the Commonwealth', *Australia*, vol. 7, part 1, *Cambridge History of the British Empire*, ed. J. Holland Rose et al., Cambridge University Press, Cambridge, 1933.

Gellman, Barton, 'Secret unit expands Rumsfeld's domain: New espionage branch delving into CIA territory', *Washington Post*, 23 January 2005, <http://www.washingtonpost.com/wp-dyn/articles/A29414-2005Jan22.html> (retrieved 22 October 2013).

German Marshall Fund, *Trans-Atlantic Trends*, German Marshall Fund of the United States, Washington, DC, 2012.

Glaser, Bonnie, 'US policy priorities and the "rebalance" to the Asia–Pacific', speech to Sydney Institute, 24 May 2013, <http://www.thesydneyinstitute.com.au>.

Goodall, Heather, 'Port politics: Indian seamen, Australian unions and Indonesian independence, 1945–47', *Labour History*, no. 94, May 2008, pp. 1–28.

Gover, Dominic, 'Britain scorned White House "fools" and "fascists" over Falklands War', *International Business Times*, 28 December 2012, <http://www.ibtimes.co.uk/articles/418968/20121228/ronald-reagan-thatcher-falklands.htm> (retrieved 22 October 2013).

Grant, Bruce, *Fatal Attraction: Reflections on the Alliance with the United States*, Black Inc., Melbourne, 2004.

Grattan, C. Hartley, 'Australia and the Pacific', *Foreign Affairs*, vol. 7, no. 1, 1928, pp. 144–9.

Grayson, George W., *Strange Bedfellows: NATO Marches East*, University Press of America, Lanham, MD, 1999.

Greenwood, Gordon, & Grimshaw, Charles (eds), *Documents on Australian International Relations 1901–1918*, Australian Institute of International Affairs, Melbourne, 1977.

Grey, Jeffrey, *The Australian Army*, Oxford University Press, South Melbourne, 2001.

——'Defence', in *Oxford Companion to Australian History*, ed. Graeme Davison, John Hirst & Stuart Macintyre, Oxford University Press, South Melbourne, 2001.

——'Defending the Dominion, 1901–18', in *Between Empire and Nation: Australia's External Relations from Federation to the Second World War*, ed. Carl Bridge & Bernard Attard, Australian Scholarly Publishing, Melbourne, 2000.

——*A Military History of Australia*, Cambridge University Press, Melbourne, 1990.

——'"A pathetic sideshow": Australians and the Russian intervention, 1918–1919', *Journal of the Australian War Memorial*, vol. 7, October 1985, pp. 12–17, <http://www.awm.gov.au/encyclopedia/north_russia/journal.asp> (retrieved 22 October 2013).

Grimshaw, Patricia, 'White women as nation builders: Gender, colonialism and the federal vote', in *Selective Democracy: Race, Gender and the Australian Voice*, ed. John Chesterman & David Philips, Melbourne Publishing Group, Melbourne, 2003.

Grubel, James, 'Bush's "sheriff" comment causes a stir', *Age*, 17 October 2003, <http://www.theage.com.au/articles/2003/10/16/1065917555365.html> (retrieved 13 November 2013).

Guardian, 'Australian general to help lead US military push into Pacific', 21 August 2012, <http://www.guardian.co.uk/world/2012/aug/21/australian-general-us-army-pacific> (retrieved 22 October 2013).

Gyngell, Alan, & Wesley, Michael, *Making Australian Foreign Policy*, 2nd edn, Cambridge University Press, Cambridge, 2007.

Haas, Richard, *War of Necessity War of Choice: A Memoir of Two Iraq Wars*, Simon & Schuster, New York, 2009.

Halberstam, David, *War in a Time of Peace: Bush, Clinton and the Generals*, Bloomsbury, London, 2002.

Hall, Mitchell K., *The Vietnam War*, 2nd edn, Pearson Education, Harlow, UK, 2008.

Halper, Stefan A., & Clarke, Jonathan, *America Alone: The Neo-Conservatives and the Global Order*, Cambridge University Press, Cambridge, 2004.

Harper, Norman, *A Great and Powerful Friend: A Study of Australian American Relations Between 1900 and 1975*, University of Queensland Press, St Lucia, Qld, 1987.

Harries, Owen, *Understanding America*, CIS Occasional Paper 80, Centre for Independent Studies, St Leonards, NSW, 2002.

Hasluck, Paul, *The Government and the People 1939–1941*, Australian War Memorial, Canberra, 1952.

Heidler, David, & Heidler, Jeanne, *Manifest Destiny*, Greenwood Press, Westport, CT, 2003.

Heilbrunn, Jacob, 'Refighting the Falklands War', *National Interest*, 30 December 2012, <http://nationalinterest.org/blog/jacob-heilbrunn/refighting-the-falklands-war-margaret-thatcher-versus-jeane-7919> (retrieved 22 October 2013).

Hirst, John, 'Federal Council of Australasia', in *Oxford Companion to Australian History*, ed. Graeme Davison, John Hirst & Stuart Macintyre, Oxford University Press, South Melbourne, 2001.

——*The Sentimental Nation: The Making of the Australian Commonwealth*, Oxford University Press, Melbourne, 2000.

Holbrooke, Richard, *To End a War*, Random House, New York, 1998.

Holding, Roger, Johnson, Vivianne, & Andre, Pamela (eds), *Documents on Australian Foreign Policy: The ANZUS Treaty 1951*, Department of Foreign Affairs and Trade, Canberra, 2001.

Holland Rose, J., Newton, A.P., & Benians, E.A. (eds), *Australia*, vol. 7, part 1, *Cambridge History of the British Empire*, Cambridge University Press, Cambridge, 1933.

Horner, David, *Inside the War Cabinet: Directing Australia's War Effort 1939–45*, Allen & Unwin, Sydney, 1996.

Hotta, Eri, *Pan-Asianism and Japan's War 1931–1945*, Palgrave Macmillan, New York, 2007.

Hudson, W.J., *Australian Diplomacy*, Macmillan Australia, Melbourne, 1970.

——*Billy Hughes in Paris: The Birth of Australian Diplomacy*, Thomas Nelson Australia, Melbourne, 1978.

——*Towards a Foreign Policy, 1914–1941*, Cassell Australia, Melbourne, 1967.

Hudson, W.J., & Sharp, M.P., *Australian Independence: Colony to Reluctant Kingdom*, Melbourne University Press, Carlton, Vic, 1988.

Hughes, W.M., *The Splendid Adventure: A Review of Empire Relations*, Ernest Benn, London, 1929.

International Monetary Fund, *World Economic Outlook: Hopes, Realities, and Risks*, IMF, Washington, <http://www.imf.org/external/pubs/ft/weo/2013/01/> (retrieved 23 October 2013).

Johnston, Senator the Hon. David, 'Minister for Defence—Defence space cooperation—space situational awareness', 15 November 2012, <http://www.minister.defence.gov.au/2012/11/15/minister-for-defence-defence-space-cooperation-space-situational-awareness> (retrieved 29 October).

Joye, Christopher, 'Free ride on US defence must stop', *Australian Financial Review*, 19 August 2013, <http://www.afr.com/p/national/free_ride_on_us_defence_must_stop_NPl6wsSIhCqzc4VTp13ZgN> (retrieved 22 October 2013).

Kakar, M. Hassan, *Afghanistan: The Soviet Invasion and the Afghan Response, 1979–1982*, University of California Press, Berkeley, CA, 1995.

Kallender-Umezu, Paul, 'Japan passes law permitting military space development', *Defense News*, 22 June 2012, <http://www.defensenews.com/article/20120622/DEFREG03/306220001/Japan-Passes-Law-Permitting-Military-Space-Development> (retrieved 22 October 2013).

Karnow, Stanley, *Vietnam: A History*, Penguin Books, New York, 1984.

Kilcullen, David, & Exum, Andrew McDonald, 'Death from above, outrage down below', *New York Times*, 16 May 2009, <http://www.nytimes.com/2009/05/17/opinion/17exum.html?_r=2&> (retrieved 22 October 2013).

Kildea, Jeff, 'Australian Catholics and conscription in the Great War', *Journal of Religious History*, vol. 26, no. 3, 2002, pp. 298–313.

Kissinger, Henry, 'China: Containment won't work', *Washington Post*, 13 June 2005, <http://www.washingtonpost.com/wp-dyn/content/article/2005/06/12/AR2005061201533.html> (retrieved 22 October 2013).

Kolko, Gabriel, *Anatomy of a War: Vietnam, the United States, and the Modern Historical Experience*, Pantheon Books, New York, 1985.

Kristensen, Hans M., 'New Chinese SSBN deploys to Hainan Island', Federation of American Scientists, 24 April 2008, <http://blogs.fas.org/security/2008/04/new-chinese-ssbn-deploys-to-hainan-island-naval-base/> (retrieved 22 October 2013).

Kristof, Nicholas, 'China's new leader, and the islands dispute', *New York Times*, 5 January 2013, <http://kristof.blogs.nytimes.com/2013/01/05/chinas-new-leader-and-the-islands-dispute/> (retrieved 22 October 2013).

Lake, Marilyn, & Reynolds, Henry, *Drawing the Global Colour Line: White Men's Countries and the International Challenge of Racial Equality*, Cambridge University Press, Melbourne, 2008.

Lauren, Paul Gordon, *Power and Prejudice: The Politics and Diplomacy of Racial Discrimination*, Westview Press, Boulder, CO, 1996.

Lebra, Joyce C. (ed.), *Japan's Greater East Asia Co-Prosperity Sphere in World War II: Selected Readings and Documents*, Oxford University Press, Kuala Lumpur, 1975.

Lee, Norman E., *John Curtin: Saviour of Australia*, Longman Cheshire, Melbourne, 1983.

Leiber, Robert, *Power and Willpower in the American Future: Why the United States is Destined Not to Decline*, Cambridge University Press, New York, 2012.

Lewis, David, 'John Latham and the Statute of Westminster', paper presented at *Looking Ahead: New Directions in Postgraduate Historical Research*, University of Newcastle, Newcastle, NSW, 1998.

Lim, Tai Wei, & Yeo, Lay Hwee, 'Trilateral congregation—Condi Rice's attempts in "containing" China', APSNet Policy Forum, 16 March 2006, <http://nautilus.org/apsnet/0607a-lim-yeo-html/#axzz2iP77fAMr> (retrieved 22 October 2013).

Lippman, Thomas, 'Clinton, Yeltsin agree on arms cuts and NATO', *Washington Post*, 22 March 1997, <http://www.washingtonpost.com/wp-srv/inatl/longterm/summit/summit.htm> (retrieved 28 October 2013).

Lipset, Seymour, *American Exceptionalism: A Double-edged Sword*, W.W. Norton & Co., New York, 1996.

Long, Gavin, *The Six Years War: Australia in the 1939–45 War*, Australian War Memorial & Australian Government Publishing Service, Canberra, 1973.

Louis, Roger, 'Australia and the German colonies in the Pacific, 1914–1919', *Journal of Modern History*, vol. 38, no. 4, 1966, pp. 407–21.

McDuling, Lieutenant Grant, 'Tri-nation naval exercise Pacific Bond kicks off', 27 June 2013, <https://www.navy.gov.au/news/tri-nation-naval-exercise-pacific-bond-kicks> (retrieved 22 October 2013).

McKernan, M., & Browne, M., *Australia: Two Centuries of War and Peace*, Australian War Memorial, Canberra, & Allen & Unwin, Sydney, 1988.

McNamara, Robert, *In Retrospect: The Tragedy and Lessons of Vietnam*, Times Books, New York, 1995.

McNamara, Robert, Blight, James, & Brigham, Robert, *Argument Without End: In Search of Answers to the Vietnam Tragedy*, Public Affairs, New York, 1999.

Maloney, Shane, & Grosz, Chris, 'Billy Hughes and Woodrow Wilson', *Monthly*, no. 28, October 2007, <http://www.themonthly.com.au/issue/2007/october/1290559133/shane-maloney/billy-hughes-woodrow-wilson> (retrieved 22 October 2013).

Marr, David, *Barwick*, Allen & Unwin, Sydney, 1980.

Marshall, Peter, 'The Balfour formula and the evolution of the Commonwealth', *Round Table*, vol. 90, no. 361, 2001, pp. 541–53.

Martin, A.W., *Robert Menzies: A Life*, Melbourne University Press, Carlton, Vic, 1996.

Masters, Jonathan, 'Targeted killings', Council on Foreign Relations, 23 May 2013, <http://www.cfr.org/counterterrorism/targeted-killings/p9627> (retrieved 22 October 2013).

Meaney, Neville, *Australia and the World: A Documentary History from the 1870s to the 1970s*, Longman Cheshire, Melbourne, 1985.

——'Look back in fear: Percy Spender, the Japanese peace treaty and the ANZUS pact', *Japan Forum*, vol. 15, no. 3, 2003, pp. 399–410.

Menzies, Robert, *Afternoon Light: Some Memories of Men and Events*, Cassell Australia, Melbourne, 1967.

Miguel, Edward, & Rowland, Gerard, *The Long Run Impact of Bombing Vietnam*, Working Paper 11954, National Bureau of Economic Research, Cambridge, MA, 2006.

Millar, T.B. (ed.), *Australian Foreign Minister: Diaries of R.G. Casey, 1951–60*, Collins, London, 1972.

Ministry of Foreign Affairs of Japan, 'Treaty of Peace and Friendship Between Japan and the People's Republic of China', 12 August 1978, <http://www.mofa.go.jp/region/asia-paci/china/treaty78.html> (retrieved 23 October 2013).

Mitchell, Alison, 'Clinton urges NATO expansion in 1999', *New York Times*, 23 October 1996.

Muirden, Bruce, *The Diggers Who Signed on for More: Australia's Part in the Russian Wars of Intervention, 1918–1919*, Wakefield Press, Kent Town, SA, 1990.

Murdoch, Walter, *Alfred Deakin*, Bookman Press, Melbourne, 1999.

Murray, Robert, *The Ironworkers: A History of the Federated Ironworkers' Association of Australia*, Hale & Iremonger, Sydney, 1982.

Nelan, Bruce, & Branegan, Jay, 'NATO plus three', *Time*, vol. 150, no. 2, 14 July 1997.

Nicholls, Bob, *Bluejackets and Boxers: Australia's Naval Expedition to the Boxer Uprising*, Allen & Unwin, Sydney, 1986.

Nicholson, Brendan, 'Marines lodging bill to hit $1.6bn', *Australian*, 22 April 2013, <http://www.theaustralian.com.au/national-affairs/defence/marines-lodging-bill-to-hit-16bn/story-e6frg8yo-1226625469670> (retrieved 22 October 2013).

Nish, I.H., 'Australia and the Anglo-Japanese alliance, 1901–1911', *Australian Journal of Politics and History*, vol. 9, no. 2, 1963, pp. 201–12.

Nish, Ian, Steeds, David, & Hotta-Lister Ayako, 'Anglo-Japanese alliance', discussion paper, Suntory Centre, London School of Economics and Political Science, April 2002, <http://sticerd.lse.ac.uk/dps/is/IS432.pdf> (retrieved 22 October 2013).

Norris, John, *Collision Course: NATO, Russia, and Kosovo*, Praeger, Westport, CT, 2005.

Norris, Ronald, *The Emergent Commonwealth – Australian Federation: Expectations and Fulfilment 1889–1910*, Melbourne University Press, Carlton, Vic, 1975.

Nye, Joseph, *Soft Power: The Means to Success in World Politics*, Public Affairs, New York, 2004.

——'Work with China, don't contain it', *New York Times*, 25 January 2013, <http://www.nytimes.com/2013/01/26/opinion/work-with-china-dont-contain-it.html?adxnnl=1&adxnnlx=1376280575-Djus41w90ES M85nskaIWWQ> (retrieved 22 October 2013).

Odgers, George, *100 Years of Australians at War*, Lansdowne Publishing, Sydney, 1999.

O'Malley, Nick, Garnaut, John, & Welch, Dylan, 'US eyes Perth naval base', *Sydney Morning Herald*, 2 August 2012, <http://www.smh.com.au/federal-politics/political-news/us-eyes-perth-naval-base-20120801-23fy9.html> (retrieved 22 October 2013).

Palmer, David, '"What might have been"—Bill Clinton and American political power', *Australasian Journal of American Studies*, vol. 24, no. 1, 2005, pp. 38–58.

Pillar, Paul, 'The errors of exceptionalism', *National Interest*, 30 November 2010, <http://nationalinterest.org/node/4497> (retrieved 13 November 2013).

Pincus, Walter, & Smith, R. Jeffrey, 'Official's key report on Iraq is faulted – "dubious" intelligence fueled push for war', *Washington Post*, 9 February 2007,

<http://www.washingtonpost.com/wp-dyn/content/article/2007/02/08/AR2007020802387_pf.html> (retrieved 22 October 2013).

Pixley, Michael, 'Eisenhower's strategy in the Taiwan Strait drove a wedge between the Soviet Union and China', *Military History*, vol. 21, no. 6, 2005.

Plokhy, S.M., *Yalta: The Price of Peace*, Penguin Books, New York, 2010.

Priest, Dana, & Arkin, William, '"Top secret America": A look at the military's joint special operations command', *Washington Post*, 3 September 2011, <http://www.washingtonpost.com/world/national-security/top-secret-america-a-look-at-the-militarys-joint-special-operations-command/2011/08/30/gIQAvYuAxJ_story.html> (retrieved 22 October 2013).

Puchala, Donald J., 'The President, the Persian Gulf War, and the United Nations', in *The Presidency and the Persian Gulf War*, ed. Marcia Lynn Whicker & James P. Pfiffner, Praeger, Westport, CT, 1991.

Putin, Vladimir, 'A plea for caution from Russia – What Putin has to say to Americans about Syria', *New York Times*, 11 September 2013, <http://www.nytimes.com/2013/09/12/opinion/putin-plea-for-caution-from-russia-on-syria.html?adxnnl=1&pagewanted=all&adxnnlx=1381885442-Un1kFM+TqgztCGoq5MPLbQ> (retrieved 22 October 2013).

Rachman, Gideon, 'Gaffe-prone Japan is a danger to peace in Asia', *Financial Times*, 12 August 2013, <http://www.ft.com/intl/cms/s/0/c4d9e34c-033a-11e3-9a46-00144feab7de.html#axzz2c1AIQ4QY> (retrieved 22 October 2013).

Redden, Thomas J., 'The US Comprehensive Anti-Apartheid Act of 1986: Anti-apartheid or anti-African National Congress?', *African Affairs*, vol. 87, no. 349, 1988, pp. 595–605.

Reese, Trevor, *Australia, New Zealand, and the United States: A Survey of International Relations 1941–1968*, Oxford University Press, Melbourne, 1969.

Remnick, David, 'The wanderer: Bill Clinton's quest to save the world, reclaim his legacy and elect his wife', *New Yorker*, 18 September 2006.

Renouf, Alan, *Let Justice Be Done: The Foreign Policy of Dr H.V. Evatt*, University of Queensland Press, St Lucia, Qld, 1983.

Reynolds, Isabel, 'Japan defense budget to increase for first time in 11 years', *Bloomberg*, 30 January 2013, <http://www.bloomberg.com/news/2013-01-29/japan-s-defense-spending-to-increase-for-first-time-in-11-years.html> (retrieved 22 October 2013).

Reynolds, John, *Edmund Barton*, Bookman Press, Melbourne, 1999.

Rhodes, Benjamin, *The Ango-American Winter War with Russia, 1918–1919: A Diplomatic and Military Tragicomedy*, Greenwood Press, New York, 1988.

Roberts, Les, & Toole, Michael, 'Cholera deaths in Goma', *Lancet*, vol. 346, no. 8984, 25 November 1995.

Robertson, J., *1939–1945: Australia Goes to War*, Doubleday Australia, Sydney, 1984.

Rogers, Paul, 'Drone wars: The new blowback', *Open Democracy*, 29 November 2012, <http://www.opendemocracy.net/paul-rogers/drone-wars-new-blowback> (retrieved 22 October 2013).

Roggeveen, Sam, 'Blunt words on China from US Navy', *Lowy Interpreter*, 5 February 2013, <http://www.lowyinterpreter.org/post/2013/02/05/Blunt-words-on-China-from-US-Navy.aspx?p=true> (retrieved 22 October 2013).

Rosenberg, David, 'Contested borderlands of the South China Sea', BBC World Service, 21 April 2009, <http://www.southchinasea.org/contested-borderlands-of-the-south-china-sea/> (retrieved 22 October 2013).

Ross, Alice K., 'Pakistani court rules CIA drone strikes are illegal', Bureau of Investigative Journalism, 9 May 2013, <http://www.thebureauinvestigates.com/2013/05/09/pakistani-court-rules-cia-drone-strikes-are-illegal-and-war-crimes/> (retrieved 17 October 2013).

Roth, Zachary, '10 years later: The architects of the Iraq War', MSNBC, 18 March 2013, <http://tv.msnbc.com/2013/03/18/architects-of-the-iraq-war-where-are-they-now/> (retrieved 15 October 2013).

Ryall, Julian, 'Japan agrees to buy disputed Senkaku islands', *Telegraph* (London), 5 September 2012, <http://www.telegraph.co.uk/news/worldnews/asia/japan/9521793/Japan-agrees-to-buy-disputed-Senkaku-islands.html> (retrieved 22 October 2013).

Saikal, Amin, 'Afghanistan during the Cold War', in Chandra Chari (ed.), *Superpower Rivalry and Conflict: The Long Shadow of the Cold War on the Twenty-First Century*, Routledge, Abingdon, UK, 2010.

Sales, Peter, 'W.M. Hughes and the Chanak crisis of 1922', *Australian Journal of Politics and History*, vol. 17, no. 3, 1971, pp. 392–405.

Saragih, Bagus B.T., 'RI brings Timor Leste a step closer to ASEAN membership', *Jakarta Post*, 27 April 2013, <http://www.thejakartapost.com/news/2013/04/27/ri-brings-timor-leste-a-step-closer-asean-membership.html> (retrieved 22 October 2013).

Sarotte, Mary Elise, 'Not one inch eastward? Bush, Baker, Kohn, Genscher, Gorbachev and the origin of Russian resentment toward NATO enlargement', *Diplomatic History*, vol. 34, no. 1, 1990, pp. 119–40.

Scahill, Jeremy, *Dirty Wars: The World is a Battlefield*, Nation Books, New York, 2013.

Schmitt, Eric, & Mazzetti, Mark, 'Secret order let US raid Al Qaeda', *New York Times*, 9 November 2008, <http://www.nytimes.com/2008/11/10/washington/10military.html?pagewanted=all&_r=2&> (retrieved 22 October 2013).

Scowcroft, Brent, 'Don't attack Saddam', *Wall Street Journal*, 15 August 2002, <http://online.wsj.com/article/SB1029371773228069195.html> (retrieved 22 October 2013).

Shaw, Han-Yi, 'The inconvenient truth behind the Diaoyu/Senkaku Islands', *New York Times*, 19 September 2012, <http://kristof.blogs.nytimes.com/2012/09/19/the-inconvenient-truth-behind-the-diaoyusenkaku-islands/?_r=0> (retrieved 22 October 2013).

Shawcross, William, *Deliver Us from Evil: Peacekeepers, Warlords, and a World of Endless Conflict*, Simon & Schuster, New York, 2000.

Sheridan, Tom, *Division of Labour: Industrial Relations in the Chifley Years, 1945–49*, Oxford University Press, Melbourne, 1989.

Shimazu, Naoko, *Japan, Race and Equality: The Racial Equality Proposal of 1919*, Routledge, London, 1998.

Siracusa, Joseph, 'John Howard, Australia and the Coalition of the Willing', *Yale Journal of International Affairs*, vol. 1, no. 2, 2006, pp. 39–49.

Stark, Joseph, *The ANZUS Treaty Alliance*, Melbourne University Press, Carlton, Vic, 1965.

Stephens, Alan, 'Scherger, Sir Frederick Rudolph (1904–1984)', *Australian Dictionary of Biography*, vol. 18, Melbourne University Press, Carlton, Vic, 2012, <http://adb.anu.edu.au/biography/scherger-sir-frederick-rudolph-15055> (retrieved 22 October 2013).

Stockholm International Peace Research Institute, 'Nuclear forces development', SIPRI, Stockholm, 2013, <http://www.sipri.org/research/armaments/nuclear-forces> (retrieved 22 October 2013).

——SIPRI Military Expenditure Database 1998–2012, <http://www.sipri.org/research/armaments/milex/milex_database> (retrieved 22 October 2013).

——*SIPRI Yearbook 2012: Armaments, Disarmament and International Security*, SIPRI, Stockholm, 2012.

Stretton, Pat, 'Indigenous Australians and the vote', Australian Electoral Commission, 2010, <http://www.aec.gov.au/voting/indigenous_vote/aborigin.htm> (retrieved 22 October 2013).

Studeman, Michael, 'Thorns in the dragon's side', *US Naval Institute Proceedings*, vol. 126, no. 7, 2000, pp. 64–8.

Tan, See Seng, 'Herding cats: The role of persuasion in political change and continuity in the Association of Southeast Asian Nations (ASEAN)', *International Relations of the Asia Pacific*, vol. 13, 2013, pp. 233–65.

Tange, Arthur, *Defence Policy-making: A Close-up View, 1950–1980*, ANU E-press, Canberra, 2008.

Tanter, Richard, 'After Obama – The new joint facilities', Nautilus Institute for Security and Sustainability, 2012, <http://nautilus.wpengine.netdna-cdn.com/wp-content/uploads/2011/12/After-Obama-Back-to-the-Bases-footnoted-version-18-April-1500.pdf> (retrieved 22 October 2013).

——'The "Joint Facilities" revisited—Desmond Ball, democratic debate on security and the human interest', Nautilus Institute for Security and Sustainability, 11 December 2012, <http://nautilus.org/napsnet/napsnet-special-reports/the-joint-facilities-revisited-desmond-ball-democratic-debate-on-security-and-the-human-interest/#axzz2iP77fAMr> (retrieved 22 October 2013).

——'Standing upright there: The New Zealand path to a nuclear-free world', NAPSNet Policy Forum, 3 October 2012, <http://nautilus.org/napsnet/napsnet-policy-forum/standing-upright-there-the-new-zealand-path-to-a-nuclear-free-world/> (retrieved 22 October 2013).

Taylor, Alastair, *Indonesian Independence and the United Nations*, Cornell University Press, Ithaca, NY, 1960.

Tennant, Kylie, *Evatt: Politics and Justice*, Angus & Robertson, Sydney, 1970.

Thompson, Raymond, 'First steps in diplomacy', in *Between Empire and Nation: Australia's External Relations from Federation to the Second World War*, ed. Carl Bridge & Bernard Attard, Australian Scholarly Publishing, Melbourne, 2000.

Tran, Thi Lien, 'The Catholic question in North Vietnam: From Polish sources, 1954–56', *Cold War History*, vol. 4, no. 4, 2005, pp. 427–49.

Trofimov, Yaroslav, 'Karzai condemns US drone strikes in Pakistan', *Wall Street Journal*, 16 June 2013, <http://online.wsj.com/article/SB100014241278873 24520904578549380829445840.html> (retrieved 23 October 2013).

Tucker, N.B. (ed.), *Dangerous Strait: The US–Taiwan–China Crisis*, Columbia University Press, New York, 2005.

Vinson, J. Chal, 'The Imperial Conference of 1921 and the Anglo-Japanese alliance', *Pacific History Review*, vol. 31, no. 3, 1962, pp. 257–66.

Wain, Barry, *Malaysian Maverick: Mahathir Mohamad in Turbulent Times*, Palgrave Macmillan, Basingstoke, 2010.

Waller, Douglas, & McAllister, J.F.O., 'How Clinton decided on NATO expansion', *Time*, vol. 150, no. 2, 14 July 1997.

Wall Street Journal, 11 January 2001.

Walt, Stephen, 'The myth of American exceptionalism', *Foreign Policy*, November 2011, <http://www.foreignpolicy.com/articles/2011/10/11/the_myth_of_american_exceptionalism> (retrieved 23 October 2013).

Wan, William, 'Defense Secretary Leo Panetta highlights US ties to Vietnam during visit', *Washington Post*, 4 June 2012, <http://www.washingtonpost.com/world/asia_pacific/defense-secretary-leon-panetta-highlights-us-ties-to-vietnam-during-visit/2012/06/03/gJQAOWcLBV_story.html> (retrieved 23 October 2013).

Waters, Christopher, *Australia and Appeasement: Imperial Foreign Policy and the Origins of World War II*, I.B. Tauris, London, 2012.

Watt, Alan, *The Evolution of Australian Foreign Policy 1938–1965*, Cambridge University Press, London, 1967.

Weisbrod, Hanno, 'Sir Garfield Barwick and Dutch New Guinea', *Australian Quarterly*, vol. 39, no. 2, 1967, pp. 24–35.

Weiss, David, & Edwards, Jason, 'Introduction: American exceptionalism's champions and challengers', in *The Rhetoric of American Exceptionalism: Critical Essays*, ed. Jason Edwards & David Weiss, McFarland & Company, Jefferson, NC, 2011.

Whaley, Floyd, 'US seeks expanded role for military in Philippines', *New York Times*, 12 July 2013, <http://www.nytimes.com/2013/07/13/world/asia/us-negotiates-expanded-military-role-in-philippines.html?_r=0> (retrieved 23 October 2013).

White, Hugh, 'Caught in a bind that threatens an Asian war nobody wants', *Sydney Morning Herald*, 26 December 2012, <http://www.smh.com.au/federal-politics/political-opinion/caught-in-a-bind-that-threatens-an-asian-war-nobody-wants-20121225-2bv38.html> (retrieved 23 October 2013).

White, Hugh, *The China Choice: Why America Should Share Power*, Black Inc., Collingwood, Vic, 2012.

Wilkinson, Frank, *Australia at the Front: A Colonial View of the Boer War*, John Long, London, 1901.

Wolverton, Joe, 'As drone tech improves, blowback from drone-targeted nations worsens', *New American*, 16 May 2013, <http://www.thenewamerican.com/usnews/foreign-policy/item/15417-as-drone-tech-improves-blowback-from-drone-targeted-nations-worsens> (retrieved 23 October 2013).

Woodard, Garry, 'Best practice in Australia's foreign policy: "Konfrontasi" (1963–66)', *Australian Journal of Political Science*, vol. 33, no. 1, 1998, pp. 85–99.

——*Asian Alternatives: Australia's Decision and Lessons on Going to War*, Melbourne University Press, Carlton, 2004.

Woodley, Naomi, 'Smith rejects proposal for US carrier base', ABC, 2 August 2012, <http://www.abc.net.au/news/2012-08-02/smith-rejects-us-base-proposal/4171086> (retrieved 23 October 2013).

Wroe, David, 'Military ties benefit from sixth satellite', *Sydney Morning Herald*, 9 August 2013, <http://www.smh.com.au/technology/sci-tech/military-ties-benefit-from-sixth-satellite-20130808-2rkp8.html> (retrieved 23 October 2013).

Zenko, Micah, *Reforming US Drone Strike Policies*, Special Report No. 65, Council on Foreign Relations, New York, January 2013.

Zinn, Howard, 'The power and the glory: Myths of American exceptionalism', *Boston Review*, 1 June 2005, <http://www.bostonreview.net/zinn-power-glory> (retrieved 23 October 2013).

Primary sources

Agence France Presse, 23 February 1998.

'American inflation rate history—1970 to 1980', 17 September 2013, <http://www.rateinflation.com/inflation-rate/usa-historical-inflation-rate?start-year=1970&end-year=1980> (retrieved 27 October 2013).

'An armistice that does less than justice to Australia and the British Empire', *Times* (London), 8 November 1918, in *Australia and the World: A Documentary History from the 1870s to the 1970s*, ed. Neville Meaney, Longman Cheshire, Melbourne, 1985.

ASEAN, 'ASEAN at 30', <http://www.asean.org/news/item/asean-at-30> (retrieved 23 October 2013).

——'History: The founding of ASEAN', <http://www.asean.org/news/item/the-founding-of-asean> (retrieved 23 October 2013).

Australian Bureau of Statistics, 'A century of change in the Australian labour market', 2007, <http://www.abs.gov.au/ausstats/abs@.nsf/0/12D509E0F07 F37BFCA2569DE0021ED48?Open> (retrieved 23 October 2013).

Australian Bureau of Statistics, 'Employee earnings, benefits and trade union membership, Australia, August 2012', <http://www.abs.gov.au/ausstats/ abs@.nsf/Latestproducts/6310.0Main%20Features2August%202012 ?opendocument&tabname=Summary&prodno=6310.0&issue=August%20 2012&num=&view=> (retrieved 13 October 2013).

'Australian inflation rate history—1970 to 1980', 23 October 2013, <http://www. rateinflation.com/inflation-rate/australia-historical-inflation-rate?start-year=1970&end-year=1980>(retrieved 27 October 2013).

Australian Labor Party, Official Report of the Proceedings of the 18th Commonwealth Triennial Conference, 27 September 1948, <http:// parlinfo.aph.gov.au/parlInfo/download/library/partypol/1331010/upload_ binary/1331010.pdf;fileType=application%2Fpdf#search=%221940s%22> (retrieved 11 November 2013)

Australian Labor Party, Official Report of the Proceedings of the 19th Commonwealth Triennial Conference, 1 March 1951.

Australian Olympic Committee, 'Moscow 1980', <http://corporate.olympics. com.au/games/1980-moscow> (retrieved 23 October 2013).

Australian War Memorial, 'Australian fatalities at Gallipoli', <http://www.awm. gov.au/encyclopedia/gallipoli/fatalities/> (retrieved 23 October 2013).

——'Australians at war', <http://www.awm.gov.au/atwar/> (retrieved 28 October 2013).

——'Vietnam War 1965', <http://www.awm.gov.au/atwar/vietnam.asp> (retrieved 27 October 2013).

Balfour Declaration, 1926, <http://foundingdocs.gov.au/scan-sid-17.html> (retrieved 23 October 2013).

Barton, E., Speech by the Prime Minister and Minister for External Affairs in the House of Representatives, 7 July 1903, extract, Commonwealth Parliamentary Debates, vol. 14, 1903, pp. 1797–8.

Boxer Protocol, signed Peking, 7 September 1901, <http://www.100jia.net/ china1900/ereignisse/boxerprotokoll.htm> (retrieved 13 November 2013).

Bureau of Investigative Journalism, 'Get the data: Drone wars', <http://www .thebureauinvestigates.com/category/projects/drones/drones-graphs/> (retrieved 23 October 2013).

Bush, George Snr, 'Address before a joint session of the Congress on the cessation of the Persian Gulf crisis', 6 March 1991, <http://www.presidency.ucsb .edu/ws/?pid=19364#axzz2hkm0xdzB> (retrieved 23 October 2013).

Bush, George W., 'Remarks accepting the presidential nomination at the Republican National Convention in New York City', 2 September 2004, <http://www.presidency.ucsb.edu/ws/index.php?pid=72727#axzz1Xs4 CwFYP> (retrieved 23 October 2013).

——'Address to the joint session of the 107th Congress', 20 September 2001, <http://georgewbush-whitehouse.archives.gov/infocus/bushrecord/documents/Selected_Speeches_George_W_Bush.pdf> (retrieved 28 October 2013).

——Joint news conference with French President, Washington, 6 November 2001, <http://edition.cnn.com/2001/US/11/06/ret.bush.coalition/index.html> (retrieved 17 November 2013.

Cabinet Decision 10552, 'Australian response to Soviet intervention in Afghanistan', 9 January 1980, NAA: A13075, 10552, <http://www.naa.gov.au/Images/1980-FA-Afghanistan-Soviet-Olympics-boycott_tcm16-45335.pdf> (retrieved 23 October 2013).

Carter, Jimmy, 'Address to the nation on the Soviet invasion of Afghanistan', 4 January 1980, <http://www.presidency.ucsb.edu/ws/?pid=32911#axzz2hevxVlUm> (retrieved 23 October 2013).

Casey, R.G., Minister for Supply and Development, to Mr R.G. Menzies, Prime Minister, cablegram, 17 November 1939, <http://www.info.dfat.gov.au/info/historical/HistDocs.nsf/(LookupVolNoNumber)/2~371> (retrieved 13 November 2013).

Central Intelligence Agency, 'Country comparison: Military expenditures', *World Factbook*, <https://www.cia.gov/library/publications/the-world-factbook/rankorder/2034rank.html> (retrieved 23 October 2013).

Churchill, Winston, British Colonial Secretary, to Lord Forster, Governor-General, cablegram (secret), 16 September 1922, AA, CP 78/32, item 1922-1923.

——UK Prime Minister (in the United States), to Mr John Curtin, Prime Minister, cablegram, <http://www.dfat.gov.au/publications/historical/volume-05/historical-document-05-271.html> (retrieved 23 October 2013).

Colony of New South Wales, *Official Record of the Debate of the Australasian Federal Convention—Second Session*, Legal Books, Sydney, 1986.

Commonwealth Bureau of Census and Statistic, *Official Book of the Commonwealth of Australia* No. 58, Commonwealth of Australia, Canberra, 1972.

Convention between Great Britain and France, signed 16 November 1887, New Hebrides, <http://www.vanuatu.usp.ac.fj/library/online/texts/Pacific_archive/New%20Hebrides/2.Convention%20between%20Britain%20and%20France%20respecting%20New%20HEbrides,%20November%2016,%201887.PDF> (retrieved 13 November 2011).

Convention of Peking, singed at Peking, 24 October 1860, <http://www.chinaforeignrelations.net/treaty_beijing> (retrieved 13 November 2013).

Curtin, John, 'Australia turns to America', *Herald* (Melbourne), 27 December 1941, <http://www.ww2australia.gov.au/japadvance/austous.html> (retrieved 23 October 2010).

'Declaration of the East Asia Summit on the principles for mutually beneficial relations, Bali, 19 November 2011', <http://www.mofa.go.jp/region/asia-paci/eas/pdfs/declaration_1111_2.pdf> (retrieved 23 October 2013).

Department of Defence, 'Defence White Paper 2009', Commonwealth of Australia, Canberra, <http://www.defence.gov.au/whitepaper2009/> (retrieved 23 October 2013).

Department of Defense, 'Deputy Secretary Wolfowitz interview with Sam Tannenhaus, *Vanity Fair*', 9 May 2003, <http://www.defense.gov/transcripts/transcript.aspx?transcriptid=2594> (retrieved 23 October 2013).

——Office of Inspector General, Review of pre-Iraqi War activities of the Office of the Under Secretary of Defense for Policy, 2007, <http://www.fas.org/irp/agency/dod/ig020907-decl.pdf> (retrieved 13 November 2013).

Department of Foreign Affairs and Trade, *The ANZUS Treaty 1951*, ed. Roger Holdich, Vivianne Johnson & Pamela Andre, Department of Foreign Affairs and Trade, Canberra, 2001.

——'ASEAN–Australia–New Zealand Free Trade Agreement', <http://www.dfat.gov.au/fta/aanzfta> (retrieved 23 October 2013).

——'History of Australia House', <http://www.uk.embassy.gov.au/lhlh/History.html> (retrieved 23 October 2013).

——'History of the Department of Foreign Affairs and Trade', <http://www.dfat.gov.au/dept/history.html> (retrieved 23 October 2013).

——'Treaty on principles governing the activities of states in the exploration and use of outer space, including the moon and other celestial bodies', 16 January 2009, <http://www.info.dfat.gov.au/Info/Treaties/treaties.nsf/AllDocIDs/89692731D2AEE0A2CA256CDF001D0E5C> (retrieved 29 October 2013).

Department of Foreign Affairs and Trade & Association of Southeast Asian Nations, 'Joint declaration on the ASEAN–Australia comprehensive partnership', <http://www.dfat.gov.au/asean/joint_dec_2007.html> (retrieved 23 October 2013).

Department of Immigration and Border Protection, 'Immigration to Australia during the 20th century—historical impacts on immigration intake, population size and population composition—a timeline', <http://www.immi.gov.au/media/publications/statistics/federation/timeline1.pdf> (retrieved 23 October 2013).

Department of Immigration and Citizenship, 'Immigration history 1945–1955', *Annual Report 2009–10*, <http://www.immi.gov.au/about/reports/annual/2009-10/html/65-years-of-nation-building/Immigration-history-1945-1955.htm> (retrieved 23 October 2013).

Department of Justice, 'Lawfulness of a lethal operation directed against a US citizen who is a senior operational leader of Al-Qa'ida or an associated force', White Paper, <http://msnbcmedia.msn.com/i/msnbc/sections/news/020413_DOJ_White_Paper.pdf> (retrieved 23 October 2013).

Derby, Lord, British Colonial Secretary, despatch, to Officer Administering the Government of Queensland, 11 July 1883, *Journals of the Legislative Council, 1883-1884 Session*, Queensland, vol. 23, pp. 3–4, in *Australia and the World:*

A Documentary History from the 1870s to the 1970s, ed. Neville Meaney, Longman Cheshire, Melbourne, 1985.

Downer, Alexander, Minister for Foreign Affairs, media conference, Beijing, 17 August 2004, <http://pandora.nla.gov.au/pan/25167/20070502-0000/www.foreignminister.gov.au/transcripts/2004/040817_ds_beijing.html> (retrieved 23 October 2013).

Dulles, John Foster, Secretary of State to the Embassy in Australia, telegram to Embassy in Australia, Washington, April 30, Department of State, Central Files, 793.00/4-3055, <http://history.state.gov/historicaldocuments/frus1955-57v02/d233> (retrieved 27 October 2013).

Edwards, Major General, report, *Argus*, 15 October 1889, <http://trove.nla.gov.au/ndp/del/printArticlePdf/8560537/3?print=n> (retrieved 13 November 2013).

Eisenhower, Dwight, 'Military–industrial complex speech', 1961, <http://coursesa.matrix.msu.edu/~hst306/documents/indust.html> (retrieved 23 October 2013).

Examiner (Launceston), 'White Australia Policy', 21 February 1950, <http://trove.nla.gov.au/ndp/del/article/52771861> (retrieved 13 November 2013).

Fitzgerald, Stephen, *Immigration: A Commitment to Australia—The Report of the Committee to Advise on Australia's Immigration Policies*, Australian Government Publishing Service, Canberra, 1988.

Fraser, Malcolm, 'Australia and some world economic issues', speech, Economic Club of New York, 4 January 1979, <http://pmtranscripts.dpmc.gov.au/transcripts/00005227.pdf> (retrieved 23 October 2013).

——Speech regarding Soviet Union invasion of Afghanistan to House of Representatives, 22 May 1980, <http://moadoph.gov.au/learning/national-history-challenge/docs/2007/fraser-text.pdf> (retrieved 13 November 2013).

Garnaut, Ross, *Australia and the Northeast Asian Ascendancy*, AGPS, Canberra, 1989.

Gleeson, Murray, 'The birth, life and death of section 74', speech, Samuel Griffith Society, Sydney, 14 June 2002, <http://www.hcourt.gov.au/assets/publications/speeches/former-justices/gleesoncj/cj_griffith2.htm> (retrieved 23 October 2013).

Global Security, 'JMSDF [Japan Maritime Self Defence Force] ships', <http://www.globalsecurity.org/military/world/japan/ship.htm> (retrieved 28 October 2013).

Goh, Chok Tong, 'Present state of the world', InterAction Council 30th Annual Plenary Meeting, 10 May 2012, Tianjin, China, <http://interactioncouncil.org/present-state-world-1> (retrieved 12 November 2013).

Hagel, Chuck, speech, International Institute for Strategic Studies, Singapore, 1 June 2013, <http://www.defense.gov/speeches/speech.aspx?speechid=1785> (retrieved 23 October 2013).

Hall, Keith R., Assistant Secretary of the Air Force (Space) and Director, National Reconnaissance Office, 'Presentation to the Committee on Armed Services Subcommittee on Strategic Forces United States Senate on Space Policy, Programs, and Operations', 8 March 2000, <http://cryptome.org/nro030800.htm> (retrieved 16 October 2013).

High Court of Australia, 'History of the High Court', <http://www.hcourt.gov.au/about/history> (retrieved 23 October 2013).

Ho Chi Minh, 'Declaration of independence', 2 September 1945, <http://www.chinhphu.vn/portal/page/portal/English/TheSocialistRepublic OfVietnam/AboutVietnam/AboutVietnamDetail?categoryId=10000103& articleId=10002648> (retrieved 23 October 2013).

Horton, Rebecca, Department of Defence, email to Malcolm Fraser, 'HMAS Sydney', 14 October 2013.

Howard, John, television interview with Laurie Oakes, *Sunday*, Nine Network, 1 December 2002, <http://pmtranscripts.dpmc.gov.au/browse .php?did=12454> (retrieved 12 November 2013).

Information Office of the State Council, 'The diversified employment of China's armed forces', Beijing, April 2013, <http://news.xinhuanet.com/english/china/2013-04/16/c_132312681.htm> (retrieved 23 October 2013).

International Maritime Law Institute, '1989 USA–USSR: Joint statement with attached uniform interpretation of rules of international law governing innocent passage, adopted at Wyoming, USA on 23 September, 1989', Centre for International Law, University of Singapore, <http://cil.nus.edu.sg>.

James, Walter, extracts from a paper, *Proceedings of the Royal Colonial Institute*, 10 April 1906, vol. 37, 1905–06, pp. 228–30.

Johnson, Lyndon B., 'Remarks of welcome to Prime Minister Holt of Australia on the South Lawn at the White House', 29 June 1966, <http://www .presidency.ucsb.edu/ws/?pid=27687#axzz2hevxVlUm> (retrieved 24 October 2013).

'Joint resolution', Public Law 107–40, 107th Congress, <http://www.gpo .gov/fdsys/pkg/PLAW-107publ40/pdf/PLAW-107publ40.pdf> (retrieved 29 October 2013).

Kennan, George F., 'The chargé in the Soviet Union (Kennan) to the Secretary of State', 'Long telegram', 22 February 1946, <http://www2.gwu .edu/~nsarchiv/coldwar/documents/episode-1/kennan.htm> (retrieved 24 October 2013).

Kissinger, Henry, *Daily Telegraph* (London), 28 June 1999.

Levin, Senator Carl, *Report of an Inquiry into the Alternative Analysis of the Issue of an Iraq-al Qaeda Relationship*, Senate Armed Services Committee, 21 October 2004, <http://www.levin.senate.gov/imo/media/doc/supporting/2004/10 2104inquiryreport.pdf> (retrieved 24 October 2013).

Liesching, P., British High Commissioner to Australia, to Lord Stanley, British Secretary for Dominion Affairs, cable, 31 August 1938, in *Australia and the*

World: A Documentary History from the 1870s to the 1970s, ed. Neville Meaney, Longman Cheshire, Melbourne, 1985.

Lloyd George, David, British Prime Minister, to W.H. Hughes, Prime Minister, letter, 31 December 1918, House of Lords Library, Lloyd George Papers, Box 38, Folder 5.

Lyons, Prime Minister, in the House of Representatives, *Commonwealth Parliamentary Debates*, 1937 Session, vol. 154, pp. 22–31, 24 August 1937.

McIlwraith, Thomas, Queensland Colonial Secretary, to Sir A.E. Kennedy, Governor of Queensland, letter, 26 February 1883, *Queensland, Votes and Proceedings of the Legislative Assembly, 1883 Session*, vol. 2: *The Annexation of New Guinea (Correspondence Respecting)*.

'Memorandum of a Conversation, Washington, March 14, 1955', US Department of State, Conference Files: Lot 60 D 627, CF 439, <http://history.state.gov/historicaldocuments/frus1955-57v02/d154> (retrieved 23 October 2013).

Menzies, R.G., Prime Minister, to S.M. Bruce, High Commissioner in London, letter, 22 February 1940, <http://www.dfat.gov.au/publications/historical/volume-03/historical-document-03-71.html> (retrieved 23 October 2013).

Ministry of Defense, *Defense of Japan* (annual White Paper), <http://www.mod.go.jp/e/publ/w_paper/index.html> (retrieved 28 October 2013).

Ministry of Economic Affairs, ROC, 'The bilateral trade between Taiwan and Mainland China', 2011, <http://www.moea.gov.tw/Mns/english/news/News.aspx?kind=6&menu_id=176&news_id=22769> (retrieved 23 October 2013).

Ministry of Foreign Affairs of Japan, 'The Basic View on the Sovereignty of the Senkaku Islands', <http://www.mofa.go.jp/region/asia-paci/senkaku/basic_view.html> (retrieved 13 November 2013).

Natalegawa, R.M.M.M., 'An Indonesian perspective on the Indo-Pacific', keynote address, Conference on Indonesia, Washington, 16 May 2013, <http://csis.org/files/attachments/130516_MartyNatalegawa_Speech.pdf> (retrieved 23 October 2013).

National Archives of Australia, 'Conscription referendums, 1916 and 1917 – Fact sheet 161', Commonwealth of Australia, Canberra, 2012, <http://www.naa.gov.au/collection/fact-sheets/fs161.aspx> (retrieved 24 October 2013).

Neale, R.G. (ed.), *Documents on Australian Foreign Policy 1937–49*, vol. 1: 1937–38, Australian Government Publishing Service, Canberra, 1975.

Neale, Robert, 'Australia's military commitment to South Vietnam', report presented to Parliament, 1975.

New South Wales Constitution Act 1855, <http://foundingdocs.gov.au/item-sdid-78.html> (retrieved 24 October 2013).

Nixon, Richard, 'Vietnamization', speech, 3 November 1969, <http://vietnam.vassar.edu/overview/doc14.html> (retrieved 13 November 2013).

Office of the Press Secretary, White House, 'Fact sheet US policy standard and procedures for the use of force in counterterrorism operations outside the United States and areas of active hostilities', 23 May 2013, <http://www.whitehouse.gov/the-press-office/2013/05/23/fact-sheet-us-policy-standards-and-procedures-use-force-counterterrorism>(retrieved 24 October 2013).

Office of the Spokesperson, 'Department of State, US–China strategic and economic dialogue outcomes of the strategic track', 12 July 2013, <http://www.state.gov/r/pa/prs/ps/2013/07/211861.htm> (retrieved 24 October 2013).

Official Record of the Debates of the Australasian Federal Convention [Sydney, 1897], Legal Books, Sydney, 1986.

Open letter to President Clinton, 26 June 1997 (NATO expansion), <http://www.bu.edu/globalbeat/nato/postpone062697.html> (retrieved 12 November 2013).

Parkes, Henry, *The Federal Government of Australasia: Speeches Delivered on Various Occasions (November, 1889–May, 1890)*, Turner & Henderson, Sydney, 1890.

Panetta, Leon, Secretary of Defence, 'Shangri-La Security Dialogue', speech, Singapore, 2 June 2012, <http://www.defense.gov/speeches/speech.aspx?speechid=1681> (retrieved 24 October 2013).

Pentagon Papers, *Direct Action: The Johnson Commitments, 1964–1968*, Part IV C 5, <http://www.archives.gov/research/pentagon-papers/> (retrieved 13 November 2013).

——*Evolution of the War. Aid for France in Indochina, 1950–1954*, Part IV, A, 2, <http://www.archives.gov/research/pentagon-papers/> (retrieved 13 November 2013).

——*Evolution of the War: Counterinsurgency: Phased Withdrawal of U.S. Forces in Vietnam, 1962-64*, Part IV B 4, <http://www.archives.gov/research/pentagon-papers/> (retrieved 13 November 2013).

——*Evolution of the War: Training of Vietnamese National Army, 1954-59*, Part IV, A, 4, <http://www.archives.gov/research/pentagon-papers/> (retrieved 13 November 2013).

Price, Charles A., 'Post-War Migration: 1947–98', W.D. Borrie Lecture, Australian Population Association National Conference, University of Queensland, Brisbane, 22 September 1998.

Project for the New American Century, 'Statement of Principles', 1997, <http://www.newamericancentury.org> (retrieved 16 October 2013).

Reagan, Ronald, 'Evil Empire' speech to the House of Commons, London, 8 June 1982, <http://www.fordham.edu/halsall/mod/1982reagan1.asp> (retrieved 13 November 2013).

'Report of meeting with Mr Averell Harriman [and Menzies' Cabinet, 1963] in Canberra', 7/6/63, NAA A4940/C3812/1338485, <http://recordsearch.naa.gov.au/scripts/Imagine.asp?B=1338485> (retrieved, 13 November 2013).

Resolution 678 (1990) Adopted by the UN Security Council at its 2963rd meeting on 29 November 1990, <http://daccess-dds-ny.un.org/doc/

RESOLUTION/GEN/NR0/575/28/IMG/NR057528.pdf?Open Element> (retrieved 13 November 2013).

Response to the German Annexation of New Guinea by the Government of Victoria.

Rumsfeld, Donald, Secretary of Defense, Department of Defense news briefing, 9 October 2001, <http://www.defense.gov/transcripts/transcript .aspx?transcriptid=2034> (retrieved 24 October 2013).

Service, James, Victorian Premier, memo to the Governor.

State Department Telegram 243, G. Ball to H.C. Lodge, 24 August 1963, FRUS, 1961–63, vol. 3, pp. 628–9, <http://2001-2009.state.gov/r/pa/ho/frus/ kennedyjf/iii/8177.htm> (retrieved 14 October 2013).

Statement of Immigration by the Minister for Immigration and Information the Hon. Arthur A. Calwell—Commonwealth Parliament, 9 August 1946, <http://www.immi.gov.au/media/history/post-war-immigration/ _pdf/19460809_ministerial_statement.pdf> (retrieved 12 October 2013).

Statute of Westminster, <http://foundingdocs.gov.au/item-did-25-aid-2-pid-23 .html> (retrieved 25 October 2013).

Sydney Morning Herald, 'Mrs O'Keefe to stay, Gamboa allowed to come here', 17 February 1950, <http://trove.nla.gov.au/ndp/del/printArticlePdf/18147 226/3?print=n> (retrieved 12 November 2013).

——'Sir Henry Parkes at Tenterfield', 25 October 1889, <http://trove.nla.gov .au/ndp/del/article/13746899> (retrieved 24 October 2013).

——'US Army problem now for Gamboa', 18 February 1950, <http:// trove.nla.gov.au/ndp/del/printArticlePdf/18146061/3?print=n> (retrieved 12 November 2013).

Taiwanese Tourism Bureau, Yearly statistics, <http://admin.taiwan.net.tw/ statistics/year_en.aspx?no=15> (retrieved 24 October 2013).

Telegram from the Governor-General to the Secretary of State for the Colonies, received 3 August, 1914, CPP, 1914-15-16-17, Vol. V, p. 1434.

Treaty of Nanking, signed at Nanking, 29 August, 1842, <http://www.london-gazette.co.uk/issues/20276/pages/3597/page.pdf> (retrieved 13 November 2013).

United Nations, Outreach Programme on the Rwanda Genocide and the United Nations, 'Rwanda: A brief history of the country', <http://www.un.org/ en/preventgenocide/rwanda/education/rwandagenocide.shtml> (retrieved 24 October 2013).

——'Somalia – UNOSOM I: Background', <http://www.un.org/en/ peacekeeping/missions/past/unosom1backgr2.html> (retrieved 23 October 2013).

——'Submission by the People's Republic of China concerning the outer limits of the continental shelf beyond 200 nautical miles in part of the East China Sea to the Commission on the Limits of the Continental Shelf',

<http://www.un.org/depts/los/clcs_new/submissions_files/submission_chn_63_2012.htm> (retrieved 24 October 2013).

——United Nations Convention on the Law of the Sea, <http://www.un.org/depts/los/convention_agreements/texts/unclos/unclos_e.pdf> (retrieved 24 October 2013).

United Nations Office for Disarmament Affairs, 'Treaty on the non-proliferation of nuclear weapons', 1 July 1968, <http://disarmament.un.org/treaties/t/npt/text> (retrieved 28 October 2013).

US Congress, *Report on Intelligence Activities Relating to Iraq Conducted by the Policy Counterterrorism Evaluation Group and the Office of Special Plans within the Office of the Under Secretary of Defense for Policy*, Washington DC, June 2008, <http://www2.hn.psu.edu/faculty/jmanis/poldocs/phase2b.pdf> (retrieved 14 November 2013).

——*Report of the Select Committee on Intelligence on the U.S. Intelligence Community's Prewar Intelligence Assessments on Iraq*, Washington DC, July 9 2004, <http://www.intelligence.senate.gov/108301.pdf> (retrieved 14 November 2011).

——Testimony of Frank J. Cilluffo, Deputy Director of the Global Organized Crime Program, to the House Judiciary Committee, Washington DC, 13 December 2000, <http://commdocs.house.gov/committees/judiciary/hju68324.000/hju68324_0f.htm> (retrieved 24 October 2013).

——Testimony of Ralf Mutschke of Interpol's Criminal Intelligence Division, to the House Judicial Committee, Washington DC, 13 December 2000, <http://commdocs.house.gov/committees/judiciary/hju68324.000/hju68324_0f.htm> (retrieved 24 October 2013).

US Department of State, Office of the Historian, 'Soviet Invasion of Czechoslovakia, 1968', <http://history.state.gov/milestones/1961-1968/soviet-invasion-czechoslavkia> (retrieved 23 October 2013).

Woods, Kevin M., *Iraqi Perspectives Project – Saddam and Terrorism: Emerging Insights from Captured Iraqi Documents, Volume 1*, Institute for Defence Analyses, Alexandria, Virginia, November 2007, <https://archive.org/details/IraqiPerspectivesReportSaddamAndTerrorismEmergingInsightsFromCaptured> (retrieved 14 November 2013).

World Bank, 'Military expenditure (% of GDP)', <http://data.worldbank.org/indicator/MS.MIL.XPND.GD.ZS> (retrieved 24 October 2013).

Yudhoyono, Susilo Bambang, 'Keynote speech at the 11th IISS Asia Security Summit, the Shangri-La Dialogue', 1 June 2012, <http://www.presidenri.go.id/index.php/eng/pidato/2012/06/01/1867.html> (retrieved 24 October 2013).

Index